U0692576

第二版

高·校·英·语·专·业·教·材

A Guide to Appreciating English Literature

英美文学鉴赏导读

■主　编　魏　健
副主编　温中兰
审　校　〔美〕Michael C. Milam

ZHEJIANG UNIVERSITY PRESS
浙江大学出版社

前　言

通过基础阶段的英语学习，英语专业的学生虽然掌握了一定的听说读写能力，但他们的文学基本知识仍相对薄弱，要真正理解和透彻赏析英美文学作品的精华所在，仍不同程度地存在一定的困难。即使他们有时能在文字层面上读懂原文，但要对作品的文学价值进行真正有效的把握，不免会有“老虎吃天、无从下手”之感。《英美文学鉴赏导读》的编写遵循文学赏析教学应坚持“掌握方法为手段、文本阅读为载体、有效赏析为目标”的宗旨，努力帮助学习者克服上述困难。

《导读》的突出特点是，编者从介绍文学原理和鉴赏方法切入，紧密结合文本分析，力图解决传统文学教学中文本阅读与鉴赏实践严重脱节的突出矛盾。古人云：“授之以鱼，不如授之以渔。”授之以“鱼”，数量再多，终会穷尽；授之以“渔”，学生掌握了捕鱼的本领，固化了审美意识，必将受用终生。笔者认为，“授之以渔”不仅是《导读》编写的指导性纲领，更是一种行之有效的教学方法和一种崭新的教育理念，对教师在文学教学过程中培养学生创造性的思维能力以及提高学生分析问题和解决问题的水平具有普遍的指导意义。

鉴于“文学作品浩如烟海、文学教学课时有限”这一客观现实，本教材对文学作品的遴选不求面面俱到，而是把重点放在对各类文学作品的鉴赏方法上。换言之，教材的设计没有将文学教学仅仅停留在字、词、句乃至篇章结构的讲解上，而是着重引导学生把握鉴赏方法，深入感受和理解不同文体的文学作品，深刻领悟作品艺术形象的本质意义和作家的真实意图，最终有效摄取作品中真正有价值的东西。

综上所述，《导读》的整体设计不但能够满足教师英美文学课堂教学的基本需要，同时又能为学生自主学习提供便捷有效的帮助，使之在学习过程中逐步掌握鉴赏方法，整体把握作品实质，最终实现有效鉴赏作品的目标。

《导读》是浙江大学宁波理工学院科研基金重点资助项目的成果，项目组其他成员还有宁波大学的李其金和吴秀琼老师，本学院的胡海鹏老师，以及美籍专家 Michael C. Milam 教授。在编著本书的整个过程中，我们得到了学校以及外国语学院领导自始至终的大力支持和帮助，在此深表谢忱，并希望该书能在英语专业的学科建设和文学课程的教学中发挥应有的积极作用。

在编著本书的过程中，我们查阅了大量相关资料，并借鉴了不少作者的思想观点。也正因如此，《导读》才有了更高的可读性和更强的实用性，我们在此表示由衷的感激和谢意。

由于我们的学识水平有限，书中难免会出现疏漏和不足之处，恳请使用者不吝赐教与斧正，以便我们及时修改与订正。

编　者

2013 年 11 月

Foreword

Professors Wei Jian and Wen Zhonglan, in their textbook *A Guide to Appreciating English Literature*, have written a thorough introduction to the study of literature and selected the indispensable classics, giving the Chinese student the essential tools for discovering the aesthetic and intellectual pleasures of literature in English.

One of the great strengths of this work is indeed its thoroughness. Considering that Chinese students have little or no background in the study of literature in English, the book begins with the basics, explaining what the special nature of literature is and what the student can gain from studying great authors. These do not become mere platitudes because this discussion moves directly into the practical aspects of thinking and writing about literature, something that they present in a lively and extremely useful manner. The first part "An Overall Guide to Appreciating Literature", for instance, ends with critical approaches and literary schools in order to prepare students to analyze texts and put them in their historical perspectives.

Moreover, the next four sections are wisely ordered on the four main genres: poetry, drama, fiction and essay. The arrangement of the four is a tribute to the compilers' understanding of western literature in general since historically literature in the west developed in this sequence. It was Homer before Sophocles and Boccaccio before Francis Bacon. Like the introduction, each of these sections shows the attention to the basic needs of the students as well. Before they tackle John Donne, they are given the basics of the mechanics and music of poetry. Before they meet Shakespeare, they are given the elements of drama necessary for reading The Bard. The presentation of the two "modern" genres follows the same felicitous pattern. Narrative point of view is explained before Faulkner's "A Rose for Emily" is perused, and the types and techniques of the essay are given before Francis Bacon is pondered. All in all, the integration of study skills and the classics is quite impressive. And the second edition of this book should undoubtedly serve Chinese students much better.

This book certainly reflects the two professors' love and dedication to the study and teaching of literature in English, revealing their passion for the written word. As a colleague and fast friend of theirs for the past six years, I hope that our friendship and dedication to teaching literature to Chinese students, in a small but significant way, has demonstrated how literature has the power to forge understanding across cultural boundaries and bring China and the west one little step closer.

Dr. *Michael C. Milam*
Professor of English
University of Indianapolis, USA
November, 2013

修订版说明

《英美文学鉴赏导读》作为高校英语专业教材，供大专院校英语专业三年级英美文学课程教学使用。自 2008 年 7 月由浙江大学出版社出版以来，因其较强的针对性和实用性，在课堂教学中产生了较好的效果，并受到了全国广大使用者的普遍欢迎。但由于本书当初编写时间仓促，考虑不周之处在所难免。为答谢广大读者的厚爱，我们决定在第一版的基础上进行更为合理的修订。本次修订主要有以下特点：

1. 最大限度地维持原书的基本架构。由于该教材专为“任务驱动型教学”所设计，重在鉴赏方法的引入和作品鉴赏两个实践环节的有机结合，而且实践证明这是一套行之有效的学习路径，所以，修订版的各部分内容力求保持与原书的一致既是广大使用者的愿望，也是编者的明智选择。

2. 修订版对第一版某些部分的内容进行合理补充，使之更趋全面和完整，旨在为使用者提供更有效的帮助。增补内容贯穿在“鉴赏方法导读”、“作品点评”、“问题与练习”、“文学术语词表”的各部分。

3. 使用过程中，我们还发现第一版对部分选读作品的注释不够全面，导致读者理解原作有一定的难度。所以，我们特意为某些作品增补了较为详尽的注释。

修订版的上述做法仅为编者的主观愿望，不妥之处仍难避免。因此，我们衷心希望使用本书的同仁能不吝赐教，多加指正。

另外，本教材遴选作品的内容较多，教师应根据各自教学的具体情况选择使用，特此提醒。

编　者

2013 年 11 月

Contents

Part 1 An Overall Guide to Appreciating Literature

Selected Readings of English Poetry

Part 3 A Guide to Appreciating English Drama

Selected Readings of English Drama

Part 4 A Guide to Appreciating English Fiction

Selected Readings of English Fiction

Selected Readings of English Essays

Part 6 Short Glossary of Literary Terms

References

Part 1

An Overall Guide to Appreciating Literature

Before we begin our discussions on any specific topics about English literature, let us first deal with some basic issues concerning literature at large so as to prepare our minds for specific studies of English literature.

The original source of literature arises from human interest in telling a story about some aspects of human experiences by arranging words in artistic forms. Initially, the literary impulse exists only in one's mind. It is the writer who turns this impulse of experience into literature, by means of language, and in such forms as fiction, poetry, drama, or essay. To a certain extent, literature may be briefly defined as fictional texts in the form of language artistically employed to achieve identifiable literary qualities and convey meaningful messages.

The word "literature" came into English from the 14th century in the sense of polite learning through reading. Thus a man of literature, or a man of letters, referred to what we would now describe as a man of wide reading, somewhat like the modern meaning of the word "literacy". From the mid-18th century, literature referred to the practice and profession of writing. And since the 19th century, literature has been the high skills of writing with exuberant imagination.

1 What Is Literature?

1.1 Types of literature

Literature may be classified into four categories or genres: prose fiction, poetry, drama, and nonfiction prose.

Prose fiction, or narrative fiction, includes myths, parables, romances, novels and short stories. The essence of prose fiction is narration, the relating of a sequence of events or actions. Fictional works usually focus on one or a few major characters who change and grow as a result of how they deal with other characters and how they attempt to solve their problems.

If prose is expansive in the use of language, poetry strives towards brevity. It offers the reader high points of emotion, reflection, thought, and feeling with highly compacted syntax. Very often, poetry expresses the most powerful and deeply felt experiences of human beings. Many exquisite poems become our lifelong friends, and we visit them over and over again for insight, understanding, and peaceful reflection about our life.

Drama is literature designed for stage or film presentation by actors for the benefit and delight of the audience. The essence of drama is the development of character and situation through speech and action. Although most modern plays use prose dialogue, on the principle that the language of drama should resemble the language of everyday speech, many plays from the past are in poetic form.

Usually, the first three are regarded as imaginative literature, while nonfiction prose consists of essays, news reports, feature articles, historical and biographical works, and the like. The main purpose of nonfiction prose is to present truths and make logical conclusions about the factual world of history, science, and current events.

Roughly speaking, the essential qualities of literature are characterized by the following four features.

1.2 Literature is language

As we all know, authors of literature use language in special ways. Most importantly, literary language emphasizes connotative rather than denotative meanings of words. Unlike scientific language which mainly emphasizes the denotative value of language, writers of literature use language in a more subtle manner—to bring into full play all the emotional associations that words may carry. A good case in point is the word *mother*, whose denotation is simply the female parent, but the connotation may include such meanings as protection, warmth, care, love, devotion, home, and a happy memory of one's childhood. Thus, literature is inseparably associated with language in terms of linguistic application.

1.3 Literature is fictional

A work of literature is fictional in two ways. On the one hand, authors make up or imagine some or all the materials. This is perhaps why literature is often thought of as imaginative literature. Even historical fiction, which chiefly relies on factual events, is also fictional, as it includes characters, dialogues, events, and settings that never existed in history.

On the other hand, the fictional quality of literature also lies in the artistic control that writers exercise over the work. This artistic control produces the effect of stylizing the materials of the work, thus setting it apart from the real. This occurs simply because there always exists an obvious disparity between literary phenomena and real life. Compare how a newspaperman and a poet describe the same event respectively, and we will see the distinction. The scientist would try to present his account as exactly as possible about the event; the poet, in contrast, would most probably manage to make his poem the object of experiencing profound emotion. In other words, the poet would adopt such literary techniques as metaphor, irony, or imagery to make his work more of an artistic creation.

1.4 Literature is true

Despite that literature is mostly "fictional", it has the innate nature of being true. Thus, there exists a paradox in literature—its imaginative properties against its representation of actual human conditions. In other words, we can find in literature a paradox between fictionality and truth. There are mainly three ways for literature to be true.

First of all, literature is true to the facts of real life. It directly states the depictions of real people, actual places, and existing events; more importantly, literature is true in the sense of its power of communicating truthful ideas of human life.

Then, literature is true because of the indirectly stated ideas that the authors present in literary works. Though all the details of a literary work make up an imaginary world, such a world is based on the author's ideas about the real world.

Finally, what we readers usually encounter in literary works are the typical characters and probable actions. By imposing order on the chaos of real life, authors present characters who typify real people, and they recount actions that would probably happen in real life. Because of this, we are often able to find characters who represent recognizable types of people in real life.

1.5 Literature is aesthetic

The aesthetic property of literature lies in its artistic beauty. Like any other art forms—music, painting, photography, and dance, literature is an end in itself. The pleasure we get from literature can be found in the way authors use literary techniques, such as metaphor, plot, character, symbolism, irony, suspense, theme, and rhythmic language. All such literary elements combine to form an organic coherence of artistic beauty.

Moreover, while experiencing the beauty of literature, we can trace the profound meanings in literature. Great authors are undoubtedly very competent to make the aesthetic qualities of literature inextricably bound up with the ideas conveyed by their works. They use pleasurable conventions to enhance and communicate their themes.

2 Why Do We Read Literature?

Literature serves quite a few purposes. Sometimes we read for pleasure only, just as sometimes we listen to music for relaxation or go to a movie for entertainment. Good and great literature, however, makes us work a little harder. It demands more because in the end it has more to give. It compels us to read actively and alertly, and insists that while reading we have to question and think hard in order to gain any profit. In short, good literature asks us to read *critically* so as to procure what we wish to get. There are at least the following five advantages in reading literature.

2.1 To acquire knowledge and wisdom

Literature is a cultural heritage and a key to acquire social knowledge and human wisdom. By learning literature, we learn fresh ideas and new concepts. Literature brings readers insight about the nature of reality. Through literature, we know more about traditions, customs, beliefs, attitudes, folklore, and the values of the era in which it is written. Whether in the form of fiction, poetry, drama, or essay, literature always furnishes us readers with some new information that broadens our knowledge of the world.

2.2 To consolidate language competence

To master the English language, to improve our understanding of its culture, or to consolidate our language competence, it is unarguably indispensable to study at least some of the great works written by outstanding authors of the language. As is widely known, as English majors, for instance, literature can serve the English learners as a useful tool for increasing vocabulary, mastering idiomatic expressions, enhancing cultural awareness, and raising communicating ability. Therefore, literature, when properly used in language classes, will undoubtedly achieve these purposes in the process of language acquisition.

2.3 To read for pleasure

Apart from its role of education, literature can bring pleasure by entertaining those who voluntarily attend to it. Generally speaking, literature offers readers narratives with an exciting world of experiences that is different from their own. One may argue that there are a variety of other ways of giving pleasure or entertainment to people, yet we discover that literature enables people to find the greatest pleasure and satisfaction when we are ultimately brought back to some sober-minded realities of human problems, feelings, and relationships. The reason lies in the fact that literature is not simply a copy of what is obviously seen by our own eyes; we are, in fact, furnished with an imaginative and interpretative reflection upon special views of human existence and social reality.

2.4 To improve understanding about life

Literature is appealing to us also because of its intimate relationship and relevant association with human existence. It sheds light on the complexity of human experiences and thus broadens the awareness of our own understanding about life. While observing the private lives of characters, our minds also begin working and our hearts beating along with the characters. An awareness of how other people feel can be a very useful way to enrich one's own personality. In this sense, literature not only gives us a chance to participate in the experience of others, but also succeeds in affecting our attitudes to and expectations about things to happen.

2.5 To cultivate capacity of artistic appreciation

Because of its good craftsmanship and the beauty of expression in terms of aesthetics, literature can be studied for artistic appreciation. A story, a poem, a play, or an essay, with its unique texture, is a self-contained piece of art, which can be analyzed in accord with literary theories. When we are able to do this, we begin to move in the direction of literary criticism. However, literary criticism is by no means negative or fault-finding; it is an attempt to clarify, explain and evaluate literature from an aesthetic point of view. In fact, the more we learn about how to analyze literature from an artistic point of view, the deeper our understanding and better our appreciation of a literary work can be obtained, and greater still the pleasure and enjoyment can be drawn from it.

3 How to Learn Literary Texts?

3.1 Copying

Since most writers work very scrupulously to get each word exactly proper and in exactly the right order, there seem to be no better words to use than those of the literary text itself. So it could be a good way for you just to copy the story over again word for word so as to remember them by heart. One may argue that, with all the technology available to us, copying texts doesn't seem very useful in our electronic age. Still, it's a good exercise for teaching yourself accuracy and attention to detail, particularly in the early phase of a literature course. Moreover, being able to copy a passage accurately will help you a lot when you want to quote a passage to illustrate a point you are making. By the way, reading aloud, a variation of copying, may be a more original exercise than copying itself, since by tone, emphasis, and pace you can clarify the implied theme of the text. Though copying or reading is not by itself writing *about* literature, having something to say can be the first and most significant step in learning to write *about* literature.

3.2 Paraphrase

When you look away from the text for a while and then rewrite the same material in your own words, you are writing a paraphrase. For example, let's paraphrase the first sentence of Jane Austen's *Pride and Prejudice*: "It is a truth universally acknowledged that a single man in possession of a good fortune must be in want of a wife." You can start by making it less formal as follows: *Everybody agrees that a rich bachelor needs a wife.*

There are several advantages of paraphrase. First of all, paraphrase enables us to test whether we really understand what we are reading. Second, certain elements of the text become clearer: we may see now that Austen means her sentence to be ironic or humorous, and we now understand the two possible meanings of "in want of". Third, we can check our paraphrase against those of others to compare with theirs our understanding of the passage. And finally, we have learned how much literature depends on words.

However, paraphrase, no matter how faithfully and precisely it follows the original text, can render only an approximate equivalent of a text's meaning. Paraphrasing, like copying, is not in itself an entirely satisfactory way of writing about literature. But, like copying, it can be a useful tool to clarify a literary text. Unlike exact copying, a paraphrase in your own words can add much of your understanding to the text, thus it becomes more valuable.

3.3 Summary

When you stand back far enough from the original text and put down briefly in your own words what you believe the whole work is about, you are writing a summary. A summary can be long and short according to your needs. For example, you could summarize the story of *Hamlet* in a single sentence: "A young man, seeking to avenge the murder of his father by his uncle, kills his uncle, but he himself and others also die tragically in the process."

If you feel that too much is left out in this one-sentence summary, you may lengthen it like this: "In Denmark, many centuries ago, a young prince avenged the murder of his father, the king, by his uncle, who had usurped the throne, but the prince himself was killed as were others, and a well-led foreign army had no trouble successfully invading the decayed and troubled state."

A summary may be written quite differently from person to person. A summary of your classmate may go like this: "From the ghost of his murdered father the young prince learns that his uncle, who has married the prince's mother, much to the young man's shame and disgust, is the father's murderer, and the prince plots revenge, feigning madness, acting erratically—even insulting the woman he loves—and, though gaining his revenge, causes the suicide of his beloved and the deaths of others and, finally, of himself."

To summarize means to emphasize and to interpret rather than replicate the text in miniature. When you write a summary, you should try to be as objective as possible; nevertheless, your summary will reflect not only the original text but also your own understanding and attitudes. A good summary can be a form of literary criticism. But beware: a mere summary, no matter how accurately done, will seldom fulfill an assignment for a critical essay.

3.4 Description

By concentrating on subject and plot, we give a summary about a particular work. A description, on the other hand, may concentrate more widely on the form, structure, or logic of the work. The following is a sample description of Shelley's *Ode to the West Wind*:

Ode to the West Wind belongs to the Horatian type, that is, it is written with stanzas of uniform length and regular arrangement. The form of the poem employed here is a unique combination of Dante's Terza rima and the Shakespearean sonnet: five 14-lined stanzas of iambic pentameter, with each stanza containing four tercets and a closing couplet, and the rhyme scheme being *aba bcb cdc ded ee.*

This is just a brief description of the complex pattern of rhymes and stanza form of the poem. Though we could describe many other elements of the poem—images and symbols, for example—the unusual and dominant element is clearly the intricate and insistent pattern of rhyme and stanza form. Moreover, you can further describe at length, in depth, and with considerable complexity certain aspects of the work without mentioning the content at all. You might describe a novel in terms of characters, plot, sentence structure, diction, voice, dramatized scenes, so on and so forth.

3.5 Analysis

Copying, paraphrase, summary, and description of a work rarely stand alone as a piece of writing about literature. It is just a tool or a means of supporting a point or opinion. Even the description we have given above borders on analysis. To analyze is to break something down into its parts to discover how they function in relation to the whole work. In order to analyze a certain aspect, you first have to decide what a work is mainly about: what its *theme* is. If you defined the theme, you could then write an analytical paper suggesting how certain writing techniques help reinforce that theme.

By analysis, you refer to interpretation or the expression of your understanding of a work and its meaning. This involves an initial general impression that is supported and often modified by your analysis. Particularly, you need to keep your mind open for modifications or changes, rather than forcing your analysis to confirm your first impressions.

This procedure should, in turn, suggest that the essay should present the overall theme and support that generalization with close analyses of the major elements of the text—showing how one or more such elements as rhyme, speaker, plot, or setting reinforce and define the theme of the story. Often the conclusion of such an essay will be a more refined statement of the theme.

Even after you have done your best, however, you must hold your interpretation as a hypothesis rather than a final truth. Your experience of reading criticism has probably already shown you that no reading can exhaust the connotative meaning of a work. In other words, an interpretation is "only an opinion". Your opinions are a measure of your knowledge, intelligence, and sensibility. They should not be lightly changed, but neither should they be obstinately held.

4 How to Write About Literature?

4.1 Having something to say

Deciding what to write about—what approach to use, which questions to ask—seems to be the first step in the process of writing a paper about a work of literature. In fact it isn't. Before that, you have to feel confident that you have something to say.

First, before you can tell anyone else about what you have read, you should be aware that writing about literature is just another form of talking about literature.

Then when you have finished that first reading, think about your first impressions. Write down any key phrases or important events that you remember, anything you might forget. Look back at any parts that puzzled you at first. After finishing a certain part, write down in one sentence what you think it is about. Then after finishing the whole work, write a longer statement—three or four sentences—summarizing the work and suggesting more fully what it seems to be about. If you get stuck, try brainstorming all of your ideas about the work for some time, and then write the summary.

4.2 Choosing a topic

Once you unconsciously have the desire to tell someone of your understanding about a work, it is quite probable that you have already chosen a topic. However, a topic itself is not enough; most of the work—writing your essay sentence by sentence or paragraph by paragraph remains ahead of you. You need to transmute your personal desire to communicate into an "objective" statement or a thesis about the work.

If your instructor assigns a topic, it almost certainly will work, and you will have a payoff if you approach it creatively. It is time-consuming, of course, to think through the implications of a topic. Yet, an instructor's directions, especially if they are detailed and can call your attention to particular questions, may help you a lot to focus on important issues and lead you to crucial evidence.

If your instructor does not give you a topic, you may sometimes have to settle for the kind of topic that will be safe for any literary work. You can always, for example, analyze devices of characterization in a story; you can also analyze such literary techniques as rhythm, verse form, imagery, or the connotative theme in a poem. Most importantly, the best papers are usually very personal in origin; even when a topic is set by the instructor, the best papers usually come from a sense of having personally found an answer to a significant question. Generally speaking, to turn a promising idea into a good paper, personal responses usually need to be supported by a considerable mass of evidence from the original texts.

By the way, you may need to *narrow* your topic so that your thesis can be supported by examples from throughout the text. If your topic is too broad, your paper will likely become long, unwieldy, and overly general.

4.3 Considering your audience

Who is your audience? And for whom are you writing? The obvious answer is your instructor, but in an important sense, that is the wrong answer. It is wrong because, although your instructor could literally be the only other person who will ever read your paper, you write about literature to learn how to write for an audience of peers, who much like yourself are sensible and educated, and appreciate having something explained so that they will understand the work more fully. So it is important to assume the audience is intelligent and has some idea of what literature is like and how it works, but that he or she has just read this particular literary work for the first time and has not yet had a chance to think about it carefully. Don't be insulting and explain the obvious, but don't assume either that your reader has noticed and considered every detail. The purpose of your paper is to inform and convince your reader about the work you have read.

4.4 Collecting evidence

Once you have decided on a topic, the first thing you do involves gathering evidence that supports your thesis. Look over the notes you have already made in the margins of that text or on separate pieces of paper. Some of these notes will be useful when you write your paper. Here are some general suggestions toward successful note-taking.

(1) Keep your topic and your thesis about your topic constantly in mind as you reread. Mark all passages in the text that bear on your topic, and write a single sentence that describes how the passage relates to your topic and thesis.

(2) When you think you have finished your note-taking, read over all your note cards slowly, and jot down any further ideas as they occur to you mind. You will have to be ruthless and leave out some of your favorite ideas that are irrelevant to your thesis.

(3) If you like to write notes in the margin of your text, systematically transfer them to uniform cards before you outline.

(4) The notes you have taken will become almost the whole content of your paper. The key is getting all your ideas into the right order—that is, into a sequence that allows them to argue your thesis most persuasively.

(5) Write all the major points you want to make, then decide which ideas should go first, which should go second, and so on. Next, match up your notes with the points on your outline.

4.5 Developing the argument

Once you have decided on your major points and assembled your evidence, you have to put your evidence together effectively—in a coherent and logical order so as to answer your readers' questions systematically and fully. However, this is only half the task in developing a persuasive argument. The other half involves choosing a voice and tone that will make readers want to read on.

The tone of your paper is the basis of your relationship with your readers. Being too positive can make your audience feel stupid, and can turn them into defensive or resistant readers who will rebel at your every point. Friendship with your readers is better than an adversarial relationship. Sounding like a nice person with the right tone should make readers receptive to your content. It has been said that all good papers should be organized in the same way: (a) Tell them what you're going to tell them; (b) Tell them; (c) Tell them what you told them. These three elements fit the most common kind of organization, which includes an introduction, a body of argument, and a conclusion.

4.6 Writing the first draft

When you set your pen to paper or put your fingers to keyboard, the main thing is to express clearly your sense of direction and arrests the attention of your readers. And then move along, word by word and sentence by sentence, as you follow your outline from one paragraph to another. If you become stuck, try working out your ideas on a separate piece of paper or free-writing for a while. Stay with your first draft until you are reasonably satisfied with it.

4.7 Revising

Revising is the final and the most important stage of all. Don't allow yourself to be too easily satisfied. You should let your work settle for a few hours, preferably overnight. All those sentences that felt so good in your earlier draft often seem flat, or even worthless, when a little time has elapsed. When a particular word or phrase turns out to be imprecise or misleading, search until you find the right one. If a paragraph is incomplete, fill it in. If a transition from one point to another does not work, look again at your outline and see if another way of ordering your points would help. Here are some things for you to watch for:

Thesis: Do you state the thesis effectively and clearly?

Organization: Does your paper have proper logic from beginning to end? Does your first paragraph set up the main issue? Do your paragraphs follow each other in a coherent and logical order? Does the first sentence of each paragraph accurately suggest what that paragraph will contain? Does your final paragraph draw a conclusion?

Use of evidence: Do you use enough, or too many, examples? Does each example prove what you say it does? Have you left out any examples useful to your thesis? Have you achieved a good balance between examples and generalizations?

Tone: How does your voice sound in the paper? Confident? Too timid? Too showy? Or too self-effacing?

Sentences: Does each sentence read clearly? Is the first sentence of your paper a strong, clear one likely to interest a neutral reader? Are your sentences varied enough?

Word choice: Have you used any words whose meaning you are not sure of? Do your figures of speech make exact sense?

Conciseness: Have you eliminated all the padding you put in when you didn't think your paper would be long enough? Have you eliminated all the unnecessary words and phrases?

Grammar and punctuation: Have you checked the syntax in each sentence? Have you checked the spelling of any words you are not sure of? Have you confirmed the punctuation of each sentence?

4.8 Documentation

Documentation or "giving credit" means identifying the sources you consult when you prepare your essays. Two kinds of sources are relevant to writing about literature: primary sources and secondary sources.

(1) Primary sources are the works of literature themselves. If your essay is about *Hamlet*, then *Hamlet* is your primary source. Primary sources are crucial for essays about literature. After all, they are what your essays are about, and what you want to interpret. Your most important facts, the ones that support your opinions, will come from primary sources.

(2) Secondary sources include *facts* from outside the work or *commentary* from people outside the work. Secondary sources are valuable for the information they give to help us form our own opinions.

Facts from secondary sources include such things as information about the author's life, the period in which the author lived, the author's philosophy, literary history, the works' influence, and similarities to other works.

In addition to facts, secondary sources also contain commentary or interpretation by critics. You can find commentary in such places as introductions to individual works, head notes in anthologies, opinion columns on websites, articles in professional journals, chapters in books, and book-length studies. Although testimony is no substitute for your own skillful argumentation, it can add to the persuasive power of your essays.

(3) Give credit to your documentation. As you use secondary sources, through either direct quotation or summary of a critic's argument, you must signal to your reader the specific source in each case. Here is a brief summary of how to adopt secondary sources in students' essay writing.

(A) In-text citation: If you use the author's name to introduce the material, give only the page number in parentheses. Example:

As Judith Fetterley notes, "Emily, like Georgiana, is a man-made object" (35).

(B) If you don't use the author's name to introduce the source, put the name and page number(s) in parentheses. Example:

One critic points out that "Emily, like Georgiana, is a man-made object" (Fetterley 35).

(C) If you cite another work by the same author elsewhere in the paper, use a title word before the page number(s). Example:

As Judith Fetterley notes, "Emily, like Georgiana, is a man-made object" ("A Rose" 35).

(D) If you don't use the author's name to introduce your source and you cite another work by the same author, use both name and title with the page number(s). Example:

One critic points out that "Emily, like Georgiana, is a man-made object" (Fetterley, "A Rose" 35).

4.9 The "Works Cited" page

Every literary research paper must include a "Works Cited" page that lists alphabetically by author's last name all secondary sources used in the paper. Here is a brief guide to the proper format for some of the most common sources:

(1) A book by one author or editor:

Morgan, Kathryn A. *Myth and Philosophy from the Presocratics to Plato.* New York: Cambridge UP, 2000.

(2) A book by two or three authors or editors:

Weliek, Rene, and Austin Warren. *Theory of Literature.* 3rd ed. Orlando: Harcourt, 1956.

(3) A book by more than three authors or editors:

Greenblatt, Stephen, et al., eds. *The Norton Shakespeare.* New York: Norton, 1997.

or:

Greenblatt, Stephen, Walter Cohen, Jeane, Howard, and Katharine Eisaman Maus. *The Norton Shakespeare.* New York: Norton, 1997.

(4) Editor's introduction to a book:

O'Prey, Paul. Introduction. *Heart of Darkness.* By Joseph Conrad. New York:

Viking, 1983.

(5) A translated book:

Boccaccio, Giovanni. *The Decameron.* Trans. G. H. McWilliam. London: Penguin, 1972.

(6) An essay or any other short work in a book:

Wihl, Gary. "Marxist Theory and Criticism." *The Johns Hopkins Guide to Literary Theory and Criticism.* Ed. Michael Groden and Martin Kreiswirth. Baltimore: Johns Hopkins UP, 1994.

(7) An article in a reference book:

"Gnostic." *Merriam-Webster's Collegiate Dictionary.* 10th ed. 1994.

(8) An article in a newspaper:

McNulty, Charles. "All the World's a Stage Door." *Village Voice,* 13 Feb. 2001: 69.

(9) An article in a magazine:

Fenton, James. "Becoming Marianne Moore." *New York Review of Books,* 24 April 1997: 40—45.

(10) Website example:

Padgett, John B. "William Faulkner." The Mississippi Writers Page. 29 Mar. 1999. 8 Feb. 2001 <http://www.olemiss.edu/depts/english/ms-writers/dir/faulkner william/>.

4.10 Sample Essay 1

Analysis of *Break, Break, Break*

Break, Break, Break is a sad lament for a lost friend. Many people think that Tennyson wrote this poem to express his deep emotion of loss over the death of his friend Arthur Hallam. In the poem a speaker near a rocky shore addresses the sea as if it were a person. While expressing his or her grief the speaker notices others who are still happily going about their daily business, unaware of the speaker's heartbreak. The speaker seems to find some solace in the unchanging sea whose waves break over and over again on the "cold gray stones". He or she sadly comes to realize, however, that the past is gone, never to return.

Tennyson has made effective use of sounds in this poem which follows a traditional form by using a clear and regular rhythm and an easy-to-follow rhyme scheme. Most lines have three strong beats; the rhyme scheme follows a simple *abcb* pattern. This traditional approach coordinates well with the mood and personality of the speaker, who seems to be focusing on the past rather than the future as he or she remembers his dead friend. At the beginning of the poem and again in the last stanza, the speaker says the word *break* three times in one line. This repetition imitates the incessant sound of waves breaking on the shore so as to reveal the speaker's heart-breaking feeling at the moment.

In addition, Tennyson uses a special kind of metaphor called apostrophe when he has the speaker talk directly to the sea. This figure of speech helps convey the speaker's loneliness, which he or she hopes the sea can somehow help to heal. Another way Tennyson shows the speaker's feelings is contrast. The poet has the speaker notice the children at play, the singing sailor, and the ships continuing their daily routines, thereby emphasizing how different the speaker's feelings are from everyone else's.

Although this poem is sad, I enjoyed it. It makes me feel less lonely to know that other people feel unhappy at times, and that if I try, I can find comfort in nature. I also like the dramatic expression in this poem and the speaker's willingness to share his or her emotions with the reader. Finally, the effective use of rhythm and rhyme in this poem will probably help me remember it for a long time to come.

Sample poem: **Break, Break, Break**

by Alfred Tennyson

Break, break, break,
    On thy cold gray stones, O Sea!
And I would that my tongue could utter
    The thoughts that arise in me.

O, well for the fisherman's boy,
    That he shouts at his sister at play!
O, well for the sailor lad,
    That he sings in his boat on the bay!

And the stately ships go on
    To their haven under the hill;
But O for the touch of a vanished hand,
    And the sound of a voice that is still!

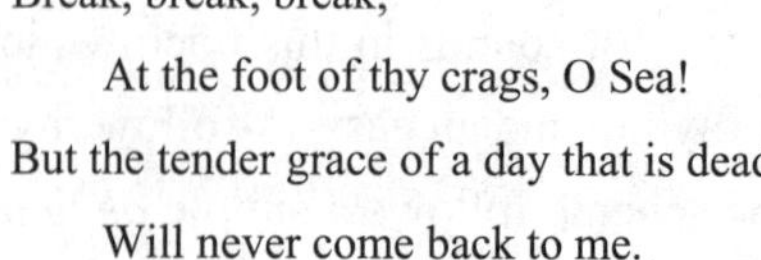

Break, break, break,
    At the foot of thy crags, O Sea!
But the tender grace of a day that is dead
    Will never come back to me.

Comment

The above essay is a discussion of the poem *Break, Break, Break* by Alfred Lord Tennyson. The writer begins with a general statement about the poem, then launches into a summary of the poem for those who have never read it. Element by element, the writer analyzes the poet's treatment of several different elements, including its use of sounds, such as rhythm, rhyme, and repetition; its effective use of figurative language; its truthful theme; and a speaker with whose feelings the writer can identify; and finally concludes the essay by sharing his or her personal, subjective reaction to the poem.

4.11 Sample Essay 2

"Like the Sand of the Hourglass..."

(A student's essay on William Faulkner's *A Rose for Emily*)

The year 1865 saw the end of the Civil War between the Union and the Confederacy, and saw the beginning of a "New South". With the many changes pressed upon the South, the so-called "Old South" could no longer exist. For example, people could not own slaves as they had in the past, and they couldn't survive anymore simply by belonging to a family with an "august name". These changes didn't happen overnight however; they took many years to occur. In William Faulkner's *A Rose for Emily*, we are shown the transition from Old South to New South as it takes place in the little town of Jefferson, and we see how Miss Emily Grierson, survivor of the Old South, resists these changes.

Jefferson was once inhabited by many well-off families who were members of the Old South's aristocratic class. As time, and the Reconstruction, marched on, these families slowly disappeared. Eventually, the last true living legacy of the Old South in Jefferson was Miss Emily Grierson. She had been raised to be a Southern Belle, an upstanding member of society, and she clung to her world of the Old South. She kept a black servant, Tobe, who did everything for her, just as if he were a slave, and she lived in "a big, squarish frame house that had once been white, decorated with cupolas and spires and scrolled balconies in the heavily lightsome style of the seventies, set on what had once been our roost select street" (para. 2). With the infiltration of the New South, however, "garages and cotton gins... encroached and obliterated even the august names of that neighborhood" (para. 2). Yet the house remained, "lifting its stubborn and coquettish decay above the cotton wagons and the gasoline pumps," just as its willful inhabitant "carried her head high... even when we believed that she was fallen" (para. 33).

The house was all that Miss Emily really had left after her father died. When he passed away, Miss Emily spent three days denying his death and not letting the doctors and ministers dispose of the body. Though it is not told first in the story, this was the first time Miss Emily had rejected the truth in order to retain her world of the past: a world in which other members of the Old South, such as Colonel Sartoris, lived on after they too had died.

Colonel Sartoris also represented the Old South, and he protected Emily when her father died. As mayor of Jefferson at the time, he remitted her taxes, and since no aristocratic woman such as Miss Emily could possibly lower herself to accept charity, came up with a story of how her father had loaned money to Jefferson and this was how

Miss Emily was to be repaid. “Only a man of Colonel Sartoris’ generation and thought could have invented it, and only a woman could have believed it.” (para. 3) So when Miss Emily was later approached by members of the generation of city authorities who wanted her taxes, she held onto the past and told them repeatedly to see Colonel Sartoris, even though he had been dead for almost ten years. Furthermore, when city authorities asked her whether or not she received “a notice from the sheriff, signed by him,” she remarks, “Perhaps he considers himself the sheriff” (paras. 9, 10). Obviously, Miss Emily didn’t accept that whoever was the new sheriff was really the sheriff. As far as she was concerned, the sheriff was still the same person it was several years ago.

We are shown not only the government of the Old South Jefferson, it sided with Miss Emily, and the government of the New South Jefferson, when it was against Miss Emily, but we also catch a glimpse of Jefferson’s government when it was still under transition. About two years after her father’s death, a smell developed around Miss Emily’s house. The “member of the rising generation” on the Board of Aldermen said that the solution to the problem was “simple enough.... Send her word to have her place cleaned up. Give her a certain time to do it in, and if she don’t...” At that point the remaining Old South revealed itself when the eighty-year-old mayor, Judge Stevens, irately asked, “[W]ill you accuse a lady to her face of smelling bad?” (paras. 22, 23). It is apparent that though there were some old-timers left, just as Jefferson changed, so did its people.

Members of the Old South were very honorable, graceful and above all, dignified. They had great respect for each other and for each other’s feelings, and were quick to help one another whenever possible. Most importantly, however, they always retained their dignity, no matter what. Miss Emily preserved her world of the Old South by hanging on to her dignity. It was because her dignity was so essential to her that a major conflict arose when Miss Emily met Homer Barren. Homer was a personification of Reconstruction and was Miss Emily’s opposite in every way. He was a Yankee, a member of the vulgar, haphazard post-war generation, and “a day laborer” having been hired to build Jefferson’s sidewalks and thereby contribute to the urbanization of the town.

When opposites attracted however, Miss Emily put her dignity on the line and was seen “on Sunday afternoons driving in the yellow-wheeled buggy and the matched team of bays from the livery stable” with Homer (para. 30). The ladies of the town said, “Of course a Grierson would not think seriously of a Northerner,” and the “older people, those of the Old South”, said “that even grief could not cause a real lady to forget *noblesse oblige*—without calling it *noblesse oblige*” (para. 31). As time passed, Homer and Miss Emily were seen again and again, until finally, “some of the ladies began to say that it was a disgrace to the town and a bad example to the young people. The men did not want to interfere, but at last the ladies forced the Baptist minister... to call upon her” (para. 44). Then “the minister’s wife wrote to Miss Emily’s relations in Alabama” (para. 44). When they arrived, Miss Emily realized she had to do something to preserve the dignity and pride that kept her Old South alive.

Her choices were few: marry Homer, or separate from him completely. At first it appeared that Miss Emily and Homer were either married or getting ready to be married, for she "ordered a man's toilet set in silver, with the letters H. B. on each piece" and she "bought a complete outfit of men's clothing, including a nightshirt" (para. 45). Unfortunately, while this may have kept her reputation from being tarnished as far as the New South people were concerned, it was still not enough for Miss Emily's Old South dignity. It demanded that she never demean herself by being married to a Northerner. Therefore, in order to keep Homer, but not what he was or what he stood for. Miss Emily killed him, then kept him in a bed where she could be with him when she chose without "compromising her dignity." This violence and necrophilia reflect her wish to hold onto the South's dead past as well as her own and the price she pays to do so.

Miss Emily retained her sense of dignity and her private version of the world of the Old South for the rest of her life. She was a "monument", "a tradition, a duty, and a care" (paras. 1, 3). Living secluded, she surrounded herself as best as she could by locking herself in her old house with only her memories and her black servant. When she died, she did so in dignity, "in a heavy walnut bed with a curtain, her gray head propped on a pillow" (para. 53). With her death went her Old South world as well, leaving behind only "the very old men—some in their brushed Confederate uniforms" to remind the New South of the past (para. 55) and to offer a rose of remembrance and respect for Emily.

Comment

The above essay is a direct response to *A Rose for Emily*. In it the writer traces the theme of resistance to change in the story. This essay is quite a success since the writer convincingly supports the thesis with examples directly from the text itself rather than citing any other sources from authoritative critics. This fully exhibits the fact that the writer has read the whole story rather carefully, and is considerably creative in composing this essay.

5 How to Take Essay Tests?

Tests or examinations are the work you do in class, usually within a given period of time. So the test essays are quite different from essays written outside the classroom. When your instructor tests you, he or she wants to know two things: how familiar you are with the course material and how creatively you can think about this material. Tests fall into two categories—*objective tests* and *essay tests*.

Objective tests ask you to account for, or identify details about the course material. *Essay tests* ask you to state your ideas about literary works and to support those ideas with reasoning and facts. Your test essays are usually arguments, which should (a) have a thesis, (b) try to convince an audience of the validity of that thesis, (c) use sound logic and apt illustrations, and (d) directly drive to the point with good organization. The following guidelines should help you perform well on essay tests.

5.1 Prepare thoroughly

Getting yourself fully prepared should always be a safe way to take essay tests. Here are some useful tips for you.

(1) Learn thoroughly the facts of the work or works on which you are being tested. Know the characters, plot, specific setting, and so on. When you are taking the test, you should know such details so well that they emerge from your memory almost automatically; otherwise you lose time for interpretation.

(2) Review the aspects of the works the instructor has emphasized in class. Focus on the elements of literature. Assume that your instructor will ask you how the author handles setting, characterization, theme, point of view, and so forth.

(3) Pay attention to your notes on the instructor's class comments. This will surely help you pinpoint important aspects of the works and help you anticipate test questions.

5.2 Plan your answer wisely

Here are three tips for you to plan your answers to an essay test in a sensible way.

(1) Think through your answer by making a short, topical outline. Making an outline will make your answers more relevant and complete. Once you have planned your answer by jotting down an outline of your plan, you can devote your writing time to a creative development of each main point.

(2) Cross out the items on your outline that do not fit the topic.

(3) Arrange the remaining items in a logical order. Descending order of importance is probably best. That way, if you run out of time, you will have covered the most important items.

5.3 Respond directly to the assignment

One or two sentences at the beginning of the essay or at strategic places throughout should work the best. Your direct response to the assignment is the thesis of your essay and therefore should usually come near the beginning or end of your essay.

The complete answer, of course, would explain and illustrate this point, but the direct response connects the whole answer to the assignment. Without a direct response, your answer may seem irrelevant. Example:

Assignment: Huck tricks Jim into believing that he dreamed they were separated in the fog. But Jim finally sees the trick for what it is. What does Huck learn from Jim's reaction?

Direct Response: Huck learns that Jim has feelings and dignity just as white people do.

5.4 Add inserts when necessary

It is acceptable, after you have read your answer through, to add new material. If the new material is short, write it in the margin, with an arrow to indicate where it fits. If the new material is long, write the words "INSERT" in the margin, accompanied with the arrow, and write the new material on the back of the page.

5.5 Write clear, simple, and correct prose

Be wary of serious errors such as sentence fragments, ambiguous pronoun references, and subject-verb disagreements. If your handwriting is usually hard to read, take care to make it legible.

5.6 Be creative

Some instructors want you to reproduce what they have said in class. Just memorize what the instructor has said and paraphrase it on the test. Other instructors, however, want your thinking, your creativity, rather than just their own. In this case, you should think for yourself! Here are some tips for you to achieve this purpose of creative thinking.

(1) Use the instructor's points, but provide your own facts from the works, showing that you are doing more than just memorizing lectures.

(2) Make your own claims. Because of limited class time, the instructor cannot cover every aspect, even all the important ones. There are usually plenty of other claims to be made. Study the work yourself, and come up with your own claims.

(3) Describe or take a stand on controversies about meaning in works of literature. Instructors often enjoy presenting controversies for class discussion. Understanding literary controversies can sharpen your perception of the work and demonstrate your creative involvement with the work.

(4) Provide detailed points in your illustration. The more details you provide, the clearer your creative involvement becomes, especially if you include details you have figured out on your own.

5.7 Sample Test Essays

Assignment: *Explain the possible symbolic meanings of the rocking horse in D. H. Lawrence's "The Rocking-Horse Winner". You should finish you essay within twenty minutes.* The following three essays all respond to this assignment.

Sample Test Essay 1

Paul seems desperately to want his mother to love him. He senses that somehow she disapproves of him, that he stands in her way of achieving happiness. He seeks solace in the rocking horse. She has told him that "luck" means having money, so he rides the horse to get money. He hopes that by giving his mother money, he can buy his way into her heart. But, unfortunately, when he gives her an enormous sum of money, she is even more unhappy than before. Paul returns to the rocking horse to get more money for her. He frantically rides the horse one last time. But although he wins the jackpot, he dies from overexcitement and exhaustion.

Comment

Although this essay has good qualities, it is nonetheless mediocre because it does not directly respond to the assignment. It clearly describes the action of the story accurately. Its organization is easy to follow. It seems to have the assignment vaguely in mind, but nowhere does it say what the rocking horse symbolizes. The instructor may guess what the writer has in mind, but he or she cannot know for sure. The essay also omits important details. The writer does not even say, for example, how Paul uses the horse to win money. The instructor may wonder whether the writer has actually read the story carefully.

Sample Test Essay 2

Paul's mother claims that she is "unlucky," and she explains to Paul that being unlucky means having no money. But the details of the story suggest that Paul's family does have money, because they live very well. The family is quite well-off—they have a nurse, a large house, comfortable furnishings, and a gardener. The mother, then, isn't really poor but is obsessed with money. Her children sense this obsession. Most sensitive of all is Paul, who hears voices saying, "There must be more money! There must be more money!" As a result, Paul sets out to win his mother's love by being "lucky". His means of achieving luck and thus his mother's love is the rocking horse. He finds that by riding the horse hard enough, he can predict winners of horse races. The rocking horse, then, symbolizes the love his mother has withheld from him. He even experiences something like the ecstasy of love when riding the horse to a winner. But his plan fails when his gift of 5,000 pounds only makes his mother's greed greater. He then becomes so desperate for love that he rides the rocking horse to his death.

Comment

This is a good essay. It not only recounts details from the story accurately, it also directly responds to the assignment, and it relates all the details cited from the story to support the thesis. In other words, the details become "evidence". Because it deals directly with the assignment, it treats the story more specifically and thoroughly than does Essay 1.

Sample Test Essay 3

In *The Rocking-Horse Winner*, the rocking horse symbolizes many things. Paul's mother complains that she has no money, and she tells Paul that to be "lucky" is to have money.

Paul is very impressed by what she says and decides to prove to her that he is lucky. He wants also to stop the voices in the house that incessantly demand more money. He feels that the rocking horse can take him to where luck is. Sure enough, when he rides the rocking horse and it takes him "there", he can predict the winners of horse races and make a great deal of money. So one thing the rocking horse symbolizes is luck, which, in turn, means money.

But the rocking horse also seems to represent a second idea. Paul's uncle says after Paul dies that Paul is better off being dead than living in a world where he had to ride a rocking horse to find a winner. The implication is that Paul was using the rocking horse to get what his mother never gave him: her love. So the rocking horse also symbolizes Paul's need for love and his parents' failure to give him love.

Finally, the rocking horse symbolizes success. When Paul rides the rocking horse far enough, it brings him financial success. But this success is only ironic, for it never brings him the "success" he desperately wants—his mother's love—and in the end it brings him death. Lawrence seems to suggest that some kinds of success are better than others; it is better to be loved than to be rich.

Comment

This is an excellent test essay. Like Essay 2, the essay responds to the assignment directly, and it plausibly and logically connects details of the story to its points. But it is more detailed and creative than Essay 2. The writer makes a strong case for the complexity of the symbolic rocking horse, by so doing, points to the multiple meanings and richness of the story.

6 Major Critical Approaches

To increase our ability to understand a work, we may choose to read books of literary criticism written by experts who describe, analyze, interpret, or evaluate a work of literature. Although one definition of *criticism* is "the act of finding fault", we should bear in mind the original meaning of the term when we speak of literary criticism. The word *criticize* actually means to discern. Criticism in this sense has the implied meaning of observing, recognizing, categorizing, making distinctions, and forming judgments. To read critically, then, is to understand it more profoundly, and to evaluate the merit of the work itself and the author's achievement in the world of literature. The following is a brief introduction of some helpful literary approaches to the interpretation of literary works.

6.1 Formalistic criticism

Perhaps the most frequently used method is the *formalistic approach*, also called *analytical criticism*, which believes that a literary work is a unified artistic whole that can be understood by analyzing its different parts. Its primary method is through a close reading or a systematic analysis of the literary text itself. First of all, this approach has to provide readers with the critical terms of the basic elements that make up the literary work, such as plot, character, setting, point of view, theme, symbol, allegory, tone, style, and so on. All these elements relate to each other and to the work as a whole. Without a good command of them, students would have almost no way to discuss literature. In a sense, such critical terms are the working tools for the study of literature.

In brief, formalists discover the central meaning of a literary work through detailed analyses of the work's formal elements rather than by going outside the work to consider other issues, whether biographical, historical, psychological, social, political, or ideological. Such additional considerations, in their eyes, are external, and so are of secondary importance, if any.

6.2 Biographical criticism

Some critics (such as the formalists) insist that biographical information at best distracts from and at worst distorts the process of understanding literary works. These critics believe that literary works must stand on their own, stripped of the facts of their writers' lives. But biographical critics argue that there are essentially three kinds of benefits readers can acquire from using biographical evidence for literary interpretation: (1) readers understand literary works better since the facts about the authors' experiences can help readers decide how to interpret those works; (2) readers can better appreciate a literary work for knowing the writers' struggles, conflicts, or difficulties in creating it; and (3) readers can better assess the writers' preoccupations by studying the ways they adjust their actual experience in their literary works.

In a certain sense, considering biographical information and using it as a help to analyze the literary work can be illuminating rather than distracting or distorting the works we read. As with any critical approach, the biographical perspective should be used helpfully in keeping the reader' focus on the literary work and using the biographical information to develop a proper interpretation.

6.3 Historical criticism

Historical critics assert that literature, as a consciously organized and highly unified work of literary craftsmanship, has a long history of development. Today's popular literary forms, either in prose, verse, or drama, originated themselves from folktales, ballads, fables, myths, or legends. So we have to know that all literature exists in time and bears the unmistakable imprint of the period in which it is written. Each age has its own prevailing mode of literary form—classicism, neoclassicism, romanticism, realism, surrealism, naturalism, transcendentalism, modernism, postmodernism, so on and so forth.

Historical critics approach literature mainly in two ways: (1) they provide a context of background information necessary for understanding how literary works were perceived in their time; (2) they show how literary works reflect ideas and attitudes of that time. They believe that this is necessary and even indispensable because every literary work is a product of its time and its world. Understanding the social background and the intellectual currents of that time and that world can undoubtedly shed some light on the literary works for readers of later generations who may know very little about the past.

6.4 Psychological criticism

Psychological critics approach a work of literature through analyzing the revelation of the author's mind and personality reflected both in the work itself and in the process of writing it. Critics who employ a psychological perspective do so to explain how a literary work reflects its writer's consciousness and mental world, and they use what they know of writers' lives to explain features of their work. Some psychological critics may study a writer's works along with letters and diaries for better understanding not just what a writer has done in life but why the writer behaved in a particular manner.

6.5 Sociological criticism

Like historical and biographical critics, sociological critics argue that literary works should not be isolated from the social contexts in which they are written. They focus on the values of a society and how those values are reflected in literary works.

Sociological critics are indebted to the political theory of Karl Marx and Friedrich Engels. Marxist critics examine literature for its reflection of how dominant elite and bourgeois values lead to the control and suppression of the working classes. They see the value of literature in promoting social and economic revolution. Such changes would include the overthrow of the dominant capitalist ideology and the loss of power by those with money and privilege.

6.6 Feminist criticism

Feminist criticism, like Marxist and historicist criticism, examines the social and cultural aspects of literary works, especially for what those works reveal about the role, position, and influence of women. Feminist critics typically see literature as an arena to contest for power and control, because feminist critics, just like sociological critics, also see literature as an agent for social transformation.

Moreover, feminist critics seek to redress the imbalance of literary study in which all important books are written by men or the only characters of real interest are male protagonists. Feminist critics have thus begun to study women writers whose works have been previously neglected. They have begun to look at the way feminine consciousness has been portrayed in literature. In these and other ways feminist critical perspectives have begun to undermine the masculinist assumptions that have dominated critical approaches to literature until rather recently.

6.7 Reader-response criticism

Reader-response criticism raises the question of *where literary meaning dwells*—in the literary text, in the reader, or in the interaction between text and reader. Some reader-response critics see the literary text as a kind of mirror in which readers see themselves. In making sense of literature, readers recreate themselves. Others focus on the text rather than on the feelings and reactions of the reader. These text-centered reader-response critics emphasize the temporal aspect of reading, suggesting that readers make sense of texts by moving through a text sentence by sentence, line by line, word by word, filling in gaps and making inferences about what is being implied by textual details as they read.

Of course, as you read, you may change your mind about your initial reaction to a work. You may experience opposite or different feelings as you read. Or you may make sense of the work differently because of discoveries you make later in the process of reading. Reading Shakespeare's *Hamlet* in high school can be a very different experience from reading it in college as an adult. And readers from different generations and different centuries interpret books differently. The crucial thing for readers is to acknowledge their own subjectivity in the process of reading. Being aware of our limitations when we read can prevent our biases and prejudices.

6.8 Cultural studies criticism

The term "cultural studies" indicates a wide range of critical approaches to the study of literature and society. It is a kind of umbrella term that not only includes approaches to the critical analysis of society such as Marxism, feminism, and historicism, but also refers to a wide range of interdisciplinary studies, including women's studies, African-American studies, Asian American studies, Latino studies, and other types of area studies.

Traditionally, and especially from the perspective of anthropology, culture has been considered as the way of life of a people, including its customs, beliefs, and attitudes, all of which cohere in a unified and organic way of life. Consequently, to analyze a work of literature from the cultural studies perspective should and can be an effective method to appreciate literature since everyone in the society must be richly loaded with cultural connotations, and writers, along with their works, are of no exception.

6.9 Practical criticism

Practical criticism, also called *applied criticism*, concerns with the discussion of particular works and writers. This approach stresses on "close reading" of single texts, which was the typical mode of practical criticism in the *American New Criticism.* Practical criticism sometimes analyzes a work from the following aspects.

(1) From an *impressionistic* perspective. The reader attempts to represent in words the felt qualities of a particular work, and to express his or her responses, namely the "impression", that the work directly evokes from the reader. At its extreme this mode of criticism becomes "the adventures of a sensitive soul among masterpieces" (Anatole France).

(2) From a *judicial* perspective. This approach tends to treat the work as an entity in itself. The reader strives to evaluate and analyze the effects of a work by referring to its subject, organization, techniques, style, and so on, to make judgments about a work on specified criteria of literary excellence.

(3) From a *mimetic* perspective. The reader views the literary work as an imitation, reflection, or representation of the world and human life. The primary criterion applied to a work is the "truth" of its representation to the subject matter that it represents. This mode of criticism, which first appeared in Plato and in Aristotle, remains characteristic of modern theories of literary realism.

(4) From a *pragmatic* perspective. The critic sees the work as something constructed in order to achieve certain effects on the audience, such as aesthetic pleasure, instruction, or emotion, and it tends to judge the value of the work according to its success in achieving those effects on the part of the readers.

(5) From an *expressive* perspective. The reader treats a work primarily in relation to its author. The expressive perspective defines literature as an expression or overflow of feelings on the part of the author. It tends to judge the work by its sincerity and the experiences of the writer who, consciously or unconsciously, has revealed himself or herself in it. Such views were developed mainly by romantic critics in the early 19th century and remain popular in our own time.

6.10 Some tips on applying critical approaches

Here are some tips on applying critical approaches:

(1) Select certain critical approaches that may be more suitable than others. Although certain works have been discussed from quite a few critical perspectives, we probably find that certain critical approaches can make a better interpretive fit than others. Select the one you feel most appropriate.

(2) Make a combination of several critical perspectives. You may wish, for example, to combine formalistic and historical perspectives. Or you may wish to combine feminist approach with biographical or psychological approaches, and the like.

(3) Do not make overuse of critical approaches. There might exist a danger in using a particular critical approach to analyze all literary texts. Some people tend to read works with an eye toward making them conform to their particular favorite theory. They may

distort the text of a literary work by quoting from it selectively or by ignoring aspects that do not conform to their theoretical approach. A possible solution to this problem is to see the various critical perspectives merely as interpretive possibilities, and select the one that is most appropriate for analyzing the work we read.

(4) Regard all the critical perspectives as heuristics. During reading, we should regard the critical perspectives we choose as heuristics, or methods for generating constructive ideas about literature. Such a perspective often takes the form of a questionnaire. If we can ask a sequence of questions as a preparation for reading literature, we may be able to get the most from what we read.

7 Major Literary Schools

To have an in-depth understanding of literary works, in addition to adopting some necessary approaches in literary criticism we also have to familiarize ourselves with some important literary schools in the course of historical development of literature.

7.1 Classicism and neoclassicism

In a broad sense, literary classicism refers to a formal orthodox work in ancient Greece and Rome that is considered first rate or excellent of its kind, and therefore standard and fit to be used as a model to be imitated. Classicism had the following two main features.

First, the early classicism supported and defended the power of the Monarchy, believing that literature should serve the administration of the kings. Thus, classicism had an apparent court tendency and neglected the artistic need of the working class.

Then classicism advocated rationalism. They think that reason should be above everything else. For them, logical thought should be the dominant element in literary creation, and romantic emotion and excessive imagination should be restricted. Therefore, precise idea, elegant form, realistic description, and standardized language are strictly required in classicism.

Neoclassicism may be taken to denote the deliberate imitation of the works of antiquity, flourishing in England in the late 17th and 18th centuries, as represented by Samuel Johnson, John Dryden, Alexander Pope, Joseph Addison, and Richard Steele. Neoclassic writers esteemed such virtuous qualities as objectivity, harmony, rationality, dignity, proportion, and moderation. They conceived literature to be primarily an art—a set of craftsmanship with artistic styles. According to neoclassicists, poetry should follow the ancient divisions, and should be epic, didactic, satiric, or dramatic, each being guided by its own principles. Prose should be precise, direct, smooth, and flexible. Drama should be characterized by such qualities as rhymed couplet instead of blank verse. The most influential rule was the three unities (time, place and action), requiring that a play should have one plot, carried out at one place in no more than 24 hours.

In the eyes of classicism and neoclassicism, the aim of literature is to yield both instruction and aesthetic pleasure to readers. Not art for art's sake, but art for humanity's sake, was the central ideal of neoclassic humanism. So many of the great neoclassic works attack human pride, avoid extremes, and keep human desires within appropriate limits. Specifically, the 18th century is known as the age of neoclassicism, and an age of reason, order, and elegance. Neoclassicists, such as Addison, Steele, Swift, Pope, Johnson, and Gray, made great effort to strive for a rational human perspective which is neither too high nor too low, but balanced, ordered, and reasoned.

The Neoclassic Period in England spans the 140 years or so after the Restoration (1660) until the publication of William Wordsworth's *Lyrical Ballads* in 1798 which declared the beginning of the Romantic Movement.

7.2 Romanticism

Romanticism is a school of literature opposed to neoclassicism. William Wordsworth's preface to the 2nd edition of *Lyrical Ballads* in 1800 was written as a poetic manifesto, in which he denounced the upper class subjects and the poetic diction of the preceding century and proposed to deal with materials from "common life" in "a selection of language really used by men". Some of the romanticists of this period include Blake, Wordsworth, Coleridge, Byron, Keats, and Shelley. Broadly speaking, romanticism has the following characteristics.

(1) For romanticists, intuitions and emotions were more crucial than reason and common sense. They held that one could find truth through one's feelings and that not everything could be explained by reason.

(2) Romanticists emphasized individualism, placing the individual against the group and the authority. They saw the individual at the very center of life and art and emphasized personal freedom and freedom from formalism, tradition, and conformity.

(3) Romanticists did not conceive of the world as stereotyped object made by God. They thought of the world as a living, breathing being, and emphasized firmly the close relationship between man and nature, which is why nature was a suitable subject of true art. They held that humanity close to nature would not be affected by civilization and could not be possibly bad. The greatest human joy was to imitate nature, absorb it, and be absorbed by it.

(4) Romanticists stressed individual and creative function of imagination, and placed individual at the very center of all life and all experience and at the center of art.

(5) American romanticists are classified into early romantics and high romantics. Early romanticists were naive, experimental conformist, self-conscious and imitative, including Irving, Bryant, and Cooper, whose works were picturesque, but lacked a deeper power. Major high romanticists include Edgar Allan Poe, Walt Whitman and Emily

Dickinson in poetry, and Nathaniel Hawthorne and Herman Melville in fiction, who tended to present the dark and brooding pictures of the United States.

7.3 Realism

According to Holman, "Realism is, in the broadest sense, simply fidelity to actuality in its representation in literature." Realism is based on the accurate, unromantic observation of human experiences. As for style and subject matter, it insists on precise description, authentic action, true-to-life dialogue, moral honesty, and a democratic openness. As a literary movement, it is a period concept, which refers to the approach of realist fiction occurred at the latter part of the 19th century. By paying less attention to general ideas and more to the immediate facts of life, realism came as a reaction against falseness and sentimentality of romanticism and sentimentalism in the earlier periods of history. The following are the major features of realist works.

(1) Realism stresses truthful treatment of material in a straightforward or matter-of-fact manner rather than abstract interest in such substantial subjects as life, death, and nature.

(2) In realist fiction, characters from all social levels are examined in depth. Realists keep examining how characters relate to each other, and stress the function of environment in shaping characters. Thus they have a strong tendency to explore the psychology of the people in the story.

(3) Open ending is an important feature of realism, implying that life is complex and cannot be fully understood. Moreover, this can leave much room for the reader to contemplate over the possible conclusions of the story.

(4) Realism focuses on common lives of the average people rather than characters as symbols. By the end of the 19th century, in particular, the reading public in America was willing to read about average folks who were just like themselves instead of stories about royal families.

(5) Realism emphasizes objectivity rather than idealistic views of human nature. Simple, clear, direct prose is the desirable style of writing. The author just presents the reader what the characters do and lets the reader decide what it really means.

(6) Realism presents moral visions. Realists are aware of the accepted social criteria and have a strong ethical sense about the right and wrong ways of doing things. They are able to probe deeply into these problems of the human conscience with completely objective methods.

7.4 Naturalism

The background of naturalism in literature originated from Charles Darwin (1809—1882), an English naturalist and author. His *Origin of Species* (1859) had a strong influence in the history of Western thought. Darwin's theory, or Darwinism, believes that the origin of species is derived by descent with variation from parent forms, and that, in the process of natural selection, only those who are best adapted to their surroundings can survive in the struggle for existence.

Darwin developed these ideas to talk about biological organism. Herbert Spencer (1820—1903) grafted Darwin's theories into the theory of social Darwinism—the weak and stupid would fall victim in the natural course of events to economic forces. His ideas, which became a metaphor for all existence, were then applied to society. The writers also found a way to explain human behavior according to Darwin's natural selection, exploring why some people were successful and why others were failures. The major features of naturalism are as follows.

(1) Naturalism applies the principles of scientific determinism to fiction. It views human beings as animals in the natural world. All their actions are controlled and determined by fate, which is called pessimistic "determinism". Humans, like anxious little ants, have no free will to make their own choices, and human desires to create great things are overpowered by the force of natural surroundings.

(2) The world is indifferent and hostile to human desires. Life becomes a struggle for survival. Hence, the individual struggle to adapt to environment and the Darwinian idea of the survival of the fittest become natural concerns of naturalist works. Social systems that destroy and dehumanize and the individual experience of loss and failure are the two recurrent concerns for naturalists.

(3) Naturalists, like realists, also describe real life, the way things really are, and do not escape into a world of illusion. But naturalists are not at all genteel; they do not simply look at the average, but rather, they pay great attention to the violent, sordid, unpleasant, and ugly aspects in life, such as selfishness, prostitution, crimes, and war. Instead of describing middle-class life, naturalists would go to the slums and write about poverty and crime.

7.5 Modernism

Most historians of literature agree that the high modernism came after World War I. The catastrophe of the war had shaken the faith in the moral basis of Western civilization and raised doubts about the adequacy of traditional literary modes in representing the harsh realities of the postwar world. Influenced by different ideas, thoughts, and various social realities, modernism was made up of many facets: symbolism, surrealism, existentialism, and so on. These different schools had their own special characteristics, but on the whole, they possessed certain common features. All of them put together constituted the school of modernism, the major features of which are as follows.

(1) Modernism involves a deliberate and radical break from the traditional art and

culture in subject matter. In this sense, important intellectual modernists are usually thinkers who had questioned the values of traditional social structure, religion, morality—thinkers such as Friedrich Nietzsche, Karl Marx, Sigmund Freud, and so on.

(2) In content, the frequent theme of modernism is for man to search for his own identity. To modernists, the world is an irrational machine from which man can never escape and in which man is an indifferent, selfish, and cruel animal. He is perplexed and does not know where he belongs. In such a world of chaos, he loses his identity and wishes to find it back. As a result, modernists deny rationalism and science. It stresses intuition, instinct, and subconsciousness in literary creation.

(3) In form, modernism is the synonym of revolution. In stressing its unconventional form, modernists advocate "art for art's sake". Art to them should be separated from life and politics. It serves nothing but itself. Modernism is the phenomenon called the *avant-garde* (a military metaphor for "advancc-guard"), a small, self-conscious group of artists and authors who deliberately undertake to "make it new" (Ezra Pound). By violating the accepted conventions, they set out to create ever-new artistic forms and styles and to introduce neglected, and sometimes forbidden, subject matter into their writing. Frequently, the *avant-garde*'s important aim is to shock the sensibilities of the conventional reader and to challenge the norms of the dominant Western culture.

Major works of modernist fiction, following Joyce's *Ulysses* and his even more radical *Finnegans Wake* (1939), subvert the basic conventions of earlier prose fiction by breaking up the narrative continuity through the use of stream of consciousness, interior monologue, psychological depth, and other innovative modes of narration. Among other writers who are central representatives of modernism are William Faulkner, William Butler Yeats, William Carlos Williams, and Eugene O'Neill.

7.6 Postmodernism

The term postmodernism is often applied to the literature and art after World War II (1939—1945), when the effects on Western morale of the first war were greatly made worse by the experience of Nazism, the threat of the atomic bomb, the advancing devastation of the natural environment, and the frightening fact of overpopulation. Postmodernism involves not only a continuation of the counter-traditional experiments of modernism, but also an attempt to break away from modernist forms of "high art" which had, in the eyes of the postmodernists, already become conventional. The major features of postmodernism are as follows.

(1) Postmodernism is to subvert the foundations of our accepted modes of thought and experience, prominently in Samuel Beckett and other authors of the literature of the absurd. They tried to reveal the meaninglessness of existence and the underlying "abyss", or "void" or "nothingness" on which any supposed security is conceived to be

precariously suspended.

(2) Postmodernism, especially in America, began to question, mock, and parody the official discourse. The line between the real and the imaginary was collapsed, and absurdity permeated on all levels of social life. Joseph Heller provided an excellent example in *Catch-22* (1961), which attacks the absurdity of World War II, and protests against the absurdity of modern America.

(3) The narrative in postmodernism became fragmented, discontinuous, ironic, and full of black humor. It carries the tone of anger and bitterness in the grotesque situations of suffering, anxiety and death. It makes readers laugh at the blackness of modern life. Modernists feel amused at their characters' vain attempt to create order in their absurd world.

(4) Postmodern writers held that the reality of modern life was too elusive and uncertain for people to rationalize and idealize. Any attempt to impose order on a disordered reality was artificial and falsifying. As a result, postmodern texts are disintegrated into a form of deliberate un-readability, chaos, and absurdity of the world which might be the only meaningful ways of life.

(5) Postmodern writers challenged the terms that defined modernist fiction as stream of consciousness, interior monologue, psychological depth. Postmodern fiction undermined the modernist tradition and rejected its mimetic function, by offering a collection of fragments, a puzzling catalogue of lists, a montage of disparate elements both in space and time. While modernists tried to control the fragmented society through the agency of art and give it an art form, postmodern writers were too skeptical to trust their own ability to give shape or significance to the absurd world. Postmodernism found itself unable to structure any ordering ideas of reality and so thought of reality as itself unreal. Rather than observing the modernist slogan "Make It New", postmodern writers slowed things down.

Questions and Exercises

1. Why learning literature in English is a must for English majors? What can be some of the effective ways to learn literature?
2. What are the major critical approaches for literary criticism? Why are they so crucial in the process of interpreting literary texts?
3. What are the major literary schools in English literature? Besides those discussed in this part of the textbook, what other literary schools do you know?

Part 2

A Guide to Appreciating English Poetry

1 Introduction

1.1 Nature of poetry

Long before people had systems of writing, they often shared stories in form of poetry. Only in the last few hundred years have some people chosen to write in prose instead of poetry.

Poetry is the form of literature in which the words and meanings of language are manipulated to enhance what is to be communicated by ear or eye; and it is characterized by special uses of *rhythm, sound,* and *language.* Properties of poetry fall into two categories: the external, including all those elements concerning the outer form of poetry; and the internal, all those concerning the inner content of poetry. (1) External qualities: You have probably noticed that poems look different on the page from other kinds of literature in prose form. The prime external characteristics of poetry are as follows. First, poetry is *metrical,* that is, the words are arranged according to some sort of rhythmical schemes. Second, the effect of the rhythm is augmented by the use of *rhyme*, and by other sound devices as assonance, consonance, alliteration and onomatopoeia. Third, the sentences of a poem are broken up into lines, and these lines are usually shorter than prose lines. Each new line often begins with a capital letter. The lines of a poem are sometimes grouped together into stanzas, and usually each stanza works to develop a single idea. (2) Internal qualities: The internal qualities constitute the true nature of poetry, including the poet's imaginative awareness, feeling, view of the experience, and attitude towards the world. These poetic thoughts are the key to inspire the emotional response on the part of the reader.

Every poem has a speaker—the person or thing that "relates" the poem. Often the speaker is the poet, but sometimes the poet speaks in the voice of another person, an animal, or an object. The inner qualities of poetry are often revealed through this speaker. And it is often the internal qualities rather than the external qualities that decide whether or not a piece of work is poetry. Consequently, many works of metrical composition seem to be but not really is poetry; and numerous real poems such as free poetry are not metrical writing, nor even in verse form at all.

1.2 Various descriptions about poetry

According to the dictionary, a poet is not only a writer of poems but also a person who demonstrates keen insight and a vivid imagination. From this we can suppose that insightfulness and imagination are major characteristics of a poem. Of course, as for what the essence of poetry is, many people have given specific descriptions from their own perspectives. Let us just refer to some of them.

Thomas Nashe: Poetry is the honey of all flowers, the quintessence of all science, the marrow of wit, and the very phrase of angels.

Lee Teng-hwee: Poetry is the expression of impassioned feeling in language.

Eric Warner & Graham Hough: A poem deserves its title only inasmuch as it excites, by elevating the soul. The value of the poem is in the ratio of this elevating excitement.

William Wordsworth: Poetry is the spontaneous overflow of powerful feelings; it takes its origin from emotion recollected in tranquility.

Charles Barber: Poetry is imaginative literature written in verse.

Emily Dickinson: If I read a book and it makes my body so cold that no fire can ever warm me, I know that is poetry. If I feel physically as if the top of my head were taken off, I know that is poetry.

Edwin Arlington Robinson: Poetry is a language that tells us, through a more or less emotional reaction, something that cannot be said.

Henry Huizinga: Poetry is thought expressed and arranged in such a way that the feelings of the author and the reader harmonize with the sound of the words. It is usually written so that the accents or stress of syllables come at regular intervals, the lines are of fixed length, with words of similar sound at the ends of the lines. The regularity of accent is called rhythm, and the similarity of sound is called rhyme.

R. M. Alden: Poetry is the art of presenting human experiences, in so far as they are of lasting or universal interest, in metrical language, usually with chief reference to the emotions and by means of the imagination.

The following example can illustrate a good case in point where poetry can express a kind of emotion in a way that prose can never do.

To Celia

Drink to me only with thine eyes,
And I will pledge with mine;
Or leave a kiss but in the cup,
And I'll not ask for wine.

Ben Johnson

If we rewrite this stanza of the poem in prose form as follows, no poetic taste can ever be found in it.

Drink to me only with your eyes, and I'll pledge my love to you with my eyes; or leave a kiss within the cup, that's all I'll want to drink.

Or you may paraphrase it more clearly as:

Let's not drink. Let's just sit down and look at each other. Or put a kiss in my cup and I won't want anything to drink.

Therefore, we can see that poetry at least has the following features. First, it should reveal human experiences of permanent or universal interest. Second, poetry may use specific poetic diction mostly used in poetry such as *thine* for *your*. Third, poetry has rhyme such as *mine—wine*. And fourth, poetry has rhythm, that is, poetry should be written in metrical language, accents or stress of syllables coming at regular intervals.

Yet the first three are not the most important distinctions, as any form of literature should reveal human experiences, poetry also uses common vocabulary, and some free verse and blank verse poems do not have rhyme either. Thus, the most important distinction between prose and poetry is that all poems have their specific "rhythmic patterns", which is the most distinctive feature of poetry.

Another thing that we should bear in mind is that the sound of poetry also contributes greatly to its distinctive qualities. Ideally, we should read a poem aloud to appreciate fully its impact. Poets seek to create an overall pattern or quality of sound that is appropriate to the particular mood and meaning of a poem, with the various techniques of rhythm, rhyme, alliteration, assonance, consonance, and so on. Therefore, it is not exaggerated to say that poetry becomes poetry only when it is read aloud with the reader's whole feelings fully involved.

1.3 Value of learning poetry

It is not inappropriate to say that poetry is the finest flower of literature and that all best things are crystallized from the human soul. Some believe that all truth, virtue and beauty, dwell in poetry, since poetic language is the loftiest and purest language, the best words in their best order. Percy Bysshe Shelley even said that poets are the unacknowledged legislators of the world. Therefore, different people may gain different benefits through reading poetry. Here are some of the eloquent sayings about the value of learning poetry.

Poetry brings blessing to our life both physically and psychologically.

Poetry brings the light of knowledge as a whole.

Poetry is a fundamental way of expressing human emotion and thought.

Appreciation of poetry helps us to foster an aesthetic taste and lofty sentiments.

It is always summer in poetry.

It would be an unimaginable loss for a student of liberal arts to be shut away from the magnificent mansion of poetry.

The following poem written by Eleanor Farjeon may intrigue our mysterious keenness to learn poetry.

Poetry

What is Poetry? Who knows?
Not a rose, but the scent of the rose;
Not the sky, but the light in the sky;
Not the fly, but the gleam of the fly;
Not the sea, but the sound of the sea;
Not myself, but what makes me
See, hear, and feel something that prose
Cannot: and what it is, who knows?

2 Scansion of Poetry

We have to know some literary terms such as "rhythm", "meter", "rhyme," "line" and "stanza" for the scansion of a poem.

2.1 Rhythm

The term "rhythm" is derived from a Greek word meaning "flow", namely, to move from place to place with a regular pattern. In poetry, rhythm refers to the regular recurrence of the stressed and unstressed syllables in a line of a poem. Rhythm exists everywhere. It is omnipresent—from the clicking of a clock to the change of seasons, motion of heavenly bodies, music playing, drum-beating, and the regular activities of human body such as breathing and heart-beating.

2.2 Meter and foot

"Meter" refers to the rhythmic pattern of a poetic line with fixed arrangement of stressed and unstressed syllables. It is the basic unit to analyze a line of poetry. But when we actually come to measure a line, we use the name "foot", the unit in which meter is measured. In other words, "foot" is used to count the number of such a rhythmic pattern repeatedly occurring in the line. For example,

∪ — | ∪ — | ∪ — | ∪ —
For men may come and men may go

The above line has four *feet* of *iambic meter*, so the metrical pattern of the line is *iambic tetrameter*.

2.3 Rhythmic patterns

When we use scansion to analyze the rhythmic patterns of a poem, we should first divide a line into syllables, and then see which are stressed syllables and which are unstressed syllables. Then use markers "—" to denote a stressed syllable, "∪" to denote an unstressed syllable, and "×" to denote an omitted syllable, thus we have the following

∪— | ∪—|∪—| ∪ —

I have to eat to live my life.

This line has four unstressed syllables and four stressed syllables respectively. Each unstressed syllable and stressed syllable make up one meter, a basic unit to scan rhythmic patterns of a line.

In scanning a poem, two factors must be taken into account: (1) how each set of unstressed syllables and stressed syllables are arranged; (2) how many times such a form appears in one line. We use foot, together with the rhythmic patterns, to scan a line of English poetry. The following rhythmic patterns or metrical forms are commonly seen in English poetry.

(1) Iambus (iambic *adj*.): one unstressed syllable followed by one stressed syllable.

∪ —| ∪ —| ∪ —|∪ —

When Daisies pied and violets blue

This line has four feet of iambic rhythmic pattern. It is also called a line of iambic tetrameter.

(2) Trochee (trochaic adj.): one stressed syllable followed by one unstressed syllable.

— ∪|— ∪ |— ∪ | — ×

Shake your chains to earth like dew

— ∪| —∪ |— ∪ |— ∪

Double double toil and trouble,

The above two line have four feet of trochaic rhythmic pattern each, which is also called a line of trochaic tetrameter.

(3) Anap(a)est [anap(a)estic adj.]: two unstressed syllables followed by one stressed syllable.

∪ ∪ —| ∪ ∪—

Like a ghost from the tomb

∪∪— |∪∪ — |∪∪—|

I arise and unbuild it again.

The first line has two feet of anapestic rhythmic pattern. It is also called a line of anapestic dimeter. And the second line has three feet of anapestic rhythmic pattern, which is also called a line of anapestic trimeter.

(4) Dactyl (dactylic adj.): one stressed syllable followed by two unstressed syllables.

— ∪ ∪ | — ∪∪ |— ∪ ∪

Dragging the corn by her golden hair

This line has three feet of dactylic rhythmic pattern, which is also called a line of dactylic trimeter.

(5) Spondee (spondaic adj.): one stressed syllable forms a meter by itself.

— | —

Break, break

This line has two feet of spondaic rhythmic pattern, which is also called a line of spondaic dimeter.

(6) Amphibrach: one unstressed syllable followed by one stressed syllable and one unstressed syllable.

∪ — ∪ | ∪ — ∪

My heart's in the highlands

This line has two feet of amphibrach rhythmic pattern, which is also called a line of amphibrach dimeter.

(7) Pyrrhic: a foot of two unstressed syllables alone, the opposite of the spondee but is less frequently found in English poetry.

∪∪ | ∪ — |∪∪| ∪ — | ∪ — |

It is the cause, it is the cause, my soul!

This line has five feet of mixed pyrrhic/iambic rhythmic patterns.

(8) Sprung rhythm: The term *sprung rhythm*, created by Gerard Manley Hopkins, is a kind of meter in which each foot contains one stressed syllable, usually the first, and followed by any number of unstressed syllables. Hopkins believed this should be the rhythm of natural speech in reading poetry.

— — —

Ding, Dong, Bell,

— ∪ ∪ ∪ —

Pussy's in the well.

Notice that the number of unstressed syllables may vary from foot to foot. Also, in sprung rhythm, two or even more accented syllables may occur together.

Among the above eight metric patterns, iambus is the commonest—approximately 90% of English poems use it. The first four are regarded as the commonly seen rhythmic patterns. Generally speaking, one poem usually contains one domineering rhythmic pattern. Yet, a mixture use of different rhythmic patterns is also rather common and quite acceptable in English poetry.

2.4 Metrical mutations

Meter in poetry marks the basic rhythmic pattern or theoretical design, from which the actual rhythm of a poem always departs. This, however, in no way suggests that the poet is inferior in talent. For putting a poem under certain strict metrical patterns is not as tough a job as it might seem. Take Doctor Samuel Johnson's little parody of simple-minded poets:

I put my hat upon my head
And walked into the Strand,
And there I met another man
Whose hat was in his hand.

This poem is obviously in the common measure. But the fact that it scans so nicely is no proof that it is good poetry, for perfectly regular metrical verse, though not hardly manageable, sounds sing-song and is often dull to read.

Metrical mutation refers to variation in metrical patterns. It is one of the most important laws of English prosody. The predominating rhythmic tendency of a given poem serves as "the model line", which sets the underlying rhythmic pattern. The model line functions as the metronome in the music of poetry. The metronome only exists in the head of the poet or the reader; to break away from the model line is rather common and natural in English poetry.

— ∪| — ∪∪|— ∪∪ |— —
Let me not to the marriage of true minds
This is a mixed variation of "trochee-dactyl-dactyl-spondee" metrical patterns.
∪ ∪ — | ∪— |
I'd a dream tonight
∪∪—| ∪— |
As I fell asleep.

3 Poetic Lines

A poetic line is an aural and visual stretch of words, and it is the basic compositional unit of a poem written in verse. English poetic lines can mainly be classified into the following six kinds according to the number of feet contained in one line.

3.1 Monometer

It is a poetic line with only one foot.

— ∪
Cuckoo
This is a line with trochaic monometer.

3.2 Dimeter

It is a poetic line with two feet.

∪ —| ∪ —
Reply, reply!
This is a line with iambic dimeter.

3.3 Trimeter

It is a poetic line with three feet.

∪ —| ∪ — | ∪ —

What man has made of man?

This is a line with iambic trimeter.

3.4 Tetrameter

It is a poetic line with four feet.

—∪∪| — ∪ ∪|— × ∪|— ××|

Merrily, swim we, the moon shines bright:

— ∪ ∪|— ∪ ∪ |—∪ ∪|— ××|

Downward we drift through the shadow and light.

Each of these two lines has four feet of dactylic tetrameter.

3.5 Pentameter

It is a poetic line with five feet.

∪ — |∪ — |∪—|∪— |∪ —

One man I missed him on the customed hill

This is a line with iambic pentameter.

3.6 Hexameter

It is the famous Alexandrine, a common classical metrical form, a line made of six iambic feet, belongs under this head. It is a quite common classical metrical form in conventional poems.

—∪∪ | ∪ —|∪ — |∪ — |∪—|∪ — ∪|

Suddenly I saw the cold and rook-delighting heaven

∪ — |∪ — |∪ — |∪ — |∪ ∪ — |— ×|

That seemed as though ice burned and was but the more ice.

4 Rhyme Schemes

Rhyme refers to the identity or strong similarity between terminal sounds of words. The use of rhyme at the ends of lines in poetry is normal, especially in the well-known stanza forms where certain rhyme patterns are prescribed. The following are some of the commonly adopted rhyme schemes in English poetry.

4.1 Full rhyme

Full rhyme, also called true rhyme or single rhyme, must be rhymed on the stressed syllables beginning with different consonants, while the vowels are the same, and the following consonant and the unstressed syllable must also be the same. Thus, "motor-cade" and "arcade", "fight" and "fight" cannot be considered as full rhyme. For example,

Had we but world enough, and *time*,
This coyness, lady, were no *crime*.

4.2 Imperfect rhyme

Imperfect rhyme exists due to various causes, especially when there is no possibility to change one word into another word. The most commonly seen imperfect rhyme is near rhyme—the final consonants are the same, the vowels before the consonants are similar but not the same as in "moon—rain", "green—gone". For example,

He who the ox to wrath has *moved*
Shall never be any women *loved.*

4.3 Positional types of rhyme

According to the positions of appearance of the rhymed words, rhyme falls into end rhyme, internal rhyme and beginning rhyme.

End rhyme occurs when the rhyming vowel is on the last syllable of the line.

True, a new mistress now I *chase*,
    The first foe in the *field*;
And with a stronger faith em*brace*
    A sword, a horse, a *shield.*

(Richard Lovelace)

The rhyme scheme here is *abab*.

Internal rhyme occurs when the stressed syllables at one or more than one places within the line may rhyme to the syllable at the end or to each other. The usual case is that the final syllable of the line rhymes with that just preceding the medial pause (*caesura*).

And a good south *wind* sprung up be*hind*,
    The Albatross did flow,
And every *day*, for food or *play*,
    Came to the mariner's hollo.

(Samuel Taylor Coleridge)

Beginning rhyme occurs in the first syllable or syllables of successive lines.

Why should I have returned?
My knowledge would not fit into theirs.
I found untouched the desert of the unknown.

(William Stanley Merwin)

4.4 Numberal types of rhyme

According to the number of the rhyming syllables at the end of a line, rhymes can be classified into masculine rhyme, feminine rhyme and triple rhyme.

(1) Masculine rhyme is also called male rhyme, single rhyme or monosyllabic rhyme, or true rhyme. It refers to one where the rhyming syllable is single or with no other syllables after it. Masculine rhyme is characterized as strong and powerful in sound effect. For example,

O World! O Life! O Time!
On whose last steps I climb.

(Percy Bysshe Shelley)

(2) Feminine rhyme is a rhyme which falls on an accented syllable followed by an unaccented one of whatever composition. Feminine rhyme is also called double rhyme, female rhyme or dissyllabic rhyme, as in *neighbor—labor*. Feminine rhyme also can be made from two or more words together, as in *limit—dim it*. Feminine rhyme can produce a light-hearted feeling or a melancholy emotion in the poem. For example,

And I will make thee beds of roses
    And a thousand fragrant posies;
And a cap of flowers, and a kirtle
    Embroider'd all with leaves of myrtle.

(Christopher Marlowe)

(3) Triple rhyme, also called multiple rhyme, is one in which the stressed syllable is followed by two unstressed syllables like in: opportunity—impurity; sincerity—prosperity; tenderly—slenderly; glorious—victorious. For example,

But Oh! ye lords of ladies intellectual,
Inform us truly: have they not hen-pecked you all?

Triple rhymes are unusual in form. They may be regarded as a variation of the feminine rhyme, but are more emphatic than the latter. It is likely to produce a comic effect either of special beauty or of grotesqueness. Therefore, the triple rhyme usually belongs to light verse. For example,

Though never nurtured in the lap
    Of luxury, yet I admonish you,
I am an intellectual chap,
    And think of things that would astonish you.

(William Schwenck Gilbert)

4.5 Other special sound effects

Some special use of sound in a poem does not actually belong to any kind of rhyme scheme. The purpose is just to produce some special effect in helping the poet to reveal his or her ideas.

(1) Alliteration: Alliteration is the repetition of consonants, especially at the beginning of several words or of stressed syllables within a line. The purpose is to achieve musical effect for the poem. For example,

The fair breeze blew, the white foam flew,
The furrow followed free.
We were the first that ever burst
Into that silent sea.

(Samuel Taylor Coleridge)

He *c*laps the *c*rag with *c*rooked hands,
*C*lose to the sun in *l*onely *l*ands.

(Alfred Tennyson)

(2) Assonance: The repetition of vowel sound, particularly in stressed syllables, is called assonance. In assonance, the vowel sound is repeated, but the consonant sounds following the vowel are different, as *in lake—fate, clean—sweep*. For example,

If the blues was whisky, I'd stay drunk all the time,
Stay drunk, baby, just to wear off my mind.

(3) Consonance: A technique in which the consonant sounds at the ends of stressed syllables stay the same but the vowel sounds preceding them change. In other words, the stressed vowels are different, but all the consonants (and the unstressed vowels, if any) remain the same, as in *chitter—chatter, pitter—patter, reader—rider, despise—dispose.*

5 Stanza Forms

Stanzas usually refer to the rhymed verse forms in the conventional poems with fixed rhyme schemes, rhythms and fixed number of lines in each unit of a poem.

5.1 Couplet

This is the shortest possible stanza form, which is made up of two lines, usually in the same meter and joined by rhyme. Couplets can be both short and long. For example,

As I in hoary winter's night stood shivering in the snow,
Surprised I was with sudden heat which made my heart to glow.

Iambic pentameter couplet, also called the heroic couplet, is the most popular and durable of couplet forms. It has ten syllables, five iambic meters. The two lines rhymed to each other. After the first line, there is a short pause; after the second line, the meaning is usually complete. Alexander Pope is a noted master in writing poems with heroic couplet. For example,

True ease of writing comes from art, not chance,

As those move easiest who have learned to dance.

5.2 Triplet

A triplet is a three-line stanza. It is also called a tristich or a tercet. But usually a triplet or a tristich is used when the three lines are on the same rhyme: *aaa*.

The Eagle

He clasps the crag with crooked hands;
Close to the sun in lonely lands,
Ringed with the azure world, he stands.

The wrinkled sea beneath him crawls;
He watches from his mountain walls,
And like a thunderbolt he falls.

(Alfred Tennyson)

However, a tercet, also called terza rima (pl.terza rime), is a form borrowed from Italy, meaning "the rhymed three", in which the first and third lines rhyme together while the middle line is left to rhyme with the first and third lines of the next tercet. The whole poem generally ends with a couplet or quatrain to avoid leaving one line unrhymed. The rhyming pattern goes like this: *aba, bcb, cdc, ded, ee.*

Make me thy lyre, even as the forest is:
What if my leaves are falling like its own!
The tumult of thy mighty harmonies

Will take from both a deep, autumnal tone,
Sweet though in sadness. Be thou, Spirit fierce,
My spirit! Be thou me, impetuous one!

Drive my dead thoughts over the universe
Like withered leaves to quicken a new birth!
And, by the incantation of this verse,

Scatter, as from an unextinguished hearth
Ashes and sparks, my words among mankind!
Be through my lips to unawakened Earth

The trumpet of a prophecy! O Wind,
If winter comes, can Spring be far behind?

(Percy Bysshe Shelley)

5.3 Quatrain

Quatrain, also called quartet, is the unit of four lines, and is among the commonest of stanza forms in English poetry. As a rule, it appears in the following varied forms.

(1) *aaab:* This is a mono-rhymed quatrain—all four lines rhyming on the same sound.

The twentieth year is well-nigh past.
Since first our sky was overcast:
Ah, would that this might be the last!
　　My Mary!

Thy spirits have a fainter flow,
I see thee daily weaker grow—
'Twas my distress that brought thee low,
　　My Mary!

(William Cowper)

(2) *aaba:* This stanza form is called the Rubaiyat, quite similar to that of the Chinese *jueju.* For example,

Whose woods these are I think I know.
His house is in the village though;
He will not see me stopping here
To watch his woods fill up with snow.

(Robert Frost)

(3) *aabb*: This kind of quatrain is actually a simple combination of two couplets put together. For example,

Was it for this I uttered prayers
　And sobbed and cursed and kicked to stairs,
That now domestic as a plate,
　I should retire at half past eight?

(Edna Millay)

(4) *abab*: This stanza form is generally regarded as the standard quatrain form in English poetry. For example,

Whenever Richard Cory went down town,
　We people on the pavement looked at him:
He was a gentleman from soul to crown,
　Clean favored and imperially slim.

(Edwin Arlington Robinson)

(5) *abba*: This is called a quatrain with an envelope stanza. For example,

Eternal spirit of the chainless Mind;

Brightest in dungeons, Liberty! thou art:
For there thy habitation is the heart,
The heart which love of thee alone can bind.
(George Gordon Byron)

(6) *abcb*: This quatrain form, also called the ballad stanza, is one of the oldest stanza forms. It is a familiar type of quatrain in short lines, particularly of alternating tetrameter with trimeter, and is mostly seen in songs, ballads and other popular types of English poetry. For example,

Fair Daffodils, we weep to see
    You haste away so soon:
As yet the early-rising sun
    Has not attain'd his noon.
(Robert Herrick)

Among the above six types of quatrain stanza forms, (4), (5) and (6) are the most popular stanza forms.

5.4 Quintet

Quintet is the name of a five-line stanza form rhymed *abaab*. For example,

As the Liberty lads o'er the sea
    Bought their freedom, and cheaply, with blood,
So we, boys, we
    Will die fighting, or live free.
And down with all Kings but King Ludd!
(George Gordon Byron)

Limerick is a short, humorous poem with five-lines. The rhyme scheme is *aabba*, Lines one, two and five have three metric feet, and lines three and four have only two feet. For example,

There was a young lady of Niger
    Who smiled as she rode on a tiger;
They returned from the ride,
    With the lady inside.
And the smile on the face of the tiger.

5.5 Sestet

Sestet is also a rather commonly used stanza form consisting of six lines. For example,

She walks in beauty, like the night
    Of cloudless climes and starry skies;
And all that's best of dark and bright

Meet in her aspect and her eyes:
Thus mellow'd to that tender light
Which heaven to gaudy day denies.
(George Gordon Byron)

5.6 Octet

Octet refers to a stanza of eight lines, which is actually made up of two quatrains. For example,

Think of the things that make you happy,
Not the things that make you sad;
Think of the fine and true in mankind,
Not its sordid side and bad;
Think of the blessings that surround you,
Not the ones that are denied;
Think of the virtues of your friendships,
Not the weak and faulty side.
(Robert E. Farley)

By the way, the octave specifically refers to the first eight lines of a Petrarchan sonnet.

5.7 Spenserian stanza

The Spenserian stanza is the nine-line stanza form of *The Faerie Queene* by Edmund Spenser: the first eight lines are iambic pentameters, the ninth line is an iambic hexameter/Alexandrine. The rhyme scheme is *abab, bcbcc.* Such an enchanting and highly distinctive stanza, unpopular in the 17th century, was revived in the mid-18th century mainly by poets seeking for archaic effects. For example:

A gentle Knight was pricking (spurring) on the plain
Y-clad (=clad) in mightie armes and silver shielde,
Wherein old dints of deepe wounds did remain,
The cruell markes of many a bloody fielde:
Yet armes till that time did he never wield:
His angry steede did chide his foming (= foaming) bitt (= bit),
As much disdayning to the curbe to yield;
Full jolly (= handsome) Knight he seemed, and fair did sitt,
As one for knightly giusts (= tournament) and fierce encounters fitt.

6 Classification of English Poetry

English poems can roughly be divided into the following eight categories in terms of both the stanza forms they carry and the main themes they reveal.

6.1 Epic

An epic is a long narrative poem in elevated style of grave and stately language presenting characters of high position in a series of adventures. The central figure of an epic is often about the history of a nation or people. The historical background of epic poems lies in the fact that, in the primitive and harsh environment of the ancient society, the hero occupied a place of great importance, since his quality of strength and wisdom and courage might save the people from evils that threatened them. So the sense of fatal doom that pervaded their world is always reflected in an epic poem.

Epics usually fall into two kinds: folk (national) epics and art (literary) epics. The folk epics deal with the tradition closely associated with the people of a nation written by unknown authors or assumed to be the product of communal composition. The art epics are supposed to be more sophisticated and more consciously moral in purpose than the folk epics.

Epics of both kinds share the following common characteristics: (1) the hero is a figure of national or international importance, and of great historical or legendary significance; (2) the setting is vast in scope, covering great nations, the world, or even the universe; (3) the action consists of great valor or requires superhuman courage; (4) the style has sustained elevation and grand simplicity; and (5) the epic poet recounts the deeds of the heroes with objectivity.

The best-known folk epics in world literature are Homer's *Iliad* and *Odyssey*. Some of the well-known art epics include Virgil's *Aeneid,* Dante's *Divine Comedy,* the Anglo-Saxon epic poem *Beowulf*, and Milton's *Paradise Lost.*

6.2 Ballad

Ballad is a form of verse to be sung or recited and characterized by its dramatic or exciting episode in simple narrative form. The folk ballad is one of the earliest forms of literature. Some common characteristics of ballads are: (1) the supernatural force plays an important role in events presented in ballads; (2) physical courage and love are their frequent themes; (3) slight attention is paid to characterization or description; (4) transitions are abrupt and the action is largely developed through dialogues; and (5) a single episode of a highly dramatic nature is presented with the utmost simplicity.

The stanza form of the folk ballad (also known as ballad meter) usually consists of four lines, rhyming *abcb,* with the first and third lines carrying four accented syllables and the second and fourth carrying three, though there is great variation in the number of unstressed syllables. The rhyme is often approximate, with assonance and consonance frequently appearing. A refrain is not uncommon in ballad poems.

The English and Scottish Popular Ballads was edited by Francis James Child between

1882 and 1898, in which there are a total of 305 ballads collected. The most significant group of ballads is the series of 37 ballads of different lengths that deal with the famous outlaw Robin Hood and his men and their activities.

6.3 Lyric

A lyric poem expresses a poet's thoughts and feelings and is usually brief. The main purpose of a lyric poem is to communicate the emotions of the poet. Most lyric poems contain vivid and imaginative images.

Usually lyric poems describe a particular moment, feeling, or memory that stirs the poet's imagination. *The Passionate Shepherd to His Love* by Christopher Marlowe is a typical example of lyric poetry. It is filled with vivid and varied images of things that effectively reveal the narrator's feelings. The word *lyric* comes from *lyre,* a guitarlike instrument that poets centuries ago played as they sang their poems. Few poets today sing their poems, but *lyric* is still used to refer to the words of songs and to poems that are brief, emotional, and musical.

6.4 Heroic couplet

Couplet means two lines of verse with similar end-rhymes. In English literature, heroic couplet specifically refers to poetic lines of iambic pentameter rhymed in pairs. It was the favorite metrical form used by Geoffrey Chaucer. However, this verse form comes into its greatest popularity in the middle of the 17th century. The form became best known with John Dryden. With Alexander Pope the heroic couplet became such an important and fixed form that its influence dominated English verse for many years. For example,

Others for language all their care express,
And value books, as women men, for dress.
Their praise is still—the style is excellent,
The sense they humbly take upon content.
Words are like leaves; and where they most abound,
Much fruit of sense beneath is rarely found.

(Alexander Pope)

6.5 Elegy

Elegy belongs to the category of formal poems concerning the poet's serious, subjective meditations upon death or some other solemn themes like love or war. The meditation is often occasioned by the death of a particular person, but it may be a generalized observation or the expression of a solemn mood. The Elizabethans used this poetic form for love poems, particularly complaints about miseries in life. Notable English elegies include John Donne's *Elegies,* and Thomas Gray's *Elegy Written in a Country Churchyard.*

The pastoral elegy is a specialized form of elegy popular with English poets. They employed conventional pastoral imagery, wrote in dignified, serious language, and took as its theme the expression of grief at the loss of a friend or important person. The elegiac stanza takes its name from Thomas Gray's *Elegy Written in a Country Churchyard,* which is composed in the iambic pentameter quatrain, rhyming *abab.*

The curfew tolls the knell of parting day,
    The lowing herd wind slowly o'er the lea,
The plowman homeward plods his weary way,
    And leaves the world to darkness and to me.

(Thomas Gray)

6.6 Ode

An ode is a long lyric poem, serious and dignified in subject, tone, and style, directed to a single purpose, dealing with one theme. The ode was originally a Greek form used in dramatic poetry, in which a chorus would follow the movements of a dance while singing the words of the ode. The odes often celebrated a public occasion of consequence such as a military victory, or to provide a vehicle for private meditation. Sometimes an ode may have an elaborate stanzaic structure. Almost all odes are poems of address, in which the poet uses apostrophe to address to a person who is usually absent or dead long ago, or to an idea or quality as if it were a person.

In spite of this definition, we must explain that the ode is perhaps the most freely defined of poetical forms. In English poetry there are three types of odes: the Pindaric ode, following the pattern originated by the ancient Greek poet Pindar, the Horatian ode, named after the ancient Roman poet Horace, and the irregular ode which has no set rhyme scheme and no set stanza pattern.

The irregular ode has employed all manner of formal possibilities, while often retaining the tone and thematic elements of the classical ode. For example, *Ode on a Grecian Urn* by John Keats was written based on his experiments with the sonnet. Dryden's *A Song for St. Cecilia's Day* is another example of the irregular ode. By contrast, the Horatian ode follows a regular stanza pattern and rhyme scheme, as do the odes by Shelley and by Keats.

6.7 Sonnet

Sonnet is a lyric poem almost invariably of 14 lines written in iambic pentameter and following one of several set rhyme schemes. The sonnet was a form developed in Italy in the 13th century and was introduced into England by Thomas Wyatt and Earl of Surrey. Petrarch, in the 14th century, raised it to its greatest Italian perfection. Sonnets can be classified into three categories: (1) Italian or Petrarchan sonnets, (2) English or Shakespearean sonnets, and

(3) Spenserian sonnets.

The Italian or Petrarchan form of sonnets is distinguished by its division into the *octave* and the *sestet:* the octave consisting of eight lines rhyming *abba, abba,* and the sestet consisting of six lines rhyming *cdecde, cdccdc,* or *cdedce.* The octave presents a narrative, states a proposition or raises a question; the sestet drives home the narrative by making an abstract comment, applied the proposition, or solves the problem.

English poets have varied these requirements and the rhyme scheme greatly. In the English or Shakespearean sonnets, instead of the octave and sestet, four divisions are used: three quatrains and a rhymed concluding couplet. The typical rhyme scheme for the English sonnet is *abab, cdcd, efef, gg.* The couplet at the end is often a commentary on the preceding three quatrains, and an epigrammatic close.

The Spenserian sonnet combines the above two forms, using three quatrains and a couplet but having linking rhymes among the quatrains, thus *abab, bcbc, cdcd, ee.*

Among the most famous sonneteers in Great Britain there have been Shakespeare, Milton, Wordsworth, Shelley, Keats, and so on.

6.8 Villanelle

Villanelle is a 19-line poem, usually of a pastoral or lyrical nature, consisting normally of five three-lined stanzas and a final quatrain, with only two rhymes throughout the whole poem. Generally the middle line of every stanza rhymes. The rhyme scheme is usually *aba aba aba aba aba abaa.*

The Villanelle had been much employed in the 19th-century France in light verse and *vers de societe*, and in the 20th century it was used to more serious purpose by such English writers as Auden, Empson, Dylan Thomas ("Do not go gentle into that good night"), and others.

The following is a sample poem written by Judith Barrington, showing the nostalgic feeling for her late mother who died by drowning in the sea. The poem is full of ocean, waves and moon, and the conventional form "Villanelle" suits very well to the mood of the writer.

When I stand on the shore, I wonder where you are
somewhere in that fathomed room behind
the waves like doors that slowly swing ajar.

Dappled stones at my feet are smeared with tar.
Sucked by the undertow, they jostle and grind
while I stand on the shore, wondering where you are.

Beyond the raging surf, beyond the bar,

in your green chamber you hide, forever blind
to the waves like doors that slowly swing ajar

inviting me in, enticing me from afar,
but their curling crests are an unmistakable sign
I should stay on shore and wonder where you are.

Your voice in the wind doesn't say where you are
and I listen less and less, resigned
to those waves like doors that slowly swing ajar.

Will the light of the crescent moon, the northern star
create a pathway we both can find
as I stand on the shore wondering where you are,
and the waves like doors slowly swing ajar.

6.9 Dramatic monologue

Dramatic monologue refers to a poem delivered in a form of speech as though by a single imagined character (also called "persona" or "mask"), frequently but not always to an imagined audience. It mainly has the following three features: (1) The speaker is not to be identified with the poet, but is dramatized, usually ironically, through his or her own words. (2) Thc speaker of the poem narrates the whole poem in a particular situation at a critical moment. (3) The general theme of the poem is mainly to reveal the speaker's nature, character, fate, and interior psychology, instead of a matter-of-fact discussion of the subject itself.

Matthew Arnold's *Dover Beach* is one example of dramatic monologue. Robert Browning, who wrote *My Last Duchess* in 1842, developed this form to a very high level. T. S. Eliot, a very influential poet of his time, enriched the form with stream of consciousness, a rather newly emerged literary technique which seeks to depict the multi-dimensional thoughts and feelings that pass through the speaker's mind. Eliot's poem *The Love Song of J. Alfred Prufrock*, an interior monologue, is a noteworthy example of this form.

6.10 Blank verse

Blank verse has generally been best accepted in dramatic verse and is commonly used for long poems whether dramatic, philosophic, or narrative. Though with no rhyme patterns, blank verse has fixed length and fixed metrical patterns in a line, often in iambic pentameter. Therefore, blank verse is also defined as the unrhymed iambic pentameter.

Shakespeare, Milton and Wordsworth elevated this form to its ultimate perfection. Shakespeare is undoubtedly regarded as a great master in using blank verse in writing his world-famous plays. For example,

Tomorrow, and Tomorrow, and Tomorrow
Creeps in this petty pace from day to day,
To the last syllable of recorded time;
And all our yesterdays have lighted fools
The way to dusty death. Out, out, brief candle!
Life's but a walking shadow, a poor player
That struts and frets his hour upon the stage,
And then is heard no more: it is a tale
Told by an idiot, full of sound and fury,
Signifying nothing—

(William Shakespeare)

6.11 Free verse

Though poetry in free verse is written without any regular metrical pattern, and usually without rhyme, it is based on the irregular rhythmic cadence of the recurrence of phrases, images, and syntactical patterns. Consequently, "rhythm" in conventional poetic forms has a different name in free verse, that is "cadence". Rhythm is present in it with greater freedom. The rhythmic unit is larger, sometimes being phrases, clauses, short sentences, and even a stanza. The Song of Solomon and The Psalms from the Bible and some of John Milton's poems are all written in free verse. And such famous modern poets as Walt Whitman, Emily Dickinson, Carl Sandburg also use this form to write their poetry.

Beat! Beat! Drums!

Beat! beat! drums! blow! bugles! blow!
Through the windows; through doors; burst like a ruthless force,
Into the solemn church, and scatter the congregation,
Into the school where the scholar is studying;
Leave not the bridegroom quiet; no happiness must he have now with his bride,
Nor the peaceful farmer any peace, ploughing his field or gathering his grain,
So fierce you whirr and pound you drums; so shrill you bugles blow.

(Walt Whitman)

7 Major Figures of Speech in Poetry

Robert Frost once said, "Poetry provides the one permissible way of saying one thing and meaning another." This statement well expresses the importance of figurative language in poetry. When reading literature, we have to admit that it is figures of speech that make language significant, moving, and fascinating. The following are some of the most commonly used figures of speech employed in poetry writing.

7.1 Allegory

Allegory occurs when one idea or object is represented in the shape of another. In some poems, abstract ideas, such as virtues and vices, are presented as human beings. In this way the reader can understand a moral or a lesson more easily.

Because I could not stop for Death—
He kindly stopped for me—
The Carriage held just but Ourselves—
And Immortality.

(Emily Dickinson)

Here Emily Dickinson uses "Death" allegorically as a figure of a coachman, kindly stopping to pick up the speaker after her death on the road to eternity.

7.2 Ambiguity

Ambiguity allows multiple meanings to coexist in a word or a metaphor. It does not mean that the word is unclear; rather, it means that it carries more than one possible interpretation at the same time.

The Chimney Sweeper

The little black thing among the snow,
Crying "Weep! Weep!" in notes of woe!
"Where are thy father and mother? Say?"
They are both gone to the church to pray.

(William Blake)

The word "weep" here has a double meaning. On the one hand, "weep" is the street cry ("sweep") of the chimney sweepers in the streets of London to advertise their services even when they were too young to articulate clearly. And on the other, the word "'weep" here is used as a pun to suggest both sweeping of the chimneys and weeping over their pitiful plight.

7.3 Apostrophe

Apostrophe is closely related to personification. Here, a thing is addressed directly, as though it were a person listening to a conversation. For example, we have William Wordsworth's "Milton! thou should'st be living at this hour," although Milton had obviously died long before. Apostrophe and personification go hand in hand in John Donne's poem of *Death, Be Not Proud.*

Death, be not proud, though some have called thee

Mighty and dreadful, for thou art not so;
For those whom thou think'st thou dost overthrow
Die not, poor Death, nor yet canst thou kill me.
(John Donne)

7.4 Conceit

A conceit is a metaphor where feeling and thought are mingled in an image that is always skillfully-made and appropriate though it may appear incongruous and far-fetched at first sight. In *A Valediction: Forbidding Mourning* by John Donne, the souls of the two lovers are presented the same as the two legs of a compass is a good example:

If they be two, they are two so
As stiff twin compasses are two;
Thy soul, the fixed foot, makes no show
To move, but doth, if th' other do.

And though it in the center sit,
Yet when the other far doth roam,
It leans and hearkens after it,
And grows erect, as that comes home.

7.5 Contrast

Contrast shows the difference between two objects. In this sense it is the opposite of comparison, which shows similarities.

It is not growing like a tree
In bulk, doth make man better be,
Or standing long an oak, three hundred year,
To fall a log at last, dry, bald, and sere:
A lily of a day
Is fairer far in May.
Although it fall and die that night,
It was the plant and flower of light.
In small proportions we just beauties see,
And in short measures, life may perfect be.

The poem, written by Ben Jonson, is a contrast between the size of a tree and the value of a man's life. The poem is divided into two symmetrical parts by two short lines in the middle: "A lily of a day / Is fairer far in May." These two terse and melodious lines contrast with the previous two lengthy, tedious and jaw-breaking lines between the long-lived, but "dry, bald, and sere" oak and the perfect short-lived life of man. Contrast is effectively used here in driving home the central theme of the poem.

7.6 Hyperbole

Hyperbole is an exaggeration or overstatement that is made to emphasize a point for a specific literary effect. The following poem consists of hyperbole intended to show how the speaker feels about his or her loved one's name—and the loved one as well.

When I Hear Your Name

My compulsion is to blast down every wall with your name,
I'd paint it on all the houses,
there wouldn't be a well
I hadn't leaned into
to shout your name there...
My compulsion is
to teach the birds to sing it,
to teach the fish to drink it...
God will sentence me to repeating it endlessly and forever.

7.7 Irony

Irony states one thing in one tone of voice when, in fact, the opposite meaning is intended. So it refers to conditions or affairs that are the tragic reverse of what the participants have expected. The main character from Shakespeare's tragedy *Macbeth* expects great happiness to follow his killing King Duncan; instead, he finds that by his deed of murdering he loses all that makes life worth living. In other words, irony involves a contrast between what is stated and what is more or less wryly suggested. The statement is somehow negated by its implications or suggestions. Thus, Alexander Pope attacks the proud man by ironically encouraging his pride:

Go, wiser thou! and, in thy scale of sense,
    Weigh thy opinion against Providence...
Snatch from his hand the balance and the rod,
    Rejudge his justice, be the God of God!

Under the term *irony* we also have irony of fate or cosmic irony, which describes the view that God, Fate, or some supernatural being is amused to manipulate human beings as a puppeteer would manipulate puppets.

7.8 Oxymoron

Oxymoron refers to the combination of contradictory or incongruous terms. Milton's description of hell as a place with "no light, but rather darkness visible" is a typical example of oxymoron. The two contradicting phenomena can achieve the effect of enhancing rather than weakening the meaning of each word. Thus, "sweet pain", "the living dead" are much more forceful in conveying certain experiences than otherwise.

7.9 Personification

Writers use personification to give human qualities to an object, animal, or idea. So, personification is the description of such inanimated phenomena as an animal, object, or idea in terms that normally would be used to describe only human beings. Expressions like "Mother Nature" and "Father Time" are common examples of personification. By using personification, an author can make an insect, an ocean, or even a coat rack come to life and endow it with human qualities. The thing that is personified might speak words, feel emotions, and even assume a human appearance. In brief, personification endows human characteristics and feelings to nonhuman lives, inanimate objects, or abstract ideas.

A stronger example of personification, however, is found in *Death, Be Not Proud.* Here, the speaker not only talks directly to an event as if it were a listening person, that event is also given the human characteristics of pride, might, arrogance, and faulty thinking, as if it were a person who is capable of hearing as well as possessing arrogant human emotions.

Death, be not proud, though some have called thee
Mighty and dreadful, for thou art not so;
For those whom thou think'st thou dost overthrow
Die not, poor Death, nor yet canst thou kill me.

7.10 Symbolism

Symbolism, as an abstract collective noun, refers to either the use of symbols in literary writing or a system of literature and art in which symbols are used to represent real things and feelings. Symbolism occurs when a concrete object stands for an abstract concept, while a symbol as a countable noun is something that stands for something else by reason of relationship, association, convention, or accidental resemblance, a visible sign of something invisible. A symbol can be a person, object, action, or event that, in addition to its literal meaning, suggests a more complex meaning. For example, a precious stone may symbolize eternal love, and a flowing river to the sea may stand for afterlife.

In a literary work, symbols appear in the form of words, images, objects, settings, events, and characters, and are often used deliberately to reinforce the theme of the work. Many symbols, however, imply different things to different people, and different cultures may react differently to the same symbols. Thus, symbols are usually classified as being universal symbols and private symbols, depending on the source of the associations that provide their meanings.

(1) Universal symbols: Universal symbols (also called archetypal, cultural, traditional, or conventional symbols) are those whose associations are the common property of a society or culture universally recognized and accepted. They embody ideas or emotions that the writer and the reader share in common as a result of their social and cultural heritage. When using this kind of symbols, both the writer and the reader know what the symbol represents. Thus, water, which is the substance in the sacrament of baptism, symbolizes life. When water springs up from a fountain, it may symbolize optimism. A stagnant pool of water may symbolize life being spoiled or is about to end. Other generally recognized universal symbols are the serpent, representing the Devil or simply evil, peacock for pride, eagle for heroic endeavor, rising sun for birth, and setting sun for death.

(2) Private symbols: Some writers repeatedly use symbols whose significance they largely generate themselves, and these pose a more difficult problem in interpretation. Private symbols are also called contextual or authorial symbols. They refer to those whose meanings are derived from the context of the work in which they are used.

As we all know, the literal meaning of a "rose", a kind of beautiful flower, signifies love or beauty. The word "rose" in Robert Burns' poem is conventionally used as a universal symbol of love. But William Blake's connotation about the rose is totally different:

The Sick Rose

O Rose, thou art sick.
The invisible worm
That flies in the night
In the howling storm

Has found out thy bed
Of crimson joy,
And his dark secret love
Does thy life destroy.

The "rose" here is not conventionally used as a simile or metaphor, since it has no paired subject like a lady as a love object. Blake wants the reader to see a real rose beset by an insect that preys on roses. The symbolic meaning is that furtiveness, deceit or hypocrisy has brought damage to what should be a frank and joyous relationship of physical love. The "rose" here as a private symbol is being endangered to its doom by a terrible force in the human world. More generally, the poem may show the destruction of all earthly health, innocence, and beauty by mysterious forces.

Symbolism, when successfully employed as an integral part of the language, can stimulate readers' imagination—which is certainly one of the major purposes of any form of literature.

7.11 Imagery

An image is a picture, or likeness, that a writer creates with words. It is a mental picture that can appeal to any of the senses—sight, hearing, taste, smell, and touch. All the images created in a poem is called *imagery*. Such mental pictures created by words help readers imagine the experiences that writers describe.

For example, in describing a piece of toast, you may mention its familiar scent (smell), the crunch (sound) of a knife spreading butter on its rough (touch), brown (sight) surface, and the salt-sweet flavor (taste) of your first bite. Because these descriptions appeal to all the senses, they are allied sensory images. Matthew Arnold's *Dover Beach* provides us with a very good example of imagery.

7.12 Simile and metaphor

A simile is a direct comparison between two unlike things, which uses the word *like* or *as* or the verb *appears* or *seems*, while a metaphor is an implied comparison between two unlike things. Without using *like, as, appears,* or *seems*, a metaphor suggests that one thing is another. The entire poem *The Waning Moon* by P. B. Shelley is a single simile. The two items being compared are the moon and a dying lady.

And like a dying lady, lean and pale,
Who totters forth, wrapped in a gauzy veil...
The moon arose up in the murky East,
A white and shapeless mass.

8 Effective Steps to Read a Poem

The following steps may prove helpful and effective in learning and reading poetry.

8.1 Read through for main ideas

You should first read through the poem once and try to grasp the main meaning as much as possible. Then read for a second time, line by line, and try to find out all the images and symbols implied in the poem. Thirdly, if you still feel it difficult to understand essential meaning of the poem, try to interpret each line into prose form. After you understand all the basic words and ideas in the poem, read it aloud a few more times to catch its entire meaning.

8.2 Identify the speaker

The speaker is the person or thing whose words and thoughts you read in a poem. Just as fiction depends on a narrator, poetry depends on a speaker who describes events, feelings, and ideas to readers. It cannot be assumed that the speaker is the poet him or herself because poets often assume different identities for every poem they write. Sometimes they "try on" new personalities to explore what a particular person or thing might be thinking about. In other words, to convey ideas or feelings most effectively, a poet may use a persona or a voice other than his or her own. Many poetic elements such as tone, theme, and meaning are intertwined with the speaker's personality, style, and attitude. For example, the *speaker* of Robert Browning's *My Last Duchess* is not Browning himself, but the selfish duke. For that reason, to understand a poem well, it is essential to have a profound understanding of the poem's speaker.

8.3 Decide the tone of the poem

The tone of the poem conveys the speaker's attitude toward his or her subject. Poets often indicate the tone by using techniques such as rhyme, rhythm, word choice, sentence structure, figures of speech, and imagery. The range of tones may be very wide: the poem's speaker may be joyful, melancholy, sad, playful, serious, comic, intimate, formal, relaxed, or ironic.

8.4 Try to follow the punctuation

When a line of verse has a pause as its end, it is called an *end-stopped line.* Pauses within a line are called *caesuras,* which means little pause. When there is no pause at the end of a line, one line flows into the next, we call it a *run-on line* or an *enjambment.* When you read poetry, follow the poet's directions. Do not insert punctuation where there is none, and do not force a word to be stressed that would not normally be stressed. The punctuation marks in poetry tell us how the author wishes the work to be read. End a line only when the punctuation (a period, question mark, or exclamation mark) indicates that it is correct to do so. A comma or a semicolon, in contrast, would be a pause or a half-stop; there is no need to stop at the end of a line unless there is some punctuation mark to indicate that we must.

8.5 Read the poem naturally

Despite the fact that reading a poem requires some attention to the rhythmic patterns, we should not, however, stress the rhythm too much, or the meaning will be lost, and the poem will become dull and tedious singsong. Instead, we should emphasize the words and their meanings, varying the flow of the rhythm by pausing now and then for emphasis or emotional effect. This is mainly achieved with the help of punctuations, line breaks, and stanza divisions, and so on. Now try to read the following poem in as natural a way as possible.

To Daffodils

Fair daffodils, we weep to see
You haste away so soon;
As yet the early-rising Sun
Has not attain'd his noon.
Stay, stay,
Until the hasty day
Has run
But to the even-song,
And, having pray'd together, we
Will go with you along.

We have short time to stay, as you,
We have as short a Spring;
As quick a growth to meet decay
As you, or anything.
We die,
As your hours do and dry
Away
Like to the Summer's rain;
Or as the pearls of morning's dew,
Ne'er to be found again.

(Robert Herrick)

Questions and Exercises

1. What is the essential nature of English poetry? What is your understanding about the value of learning poetry?
2. To analyze the external qualities of an English poem, rhyme schemes, rhythmic patterns, and stanza forms are the three main elements to be included. Please write down the commonly adopted steps to scan a poem written in English.
3. Reading aloud is an indispensable part of appreciating the beauty of poetry. What are the most effective skills to read an English poem?

Selected Readings of English Poetry

Christopher Marlowe

Christopher Marlowe (1564—1593) is an influential English dramatist, a great Elizabethan poet, and Shakespeare's most important predecessor in English drama. He is noted especially for his establishment of dramatic blank verse in the history of English literature. On January 14, 1579, he entered the King's School in Canterbury as a scholar. A year later he went to Cambridge and got his Bachelor of Arts degree there in 1584. He continued in residence at Cambridge until he was killed in a brawl at the age of just twenty-nine. Some maintain the brawl at a tavern was over the payment of a bill. Others think that he was killed as a result of espionage work he had done for the government.

Marlowe is regarded to be the greatest discoverer and the most daring pioneer in all our poetic literature. Before him there was neither genuine blank verse nor genuine tragedy in the English language. But after his arrival the way to great tragedies was prepared, the paths were made straight for Shakespeare.

In a playwriting career that lasted a little more than six years, Marlowe's best known tragedies—*Tamburlaine*, *Faustus*, *The Jew of Malta,* and *Edward II* earned him the title "father of English tragedy". In addition to his plays, he also wrote many shorter poems. *The Passionate Shepherd to His Love* is one of his most famous Elizabethan lyrical poems.

The Passionate[1] Shepherd to His Love

Come live with me and be my love,
And we will all the pleasures prove[2]
That valleys, groves, hills, and fields,
Woods, or steepy mountain yields.[3]

And we will sit upon the rocks,
Seeing the shepherds feed their flocks,
By shallow rivers to whose falls
Melodious birds sing their madrigals.[4]

And I will make thee beds of roses
And a thousand fragrant posies,
A cap of flowers, and a kirtle[5]
Embroidered all with leaves of myrtle;

A gown made of the finest wool
Which from our pretty lambs we pull;
Fair lined slippers for the cold,
With buckles of the purest gold;

A belt of straw and ivy buds,
With coral clasps and amber studs:
And if these pleasures may thee move,
Come with me, and be my love.

The shepherds' swains[6] shall dance and sing
For thy delight each May morning:
If these delights thy mind may move,
Then live with me and be my love.

Notes

[1] passionate: in love; in the state of tender passion.

[2] prove: test; experience.

[3] That…yields: These two lines modify the proceeding word "pleasures". Note the lucid and sprightly rhythm and sound effect that enforce the pleasures of country life.

[4] madrigals: harmonious lyrical songs.

[5] kirtle: petticoat; skirt; dress.

[6] swain: (archaic) a young man in the rustic village.

Commentary

The Passionate Shepherd to His Love, a pastoral lyric of invitation, was first published in a collection called *England's Helicon* (1600) in which country life is idealized and shepherds and shepherdesses are described as enjoying happy peaceful ease and comfort and making love all day long. The poem contains six quatrains. Each poetic line consists of octosyllabics (eight syllables) of iambic tetrameter, rhyming *aabb*.

The Elizabethan love lyrics are one of the glories in English literature. Within the strict conventions of their time, this kind of poems succeed time after time in giving love a voice in people's life. Descending from the courtly love tradition of the Middle Ages, in which a man worshipped a highborn lady from afar, Elizabethan lyrics brilliantly blend passion and elegance, body and mind by uniting the timeless power of love and the life-giving power of poetry itself. The above selected poem successfully sings praise of love as both a mortal delight and an immortal possibility for the rural young people.

Questions and Exercises

1. What is the theme of the poem? What kind of life is idealized in the poem?
2. In order to win her love, what does the shepherd promise to make for her? What do those pleasures suggest?
3. Read the following poem written by Sir Walter Raleigh, then see how the speaker replies to Marlowe's famous "passionate shepherd". Then write your own reply in the form of a letter to the shepherd by pretending yourself to be the woman to whom the shepherd addresses. Explain why you accept or refuse the offer.

The Nymph's Reply to the Shepherd

If all the world and love were young,
And truth in every shepherd's tongue,
These pretty pleasures might me move
To live with thee and be thy love.

Time drives the flocks from field to fold,[1]
When rivers rage and rocks grow cold,
And Philomel[2] becometh dumb,
The rest complains of cares to come.

The flowers do fade, and wanton[3] fields
To wayward winter reckoning yields;
A honey tongue, a heart of gall,[4]
Is fancy's spring, but sorrow's fall.

Thy gowns, thy shoes, thy beds of roses,
Thy cap, thy kirtle, and thy posies
Soon break, soon wither, soon forgotten—
In folly ripe, in reason rotten.

Thy belt of straw and ivy buds,
Thy coral clasps and amber studs,
All these in me no means can move
To come to thee and be thy love.

But could youth last and love still breed,[5]
Had joys no date[6] nor age no need,
Then these delights my mind might move
To live with thee and be thy love.

(Sir Walter Raleigh)

Notes

[1] fold: enclosure or pen for sheep.

[2] Philomel: According to Greek myth, Princess Philomela's tongue was cut out to prevent her from revealing a scandal. Later the gods turned Philomela into a nightingale.

[3] wanton: profuse or ample.

[4] gall: bitterness.

[5] still breed: always thrive.

[6] date: ending.

William Shakespeare

William Shakespeare (1564—1616), great English playwright and poet, was born of a merchant's family on 23 April, 1564, at Stratford- on-Avon. He has been universally acknowledged to be the summit of the English Renaissance, the greatest writer of the English language, one of the greatest man of letters in Western literature, and the world's preeminent dramatist. In addition, Shakespeare is the most quoted writer in the history of the English-speaking world. He is often considered to be England's national poet and is sometimes referred to as the "Bard of Avon" (or simply "The Bard") or the "Swan of Avon".

Apart from 37 plays, he wrote 154 sonnets; he was also skilled in many other poetic forms: the song, the couplet, and his most famous dramatic blank verse in all his plays. The following are just two of his widely-read sonnets.

Sonnet 2

When forty winters shall besiege thy brow,
And dig deep trenches in thy beauty's field,[1]
Thy youth's proud livery,[2] so gazed on now,
Will be a tatter'd weed[3] of small worth held:
Then being ask'd where all thy beauty lies,
Where all the treasure of thy lusty[4] days,
To say within thy own deep-sunken eyes,
Were an all-eating shame and thriftless[5] praise.
How much more praise deserv'd thy beauty's use,[6]
If thou couldst answer, "This fair child of mine
Shall sum my count,[7] and make my old excuse,[8]
Proving this beauty by succession thine!
    This were to be new made when thou art old,
    And see thy blood warm when thou feel'st it cold.

Notes

[1] deep trenches in thy beauty's field: deep wrinkles on your beautiful face.

[2] livery: (poetic) dress or covering. Here it means the outward appearance of the young man addressed.

[3] tatter'd weed: torn or ragged garment.

[4] lusty: vigorous.

[5] thriftless: unprofitable; wasteful.

[6] use: investment; value.

[7] sum my count: even out or pay off my account.

[8] make my old excuse: explain why I am old; give excuse for my old age.

Commentary

Shakespeare was the most distinguished practitioner of English sonnets during the Elizabethan

Age. Just for this reason the English sonnet is often called Shakespearean sonnet, which has fourteen lines with three quatrains and one couplet that makes an effective climax of the whole poem. It has a consistent rhyme scheme of *abab cdcd efef gg*.

In this sonnet, the speaker says that when one gets old, his beauty will be gone; but if he gets married and lets his child carry on his life, his beauty will remain immortal. The first quatrain says that at forty, the "livery of his youth" (the uniform) will have to become a tattered garment (weed). Then he feels ashamed of his present sunken-eyed appearance when people ask him what has become of his beauty. The sonneteer then points out that it would be much better if this man could answer that his beauty has been carried on with the beauty of his child. Finally the couplet draws a conclusion: The beauty that is renewed in one's offspring would become a kind of immortality.

The theme of the poem might be somewhat like this: Don't be afraid of becoming old, since ageing is a natural process in one's life; and what's more, beauty can be renewed in your next generation, and therewith it is made to become a kind of immortality.

Questions and Exercises

1. What does the poet advise the young man to do when asked where all his beauty lies? And why?
2. Scan the poem and tell how its metrical and rhyming pattern is related to the thought division of the poem.

Sonnet 18

Shall I compare thee to a summer's day?[1]
Thou art more lovely and more temperate.
Rough winds do shake the darling buds of May,
And summer's lease[2] hath all too short a date,[3]
Sometime too hot the eye of heaven[4] shines,
And often his gold complexion dimm'd,
And every fair from fair[5] sometime declines,
By chance or nature's changing course, untrimm'd.[6]
But thy eternal summer shall not fade,
Nor lose possession of that fair thou ow'st;
Nor shall Death brag thou wand'rest in his shade,
When in eternal lines to time thou grow'st.
So long as men can breathe, or eyes can see,
So long lives this, and this gives life to thee.[7]

Notes

[1] a summer's day: In England summer days are of sunny, untroubled, happy days. Here it refers to a warm and happy personality of someone that people are glad to see.

[2] lease: the length or duration of a period of time.

[3] date: a limited duration of time.

[4] the eye of heaven: the sun.

[5] every fair from fair: the beauty of every beautiful object or person.

[6] By chance…untrimm'd: Stripped of beauty by fortune or by the normal course of change in the natural world.

[7] When in eternal lines…: When in the lines of this immortal poem you become even or eternal with time, and you shall live to all time, that is, you still live in my poem after you are physically dead or gone.

Commentary

On the surface this sonnet is a eulogy of his beloved, but it is also about the power of poetry. The boast of immortality for one's verse is a Renaissance convention and such a theme frequently goes to the classics. It is not egotism on the part of the poet, but a faith in the permanence of poetry. In *Sonnet 18*, the poet writes beautifully on the conventional theme that his poetry will bring eternity to the one he loves and eulogizes.

In the first two quatrains, the poet says that his beloved person is nicer and better than a summer's day; in the third quatrain he tells the reader that if his love can live in the lines of his poetry, she will never lose her beauty. In the couplet the poet concludes that even after his beloved is dead and gone, in his poem she will live on. This poem is rich in figurative language and delicate imagery, and the comparative device is in particular central to the expression of the theme.

Questions and Exercises

1. What qualities does the poet expect the reader to find by comparing the person he loves to a "summer's day"? And by means of what comparisons does Shakespeare achieve this movement from tangible to intangible?
2. In this poem, there are quite a few applications of figurative language. Point out what rhetorical devices the poet employs in it.

Thomas Nashe

Thomas Nashe (1567—1601) was a lyric poet, playwright and pamphleteer. He was once graduated from Cambridge University and later became one of the "university wits" during the Renaissance period. His sharp satire and dashing lyricism made his drama *Life of Jack Wilton* (1594) the earliest approach to the picaresque novel or rogue story of a later age. The following selection is one of his best known lyric poems.

Spring

Spring, the sweet Spring, is the year's pleasant king,
Then blooms each thing, then maids dance in a ring.
Cold doth not sting, the pretty birds do sing:
    Cuckoo, jug-jug, pu-we, to-witta-woo![1]

The palm and may[2] make country houses gay,
Lambs frisk and play, the shepherds pipe all day,
And we hear ay[3] birds tune this merry lay:[4]
    Cuckoo, jug-jug, pu-we, to-witta-woo!

The fields breathe sweet, the daisies kiss our feet,
Young lovers meet, old wives a-sunning sit,
In every street these tunes our ears do greet:
    Cuckoo, jug-jug, pu-we, to-witta-woo!
        Spring! The sweet Spring!

Notes

[1] Cuckoo jug-jug, pu-we, to-witta-woo: These are conventional, imitative sounds (onomatopoeia) made respectively by cuckoos, nightingales, pewits or plover, and owls.

[2] may: hawthorn or its blossoms.

[3] ay: or aye, old use for "always".

[4] lay: short narrative poem or song.

Commentary

Song writing reached its peak in Elizabethan times, and lyrics often overshadowed music. Elizabethan madrigals—lyric poems designed to be sung without instrumental accompaniment—mainly spoke of love and the joys of pastoral life. The songs may make what is merry merrier or what is sad sadder. They include love songs, nonsense songs, and melancholy dirges.

The present poem is a song taken from *Summer's Last Will and Testament.* The poet in this poem intends to convey the feeling of joyfulness and pleasantness of springtime, and he succeeds in doing so mainly by three means: the use of vivid imagery, the use of proper sounds, and a skillful choice of diction. Imagery is a peculiarly effective way to evoke sensory experiences. Onomatopoeia and internal rhyme are just two of the most common uses of proper sounds that can, to some extent, subtly reinforce the meanings of words, produce more pleasing, melodious effect by conveying a light and happy mood to us readers especially when we are reading. In this poem, we can feel the sounds to be marvelously adapted to the sense by the poet.

Questions and Exercises

1. Read the poem carefully, pay attention to those image-bearing words, and see how many images the poet created in the poem and what sense impressions you can get from those images.
2. Rhythm and sound cooperate to produce what we call the music of poetry. Can you point out and explain the sounds and their musical effect in the poem?

The King James Bible

The Bible means "books". The Christian Bible consists of the books of the Old Testament, originally in Hebrew, and the New Testament, originally in Greek. Before the Protestant Reformation the Bible was ordinarily read in Latin. With the Reformation came many translations into the vernacular language, the language of the common people.

The Bible which has been called "the noblest monument of English prose" appeared in 1611 during Shakespeare's lifetime. It was the result of seven years of labor by a group of notable scholars and clergymen under orders of King James I. Many other translations of the Bible are in existence today, but the King James Bible, as it came to be called, was the first English translation to receive widespread and lasting acceptance among people in the English-speaking world.

Psalm 8

O Lord our Lord,
How excellent is thy name in all the earth!
Who hast set thy glory above the heavens.
Out of the mouths of babes and sucklings hast thou ordained[1] strength because of thine enemies,
That thou mightiest still[2] the enemy and the avenger.
When I consider thy heavens, the work of thy fingers,
The moon and the stars, which thou hast ordained;
What is man, that thou art mindful of him?
And the son of man, that thou visitest him?
For thou hast made him a little lower than the angels,
And hast crowned him with glory and honor.
Thou madest him to have dominion[3] over the works of thy hands;
Thou hast put all things under his feet:
All sheep and oxen,
Yea, and the beasts of the field;
The fowl of the air, and the fish of the sea,
And whatsoever passeth through the paths of the seas.
O Lord our Lord,
How excellent is thy name in all the earth!

Psalm 23

The Lord is my shepherd; I shall not want.[4]
He maketh me to lie down in green pastures: he leadeth me beside the still waters.
He restoreth my soul:[5] he leadeth me in the paths of righteousness for his name's sake.
Yea, though I walk through the valley of the shadow of death, I will fear no evil: for thou art with me; thy rod and thy staff they comfort me.
Thou preparest a table before me in the presence of mine enemies: thou anointest my head with oil; my cup runneth over.
Surely goodness and mercy shall follow me all the days of my life: and I will dwell in the house of the Lord forever.[6]

Notes

[1] ordained: ordered to establish.

[2] still: make quiet or silenced; prevent from moving.

[3] dominion: control.

[4] want: be in need.

[5] soul: vitality.

[6] dwell... forever: worship in the temple of the Lord as long as I live.

Commentary

The King James Bible is written chiefly in prose, but some portions use *free verse*, poetry without rhyme or regular rhythm but poetry nevertheless. This is true of the Book of Psalms, or songs of praise, perhaps the most frequently read book of the Old Testament.

Psalm 8 is an appropriate praise of Lord for His selfless endeavors to protect man from any possible harm and His effort to help man lead a peaceful life.

Psalm 23 is widely used as a good example of symbolism in world literature. It begins with a metaphor: God is like a shepherd and I (the speaker) am one of His sheep; just as a shepherd takes care of his sheep, so will God take care of me. Then the poem shifts from metaphor to symbol with phrases such as "green pastures", "still waters", and particularly "the valley of the shadow of death". The meanings of "green pastures" (nourishment, security, ease) and "still waters" (peace, calm, sustenance) are quite easy to catch. But the subtle meaning of "the valley of the shadow of death" is more difficult. It does not seem to mean just death, but a kind of life experience, both psychological and spiritual, that is somehow related to death. As human beings, no matter how hard the trip is, we must journey through this "valley". Fortunately, with Lord's help, our fears for the evils on the journey are greatly trivialized.

Questions and Exercises

1. What facts does the speaker give in *Psalm 8* to support his idea that Lord is excellent in all the earth?
2. How is the relationship between the Lord and man in *Psalm 8*? And how is man treated by the Lord?
3. In *Psalm 23*, why does the speaker say that he will dwell in the house of the Lord forever?
4. Read the two psalms aloud and try to catch the rhythm of the free verse.

Ben Jonson

Ben Jonson (1572—1637) was one of many contemporaries and successors of William Shakespeare. He wrote many tragedies, comedies and masques. It is believed that he fought bravely for two things in his life: to restore the classical form of drama, and to keep the stage from its downward course. Though he apparently failed, yet his influence on English literature remained to grow increasingly powerful and finally resulted in the so-called classicism of the 18th century.

Jonson's poetry was essentially moral. His sociable and didactic nature made him the temporary adviser of younger writers, the so-called "Sons of Ben", who followed him in the effort of raising "the despised head of poetry" again, a program for a new poetic renaissance in Britain. Ben Jonson was the first poet laureate in English literary history. When he died in 1637, he was buried with all honor in Westminster Abbey, where his tomb bears the terse inscription: "O Rare Ben Jonson".

Song: To Celia

Drink to me only with thine eyes,
 And I will pledge with mine;[1]
Or leave a kiss but in the cup,
 And I will not look for wine.
The thirst that from the soul doth rise
 Doth ask a drink divine;
But might I of Jove's nectar sup,[2]
 I would not change for thine.[3]

I sent thee late[4] a rosy wreath,[5]
 Not so much honouring thee
As giving it a hope that there
 It could not wither'd be;
But thou thereupon did'st only breathe,
 And sent'st it back to me;[6]
Since when it grows, and smells, I swear,
 Not of itself, but thee.[7]

Notes

[1] pledge: drink a toast.

[2] But might I of Jove's nectar sup: But even if I might be able to drink Jove's nectar. Jove's nectar is the drink of gods. Jove: Jupiter, gods and men, according to Roman mythology.

[3] change for thine: take it in exchange for yours.

[4] late: lately; recently.

[5] rosy wreath: a symbol of love.

[6] But thou…back to me: So long as you did breathe on the rosy wreath, your breath would be sent back to me.

[7] Since when it… / Not of itself, but thee: It grows and smells not of the rosy wreath but you, which suggests that the growth of the flowers and their pleasant scent are derived from his lover.

Commentary

The poem is a compliment to a lady, which has rarely been put in language more graceful, more wealthy with interesting sounds. The use of figures of speech and the adopted pleasing sound and rhythm make this poem all the more memorable.

This lyric is from a collection of Ben Jonson's poems entitled *The Forest* published in 1616. It is written in what is known as the ballad meter—in alternate 8-syllable lines of tetrameter and 6-syllable lines of iambic trimester with a rhyme scheme of *abcb* in each stanza.

Questions and Exercises

1. What signs is the speaker looking for in lines 1—4? What would the speaker prefer over Jove's divine nectar?
2. Why did the speaker send a wreath of roses to his beloved? What did she do with it? What proof does the poem offer that the speaker will be persistent in his love?

It Is Not Growing Like a Tree

It is not growing like a tree
    In bulk, doth make man better be,[1]
Or standing long an oak, three hundred year,
To fall a log at last, dry, bald, and sere:[2]
        A lily of a day
        Is fairer far in May.[3]

Although it fall and die that night;
It was the plant and flower of light.
In small proportions we just beauties see,[4]
And in short measures, life may perfect be.[5]

Notes

[1] It is not growing…better be: It is not simply by growing in great size as an oak tree does that makes a man more excellent.

[2] Or standing long…and sere: Nor is it standing as long as three hundred years only to fall a log, dry, and sere, that does make an oak tree be better.

[3] Is fairer far in May: Is much more beautiful in May than the oak tree.

[4] In small proportions we just beauties see: We may see perfect beauties in things of small size.

[5] And in short measures, life may perfect be: Man's life may be most excellent though very brief. It should be measured by its excellence rather than by its length.

Commentary

The poem selected here is a part of the ode *To the Immortal Memory and Friendship of That Noble Pair, Sir Lucius Gary and Sir Henry Morison*, entitled *Underwoods* (1640). The stanza selected here is perfect not only in idea, but also in form, imagery, rhythm, and the subtle combination of sound and meaning. It is divided into two symmetrical parts by two short lines in the middle: "A Lily of a day / Is fairer far in May." These two terse and melodious lines contrast with the previous two long and jaw-breaking lines about the long-lived, but "dry, bald, and sere" oak, and represent the "small proportions", "just beauties" and "short measures" that Jonson speaks of in the last two lines. Moreover, there is a circularity of couplet rhyme scheme and a complete circularity in idea with the shift from "better be" to "perfect be".

Questions and Exercises

1. What is your impression about the contrast between the oak tree and the life of a man?
2. Rewrite the poem in prose form, then make some brief comments on the theme of the poem.

John Donne

John Donne (1572—1631) was born into a Roman Catholic family and educated at both Oxford and Cambridge universities without gaining a degree probably for religious reasons. In 1615, at the suggestion of King James I, he took Anglican orders and in 1621 was made dean of St. Paul's Cathedral. He was a churchman famous for his spellbinding sermons. He lived and wrote during the successive reigns of Elizabeth to Charles I. John Donne was widely acknowledged, and in fact was regarded as the founder of the metaphysical school of poetry.

The works of metaphysical poets are generally characterized by mysticism in conceit and fantasticality in form. Metaphysical poets investigated the world through rational discussion of its phenomena rather than by their intuition. They adopted a style that is energetic, uneven, and rigorous, which has also been labelled the "poetry of strong lines". A conceit comes from the Italian word *concetto,* meaning "concept". It is an elaborate metaphor or simile that makes a comparison between two significantly different things. The comparison may seem far-fetched at first sight, but when thoughtfully examined, it gains clarity and persuasion. In other words, the conceit brings together two entirely different images or ideas, and then develops the comparison in detail, so as to highlight the similarities between the two significantly different phenomena.

Donne's vigorous poetry is argumentative in method and colloquial in tone. His love poems vary from light-hearted contempt for women (*Go and Catch a Falling Star*) to serious declarations of devotion to love (*A Valediction: Forbidding Mourning*).

Song

Go and catch a falling star,
    Get with child a mandrake root,[1]
Tell me where all past years are,
    Or who cleft the devil's foot,
Teach me to hear mermaids[2] singing,
    Or to keep off envy's stinging,
        And find
        What wind
Serves to advance an honest mind.

If thou be'st borne to strange sights,
    Things invisible to see,
Ride ten thousand days and nights,
    Till age snow[3] white hairs on thee,
Thou, when thou return'st, wilt tell me
    All strange wonders that befall thee,
        And swear

Nowhere
Lives a woman true and fair.

If thou findst one, let me know,
Such a pilgrimage were sweet;
Yet do not, I would not go,
Though at next door we might meet;
Though she were true when you met her,
And last, till you write your letter,
Yet she
Will be
False, ere I come, to two, or three.

Notes

[1] mandrake root: The root of a type of large plant called mandrake or mandragora, resembling a human body, forked at the lower part like a man's legs. As a medicine, it was supposed to promote conception. The first two lines simply mean that to beget a child on a mandrake root is as impossible as it is to catch a falling star.

[2] mermaids: This word here is identified with the sirens. According to Greek mythology, a siren is a woman or half-woman half-bird who lured ships onto rocks by enchanting the sailors with her singing.

[3] snow: whiten; make grey. The word snow here is a verb in subjunctive mood.

Commentary

As a brilliant and dashing young man, Donne found the Renaissance idea of pure love difficult to accept. He made fun of the Elizabethan poets who were so keen on the presentation of the so-called permanent true love. This cynical poem represents his reaction against the idea of Platonic love which was rife in the sentimental Elizabethan sonnets.

The whole poem is basically written in trochaic tetrameter, though it tends to become more iambic towards the end. The tone of the speaker is angry, bitter, and cynical. The reason for this anger is revealed at the end of the second stanza: there are no true women; if there were one, he would immediately go on such a "pilgrimage", but he immediately rejects even the possibility of finding such a faithful woman.

The poem bears a typical theme of misogyny—hatred of a woman. Yet we readers may infer from the whole poem that the connotative meaning might be about the poet's hatred about the deep-rooted evils in the then society. The speaker of the poem seems to say: Nothing can be true in this world of evils, so don't be easily taken in by anyone who tells you that something will be hopefully good in such a world of injustices.

Questions and Exercises

1. What is the tone of the poem? What sort of indications is there that the speaker has implied by his exaggerated description of misogyny?
2. Scan the poem and see how the poet joined quatrain, couplet and tercet together to write his longer stanza.

A Valediction: Forbidding Mourning

As virtuous men pass mildly away,
　　And whisper to their souls to go,
Whilst some of their sad friends do say
　　The breath goes now, and some say no;

So let us melt, and make no noise,
　　No tear-floods nor sigh-tempests move;[1]
'Twere profanation of our joys
　　To tell the laity our love.

Moving of th' earth brings harms and fears;
　　Men reckon what it did and meant;
But trepidation of the spheres,[2]
　　Though greater far, is innocent.[3]

Dull sublunary lovers' love
　　(Whose soul is sense) cannot admit
Absence, because it does remove
　　Those things which elemented it.

But we, by a love so much refined
　　That ourselves know not what it is,
Inter-assured of the mind,
　　Care less, eyes, lips and hands to miss.

Our two souls, therefore, which are one,
　　Though I must go, endure not yet
A breach, but an expansion,

Like gold to airy thinness beat.[4]

If they be two, they are two so
As stiff twin compasses are two:
Thy soul, the fixed foot, makes no show
To move, but doth, if th' other do.

And though it in the center sit,
Yet when the other far doth roam,
It leans and harkens after it,
And grows erect as that comes home.

Such wilt thou be to me, who must,
Like th' other foot, obliquely run;
Thy firmness draws my circle just,[5]
And makes me end where I begun.

Notes

[1] No tear-floods nor sigh-tempests move: Do not stir up such strong emotions as shedding tears like floods or giving sighs like violent storms.

[2] Moving of th' earth: The destructive earthquakes. trepidation of the spheres: quick but natural motion of the heavenly planets.

[3] innocent: harmless.

[4] Like gold to airy thinness beat: Their love is so fine and steady that it can be infinitely extended over vast distances, just as a piece of gold can be beaten to an incredible thinness like gold foil without being broken. This is a keen metaphysical image in comparing pure and steady love to the enduring fine quality of gold.

[5] just: perfect.

Commentary

It is said that Donne wrote this poem for his wife in 1611, when he was about to depart on a diplomatic mission to France. The poem is written generally in quatrains with iambic tetrameter. The speaker bids farewell to his beloved wife, attempting to convince her that because of the special nature of their love, she need not mourn their parting. The poet creates excellent images of refinement by developing a series of unusual contrasts which is called metaphysics.

Donne and the other so-called metaphysical poets used conceits frequently. Of all the conceits they devised, none is more famous than the one developed here through the final three stanzas of this poem. As we have seen, there the souls of the two lovers are compared to the two legs of a geometrical compass—a startling image at first but one that becomes clearer in sense the more we think about it.

Questions and Exercises

1. What is a "valediction" any way? Is the speaker in the poem about to die? Why does the speaker forbid mourning? Explain the metaphors in the poem.
2. The metaphor in the last three stanzas is one of the most famous in English literature. Demonstrate its appropriateness through drawing a circle by using a compass or two pencils to imitate the two legs, and then explain the appropriateness of the metaphor.

Death, Be Not Proud

Death, be not proud, though some have called thee
Mighty and dreadful, for thou art not so;
For those whom thou think'st thou dost overthrow
Die not, poor Death, nor yet canst thou kill me.
From rest and sleep, which but thy pictures[1] be,
Much pleasure, then from thee much more must flow,
And soonest our best men with thee do go,
Rest of their bones, and souls delivery.[2]
Thou art slave to fate, chance, kings, and desperate men,
And dost with poison, war, and sickness dwell,
And poppy,[3] or charms can make us sleep as well,
And better than thy stroke;[4] why swell'st[5] thou then?
    One short sleep past, we wake eternally,[6]
    And death shall be no more; Death, thou shalt die.

Notes

[1] pictures: images; incarnations.

[2] Rest of their bones, and soul's delivery: to find rest for their bones and freedom for their souls.

[3] poppy: opium.

[4] better than thy stroke: easier than your attack.

[5] swell'st: brag or swell with pride.

[6] One short sleep, we wake eternally: Shortly after we die we will wake up and live eternally.

Commentary

Donne's love poetry was written in his youth, but later in life he concentrated himself on religious subjects. Composed after the death of his wife in 1617, Donne's *Holy Sonnets,* nineteen in all, reveal his complex thoughts on divine love and death. In *Death, Be Not Proud* (Sonnet 10), Donne addresses the subject of death.

The sonnet is written strictly in Petrarchan form. The first eight lines constitute the octave (two enveloped quatrains rhyming *abba abba*), and the following six lines form the sestet, rhyming *cdd cee*.

This sonnet is an almost startling put-down of poor Death, which is personified as an adversary swollen figure with false pride and unworthy of being called "mighty and dreadful". Donne gives various reasons in accusing Death of being little more than a slave bossed about by fate, chance, kings, and desperate men—a coward that keeps bad company with poison, war and sickness. Finally, Donne taunts Death with a world-famous paradox: "Death, thou shalt die." The sonnet is a revelation of the poet's belief in life after death—death is but momentary while happiness after death is eternal. So there is nothing to be afraid about death. The following is a translated version in prose form that may be helpful for you to understand the whole poem better.

Death, don't be proud of yourself, though some people have said that you are powerful and frightening, because you are not so. As for those whom you think you have ruined, they didn't die, and you can't kill me, either. Rest and sleep are simply your incarnations, from which we can obtain much pleasure. Thus it is sure that we can get much more pleasure from you Death. The sooner our best men go with you, the faster they can find rest of their bones and freedom of their souls. What is more, you just act as a slave for fate, chance, kings, and desperate men. You also keep bad company with opium, war, and sickness. Moreover, opium and incantation can help us sleep as well as and even more easily than your "attack". Then what reason do you have to brag about yourself? With one short sleep past, we wake forever, and death will be non-existent. Death, it is no one else but you that shall die!

Questions and Exercises

1. What logical argument does Donne use to prove that Death is nothing to fear? What is the conclusion of the sonnet? And which part of the argument seems to you the most effective in expressing the main theme?
2. The speaker's defiance of death in this poem might be thought of as orthodox Christian attitude typical of Renaissance humanism. How do you explain the contradiction of the poet's attitude towards death?

Robert Herrick

Robert Herrick (1591—1674) is one of the popular lyricists in the 17th-century England. He has some 1,400 poems to his credit, the best of which are *To the Virgins*, *To Make Much of Time*, and *To Daffodils*. His works are remarkable for their exquisite sentiments and their graceful, melodious expressions. His poetry is perhaps the finest example of the kind of lyrics for which the Cavaliers have become well-known—playful, delicate, witty verses. The poetic lines are seemingly as light as snowflakes. Readers cannot help feeling as if they had been chiseled in marble. Herrick is often remembered for the first line in the following selected poem "Gather ye rosebuds while ye may".

To the Virgins, To Make Much of Time

Gather ye rosebuds while ye may,
  Old Time is still a-flying;[1]
  And this same flower that smiles today
    Tomorrow will be dying.

The glorious lamp of heaven, the Sun,
    The higher he is a-getting,
The sooner will his race be run,[2]
    And nearer he's to setting.

That age is best which is the first,
    When youth and blood are warmer;
But being spent, the worse, and worst
    Times still succeed the former.[3]

Then be not coy, but use your time;
    And while ye may, go marry;
For having lost but once your prime,[4]
    You may forever tarry.[5]

Notes

[1] Old Time is still a-flying: The personified Time like an old man is always flying.

[2] his race be run: the onward course of his life and time will come to an end.

[3] But being spent, the worse, and worst / Times still succeed the former: But after the youth is spent, the increasingly old age will always take the place of your former youthful years.

[4] prime: the springtime of life; youth.

[5] tarry: be delayed; regret for being slow in catching your golden opportunities.

Commentary

This poem is a counsel to the girls to enjoy life and go marry while they are young. The first line is the theme which is so familiar that it has a special name "carpe diem" for it (Latin for "seize the day"), which is a favorable argument for poets of all times. The motif of life reflected in this poem can be viewed as the Cavalier reaction towards asceticism and other worldliness of Medieval Christian Church and Puritanism. The poem is written in ballad form, that is, in four quatrains rhyming *abab* and with the rhythmic pattern of alternate iambic tetrameter and trimester. The feminine ending to each trimeter line brings the poem a light-hearted musical tone.

Questions and Exercises

1. There are quite a number of symbols in the poem, such as rosebuds and virgin. List them and point out what they actually symbolize.
2. Sometimes it is almost impossible to replace one word by another in a well-written classic poem. How can the connotative meanings be changed if the words "blooms" is changed for "smiles", "course" for "race", and "used" for "spent"?

George Herbert

George Herbert (1593—1633) was regarded as "the saint of the Metaphysical school" in the 17th-century England. He was a devout Anglican who believed that a poet should sing the glory of God. Professor Palmer once called Herbert the first English poet who spoke face to face with God.

Herbert's chief work *The Temple* consists of over 150 short poems. Since Herbert's Anglican Christianity is strong and deep, his poems are deeply religious. Sometimes he resorts to tricks of typographical layout to express his religious piety as shown by his *Easter Wings* and *The Altar*, which suggest in the printed form of the poem the thing which the poet sings praise of.

In Many of his poems, Herbert describes his joys, fears and doubts in a symbolic way. Sometimes, they are overloaded with far-fetched conceits, too obscure to be appreciated. But he tends to use the direct, unassuming language of the common people, and unites it with philosophical insight, sensuous response, and courtly graciousness. All such qualities of his have made his poems all the more welcome by readers of all ages.

Virtue

Sweet day, so cool, so calm, so bright,
　　The bridal[1] of the earth and the sky;
The dew shall weep thy fall to night,
　　For thou must die.

Sweet rose, whose hue, angry and brave,[2]
　　Bids the rash gazer wipe his eye;
Thy root is ever in its grave,
　　And thou must die.

Sweet spring, full of sweet days and roses,
　　A box where sweets compacted lie;
My music[3] shows ye have your closes,
　　And all must die.

Only a sweet and virtuous soul,
　　Like seasoned timber,[4] never gives;[5]
But though the whole world turn to coal,[6]
　　Then chiefly lives.

Notes

[1] bridal: wedding; marriage.

[2] angry and brave: "Angry" here refers to the red color as appearing on an angry face. "Brave" means splendid in action. Both adjectives indicate the arrogant yet pathetic defiance of beauty in the face of time.

[3] My music: My poem.

[4] seasoned timber: dried and hardened wood.

[5] give: bend; yield to pressure.

[6] the whole world turn to coal: According to Christian religion, the whole world will be burned to ashes on Doomsday.

Commentary

This poem stresses in simple and lyrical language the Christian belief that all worldly matters, however beautiful, will perish whereas a humane and virtuous soul remains immortal. Herbert uses many monosyllabic words and such rhetorical devices as contrast and repetition in order to achieve the effect of brevity, forcefulness and solemnity. The poem contains four stanzas. The first three lines in each stanza are in octosyllabics while the last line contains two feet in iambic. The rhyme scheme is *abab*.

Questions and Exercises

1. Can you identify some of the imageries of the poem? How are the four stanzas logically interconnected? How do they build to a climax? And how does the fourth stanza make a clear contrast with the first three stanzas?
2. Write a paragraph to state the central idea of the poem.

Andrew Marvell

Andrew Marvell (1621—1678), another metaphysical poet, was a Puritan who became tutor to Cromwell's ward in 1653, and later served as Milton's assistant in the Commonwealth in the foreign secretaryship in 1657.

As a poet, Marvell is one of the central figures of the 17th century. His total output of poetry is small, but it includes some of the most famous poems in the English language, such as *To His Coy Mistress*, *The Definition of Love* and *The Garden*. His poetry excellently combines ingenious thought, delicate observation and elegant music together. On analyzing his poems it is not difficult to find that they have a quality of "a tough reasonableness beneath the slight lyric grace". In other words, his fine combination of metaphysical feature and lyrical elegance constitutes Marvel's unique style of poetry writing.

To His Coy Mistress

Had we but world enough, and time,
This coyness, lady, were no crime.
We would sit down, and think which way
To walk, and pass our long love's day.
Thou by the Indian Ganges' side

Shouldst rubies find; I by the tide
Of Humber[1] would complain. I would
Love you ten years before the Flood,[2]
And you should, if you please, refuse
Till the conversion of the Jews.[3]
My vegetable love should grow
Vaster than empires, and more slow;[4]
An hundred years should go to praise
Thine eyes, and on thy forehead gaze;
Two hundred to adore each breast,
But thirty thousand to the rest;
An age at least to every part,
And the last age should show your heart.
For, lady, you deserve this state,[5]
Nor would I love at lower rate.

But at my back I always hear
Time's winged chariot hurrying near;
And yonder all before us lie
Deserts of vast eternity.[6]
Thy beauty shall no more be found,
Nor, in thy marble vault, shall sound
My echoing song; then worms shall try
That long-preserved virginity,[7]
And your quaint honour turn to dust,
And into ashes all my lust;
The grave's a fine and private place,
But none, I think, do there embrace.

Now therefore, while the youthful hue
Sits on thy skin like morning dew,
And while thy willing soul transpires
At every pore with instant fires,[8]
Now let us sport us[9] while we may,
And now, like amorous birds of prey,[10]
Rather at once our time devour
Than languish in his slow-chapped power.
Let us roll all our strength and all

Our sweetness up into one ball,
And tear our pleasures with rough strife
Thorough the iron gates of life:[11]
Thus, though we cannot make our sun
Stand still, yet we will make him run.[12]

Notes

[1] Humber: a river that flows by Hull, where Marvell lived.

[2] the Flood: (in the Bible) the flood in the time of Noah. Here it suggests the beginning of the world.

[3] the conversion of the Jews: This refers to an event, according to St. John the Divine, that is to take place before the end of the world. Here it implies that she could be as coy as she liked if there were enough time in the world.

[4] My vegetable love…and more slow: If we had enough space and time my love should grow and spread as do the empires, even vaster and slower than the empires expand. Here "love" is metaphysically compared to a growing plant.

[5] state: stately ceremony or grandeur. The line means that you deserve this grand solemn ceremonial show during which my love is shown to you.

[6] Deserts of vast eternity: Eternal time and boundless empty land, that is, the nether world.

[7] then worms shall try / That long-preserved virginity: This is one of the well-known hard images in the poem, suggesting that time shall have its own way of ravishing virginity after she is dead.

[8] while thy willing soul transpires / At every pore with instant fires: as long as you are willing and eager to make love. transpire: give off (eager passion); instant: eager.

[9] sport us: enjoy or amuse ourselves.

[10] amorous birds of prey: greedy birds that kill and eat other animals. The speaker compares lovers to devouring beasts and urges to "devour" time instead of being slowly "devoured" by time. amorous: easily moved to love or easily showing one's passionate love, here it means eager or craving.

[11] Let us roll all our strength…the iron gates of life: We should concentrate our endeavor and enjoy pleasure as much as possible while we live. The speaker urges strongly that they should tear back their pleasure from their transient life in the way that man pulls his life back through the iron gates of death. thorough: through.

[12] Thus, though we cannot…make him run: Although we cannot make time stand still, we can make it fly, that is, we can live with such intensity and such speed that time will have to run his swiftest to keep up with us.

Commentary

To His Coy Mistress consists of rhyming couplets of iambic tetrameter. The whole poem is carefully divided into three long stanzas (strophes), each with a logical bearing upon the central issue, "carpe diem". A witty, persuasive proposition on the surface, the poem as a whole shows the daunting awareness of mortality of man. The whole poem is a moving metaphor symbolizing the importance of living fully in the moment. However, while reading, we get the impression that the poem makes truth a little more disturbing for us readers. Hyperbole, hard images, and the witty figures of speech constitute the unique features of this poem.

Questions and Exercises

1. What is the logical division of the poet? And how is the poet advancing his philosophy in this poem?
2. Discuss with your partner about the important figures of speech employed in this poem.
3. Does the speaker seem playful, ironical or serious in terms of the tone in the poem? Give examples to support yourself.

John Milton

John Milton (1608—1674) has been generally admitted to be England's greatest poet only after Shakespeare. He was educated at St. Paul's school and Christ's College, Cambridge. Under Cromwell, he held the government post of Secretary for Foreign Tongues. During this period of time, he wrote a number of pamphlets defending the English Revolution. After the Restoration (1660), he suffered a short period of imprisonment. Milton's blindness, which had been coming on for ten years, became complete blind in 1652 at the age of forty-four. He died at the age of sixty-six.

It should be noted that it was after Milton went stone-blind that he finished his three great works: two epic masterpieces *Paradise Lost* and *Paradise Regained*, and one biblical tragedy *Samson Agonistes*. Milton also wrote a small number of exquisite minor poetry, including 24 sonnets. His works had a powerful influence on English literature throughout the 18th century and was at its greatest in the 19th century. But Milton has sometimes been accused of using pompous and unusual words and writing Latin rather than English sentence structures. His vocabulary often draws meaning from Latin origin, and his sentences are usually long and complicated, often full of inversions. His well-known Miltonic style is magnificently dignified. For these reasons, his works are sometimes not very easy for modern readers to read.

On His Blindness

When I consider how my light is spent[1]
Ere half my days, in this dark world and wide,
And that one talent[2] which is death to hide,[3]
Lodged with me useless,[4] though my soul more bent
To serve therewith my Maker, and present
My true account, lest He returning chide;
"Doth God exact day labour, light denied?"
I fondly[5] ask. But Patience, to prevent
That murmur,[6] soon replies, "God doth not need
Either man's work, or His own gifts; who best
Bear His mild yoke, they serve Him best. His state
Is kingly: thousands at His bidding speed
And post o'er land and ocean without rest;
They also serve who only stand and wait."[7]

Notes

[1] my light is spent: The word "light" may refer to either Milton's loss of eye-sight or his life.

[2] that one talent: To understand the word "talent", we should know the Parable of the Talents in Matthew 25. The tale goes like this: Before the master started off to a foreign country, he gave some talents (the unit of money in Greece) to his three servants, five to the first, two to the second, and one to the third. During the absence of the master, the first two servants used the money to trade, each doubling his original amount; while the third, being afraid to lose the only one talent, buried it underground. On his returning, the master asked each of the servants "to present his account". Knowing what each had done, he blessed the first two servants but chided the third for his foolish and futile act. "Talent" is here used as a pun which probably also refers to Milton's declining writing ability resulted from his blindness.

[3] which is death to hide: The normal order is "To hide (the talent) is death."

[4] Lodged with me useless: His blindness had rendered his "one talent" (writing ability) useless. Yet it should be particularly pointed out that the three major works *Paradise Lost*, *Paradise Regained* and *Samson Agonistes* were all written after he had become totally blind. So from this sonnet, we can feel Milton's personality of religious piety and his virtuous modesty.

[5] fondly: foolishly.

[6] murmur: complaint.

[7] They also serve who only stand and wait: In the grandeur of the court of Heaven, there are messengers and sentries serving God by travel busily across land and ocean. But there are also those whose duty is to stand and wait on God rather than traveling busily. In a sense, these people also serve God best. Quite possibly, Milton also suggests that he himself is waiting to be given a task by God so that he can carry out his duty of writing.

Commentary

This famous sonnet was probably written in 1652 when Milton became completely blind. While usually taken to refer to the poet's lost eyesight, the sonnet may not just about blindness. The familiar title *On His Blindness* was not given the poem by Milton, but by a printer a century later. The theme of the poem is about frustration in life (perhaps about Milton's declining power of poetry or his fame as a Puritan apologist) and reconciliation to his lot. The struggle with which this short poem enacts is between protest and resignation, between bitterness and acceptance.

The poem belongs to a Petrarchan sonnet in form. The natural ordering is protest in the octave rhyming *abba abba*, and acceptance in the sestet *cde cde*. In the octave, the speaker complains about the unfairness of God; meanwhile, he is afraid that God might reproach him for not using his abilities to the full, even though he is blind. Before he can foolishly complain that God asks too much of him, Patience tells him (in the sestet) that God does not need man's gifts because He is self-sufficient. The best service to God is devout obedience; whatever we do, we are acting according to God's will.

Questions and Exercises

1. What is the speaker lamenting in lines 1—2?
2. What two meanings does talent have? What happens if the talent is hidden? What does the speaker want to do with it?
3. What are the two kinds of activity pictured in lines 9—14? In what category does the speaker place himself?
4. Scan the sonnet, and then try to tell its thought divisions.

John Dryden

John Dryden (1631—1700) was born to a Puritan family in London and was graduated from Cambridge University in 1654. He was the outstanding English poet from the

Restoration in 1660 to the end of the 17th-century England.

Dryden wrote verse in several forms: odes, poetic drama, biting satires, and translations of classical authors. Unlike many of his predecessors, Dryden wrote in celebration of noteworthy occasions more often than in response to more personal experiences. He was made poet laureate from 1668 to 1688. Among Dryden's most important legacy to the poets of the next century was his mastery of the heroic couplet, paired lines of rhyming iambic pentameter. Another major contribution is Dryden's dignified, unaffected, and always musical language.

Dryden wrote notable prose as well, including literary criticism of Shakespeare, Chaucer, and others that is as sound in judgment now as when he conceived it. In fact, he is sometimes considered the father of English criticism. His prose is the first that strikes us as modern because it is written in a manner that resembles speech.

A Song for St. Cecilia's Day

[1]

From harmony, from heavenly harmony
This universal frame[1] began;
When Nature underneath a heap
Of jarring atoms[2] lay,
And could not heave her head,
The tuneful voice was heard from high:
"Arise, ye more than dead."
Then cold, and hot, and moist, and dry[3]
In order to their stations leap,
And music's power obey.
From harmony, from heavenly harmony
This universal frame began:
From harmony to harmony
Through all the compass of the notes it ran,
The diapason[4] closing full in man.

[2]

What passion cannot music raise and quell!
When Jubal struck the corded shell,[5]
His listening brethren stood around,
And, wondering, on their faces fell
To worship that celestial sound.

Less than a god they thought there could not dwell
Within the hollow of that shell
That spoke so sweetly and so well.
What passion cannot music raise and quell!

[3]

The trumpet's loud clangor
Excites us to arms,
With shrill notes of anger,
And mortal alarms.
The double, double, double beat
Of the thund'ring drum
Cries, "Hark, the foes come;
Charge, charge, 'tis too late to retreat."

[4]

The soft complaining flute
In dying notes discovers[6]
The woes of hopeless lovers,
Whose dirge is whispered by the warbling lute.

[5]

Sharp violins proclaim
Their jealous pangs and desperation,
Fury, frantic indignation,
Depth of pains and height of passion,
For the fair, disdainful dame.

[6]

But Oh! What art can teach,
What human voice can reach,
The sacred organ's praise?
Notes inspiring holy love,
Notes that wing their heavenly ways
To mend the choirs above.

[7]

Orpheus[7] could lead the savage race,
And trees unrooted left their place,
Sequacious of[8] the lyre;
But bright Cecilia raised the wonder higher;
When to her organ vocal breath was given,
An angel heard and straight appeared,

Mistaking earth for heaven.

Grand Chorus

As from the power of sacred lays[9]
The spheres began to move,
And sung the great Creator's praise
To all the blest above;
So, when the last and dreadful hour
This crumbling pageant[10] shall devour,
The trumpet[11] shall be heard on high,
The dead shall live, the living die,
And music shall untune the sky.[12]

Notes

[1] universal frame: the structure of the universe.

[2] jarring atoms: chaos preceding the arrangement of the universe.

[3] Then cold, and hot, and moist, and dry: According to the Bible, the world at the beginning was dark, void and without form. It was God who created nature and saved it out of chaos. This line describes nature as composed of the four discordant elements: earth, fire, water, and air.

[4] diapason: the whole range of tones of a musical scale; complete harmony. Dryden is also thinking of the Chain of Being, a view that ordered creation from inanimate nature up through humankind both of which are the result of harmony.

[5] When Jubal struck the corded shell: According to Genesis 4.21, Jubal was the inventor of the lyre and the pipe made of a tortoise shell.

[6] discovers: reveals.

[7] Orpheus: A legendary poet, son of Muses, who, in Greek mythology, played so wonderfully on the lyre that the trees and stones are enchanted and the savage race or wild beasts are tamed.

[8] Sequacious of: Following blindly.

[9] lays: songs.

[10] pageant: the stage on which the drama of man's salvation has been acted on. Here it refers to the universe and the spectacle it represents.

[11] trumpet: the last trumpet, which announces the biblical Judgment Day, or end of the universe.

[12] And music shall untune the sky: Just as music had once been able to "tune" the sky—to have brought the universe into complete harmony, it also has the ability to "untune" the sky, that is, to reduce the cosmos to its original state of chaotic jarring atoms.

Commentary

Dryden wrote *A Song for St. Cecilia's Day* in memory of a Roman woman and Christian martyr who has traditionally been regarded as the patron saint of music and the inventor of the organ. The legend goes that an angel was drawn from heaven to listen to her music playing. Dryden composed the poem in the form of an irregular ode for a celebration in her memory on November 22, 1687. Throughout the ode, Dryden eulogizes the power of music. In 1739 composer George Frederick Handel composed a score to accompany this ode.

In this ode, sound and meaning are very well intertwined and interdependent. Dryden marvels at the power of music to move us in countless ways. He examines the different effects of musical instruments. To emphasize the rousing, rhythmic, pounding qualities of the drum, he twice repeats the word "double". He mainly uses heavy, percussive consonant sounds like "double", "beat", "thund'ring", "drum" to obtain the effect of strength. Moreover, the very words "drum" and "beat" sound their meanings; they are, in short, *onomatopoetic* words. One result of these choices is that when we read these lines, we hear the strong, steady beat of a drum. In contrast, Dryden uses quieter, softer consonants to evoke the gentle, and sometimes mournful sound of the flute, like "soft", "complaining", "flute", "hopeless", "lovers". When sound and sense are merged together, as they are in this poem, the impact can be emotional as well as intellectual. The poem can reach us and move us with surprising immediacy much like music itself can.

Questions and Exercises

4. From what, according to the first stanza, did the universe begin?
5. According to stanza 7, why did an angel pay a visit to the earth?
6. With what sound will the world end, according to the Grand Chorus? What passions are stirred up by different instruments in stanzas 3—6?
7. On what occasions in our daily life does music reflect or heighten our emotions? Write a passage to express your own thought or feeling about the powerful effect of music on a certain occasion.

Alexander Pope

Alexander Pope (1688—1744) was plagued by ill health from birth. Weak and crippled from childhood, he was deprived of the common pleasures of life. In addition, his Catholicism prevented him from attending any university or holding any public office. But he turned all these disadvantages into a positive good. Encouraged by his father, he taught himself by wide reading and translating Latin, French, Italian and Greek poets, with the help of grammar books and dictionaries. His literary endeavors gave him ample means to win profit. In fact, Pope was the first English writer to demonstrate that literature alone could be a gainful profession. At twenty-three in 1711, he published his masterpiece *An Essay on Criticism.*

The Rape of the Lock, written in the form of mock epic, was published in 1714. It is a satire on the idle meaningless life of the aristocracy of the time. In the field of satiric and didactic verse, Pope was the undisputed master. He was at his best in the heroic couplet and it was he who brought this metrical medium to perfection. Besides, Pope was a master of style, too. Throughout his writing career, his verse is notable for its rhythmical variety (in spite of his apparently rigid metric unit of the heroic couplet), the precise expressiveness of meaning, and the harmony of his language.

An Essay on Criticism

(Lines 215—232)

A little learning is a dang'rous thing;
Drink deep, or taste not the Pierian spring.[1]
There shallow droughts intoxicate the brain,
And drinking largely sobers us again.
Fired at first sight with what the Muse imparts,
In fearless youth we tempt[2] the heights of arts,
While from the bounded level of our mind
Short views we take, nor see the lengths behind;
But more advanced, behold with strange surprise
New distant scenes of endless science[3] rise!
So pleased at first the towering Alps[4] we try,
Mount o'er the vales, and seem to tread the sky,
The eternal snows appear already past,
And the first clouds and mountains seem the last;
But, those attained, we tremble to survey
The growing labors of the lengthened way,
The increasing prospect tires out our wandering eyes,
Hills o'er hills, and Alps on Alps arise!

Notes

[1] the Pierian spring: The spring in Pieria on Mount Olympus, sacred to the Muses.
[2] tempt: attempt.

[3] science: knowledge.
[4] the towering Alps: the high mountain range separating France and Italy.

Commentary

An Essay on Criticism, a didactic verse written in heroic couplets, is Pope's chief contribution to literary criticism. The poem contains 744 lines and is divided into three parts, opening with the author bewailing the death of true taste in critics and stating the need to turn to nature as the best guide for critical judgment. Though written in heroic couplets, we hardly consider this as a poem but rather as an essay like a storehouse of critical maxims. "A little learning is a dang'rous thing"; "To err is human, to forgive, divine"; "For fools rush in where angels fears to tread"; —these lines and many more of the like are so popular that they have found their way into our common speech.

The above excerpt gives some advice to critics to avoid the danger of little learning. It is in fact an extended metaphor, emphasizing that a possession of large quantity of knowledge is an indispensable must for the critics to evaluate or appreciate the beauty of arts. The central idea actually lies in the first and last lines of the selection.

Questions and Exercises

1. Give a subtitle to this excerpt and then write a comment on the following critical maxims: "A little learning is a dang'rous thing; / Drink deep, or taste not the Pierian spring." and "The increasing prospect tires out our wandering eyes, / Hills o'er hills, and Alps on Alps arise!"
2. What are the main characteristics of heroic couplet? How do you like this poetic form?

William Blake

William Blake (1757—1827) was a painter, engraver, and poet. He engraved, instead of printing, his poems, and combined each with pictorial engraving that displayed the poetic theme in visual terms, thus inventing a new form by which the poem was visually completed.

Blake's first collection of poems is the *Poetical Sketches* written when he was between twelve and twenty. But the most famous of his works are *Songs of Innocence* (1789) and *Songs of Experience* (1794). In his *Songs of Innocence* Blake assumes the stance that he is writing "happy songs / Every child may joy to hear" and insists on the qualities in human nature that are the source of love, compassion and sympathy. *Songs of Experience* shows the ruthlessness in nature and injustice in society. The vision in *Songs of Experience* is an ugly and terrifying one of poverty, disease and prostitution epitomized in the ghastly representation of modern London. The worlds as depicted in these two groups of lyrics are, as Blake calls them, the "two contrary states of the human soul": innocence and experience, energy and control, cruelty and meekness.

Blake is regarded as an important pre-romantic forerunner of the Romantic poetry in the 19th century. He is seen as a liberator of human spirit and a rebellious genius in art, challenging the classical tradition of that age. His lyric poetry displays the characteristics of the Romantic spirit, and it was Blake himself that prophesied the coming of Romanticism in the history of English literature.

The Chimney Sweeper

(From *Songs of Innocence*)

When my mother died I was very young,
And my father sold me while yet my tongue
Could scarcely cry " 'weep! 'weep! 'weep!"[1]
So your chimneys I sweep, and in soot I sleep.

There's little Tom Dacre, who cried when his head,
That curled like a lamb's back, was shaved; so I said,
"Hush, Tom! never mind it, for, when your head's bare,
You know that the soot cannot spoil your white hair."

And so he was quiet, and that very night,
As Tom was asleeping, he had such a sight!—
That thousands of sweepers, Dick, Joe, Ned, and Jack,[2]
Were all of them locked up in coffins of black.

And by came an Angel, who had a bright key,
And he opened the coffins, and set them all free;
Then down a green plain, leaping, laughing, they run
And wash in a river, and shine in the sun.

Then naked and white, all their bags left behind,
They rise upon clouds and sport[3] in the wind;
And the Angel told Tom, if he'd be a good boy,
He'd have God for his father, and never want[4] joy.

And so Tom awoke, and we rose in the dark,

And got with our bags and our brushes to work.
Though the morning was cold, Tom was happy and warm;
So, if all do their duty, they need not fear harm.[5]

Notes

[1] "'weep! 'weep! 'weep!": This is the street cry ("sweep!") of the chimney sweepers, sent by their parents through London streets to advertise their services even when they were too young to articulate clearly the word "sweep". "'weep" is here used as a pun to suggest both sweeping of the chimneys and weeping over their pitiful plight.

[2] Dick, Joe, Ned, and Jack: common names for children.

[3] sport: have fun; play joyfully.

[4] want: suffer from lack of.

[5] So, if all do their duty, they need not fear harm: If all of us do our duty well in this world, we need not worry that God will do any harm to us. This line is an indirect criticism to God, church, and the adult world, who have actually failed to do their own duties of taking care of the children.

The Chimney Sweeper

(From *Songs of Experience*)

The little black thing among the snow,[1]
Crying "'weep! 'weep!" in notes of woe!
"Where are thy father and mother? Say?"
They are both gone to the church to pray.

Because I was happy upon the heath,
And smil'd among the winter's snow,
They clothed me in the clothes of death,
And told me to sing the notes of woe.

And because I am happy and dance and sing,
They think they have done me no injury,
And they are gone to praise God and his priest and king,
Who make up a heaven of our misery.[2]

Notes

[1] The little black thing: The little chimney-sweeper whose job has made him look black.

[2] Who made up a heaven of our misery: (God and His Priest and King) together build

a Heaven out of our misery.

Commentary

In the 18th century, small boys, sometimes no more than four or five years old, were employed to climb up the narrow chimney flues and clean them, collecting the soot in bags. Such boys, sometimes sold to the master sweepers by their parents, were miserably treated by their masters and often suffered disease and physical deformity.

Two vastly different versions of *The Chimney Sweeper* appeared respectively in *Songs of Innocence* and *Songs of Experience.* The first from *Songs of Innocence* is in fact a protest against the harm that society does to its children by exploiting them for labor of this kind. It was written in the child's point of view, and the dramatic irony arises from the poet's knowing more or seeing more than the child does. What the speaker says in the poem is different from what the poet means.

The second poem is from *Songs of Experience*. The short lyric, consisting of three quatrains of rhymed lines with combined iambic and anapestic feet, contains chiefly the simple yet somewhat ironical speech of a boy chimney-sweeper as he describes his life of misery and its relation to "God and His Priest and King".

Questions and Exercises

1. The above two poems are full of implications. Try to find out and interpret their implied meanings in your own words.
2. What might be the respective tones of the two poems? Angry, hopeful, sorrowful, or compassionate? Give reasons to support yourself.

The Tyger

Tyger![1] Tyger! burning bright
In the forests of the night,
What immortal hand or eye
Could frame thy fearful symmetry?[2]

In what distant deeps or skies
Burnt the fire of thine eyes?
On what wings dare he aspire?[3]
What the hand dare seize the fire?

And what shoulder, and what art,
Could twist the sinews of thy heart?

And when thy heart began to beat,
What dread[4] hand? and what dread feet?

What the hammer? What the chain?
In what furnace was thy brain?
What the anvil? What dread grasp
Dare its deadly terrors clasp?

When the stars threw down their spears,
And watered heaven with their tears,[5]
Did he[6] smile his work to see?
Did he who made the Lamb[7] make thee?

Tyger! Tyger! burning bright
In the forests of the night,
What immortal hand or eye
Dare frame thy fearful symmetry?

Notes

[1] Tyger: (archaic) Tiger.

[2] thy fearful symmetry: the bodily frame of the tiger which is of balanced proportions but at the same time evokes fear.

[3] aspire: (archaic) rise high; fly upward.

[4] dread: (archaic) dreadful.

[5] When the stars threw down their spears, / And watered heaven with their tears: The "spears" and "tears" here both refer to the light coming from the stars.

[6] he: the Maker; the God.

[7] the Lamb: the symbol of innocence and simplicity, alluding to Jesus Christ, who called himself and often has been called by others a lamb.

Commentary

The key symbol of *Songs of Experience* is the tiger; the corresponding image in *Songs of Innocence* is the lamb. The tiger is the subject of the famous poem that stands at the peak of Blake's lyrical achievement.

Tyger! Tyger! burning bright
In the forests of the night,
What immortal hand or eye
Could frame thy fearful symmetry?

The tiger in this poem is the incarnation of energy, strength, lust, and cruelty. And the tragic dilemma of mankind is poignantly summarized in the final question "Did he who made the Lamb make thee?"

The Tyger, included in *Songs of Experience*, usually considered to be a companion piece to *The Lamb*, is one of Blake's best-known poems. It seemingly praises the great power of tiger, but what the tiger symbolizes remains disputable: the power of man? the revolutionary force? the evil? or, as it is usually interpreted, the Almighty Maker who created both the meek and gentle lamb and the terrible and awesome tiger? The poem is highly symbolic with a touch of mysticism and it is open to various interpretations.

The poem contains six quatrains in rhyming couplets, and its language is terse and forceful with an anvil rhythm. The dominant rhyme scheme is trochaic tetrameter, though in the latter part of the poem it gradually becomes more iambic in rhythm.

Questions and Exercises

1. What is the symbolic meaning of the tiger? What paradox can you find in the poem?
2. *The Lamb* is a poem from Blake's *Songs of Innocence* in contrast to *The Tyger* in *Songs of Experience*. Read the following poem, and then explain what philosophical views the poet intends to reveal in this pair of companion poems.

The Lamb

Little Lamb, who made thee?
Dost thou know who made thee?
Gave thee life, and bid thee feed, [1]
By the stream and o'er the mead; [2]
Gave thee clothing of delight,
Softest clothing, wooly, bright;
Gave thee such a tender voice,
Making all the vales rejoice,
Little Lamb, who made thee?
Dost thou know who made thee?

Little Lamb, I'll tell thee,
Little Lamb, I'll tell thee:
He is called by thy name,
For he calls himself a lamb.
He is meek, and he is mild;
He became a little child.
I a child, and thou a lamb,

We are called by his name.
  Little Lamb, God bless thee!
  Little Lamb, God bless thee!

Notes

[1] bid thee feed: offer you food.

[2] mead: meadow.

Robert Burns

Robert Burns (1759—1796) is undoubtedly the Scotland's greatest poet, as he is at his best at writing poetry in the Scottish dialect and the feelings he expresses are those of the Scottish peasants, too. Burns had a profound sympathy for the downtrodden, whether man or mouse; and his emotions were deeply sincere for the lower class people. For these reasons, he is universally regarded as a patriotic poet as well as a national symbol of Scotland.

Burns was born of a poor, honest peasant's family in Ayrshire, Scotland. As a boy he toiled on the farm with the rest of the family, and at thirteen, he was doing a peasant's full day labour. With little schooling, he managed to squeeze out some time every day for reading. As a result he became well-read in some parts of English literature. From his early years he had an intimate knowledge of Scottish folk songs, and while working in the fields, he used to sing to himself, composing new songs in his mind to the old popular Scottish tunes he knew. In this way he wrote his poems. In July 1786, his *Poems Chiefly in the Scottish Dialect* were printed, and from then on he devoted all his free time to collecting, restoring, imitating and editing traditional Scottish songs.

The greater part of Burns' life was a hard and bitter struggle against poverty and misfortune. A long illness cut short his great poetic genius, and in 1796 he died miserably at the age of thirty-six.

A Red, Red Rose

O my Luve's like a red, red rose
  That's newly sprung in June;
O my Luve's like the melodie, [1]
  That's sweetly play'd in tune. [2]

As fair art thou, my bonnie lass,
  So deep in luve am I; [3]
And I will luve thee still, [4] my dear,

Till a' the seas gang dry,[5]

Till a' the seas gang dry, my dear,
And the rocks melt wi' the sun;
I will luve thee still, my dear,
While the sands o' life shall run.[6]

And fare thee weel,[7] my only Luve!
And fare thee weel a while!
And I will come again, my Luve,
Tho' it were ten thousand mile! [8]

Notes

[1] O my luve's…like the melodie: luve: love; sprung: come out; melodie: music.

[2] in tune: in harmony.

[3] As fair…in luve am I: My sweetheart, you are as beautiful as I am in deep love of you.

[4] still: always.

[5] Till a' the seas gang dry: Till all the seas go dry.

[6] While the sands o' life shall run: As long as I live; Till the end of my life. "Sands" here refers to the sands in a sandglass in old times as an instrument for measuring time.

[7] fare thee weel: farewell to you.

[8] Tho' it were ten thousand mile: Even though ten thousand miles should separate us.

Commentary

This is one of Robert Burns' most popular love lyrics written essentially in the metrical form of the ballad stanza. This poem is a good example of how the poet made use of old Scottish folk poetry and created immortal lines by revising the old folk material. Since Burns wrote this poem, the "red rose" has been well established as a symbol of beauty and love. The extreme simplicity of the language and the charming rhythmic beat of the verse match excellently to the poet's true sentiments towards his dear love. Besides, the use of various figures of speech abound in this famous lyric, such as simile, metaphor, and overstatement, making the lyric all the more charming for readers to read.

Questions and Exercises

1. Try to scan the poem in terms of stanza, line, meter and rhyme, and see which category this poem belongs to.

2. Find out the figurative language used in the poem, and explain the appropriateness of their use.

To a Mouse

On Turning Her up in Her Nest with the Plough, November 1785

Wee, sleekit, cow'rin', tim'rous beastie,[1]
Oh, what a panic's in thy breastie!
Thou need na start awa sae hasty,[2]
    Wi' bickering brattle![3]
    I wod be laith to rin an' chase thee,[4]
Wi' murd'ring pattle![5]

I'm truly sorry man's dominion
Has broken nature's social union,
An' justifies that ill opinion
    Which makes thee startle
    At me, thy poor earth-born companion,
An' fellow-mortal!

I doubt na, whyles,[6] but thou may thieve;
What then? Poor beastie, thou maun[7] live!
A daimenicker in a thrave[8]
    'S a sma' request:
I'll get a blessin' wi' the lave,[9]
    And never miss't!

Thy wee bit housie, too, in ruin!
Its silly wa's the win's are strewin'!
An' naething, now, to big[10] a new ane,
    O' foggage[11] green!
An' bleak December's winds ensuin',
    Baith snell and keen![12]

Thou saw the fields laid bare an' waste,
An' weary winter comin' fast,
An' cozie here, beneath the blast,

Thou thought to dwell,
Till crash! the cruel coulter[13] past
Out thro' thy cell.

That wee bit heap o' leaves an' stibble
Has cost thee mony a weary nibble!
Now thou's turn'd out, for a' thy trouble,
But[14] house or hald,
To thole the winter's sleety dribble,[15]
An' cranreuch cauld![16]

But, Mousie, thou art no thy lane,[17]
In proving foresight may be vain:
The best laid schemes o' mice an' men,
Gang aft agley, [18]
An' lea' e us nought but grief and pain
For promis'd joy!

Still thou art blest, compared wi' me!
The present only toucheth thee:
But, och! I backward cast my e'e
On prospects drear! [19]
An' forward, tho' I canna see,
I guess an' fear!

Notes

[1] Wee, sleekit, cow'rin', tim'rous beastie: Tiny, smooth, cowering, timid little beast.

[2] Thou need na start awa sae hasty: You need not run away in such a hurry.

[3] Wi' bickering brattle: In sudden fright.

[4] I wod be laith to rin an' chase thee: I would be loath or unwilling to chase and run after you.

[5] pattle: a small spade-like implement of a plow.

[6] whyles: sometimes.

[7] maun: must.

[8] A daimenicker in a thrave: An occasional ear of grain from a sheaf.

[9] lave: rest.

[10] big: build.

[11] foggage: rough grass.

[12] Baith snell and keen: Both sharp and cold.
[13] coulter: cutter on a plow.
[14] But: Without.
[15] To thole the winter's sleety dribble: To endure the winter's snowy drizzle.
[16] cranreuch cauld: hoar-frost cold.
[17] lane: alone.
[18] Gang aft agley: Often go wrong.
[19] I backward cast my e'e on prospects drear!: I must look back into the dull miseries of the past!

Commentary

This poem, written chiefly in Scottish dialect, was composed, according to Burn's brother, while the poet was actually holding the plow in the fields. Burns had such a compassionate understanding of human misery that it extends even to the miserable conditions of a helpless small animal such as a mouse. When the farmer plows into the mouse's nest, he apologizes and meditates on the respective conditions of both mouse and man.

The monologue is humorous because the farmer addresses the mouse as an equal being. He insists that he, as a human, has interfered with the mouse and not vice versa. He accepts the fact that the mouse is entitled to have an ill opinion of man. The poem rather convincingly arouses sympathy without sentimentality. Both man and mouse are victims, but compared with a mouse, man, in addition to his miserable present conditions to suffer from, is capable of experiencing great fear about the unknown future. He is also inclined to indulge himself in the sorrows about his painful past. Therefore, man suffers more than does the mouse.

Questions and Exercises

1. According to stanza 2, what has man's dominion broken? Who are the fellow-mortals of man?
2. According to stanza 7, what often happens to the "best-laid schemes"? What are we left with in the end?
3. Why is the mouse blessed compared with man, according to the last stanza? What is Burns's view of the mouse's misfortune? And what does this view suggest about his attitude toward nature?

William Wordsworth

William Wordsworth (1770—1850) became an orphan when he was eight, and was taken in charge by relatives, who sent him to school at Hawkshead in the beautiful lake region.

There the unroofed school of nature attracted him. He lived alone, but never felt lonely with nature. As a poet, Wordsworth was as sensitive as a barometer to every change around him, and was thought to be the world's greatest interpreter on nature's message. He made a god out of nature, and looked upon himself as "Nature's priest". Nature was a major theme for many of his poems. Much of his poetry focuses on nature and the harmony between humans and the natural world.

Wordsworth made friends with R. Southy and S. T. Coleridge and the three were known as the "Lake Poets". Together with Coleridge, Wordsworth wrote and published in 1798 a collection of poems entitled *Lyrical Ballads* which is regarded as the effective starting point of the English Romantic Movement, the great period that extended until 1830. His poetic eminence was greatly acknowledged and he was made Poet Laureate in 1845.

I Wandered Lonely as a Cloud

I wandered lonely as a cloud
    That floats on high o'er vales and hills, [1]
When all at once I saw a crowd,
    A host of[2] golden daffodils,
Beside the lake, beneath the trees,
Fluttering and dancing in the breeze.

Continuous as the stars that shine
    And twinkle on the Milky Way, [3]
They stretched in never-ending line
    Along the margin of a bay,
Ten thousand saw I at a glance
Tossing their heads in sprightly[4] dance.

The waves beside them danced, but they
    Out-did[5] the sparkling waves in glee.
A poet could not but be gay
    In such a jocund[6] company
I gazed—and gazed—but little thought
What wealth[7] the show to me had brought:

For oft, when on my couch I lie
    In vacant or in pensive mood, [8]
They flash upon that inward eye
    Which is the bliss of solitude, [9]

And then my heart with pleasure fills,
And dances with the daffodils.

Notes

[1] That floats on high o'er vales and hills: That continuously drifts high above valleys and hills.

[2] A host of: A great number of.

[3] the Milky Way: the broad luminous band of stars encircling the sky; the Galaxy.

[4] sprightly: vigorous; light and gay.

[5] Out-did: Excelled.

[6] jocund: cheerful; merry.

[7] wealth: spiritual wealth; the great pleasure or happiness.

[8] In vacant or in pensive mood: In an unthinking or seriously thoughtful mood.

[9] They flash upon that inward eye / Which is the bliss of solitude: To recall the breathtaking beauty afterward in quietness or tranquility is a sort of real happiness in the soul. According to William Wordsworth, poetry should be "the spontaneous overflow of powerful feelings; it takes its origin from emotion recollected in tranquility."

Commentary

This poem was written in 1804 and printed in the *Poems of 1807*. It is likely that the experience of daffodil-watching was derived in part from the recollections his sister Dorothy Wordsworth had set down in her journal of April 15, 1802, two years before he first drafted his poem:

"When we were in the woods beyond Gowbarrow Park we saw a few daffodils close to the waterside. We fancied that the lake had floated the seeds ashore, and that the little colony had so sprung up. But as we went along there were more and yet more; and at last, under the boughs of the trees, we saw that there was a long belt of them along the shore, about the breadth of them along the shore, about the breadth of a country turnpike road. I never saw daffodils so beautiful. They grew among the mossy stones about and about them; some rested their heads upon these stones as on a pillow for weariness; and the rest tossed and rolled and danced and seemed as if they verily laughed with the wind, that flew upon them over the lake; they looked so gay, ever glancing, ever changing. This wind blew directly over the lake to them. There was here and there a little knot, and a few stragglers a few yards higher up; but they were so few as not to disturb the simplicity, unity, and life of that one busy highway."

Obviously Wordsworth's poem echoes a few of his sister's observations. At the beginning of the poem, the poet compares himself with a cloud so that both of them can have a free chance of observing the natural beauty with a bird's eye-view. The poem is one of the many poems by Wordsworth on the beauty of nature. There is a vivid picture of the daffodils here, mixed with the poet's philosophical and somewhat mystical thoughts.

The poem consists of four sestets of iambic tetrameter with a rhyme scheme of *ababcc* in each stanza, known as stave of six.

Questions and Exercises

1. Do you think nature can have healing effect on man's mind? What is the relation between the poet and nature as described in the poem?
2. Think about the way the speaker's feelings changed when he or she spied the "host of golden daffodils". Have you ever experienced a similar change of emotion after you saw a particular sight? Perhaps, instead of making you joyful, what you saw saddened or frightened you. Discuss with a partner an occasion you felt both before and after you saw the sight.
3. Write a short essay and explain by what means the poet has made this poem sound so beautiful.

Composed Upon Westminster Bridge

Sept. 3, 1802

Earth has not anything to show more fair!
Dull would he be of soul who could pass by
A sight so touching in its majesty! [1]
This city now doth, like a garment, wear

The beauty of the morning: silent, bare.
Ships, towers, domes, theatres, and temples lie
Open unto the fields, and to the sky,
All bright and glittering in the smokeless air. [2]

Never did sun more beautifully steep[3]
In his first splendor, valley, rock, or hill;
Ne'er saw I, never felt, a calm so deep!

The river glideth at his own sweet will; [4]
Dear God! the very houses seem asleep;
And all that mighty heart is lying still! [5]

Notes

[1] Dull would he…in its majesty: His soul or sense would not be excellent enough if he could not be touched by such a majestic sight.

[2] This City now doth…in the smokeless air: In the early morning the air was smokeless and the sky clear, so everything was visible from the outskirts of the city.

[3] steep: bathe or shine on.

[4] The river glideth at his own sweet will: The river water flows at a leisurely and quiet pace.

[5] And all that mighty heart is lying still: Everything on this earth is still lying motionless. The last line stresses the serenity of the whole scene within the poet's view. Just as the landscape is saturated with the bright sunshine, so is the poet's soul saturated with deep calm in the river, the houses and all that powerful earth.

Commentary

It is said that this sonnet was written on the roof of a coach as Wordsworth was on his way to France in 1807. The poem presents the speaker's view of London in the early morning. Westminster Bridge is the bridge crossing the Thames near Westminster Abbey and the Houses of Parliament. The speaker is not only profoundly touched by its beauty and tranquility in the early morning, but even surprised to realize that London is part of Nature just as much as is his own beloved Lake Areas.

The poem is written after the pattern of the Italian sonnet. The octet (the first eight lines consisting of two enveloped quatrains rhyming *abba abba*) recreates the poet's experience of London in the morning, and the sestet (the last six lines rhyming *cdcdcd*) enlarges on his thoughtful reaction to majesty of the scene.

Questions and Exercises

1. What is the idea that underlies this poem? In what sense is this poem concerned with the relation of man and nature?
2. Point out examples of personification used in the poem, and see what effect this figure of speech brings to the whole poem.
3. What is the rhyme scheme of this sonnet? What thought divisions correspond to the scheme divisions between the octave and the sestet?

The Solitary Reaper

Behold here single in the field,
    Yon solitary Highland Lass! [1]
Reaping and singing by herself;

Stop here, or gently pass!
Alone she cuts and binds the grain
And sings a melancholy strain:[2]
O listen for the vale profound
Is overflowing with the sound.

No nightingale did ever chant
More welcome notes to weary bands
Of travelers in some shady haunt
Among Arabian sands [3];
A voice so thrilling ne'er was heard
In spring-time from the cuckoo-bird,
Breaking the silence of the seas
Among the farthest Hebrides.[4]

Will no one tell me what she sings? —
Perhaps the plaintive numbers[5] flow
For old, unhappy, far-off things,
And battles long ago;
Or is it some more humble lay,[6]
Familiar matter of today?
Some natural sorrow, loss, or pain,
That has been, and may be again?

Whate'er the theme, the maiden sang
As if her song could have no ending;
I saw her singing at her work,
And o'er the sickle bending;
I listened, motionless and still,
And, as I mounted up the hill,
The music in my heart I bore,
Long after it was heard no more.

Notes

[1] Yon: Yonder; over there. Highland: Scottish upland (the northern part of Scotland).

[2] strain: tune.

[3] in some shady haunt among Arabian sands: in some dark and horrible place among Arabian desert.

[4] Hebrides: islands off northwest tip of Scotland.
[5] the plaintive numbers: the mournful musical measures or the sad songs.
[6] humble lay: a not very refined song.

Commentary

"Solitary Reaper" describes vividly a young peasant girl who is working alone in the fields and singing as she works. The poem was written sometime between 1803 and 1805. In writing this poem, Wordsworth acknowledged his debt to his friend Thomas Wilkinson's *Tours to the British Mountains*, where a sentence reads: "Passed a female who was reaping alone; She sung in Erse as she bended over her sickle; the sweetest human voice I ever heard: her strains were tenderly melancholy, and felt delicious, long after they were heard no more."

This poem is deceptively simple, but it has long been a favorite of the English-speaking peoples. The plot of the little incident is told straightforwardly in stanzas 1,3, and 4. Stanza 2, with its comparison of the girl's song to the singing of the cuckoo and the nightingale shows the peaceful harmony of nature and the security of rural life. The impression of the girl's singing on the traveler is amazingly heightened through such comparisons.

Questions and Exercises

1. A bird sings for no audience—it is merely overheard. On hearing a bird sing, we sometimes feel that we are hearing the voice of nature itself. In what way does the girl's song resemble the song of nature?
2. Paraphrase the poem in prose form and then make comments on the different effects between the two versions.

George Gordon Byron

George Gordon Byron (1788 — 1824) belonged to an old aristocratic but impoverished family. His father was a drunkard and a faithless husband who deserted his wealthy Scottish wife after squandering her fortune, and the boy was brought up by the mother. At the age of ten, upon the death of his great uncle, Byron inherited the baronial title and a large estate.

After graduation from Cambridge University, Byron entered the House of Lords, and shortly afterwards started on a tour of Europe and the Orient. On his return he published the first two cantos of *Childe Harold's Pilgrimage,* which brought him great fame. On

February 27, 1812 he delivered his maiden speech in the House of Lords, opposing the bill introducing Capital Punishment for breaking machinery to show his deep sympathy for the condition of the weavers.

Byron was a great romantic freedom-loving poet. *Don Juan*, Byron's masterpiece, was written while he lived in Italy (from 1818 to 1824). The poem was left unfinished owing to the poet's premature death. In writing the poem Byron tried to remove the cloak of high society by laying bare its sins to the world. As a sociopolitical satiric poem, the work has tremendous force of exposure and a high artistic quality.

Don Juan

(From *Canto IX*)

Oh, Wellington! [1] (or "Villainton"[2]—for Fame
　Sounds the heroic syllables both ways;
France could not even conquer your great name,
　But pinn'd it down to this facetious phrase—
Beating or beaten she will laugh the same),
　You have obtain'd great pensions and much praise:
Glory like yours should any dare gainsay,
　Humanity would rise, and thunder "Nay!"

I don't think that you used Kinnaird quite well
　In Marinet's affair[3]—in fact, 'twas shabby,
And like some other things won't do to tell
　Upon your tomb in Westminster's old abbey.
Upon the rest 'tis not worthwhile to dwell,
　Such tales being for the tea-hours of some tabby; [4]
But though your years as man tend fast to zero,
In fact your grace is still but a young hero. [5]

Though Britain owes (and pays you too) so much,
　Yet Europe doubtless owes you greatly more:
You have repair'd Legitimacy's crutch, [6]
　A prop not quite so certain as before:
The Spanish, and the French, as well as Dutch,
　Have seen, and felt, how strongly you restore;
And Waterloo[7] has made the world your debtor
(I wish your bards would sing it rather better).

You are "the best of cut-throats": [8]—do not start;
  The phrase is Shakespeare's, and not misapplied:
War's a brain-spattering, windpipe-slitting art,
  Unless her cause by right be sanctified.
If you have acted once a generous part,
  The world, not the world's masters, will decide,
And I shall be delighted to learn who,
Save you and yours, [9] have gain'd by Waterloo?

I am no flatterer—you've supp'd full of flattery:
  They say you like it too—'tis no great wonder.
He whose whole life has been assault and battery,
  At last may get a little tired of thunder;
And swallowing eulogy much more than satire, he
  May like being praised for every lucky blunder,
Call'd "Saviour of the Nations"—not yet saved,
And "Europe's Liberator"—still enslaved.

I've done. Now go and dine from off the plate
  Presented by the Prince of the Brazils, [10]
And send the sentinel before your gate
  A slice or two from your luxurious meals:
He fought, but has not fed so well of late.
  Some hunger, too, they say the people feels:—
There is no doubt that you deserve your ration,
But pray give back a little to the nation.

I don't mean to reflect[11]—a man so great as
  You, my lord duke! is far above reflection:
The high Roman fashion, too, of Cincinnatus, [12]
  With modern history has but small connection:
Though as an Irishman you love potatoes,
  You need not take them under your direction; [13]
And half a million for your Sabine farm[14]
Is rather dear!—I'm sure I mean no harm.

Great men have always scorn'd great recompenses:
  Epaminondas[15] saved his Thebes, and died,

Not leaving even his funeral expenses:
George Washington had thanks and nought beside,[16]
Except the all-cloudless glory which few men's is
To free his country: Pitt[17] too had his pride,
And as a high-soul'd minister of state is
Renown'd for ruining Great Britain gratis.

Never had mortal man such opportunity,
Except Napoleon, or abused it more:
You might have freed fallen Europe from the unity
Of tyrants, and been blest from shore to shore:
And now—what is your fame? Shall the Muse tune it ye?
Now—that the rabble's first vain shouts are o'er?
Go! hear it in your famish'd country's cries!
Behold the world! and curse your victories!

Notes

[1] Wellington: The Duke of Wellington (1769—1852) was born in Dublin, Ireland, educated at Eton in England, and trained as a commander at a French military academy. In 1807, 1808 and 1814 he won a series of minor victories over the armies of Napoleon, and finally in 1815, as commander of the Allied Armies, completely defeated Napoleon at the Battle of Waterloo. He died in 1882 and was buried in Westminster Abbey, the resting place of Britain's national heroes.

[2] Villainton—a pun on Wellington first used by a French poet to ridicule and scorn this British general. (Note the ironical connotation in both sense and sound. Villain: a person who is guilty and capable of evil wickedness; a character whose evil actions or motives are important to the plot.)

[3] I don't think that you used Kinnaird quite well / In Marinet's affair: In 1818 Wellington barely escaped an assassination attempt in Paris. Prior to this, Lord Kinnaird had informed the British Command of such an attempt. On the pledge that no action would be taken against the informer, Lord Kinnaird asked a politician named Marinet to come to Paris to meet the local British authorities. But Marinet was arrested even as Wellington was feasting Kinnaird. Hence Byron's comment "'twas shabby."

[4] tabby: female cat; gossiping old woman.

[5] But though your years as man tend fast to zero, / In fact your Grace is still but a young hero: When Byron wrote Canto IX of *Don Juan* in 1822, Wellington was already 53 years old, but he was quite well-preserved and didn't look his age at all.

Hence Byron's satirical remark "still but a young hero".

[6] You have repair'd Legitimacy's crutch: The French bourgeois Revolution (1789—1794), which sent Louis XVI and his wife Marie Antoinette to the guillotine, challenged the principle of "the divine right of kings", and Napoleon's victories overthrew a number of hereditary monarchies on the European Continent. But with Wellington's defeat of Napoleon, a period of political reaction set in, and the monarchies were restored, or, in Byron's graphic language, "Legitimacy's crutch" was repaired.

[7] Waterloo: a small town south of Brussels in Belgium, where Wellington won his decisive victory over Napoleon in 1815.

[8] "the best of cut-throats"—an allusion to Shakespeare's *Macbeth,* Act III, Scene 4, in which Macbeth called one of his hired murderers "the best of cut-throats".

[9] Save you and yours: Except you and those connected with you (implying the British ruling class).

[10] the Prince of the Brazils: originally the Regent Prince of Portugal, who fled to the Brazils on Napoleon's invasion. After Waterloo he presented an enormous silver plate to Wellington as a gift.

[11] to reflect: to disparage; to blame; to speak ill of.

[12] Cincinnatus: Roman general in the 5th century B.C. He was a farmer who left his fields to save Rome from foreign attackers. After his victory, he refused honors and went back to farming.

[13] You need not take them under your direction: reference to the fact that Wellington was appointed to be Secretary to Ireland in 1805.

[14] half a million for your Sabine farm: In 1814, after his victory in Spain and Portugal, Wellington was given a dukedom, with an endowment of half a million pounds. The endowment is here compared to the Sabine farm, which was the gift of Meacenas, a wealthy Roman, to Horace the famous Roman poet.

[15] Epaminondas: Greek general of Thebes, in the 5th century B.C.

[16] nought beside: nothing besides; nothing else.

[17] Pit: William Pitt (1759—1806), English politician who was made Prime Minister by George III. After the French Revolution he repressed the progressive elements in England and imposed very heavy taxes on the people. So Byron blamed him for "ruining Great Britain". At the same time Pitt himself got into debt, but refused the offer of George III to pay it off. Hence Byron's satirical remark that he "had his pride" and that he ruined Great Britain "gratis".

Commentary

Don Juan, Byron's greatest work, is an epic satire in 16 cantos (the 17th is unfinished), published in 1819—1824. The verse form is *octavo rima*—iambic pentameter with the rhyme scheme *aba bab cc.*

A legendary Spanish libertine, Don Juan was much represented in English and European literature as a superhuman "Byronic hero", a melancholy but self-confident and defiant man. In Byron's poem, Don Juan was forced to leave Spain at 16 because of his scandalous affair with Donna Julia, the young wife of an elderly gentlemen. During the voyage he is shipwrecked and cast ashore on a Greek island, where he is saved by Haidee, the beautiful daughter of a pirate. Her father disapproved their love and sold Juan as a slave in Constantinople. He was bought by a Turkish Sultana, who falls in love with him and keeps him in a harem in the guise of a woman. He escaped to the Russian army which was in action in the area and distinguished himself through courage and bravery. Then he was sent with dispatches to St. Petersburg where he won favor with Empress Catherine who sent him again on a diplomatic mission to England.

Don Juan, the protagonist of the story, is in fact not the hero of the poem. His many adventures serve only as the thread of narration. In the course of telling the story, the narrator has created a long social comedy—a verse novel of great satirical fervor and wit, attacking hypocrisy, oppression, greed and lust, and implicitly promoting virtues of courage, loyalty and candor.

The above selection is taken from Canto IX, in which Byron fiercely attacks and satirizes Lord Wellington for his ignominious role in restoring the reactionary, monarchic rule in Europe.

Questions and Exercises

1. Discuss in groups the life story of General Wellington and the main purpose of this part of the poem.
2. Give examples to illustrate the poet's use of figurative language such as "pun", "irony", "sarcasm", "metaphor", and "understatement".

She Walks in Beauty

She walks in beauty, like the night
  Of cloudless climes and starry skies; [1]
And all that's best of dark and bright
  Meet in her aspect[2] and her eyes:
Thus mellow'd to that tender light
  Which heaven to gaudy day denies. [3]

One shade the more, one ray the less,

Had half impair'd the nameless grace[4]
Which waves in every raven tress, [5]
Or softly lightens o'er her face;
Where thoughts serenely sweet express
How pure, how dear their dwelling-place. [6]

And on that cheek, and o'er that brow,
So soft, so calm, yet eloquent, [7]
The smiles that win, the tints that glow, [8]
But tell of days in goodness spent, [9]
A mind at peace with all below, [10]
A heart whose love is innocent!

Notes

[1] like the night...starry skies: "clime" is poetic language meaning "climate". The poet employs this image because she wears a mourning black all over with spangles twinkling like stars in the sky.

[2] aspect: look; appearance.

[3] Which heaven to gaudy day denies: The normal order should be "Which heaven denies to gaudy day." Literally it means even heaven would refuse to give such tender light to a gaudy day, suggesting that even the colourful, gay, showy light on a celebration day cannot match the tenderness of her light.

[4] One shade the more...the nameless grace: Her beauty is so perfect that no modification or improvement is needed at all; it would have spoiled the superb beauty should one shade of dark was added or one ray of light was reduced. half impair'd: nearly damaged.

[5] raven tress: black hair.

[6] Where thoughts serenely sweet express...their dwelling-place: Her waving hair and her softly bright face indicate that her mind is pure and noble. sweet: sweetly; in a sweet manner.

[7] eloquent: movingly expressive; able to convey the feelings without words.

[8] The smiles that win, the tints that glow: the charming smiles, the glowing colours on her face that would attract people.

[9] But tell of days in goodness spent: But tell of days spent in goodness. but: only; goodness: good conduct or virtue. Here "days", "mind", and "heart" are all objects to the verb "tell".

[10] at peace with all below: in harmony with all the things in the world.

Commentary

Written in 1814, when Byron was twenty-six years old, the poem of praise *She Walks in Beauty* was inspired by the poet's first sight of his young cousin Anne Wilmot by marriage. According to literary historians, Byron's cousin wore a black gown that was brightened with spangles. This description helps the reader comprehend the origin of the poem, and its mixing together of images of darkness and light.

However the poem itself cannot just be reduced to its origins, as its beauty lies in its powerful description not only of a woman's physical beauty, but also of her interior strengths. There is no mention in the poem of spangles of a gown, no images of a woman actually walking, which may explain the fact that the poet is in pursuit of something larger than mere physical description of beauty.

The content of this poem is healthy, the tone is lively and of sincere admiration, and the imagery to make abstract beauty concrete is impressive. The simile "like the night" is especially striking, and the balance of dark and light gives the "nameless grace" of the lady. The whole poem is lucid and overflowing with unrestrained but genuine feelings on the part of the poet.

Questions and Exercises

1. What external and internal beauties does the woman possess? How are they supported by the details?
2. Try to identify the main rhetoric devices of simile, antithesis, and parallelism in the poem and explain their functions in achieving the poetic effects.
3. Why "One shade the more, one ray the less" would impair the nameless grace? Read the whole poem and then use your mind to explain which lines of the poem have impressed you the most.

Percy Bysshe Shelley

Carl Marx once said, P. B. Shelley (1792 — 1822) "was essentially a revolutionist and he would have always belonged to the vanguard of socialism." Being the most progressive among the Romanticists, Shelley was a rebel and an enemy of the then society.

Shelley was first educated at Eton where he suffered a lot for his rebelling character. He early displayed an inclination for independent thinking. Before 18, he had written two romances and published a collection of poems, in which he glorified freedom, exposed tyranny and expressed his sympathy for the oppressed. Later he actively took part in the Irish national liberation movement.

Shelley was highly talented and with a great physical beauty, yet he was full of blunders. Being regarded as a "noble foolish" and "a folly of the age", he was detested and attacked in England, and at last in 1818 compelled to leave England for Italy where he was drowned in a boat during a sudden storm in 1822.

Shelley's works include *Queen Mab* (1813), *The Revolt of Islam* (1818), *Prometheus Unbound* (1819), *The Mask of Anarchy, Ode to the West Wind* (1819), and so on. His short lyrical poems form an important part of his literary works. They are particularly worth reading because they are in essence a magnificent psalm of man's ideal for independence and liberty.

A Song: "Men of England"

Men of England, wherefore[1] plough
For the lords who lay ye low?[2]
Wherefore weave with toil and care
The rich robes your tyrants wear?

Wherefore feed, and clothe and save,
From the cradle to the grave,
Those ungrateful drones[3] who would
Drain your sweat—nay, drink your blood?

Wherefore, Bees of England,[4] forge
Many a weapon, chain, and scourge,
That these stingless drones may spoil
The forced produce of your toil?[5]

Have ye leisure, comfort, calm,
Shelter, food, love's gentle balm?[6]
Or what is it ye buy so dear[7]
With your pain and with your fear?

The seed ye sow, another reaps;
The wealth ye find, another keeps;
The robes ye weave, another wears;
The arms ye forge, another bears.

Sow seed—but let no tyrant reap;
Find wealth—let no impostor keep;
Weave robes,—let not the idle wear;
Forge arms—in your defence to bear.

Shrink to your cellars, holes, and cells.
In halls ye deck[8] another dwells.
Why shake the chains ye wrought?[9] Ye see
The steel ye tempered glance on ye.[10]

With plough and spade, and hoe and loom,
Trace your grave,[11] and build your tomb,
And weave your winding-sheet[12] till fair
England be your sepulchre.[13]

Notes

[1] wherefore: for what reason; why.

[2] lay ye low: strike you down.

[3] Those ungrateful drones: The male of the honey-bees that do not work. Here it refers to the parasitic class in human society.

[4] Bees of England: The laboring people of England.

[5] That these stingless drones may spoil / The forced produce of your toil: The stingless drones may rob or plunder the fruits of your labor which are produced under compulsion.

[6] balm: a sweet-smelling ointment. Here it refers to something which relieves the mind of pain and worry.

[7] buy so dear : pay such a high price for.

[8] deck: adorn; decorate.

[9] wrought: past tense of "work". Here it means "forged or shaped".

[10] The steel ye tempered glance on ye: The weapon you forged is flashed in your face.

[11] Trace your grave: mark out your grave; follow the course to your tomb.

[12] winding-sheet: the sheet of cloth used to wrap up the corpse.

[13] sepulchre: tombs; burial ground. The last two stanzas are ironically addressed to those workers who submit passively to the capitalist exploitation. The purpose is to give a warning to the working people—If you should give up your struggle you would be digging graves for yourselves with your own hands.

Commentary

The poem, one of Shelley's greatest political lyrics, was written almost at the same time with *The Mask of Anarchy,* the year of 1819 when Peterloo Massacre occurred. In the poem Shelley pictured the capitalist society as divided into two hostile classes: the parasitic class (drones) and the working class (bees). The whole poem is not only a forceful calling on the working people of England to rise up against their political oppressors and economic exploiters, but also a warning address to point out to them that they would be doomed to perish if they remain passively submitted to the rule of the merciless exploiting class. The poem has since become a hymn for the British labor movement.

Questions and Exercises

1. Outline the logic of the argument of the poem so as to show how its structure is developed.
2. What chief rhetoric devices does the poet use in the poem to gain its power of fighting spirit for the working class people?
3. Whom is the poet addressing to in the last two stanzas? Why does the poet speak in such a tone?

Ode to the West Wind

[1]

O wild West Wind, thou breath of Autumn's being,
Thou, from whose unseen presence the leaves dead
Are driven, like ghosts from an enchanter fleeing,

Yellow, and black, and pale, and hectic red,
Pestilence-stricken multitudes: O Thou
Who chariotest to their dark wintry bed

The winged seeds, where they lie cold and low,
Each like a corpse within its grave, until
Thine azure sister of the Spring[1] shall blow

Her clarion[2] o'er the dreaming earth, and fill
(Driving sweet buds like flocks to feed in air)
With living hues and odours plain and hill:

Wild Spirit, which art moving everywhere;
Destroyer and Preserver;[3] hear, O, hear!

[2]

Thou on whose stream, 'mid the steep sky's commotion,
Loose clouds like earth's decaying leaves are shed,
Shook from the tangled boughs of Heaven and Ocean,[4]

Angels of rain and lightning: they are spread
On the blue surface of thine aery[5] surge,
Like the bright hair uplifted from the head

Of some fierce Maenad,[6] even from the dim verge
Of the horizon to the zenith's height,
The locks[7] of the approaching storm. Thou dirge

Of the dying year, to which this closing night
Will be the dome of a vast sepulchre,
Vaulted with all thy congregated might

Of vapours, from whose solid atmosphere
Black rain, and fire, and hail, will burst: O, hear!

[3]

Thou who didst waken from his summer dreams
The blue Mediterranean, where he[8] lay,
Lull'd by the coil[9] of his crystalline streams,

Beside a pumice isle[10] in Baiae's bay,[11]
And saw in sleep old palaces and towers
Quivering within the wave's intenser day,

All overgrown with azure moss and flowers
So sweet, the sense faints picturing them! Thou
For whose path the Atlantic's level powers[12]

Cleave themselves into chasms, while far below
The sea-blooms and the cozy woods which wear
The sapless foliage of the ocean, know

Thy voice, and suddenly grow gray with fear,
And tremble and despoil themselves: [13] O, hear!

[4]

If I were a dead leaf thou mightiest bear;
If I were a swift cloud to fly with thee;
A wave to pant beneath thy power, and share

The impulse of thy strength, only less free
Than thou, O uncontrollable! If even
I were as in my boyhood, and could be

The comrade of thy wanderings over Heaven,
As then, when to outstrip the skiey speed[14]
Scarce seemed a vision, I would ne'er have striven

As thus with thee in prayer in my sore need.
O! lift me as a wave, a leaf, a cloud!
I fall upon the thorns of life! I bleed!

A heavy weight of hours has chained and bowed
One too like thee:[15] tameless, and swift, and proud.

[5]

Make me thy lyre, even as the forest is:
What if my leaves are falling like its own!
The tumult of thy mighty harmonies[16]

Will take from both[17] a deep, autumnal tone,
Sweet though in sadness. Be thou, Spirit fierce,
My spirit! Be thou me, impetuous one!

Drive my dead thoughts over the universe
Like withered leaves to quicken a new birth!
And, by the incantation of this verse,

Scatter, as from an unextinguished hearth
Ashes and sparks, my words among mankind!
Be through my lips to unawakened Earth

The trumpet of a prophecy![18] O Wind,
If Winter comes, can Spring be far behind?

Notes

[1] Thine azure sister of the Spring: the wind in spring season during which the sky is often blue, so the spring wind here is regarded as the blue sister of the west wind.

[2] clarion: loud, shrill call.

[3] Destroyer and Preserver: The west wind is considered the "Destroyer" for it drives the last sign of life from trees. It is considered the "Preserver" because it scatters the seeds which will come to life in the next spring.

[4] the tangled boughs of Heaven and Ocean: the line between the sky and the stormy sea is indistinguishable, the whole space from horizon to the zenith being covered with trailing storm clouds.

[5] aery: airy. Here it means "light".

[6] Maenad: the God of wine in Greek mythology.

[7] locks: portions of hair that naturally hangs and clings together. Here it refers to clouds.

[8] he: refers to the Mediterranean.

[9] coil: the noise of tide.

[10] pumice isle: the name of an isle near Naples, Italy, which is formed by deposits of lava from a volcano.

[11] Baiae's bay: a favorite resort of the ancient Romans on the coast of Campania, at the western end of the Bay of Naples.

[12] the Atlantic's level powers: the waves of the Atlantic Ocean moving on its flat surface.

[13] The sea-blooms and the cozy woods which wear / The sapless foliage of the ocean, know / Thy voice, and suddenly grow gray with fear, / And tremble and despoil themselves: The lands at the bottom of the ocean, the rivers and the lakes also fall under the influence of the west wind which announces the change of the season.

[14] thy skiey speed: thy airy and ethereal speed (skiey = skyey: of the sky, ethereal).

[15] One too like thee: "One" here refers to Shelley himself.

[16] thy mighty harmonies: referring to the sound of the west wind.

[17] both: the poet himself and the forest.

[18] The trumpet of a prophecy: The clarion call for a new era.

Commentary

Ode to the West Wind is of the Horatian type, that is, it is written with stanzas of uniform length and regular arrangement. The form of the poem employed here is a unique combination of Dante's Terza rima and the Shakespearean sonnet: five 14-lined stanzas of iambic pentameter, with each stanza containing four tercets and a closing couplet, and the rhyme scheme being *aba bcb cdc ded ee.*

This ode was thought to be the best known of Shelley's shorter poems. In the poem the poet describes vividly the activities of the West Wind on the earth, in the sky and on the sea, and then he continues to express his envy for the boundless freedom of the West Wind and his wish to be freely roaming on earth like the unrestrained West Wind to scatter his prophecy through poetry among mankind.

The first stanza expresses the main theme of the poem: the West Wind has the strong power as "Destroyer" and "Preserver". As Destroyer, it mercilessly sweeps off the dead leaves in autumn, and as Preserver, it carries the seeds into wintry soil waiting to grow and bloom till spring comes.

The second stanza uses cloud, lightning, hail, and storm to enhance the powerful strength of the West Wind. Upon coming, it carries with it such fierce natural phenomena as fearful rain, storm, hail, and lightning, so frightful that even the sapless foliage of the ocean suddenly grow pale with fear.

The third stanza shows the sweeping impact of the West Wind on the blue Mediterranean Sea. When the wind does not show itself, the sea appears calm; but when it does come, it suddenly stirs up such violent waves that even the sea plants "tremble and despoil themselves".

In the fourth stanza, the poet exhibits his own emotions inspired by the West Wind. He dreams of himself to be a part of it. Yet, when pondering on the cruel reality in life, he desperately falls back upon the thorns of life again.

In the final stanza, the poet bravely shows his firm resolution in conquering the injustices of the world. The famed final line "If Winter comes, can Spring be far behind?" reveals Shelley's optimistic belief in the hopeful prospect of the whole mankind.

From the whole poem, we see Shelley's West Wind is a dynamic, destructive, universal force, both as "Destroyer" and "Preserver", that will be ultimately beneficial for the whole mankind.

Questions and Exercises

1. Work out an outline of the poem so as to see its logical order of development. Then explain in what sense the poet regards the West Wind both as "Destroyer" and "Preserver".
2. How has the speaker's attitude progressed in stanza five? Explain in your own words what hopes the speaker wishes to accomplish in this stanza.
3. Discuss the connotative meaning of the West Wind, and then write a short essay to interpret the theme of this ode as you understand it.

John Keats

John Keats

John Keats (1795—1821), the son of a stable keeper, was of lowly origin. Before he was 15, both of his parents died and his guardian, a merchant, took him from school and apprenticed him to a village apothecary. Then he studied surgery at a London hospital, and though he passed the medical examination he abandoned medicine in 1817 and devoted himself to poetry.

Keats's work was mainly published in three short years from 1817 to 1820. His longer poems include *Hyperion*, *Edymion, Lamia,* and *The Eve of St. Agnes*. But Keats is better known to readers by his exquisite shorter poems. Those who study only the *Ode to a Nightingale* may find four things—a love of sensuous beauty, a touch of pessimism, a purely pagan conception of nature, and a strong individualism, which are heavily characteristic of Romantic poets.

Keats was not only the last but the most perfect of Romanticists. The one artistic aim in his poetry was always to create a beautiful world of imagination as opposed to the sordid reality of his day. His leading principle is "Beauty is truth, truth beauty." He pursues this principle in all things, yet at the bottom of his poems lies his dissatisfaction with the society in which he lived and experienced great miseries and sufferings in his life.

Ode to a Nightingale

[1]

My heart aches, and a drowsy numbness pains
My sense, as though of hemlock[1] I had drunk,
Or emptied some dull opiate to the drains, [2]
One minute past, and Lethe-wards had sunk. [3]
'Tis not through envy of thy happy lot,
But being too happy in thine happiness—
That thou, light-winged Dryad[4] of the trees,
In some melodious plot
Of beechen green, [5] and shadows numberless,
Singest of summer in full-throated ease. [6]

[2]

O for a draught of vintage! that hath been

Cool'd a long age in the deep-delved earth, [7]
Tasting of Flora[8] and the country green,
Dance, and Provencal[9] song, and sunburnt mirth!
O for a beaker full of the warm South, [10]
Full of the true, the blushful Hippocrene, [11]
With beaded bubbles winking at the brim.
And purple-stained mouth; [12]
That I might drink, and leave the world unseen,
And with thee fade away into the forest dim;

[3]

Fade far away, dissolve, and quite forget
What thou among the leaves hast never known,
The weariness, the fever, and the fret
Here, where men sit and hear each other groan;
Where palsy[13] shakes a few, sad, last gray hairs,
Where youth grows pale, and spectra-thin, and dies; [14]
Where but to think is to be full of sorrow
And leaden-eyed despairs,
Where Beauty cannot keep her lustrous eyes,
Or new Love pine at them beyond tomorrow.

[4]

Away! away! for I will fly to thee,
Not charioted by Bacchus and his pards, [15]
But on the viewless wings of Poesy, [16]
Though the dull brain perplexes and retards;
Already with thee! tender is the night,
And haply the Queen-Moon is on her throne,
Cluster'd around by all her starry Fays: [17]
But here there is no light,
Save what from heaven is with the breezes blown
Through verdurous glooms and winding mossy ways.

[5]

I cannot see what flowers are at my feet,
Not what soft incense[18] hangs upon the boughs,
But, in embalmed darkness, guess each sweet[19]
Wherewith the seasonable month endows
The grass, the thicket, and the fruit-tree wild;
White hawthorn, and the pastoral eglantine;

Fast fading violet covered up in leaves;
    And mid-May's eldest child, [20]
The coming musk-rose, full of dewy wine,
    The murmurous haunt of flies on summer eves.

[6]

Darkling[21] I listen; and for many a time
    I have been half in love with easeful Death,
Call'd him soft names in many a mused rhyme, [22]
    To take into the air my quiet breath;
Now more than ever seems it rich to die,
    To cease upon the midnight with no pain,
        While thou art pouring forth thy soul abroad
            In such an ecstasy!
Still wouldst thou sing, and I have ears in vain
    To thy high requiem become a sod.

[7]

Thou wast not born for death, immortal Bird!
    No hungry generations tread thee down;
The voice I hear this passing night was heard
    In ancient days by emperor and clown: [23]
Perhaps the self-same song that found a path
    Through the sad heart of Ruth, [24] when, sick for home,
She stood in tears amid the alien corn;
    The same that oft-times hath
Charm'd magic casements, opening on the foam
    Of perilous seas, in faery lands forlorn. [25]

[8]

Forlorn! the very word is like a bell
    To toll me back from thee to my sole self!
Adieu! the fancy cannot cheat so well
    As she is fam'd to do, deceiving elf. [26]
Adieu! adieu! thy plaintive anthem fades
    Past the near meadows, over the still stream,
        Up the hill-side; and now 'tis buried deep
            In the next valley-glades:
Was it a vision, or a waking dream?
Fled is that music:—Do I wake or sleep?

Notes

[1] hemlock: a poisonous herb which produces a numbing effect on one who drinks it.

[2] emptied…to the drains: drank up to the last drop some sleep-inducing drug containing opium.

[3] Lethe-wards had sunk: had sunk towards Lethe. In the mythology of the ancient Greeks, Lethe is the river of forgetfulness in the underworld.

[4] Dryad: wood-nymph, here it refers to the nightingale.

[5] plot / Of beechen green: piece of land which is green with beech trees.

[6] in full-throated ease: with all the power of his voice in absolute fearlessness of man.

[7] In the deep-delved earth: in the deep underground.

[8] Flora: the Roman goddess of Spring and flowers, here referring to fragrant flowers in general.

[9] Provence: a place in southern France, in the late Middle Ages renowned for its troubadours, the writers and singers of love songs.

[10] for a beaker full of the warm South: for a cup over-brimmed with the wine brewed in the warm climate of southern Europe.

[11] Hippocrene: In Greek mythology, a fountain in Mount Helicon, the supposed residence of Apollo and the Muses. Here "true, blushful Hippocrene" refers to the pure red wine mentioned above.

[12] mouth: the lip of the beaker.

[13] palsy: the paralyzed old men.

[14] Where youth grows pale, and spectre-thin, and dies: Keats's brother Tom, wasted by tuberculosis, had died the preceding winter. Here the description points to the youth like his brother. spectre-thin: frighteningly thin and weak.

[15] Bacchus and his pards: Bacchus was the god of wine who was represented in a chariot drawn by "pards" (leopards).

[16] But on the viewless wings of Poesy: not by getting drunk on wine but on the invisible wings of the poetic imagination.

[17] Fays : (archaic) Fairies.

[18] soft incense: fragrance given off by the blossoms.

[19] But, in embalmed darkness, guess each sweet: But, in the perfumed darkness, I can guess what sweet odors they must be.

[20] And mid-May's eldest child: And the first blooming flowers in the middle of May.

[21] Darkling: In the dark.

[22] mused rhyme: long thought-on verse.

[23] by emperor and clown: by all the people high and low.

[24] Ruth: The young widow in the Biblical Book of Ruth. After the death of her husband

and her father, she, together with her only daughter, went to a strange foreign country and made a living by gleaning the corns in the fields.

[25] charming magic casement: Perhaps some fair ladies confined behind the charming mysterious window in the castle. They throw it open to look forward to some brave knight to come and free them from the wizard. The quotation suggest that it was perhaps this same song of the nightingale that touched the hearts of Ruth and some legendary fair ladies long, long ago.

[26] the fancy…deceiving elf: imagination or the viewless wings of poesy. The poet here has been brought back from his ecstasy to the world of realities.

Commentary

Ode to a Nightingale was inspired by the singing of a nightingale building her nest near the house of his friend in Hampstead. The poem has been justly distinguished for the magic of the poet's imagination and the richness of the poem's sensual imagery. It is not only a piece of intricate verbal art in literature, nor merely a luxuriant revealing of emotion, but a profound statement about the human predicament.

At the time when the poem was written, Keats brother Tom had just died, he himself was threatened with consumption, a chronic lung disease incurable at the time. The nightingale's song reminded him of a lasting beauty which temporarily lured him with appealing desire to get away from his tremendous misery into the forest with the bird. The poet exquisitely expresses his yearning to free himself from the burden of human anxieties by immersing himself into a world of beauty.

The logical thinking of the poem is as follows. First, the poet describes his mixed feeling of pain and drowsy numbness of his senses on hearing the bird's singing. The cheerfulness of the bird forms a sharp contrast to the human sufferings. Thus he wishes that he could get rid of his painful memories by the power of wine, by escaping into the dim forest together with the bird, and even by hoping to fly to the "Queen-Moon" in some distant lands. All these fantasies help him forget his pain on earth. But unfortunately, the nightingale flies away with her sweet song, and the poet himself is awakened to face the cold reality in life.

The whole poem has eight stanzas, each stanza consisting of ten lines of iambic pentameter rhyming *abab cde cde*, with the exception of the eighth line which is one of iambic trimeter.

Questions and Exercises

1. What makes the poem's speaker yearn to fade away into the ethereal world?
2. In what sense do we determine this is a typical romantic poem?
3. Why does the speaker wish to have a draught of vintage? Write a passage on the

special way or ways that the speaker wishes to fly to the world of the nightingale.

Matthew Arnold

Matthew Arnold (1822—1888) was born in Laleham, a village in the valley of the Thames where clear-flowing streams were later to appear in his poems as symbols of serenity. After graduation from Oxford, where he attracted attention as a hard-working student, Matthew Arnold became an inspector of schools, the position of which he held for 35 years from 1851 to 1886. In his spare time, he went in for literary work in verse and prose. In 1849, he published *The Strayed Traveler,* the first volume of his poetry. Eight years later, in 1857, as a tribute to his poetic achievement, he was elected to the professorship of poetry at Oxford. Later he toured America in order to make money by lecturing. Arnold died of a sudden heart attack two years later after his second visit to the United States.

Arnold's poetry provides a record of a sick individual in a sick society. Many of his works express a tone of regret, disillusionment and melancholy, yet his poetry is highly intellectual, elevated and meditative. As a humanist and lover of ancient classical art and literature, Arnold is restrained in emotions and lucid in expression.

Dover Beach

The sea is calm to-night.
The tide is full, the moon lies fair
Upon the straits; [1] on the French coast the light
Gleams and is gone; the cliffs of England stand,
Glimmering and vast, out in the tranquil bay.
Come to the window, sweet is the night-air!
Only, [2] from the long line of spray
Where the sea meets the moon-blanched land,
Listen! you hear the grating roar
Of pebbles which the waves draw back, and fling,
At their return, up the high strand,
Begin, and cease, and then again begin,
With tremulous cadence slow, [3] and bring
The eternal note of sadness in.

Sophocles long ago
Heard it on the Aegean, and it brought
Into his mind the turbid ebb and flow
Of human misery; [4] we
Find also in the sound a thought,
Hearing it by this distant northern sea.

The Sea of Faith
Was once, too, at the full, and round earth's shore
Lay like the folds of a bright girdle furled. [5]
But now I only hear
Its melancholy, long, withdrawing roar,
Retreating, to the breath
Of the night-wind, down the vast edges drear
And naked shingles[6] of the world.

Ah, love, let us be true
To one another! for the world, which seems
To lie before us like a land of dreams,
So various, so beautiful, so new,
Hath really neither joy, nor love, nor light,
Nor certitude, [7] nor peace, nor help for pain;
And we are here as on a darkling plain[8]
Swept with confused alarms of struggle and flight,
Where ignorant armies[9] clash by night.

Notes

[1] the straits (of Dover): Here it refers to the Straits of Dover. Dover is a port city and a popular resort in Kent, England. Between Dover Beach and French coast is the Straits of Dover about 34 km long and 33 km across.

[2] Only: This word is, in fact, followed by "Listen"—"Only listen!" It supplies a sense of contrast, that is, the beginning six lines present a quiet, reassuring scene, while starting from "only" the images and tone change entirely to the ominous and sad.

[3] cadence slow: slow rhythm.

[4] Sophocles… Of human misery: Sophocles is the great ancient Greek tragedian who makes this comparison in his tragedy *Antigone*. Antigone is the daughter of Oedipus; she was condemned by her uncle to be buried alive for insisting on carrying out burial rites for her dead brother—a rebel when he was alive.

[5] Lay like the folds of a bright girdle furled: At high tide the sea envelops the land closely. Its forces are gathered up like the "folds" of bright clothing ("girdle") which have been compressed ("furled"). At ebb tide, it is unfurled and spread out. (The subject of "lay" is "The Sea of Faith".)

[6] naked shingles: pebbled beaches.

[7] certitude: conviction; faith; condition of feeling certain.

[8] a darkling plain: a stretch of dark wilderness.

[9] ignorant armies: The date of composition of the poem is generally assumed to be 1851. "Ignorant armies" here perhaps refers to the revolutions of 1848 or the siege of Rome by the French in 1849.

Commentary

The poem is composed in the form of a dramatic monologue, describing the despair at the loss of faith. The speaker stands at a window describing the view to his love in the room behind him, and then making comments on what he sees and hears. The lines are broken and uneven, and the scene is highly symbolic. Arnold uses both descriptive and metaphorical imageries to achieve his purpose.

First we are impressed by the descriptive imagery in the poem. Arnold emphasizes two senses: the visual and the aural. The poem begins with the visual—the moon, the lights of France across the water, the cliffs, the tranquil bay—to associate hope and beauty with what he sees. The poem then introduces the aural sense—the sounding of the roaring sea—which serves as an antithesis to the visual sense. These two senses create a tension and a conflict in the speaker's mind, by means of connecting sight with hope and sound with sadness.

By the third stanza, the speaker has become intellectually alert to the full implications of the conflict. He signals this alertness with a carefully worked out analogy—his comparison of the sea with faith. In the fourth stanza, he sums up his despairing conclusion with a stunning and famous simile: And we are here as on a darkling plain / Swept with confused alarms of struggle and flight, / Where ignorant armies clash by night.

This final analogy achieves several purposes. First, it brings the implication of the descriptive imagery to a logical conclusion. No longer can the speaker draw hope from visual beauty, since he cannot see at all—it is night, the plain is dark. He can only hear, but the sound now is more chaotic and threatening than the mere ebb and flow of the sea. Second, the analogy provides an abrupt change of setting. Whereas before, the speaker visualized an unpeopled plain, now he imagines human beings as agents of destruction. He implies that a world without faith must be arbitrary and violent. Finally, the analogy allows the speaker to identify his own place in this new world order. Only loyalty is pure and good. So he and his companion must cling to each other and maneuver throughout the world's battlefields as best they can.

Questions and Exercises

1. This poem is a typical example of dramatic monologue. Who are the speaker and the listener? What types of imagery does the poet employ to convey his feeling of anxiety?
2. Do you think the view of human life depicted in "Dover Beach" is applicable to the present world? What is the poet's suggested cure for this faithless world?

Robert Browning

Robert Browning (1812—1889) was the first child of Robert and Sarah Anna Browning. Though he studied at the University of London for a short period, most of his education came at home. He was an extremely bright child and learned Latin, Greek, French and Italian by the time he was fourteen.

In 1845 he saw Elizabeth Barrett's *Poems* and contrived to meet her. Although she was an invalid, six years older than he was, and very much under the control of his domineering father, the two married in September 1846 and a few days later eloped to Italy, where they lived until her death in 1861. The years in Florence were among the happiest for both of them. Her love for him was demonstrated in the *Sonnets from the Portuguese*, and to her he dedicated *Men and Women*, which contains his best poetry. Browning and Tennyson were now mentioned together as the foremost poets of the age.

Browning's special contribution to English literature is his peculiar practice of the dramatic monologue. He chose characters out of history and made them think aloud so as to display their distinctive mentalities. His influence continued to grow is his life time, and finally led to the founding of the Browning Society in 1881. He died in 1889, and was buried in Poet's Corner of Westminster Abbey.

My Last Duchess

Ferrara[1]

That's my last Duchess painted on the wall,
Looking as if she were alive. I call
That piece a wonder, now: Frà Pandolf's hands[2]
Worked busily a day, and there she stands.
Will't please you sit and look at her? I said

"Frà Pandolf" by design, for never read
Strangers like you that pictured countenance,
The depth and passion of its earnest glance,[3]
But to myself they turned (since none puts by
The curtain I have drawn for you, but I)
And seemed as they would ask me, if they durst,[4]
How such a glance came there; so, not the first
Are you to turn and ask thus. Sir, 'twas not
Her husband's presence only, called that spot
Of joy into the Duchess' cheek:[5] perhaps
Frà Pandolf chanced to say "Her mantle laps
Over my Lady's wrist too much," or "Paint
Must never hope to reproduce the faint
Half-flush that dies along her throat": such stuff
Was courtesy, she thought, and cause enough
For calling up that spot of joy. She had
A heart—how shall I say?—too soon made glad,
Too easily impressed; she liked whate'er
She looked on, and her looks went everywhere.
Sir, 'twas all one![6] My favour at her breast,[7]
The dropping of the daylight in the West,
The bough of cherries some officious fool
Broke in the orchard for her, the white mule
She rode with round the terrace—all and each
Would draw from her alike the approving speech,
Or blush, at least. She thanked men—good! but thanked
Somehow—I know not how—as if she ranked
My gift of a nine-hundred-years-old name
With anybody's gift. Who'd stoop to blame
This sort of trifling?[8] Even had you skill
In speech—(which I have not)—to make your will
Quite clear to such an one, and say, "Just this
Or that in you disgusts me; here you miss,
Or there exceed the mark"—and if she let
Herself be lessoned so, nor plainly set
Her wits to yours, forsooth, and made excuse,[9]
—E'en then would be some stooping, and I choose
Never to stoop. Oh sir, she smiled, no doubt,

Whene'er I passed her; but who passed without
Much the same smile? This grew; I gave commands;[10]
Then all smiles stopped together. There she stands
As if alive. Will't please you rise? We'll meet
The company below, then. I repeat,
The Count your master's known munificence[11]
Is ample warrant that no just pretence[12]
Of mine for dowry will be disallowed;
Though his fair daughter's self, as I avowed
At starting, is my object. Nay, we'll go
Together down, sir. Notice Neptune, [13] though,
Taming a sea-horse, thought a rarity,
Which Claus of Innsbruck[14] cast in bronze for me!

Notes

[1] Ferrara: a city in northern Italy.

[2] Frà Pandolf: Brother Pandolf, an imaginary painter who painted the duchess' portrait.

[3] I said "Frà Pandolf" by design…its earnest glance: I said "Frà Pandolf" on purpose, for strangers like you never understand the facial feeling, the depth and passion of the earnest glance of that picture.

[4] durst: (arch.) past form of "dare".

[5] Sir, 'twas not…the Duchess' cheek: Sir, it was not her husband's presence only that called that spot of joy into the Duchess' cheek.

[6] 'twas all one: it makes no difference to her.

[7] My favour at her breast: The precious ornament at her breast which was sent by me.

[8] Who'd stoop to blame / This sort of trifling: Who would give in to argue with her about this kind of insignificant things?

[9] if she let…and made excuse: if I gave her a lesson, if she would not argue with me, and indeed, she would not made false excuse for what she had done.

[10] I gave commands: I ordered her killed (so that all her smiles stopped).

[11] munificence: great generosity.

[12] pretense: claim; demand.

[13] Neptune: In Roman myth, the god of the sea, whose character was generally wild and cruel, since he may use his power to lash the sea into storm and to cause earthquakes. Like Ares, Neptune is regarded as god of war, the enemy of the goddess of wisdom, Athene. The remarks in the last three lines constitute an indirect threat to the Duke's next wife.

[14] Claus of Innsbruck: the name of an imaginary sculptor in Innsbruck, a city in the west of Austria.

Commentary

My Last Duchess, a famous poem from the Victorian period, was first published among the sixteen poems in *Dramatic Lyrics* (1842). The story is based on real incidents in the life of Alfonso II, Duke of Ferrara in northern Italy. His first wife Lucrezia, a young girl of 14, died in 1561 after three years of their marriage. Then the Duke opened negotiations in the process of courtship for the niece of Tyrol who sent an envoy to discuss with the Duke about the dowry.

The poem is typical of the type called dramatic monologue, because it consists entirely of the words of a single persona who reveals in his speech his own nature and the dramatic situation he is in. One thing that is particularly worthy of notice is the *speaker* of the poem—the duke whose first wife died suddenly after the duke decided she was too free with her smiles. Now he wants to marry again, this time choosing the daughter of a count. In the poem, the Duke is negotiating with the envoy for the hand of his next Duchess. The speaker ironically paints a picture of himself as being selfish, vain, arrogant, cold-blooded and heartless. Just because his last Duchess was young, innocent, friendly, outgoing, blushed easily and smiled frivolously too often, the Duke thought she was not sufficiently qualified in the Duke's long family origin. This was what the Duke could not bear. So he ordered her to be killed. Moreover, his intent of describing his dead wife to the envoy is simply to loom a warning about his harsh expectations to the would-be Duchess.

The poetic form of dramatic monologue, the loose syntactical structure, and the run-on lines together make the poem easy to read and sound more of everyday speech. The success of the poem also lies in the poet's ability to develop the voice of this Duke's complex character, who embodies both superficial elegance and shocking cruelty. For example, he ironically claims that he has little skill in speaking when actually he is cleverly manipulating the conversation. Though the poem is written in the conventional form of heroic couplet, the rhyme flows out very naturally. On the whole, both the form and the style of the poem are quite appropriate to the speech of a Duke from the higher class.

Questions and Exercises

1. In this dramatic monologue, who and on what occasion is speaking to whom? What sort of person is the Duke's last Duchess? And what became of her in the end?
2. Characterize the art-collecting Duke, then point out words or lines that especially convey his arrogance, vanity, egoism and coldness.
3. In all likelihood, the Duke will not succeed in his suit because the envoy will warn his master about the dangerous possessiveness of the prospective son-in-law. Do you agree or disagree? Cite evidence from the poem to support yourself.

William Butler Yeats

W. B. Yeats (1865—1939) was born in Sandymount, near Dublin, Ireland, the son of a portrait painter. Yeats spent his childhood and youngmanhood between Dublin, London, and his mother's native county of Sligo. Each of these places contributed something to his poetic development. From the countryside around Sligo he got something extremely vigorous—a knowledge of life of the peasantry and their folklore. In Dublin he was greatly influenced by the currents of Irish nationalism and his own poetry was regarded as a fine contribution to a new Irish culture.

Yeats began writing poetry when he was eighteen. During his life career as a writer he produced a succession of lovely works, including romantic lyric, political satire, verse drama, aesthetic criticism, etc. Yeats is considered the greatest English-speaking poet of the 20th century, and in December 1923, he was awarded the Nobel Prize in literature.

The Lake Isle of Innisfree

I will arise and go now, and go to Innisfree,
　And a small cabin build there, of clay and wattles[1] made:
Nine bean-rows will I have there, a hive for the honey bee,
　And live alone in the bee-loud glade. [2]

And I shall have some peace there, for peace comes dropping slow,
　Dropping from the veils of the morning to where the cricket sings;
There midnight's all a glimmer, and noon a purple glow,
　And evening full of the linnet's wings.

I will arise and go now, for always night and day
　I hear lake water lapping with low sounds by the shore; [3]
While I stand on the roadway, or on the pavements grey,
　I hear it in the deep heart's core. [4]

Notes

[1] wattles: frameworks of interwoven twigs or branches, used to make walls or roofs of a cottage.

[2] bee-loud glade: an open place in the wood where bees are buzzing loudly.

[3] lapping with low sounds by the shore: moving gently in small waves against the shore.

[4] in the deep heart's core: at the bottom of my heart.

Commentary

As a young man in London in 1887—1891, Yeats found himself hating the city life and wanted to escape into an ideal place where he could live calmly as a hermit and enjoy the beauty of nature. In his opinion, the best remedy for the emptiness of his age seemed to exist in a return to the simplicity of the past. While in London he sometimes imagined himself living in imitation of Thoreau on Innisfree, a little island in Lough Gill, to ponder over the true meaning of human existence. So this poem was clearly inspired by the American writer and philosopher Henry David Thoreau who was best known for his *Walden*, describing his retreat from the city into a simple cabin by a forest pond to observe the life of the woods.

In *The Lake Isle of Innisfree*, Yeats refers to the island in Lough Gill in Sligo in the west of Ireland. Here it symbolizes a peaceful place for hermitage. The poem was one of Yeats's early works, and was regarded as one of his best known lyrical poems. The richness in sound, such as assonance, onomatopoeia, initial alliteration, internal rhyme, etc. makes the poem all the more musical for being read.

Questions and Exercises

1. According to the poem, what does the name "Innisfree" signify? Where does the speaker intend to go, what will he do there, and how will he live?
2. Describe the speaker's current emotional state. Is he contented or frustrated? Write a paragraph to state the central theme of the poem.
3. This poem is full of images. Explain how Yeats uses sound images to heighten the emotional effect of the poem.

Sailing to Byzantium

[1]

That is no country[1] for old men. The young
In one another's arms, birds in the trees
—Those dying generations—at their song,
The salmon-falls, the mackerel-crowded seas,
Fish, flesh, or fowl, commend all summer long
Whatever is begotten, born, and dies.
Caught in that sensual music all neglect
Monuments of unageing intellect. [2]

[2]

An aged man is but a paltry thing,
A tattered coat upon a stick, unless
Soul clap its hands and sing, and louder sing
For every tatter in its mortal dress, [3]
Nor is there singing school but studying
Monuments of its own magnificence; [4]
And therefore I have sailed the seas and come
To the holy city of Byzantium.

[3]

O sages standing in God's holy fire
As in a gold mosaic of a wall, [5]
Come from the holy fire, perne in a gyre, [6]
And be the singing-masters of my soul.
Consume my heart away; [7] sick with desire
And fastened to a dying animal[8]
It knows not what it is; and gather me
Into the artifice of eternity.

[4]

Once out of nature I shall never take
My bodily form from any natural thing, [9]
But such a form as Grecian goldsmiths[10] make
Of hammered gold and gold enamelling
To keep a drowsy Emperor awake;
Or to set upon a golden bough to sing
To lords and ladies of Byzantium
Of what it past, or passing, or to come.

Notes

[1] country: It may probably refer to the ordinary sensual world at large without the sense of a political nation, or the cycle of birth and death in which human beings are trapped and from which the speaker is about to escape.

[2] The young / In one another's arms… / Monuments of unageing intellect: This first stanza indicates that all the living creatures in the sensual world are doomed to death because they are all too deeply involved in sensual happiness without paying adequate attention to their spiritual dimensions. The salmon-falls, the mackerel-crowded seas: Both salmons and mackerels are sea food fish. Salmon adults live in the sea, but ascend rivers or waterfalls in winter to lay eggs in shallow streams.

[3] tattered coat…mortal dress: symbols of human life and the state of being aged.

[4] Nor is there singing school but… / Monuments of its own magnificence: No music school teaches the soul to sing for its senility, the soul must study the magnificent work of itself—the art as those on the walls of the Byzantine Cathedral of St. Sophia. That is why the speaker has sailed across the seas and come to the holy city of Byzantium to accomplish his task.

[5] O sages… / As in the gold mosaic of a wall: The mosaic images on the walls of the Byzantine Cathedral, in which the figures of saints are inlaid against the background of gold.

[6] perne in a gyre: whirl or turn round in a spiral motion. In these lines the speaker asks the saints on the wall to come and whirl down from the holy fire and teach his soul to sing.

[7] Consume my heart away: Destroy my flesh heart, since I think the flesh heart is the source of all sins, and now is sick and dying.

[8] fastened to a dying animal: The human heart or soul is trapped by the flesh body which is doomed to perish.

[9] Once out of nature…any natural thing: I wish to free myself from the bodily confinement and escape from the worldly life. nature: biological form or natural being of the human body.

[10] Grecian goldsmiths: This refers to the mechanical golden clockwork birds the Byzantine Emperor Theophilus had made for himself, which sang upon the branches of a golden tree to announce the hours. Yeats himself wrote: "I have read somewhere that in the Emperor's palace at Byzantium was a tree made of gold and silver, and artificial birds that sang." Later, in 1937, Yeats said in addition that he used the golden tree and the artificial bird as a "symbol of the intellectual joy of eternity".

Commentary

This poem was written in 1926 when Yeats was past his sixty. Yeats viewed human life as a cosmic dance in which harmony exists in the process of dancing. What is past, what is passing, and what is to come, are all necessary parts in the formation of the cycle of life.

In *Sailing to Byzantium*, he faces old age with a courage that comes from intellectual wisdom. Though "An aged man is but a paltry thing, / A tattered coat upon a stick", aging is a sign of maturity, and a spiritual freedom grows as one becomes old. The speaker feels that this natural world is "no country for old men". But at the meanwhile, an old man will become a worthless thing unless his soul is freed from human passions and learns to participate in the realm of spirit; the speaker, therefore, being an old man, wishes to leave the dying world of flesh for the world of spirit, where things are beautiful and permanent, as symbolized by the art inlaid on the walls of the ancient city Byzantium.

Byzantium was the capital city of the ancient Eastern Roman Empire between 395 A.D. and 1453. It was renamed Constantinople in 330 A. D. by the Roman Emperor Constantine I. In 1930, it was again changed to the modern name Istanbul in Turkey. The ancient Byzantium was famous for its mosaics and other forms of art. In Yeats's mind Byzantium is not merely a physical city, but a symbol of beauty and paradise—an ideal and eternal world in which religious, aesthetic and practical life were one. Therefore, what is sought by the speaker of the poem is not the rural peace in *The Lake Isle of Innisfree*, but the concentrated unity of life in an ideal spiritual world.

Questions and Exercises

1. What do you know about Byzantium? What is the symbolic meaning of Byzantium used in the poem?
2. How can one, both old and young, enter into an ideal world of spirit according to the poet? Write a short paragraph to explain it.

Dylan Thomas

Dylan Thomas (1914—1953), the son of a schoolteacher, was born in Swansea, Wales, and educated in Swansea Grammar School. From the age of twenty until his death, he worked as a writer in New York. Besides writing poetry, Dylan Thomas also did some broadcasting, wrote radio and movie scripts, and gave many poetry readings. It was after he became a familiar radio voice that more and more readers were attracted to his work, recognizing him as a writer of significance.

The themes of his poems are highly individual yet closely related to those of humanity: birth, death, hate, and love. Although his life was disorderly and his outlook on life sometimes seem dark and pessimistic, he was never cynical. Dylan Thomas, judging from the themes and writing techniques, was generally accepted as a surrealist in English literature.

Do Not Go Gentle into That Good Night[1]

Do not go gentle into that good night,
Old age should burn and rave at close of day; [2]
Rage, rage against the dying of the light.

Though wise men at their end know dark is right,
Because their words had forked no lightning[3] they

Do not go gentle into that good night.

Good men, the last wave by,[4] crying how bright
Their frail deeds might have danced in a green bay,
Rage, rage against the dying of the light.

Wild men who caught and sang the sun in flight,
And learn, too late, they grieved it on its way,
Do not go gentle into that good night.

Grave men,[5] near death, who see with blinding sight
Blind eyes could blaze like meteors and be gay,
Rage, rage against the dying of the light.

And you, my father, there on the sad height, [6]
Curse, bless, me now with your fierce tears, I pray,
Do not go gentle into that good night.
Rage, rage against the dying of the light.

Notes

[1] Do not go gentle into that good night: Do not go gently without resistance into the death world. The word "gentle" here serves as an adverbial to modify the verb "go".

[2] rave at close of day: shout violently at the last stage of one's life.

[3] Because their words had forked no lightning: Because they had not made eminent achievements by means of language; they were not capable of using words.

[4] the last wave by: with the last day of their life passing by.

[5] Grave men: Men who are serious about life.

[6] on the sad height : on the verge of death.

Commentary

In this poem, Dylan Thomas is speaking to his aged father. Contrary to most common poetic treatments of the inevitability of death which argue for serenity or celebrate the peace that death provides, this poem urges his old father to resist death and be violently brave in the face of it. The poem was written in the form of villanelle, which consists of five tercets and a final quatrain with only two rhymes throughout. The first stanza states the main theme: old people should courageously resist death even facing the final moment of death. The second part (stanzas two to four) provides specific examples about old people (the wise, the good, the wild, and the grave) who do resist dying, and they all have their reasons for not going "gentle into that good night". In the final quatrain, the speaker urges his father to resist, to rage against, death in any way he wishes.

Questions and Exercises

1. What is the meaning of "that good night"? How many ways does the poet use to refer to death in this poem?
2. How many types of men who have faced death are depicted in stanzas 2—4? What types of men are they? And what are the reasons for each of them to resist death?
3. Write a short essay to comment on the poet's attitude towards death.

Edgar Allan Poe

Edgar Allan Poe (1809—1849), born in Boston, Massachusetts, the son of itinerant actors, lost his parents in his early childhood, and was taken into the household of John Allan, a tobacco exporter of Richmond; he took his foster-father's name as his middle name from 1824 onwards. He came to England with the Allans (1815—1820) and attended Manor House School at Stoke Newington; he spent a year at the University of Virginia, which he left after incurring debts and gambling to relieve them. He published his first volume of verse, *Tamerlane and Other Poems* (1827) anonymously at his own expense; he was then enlisted in the US army. Later he turned to journalism and married his cousin Virginia in 1836. He worked as editor on various papers, including the *Southern Literary Messenger,* and began to publish his stories in magazines.

In 1845 his poem *The Raven*, published in a New York paper and then as the title poem of *The Raven and Other Poems* (1845), brought him fame, but not security. He continued to suffer poverty and ill health. After his wife died in 1847, he himself was struggling with alcohol addiction and nervous instability. His end was characteristically tragic; he died in Baltimore, five days after having been found semi-conscious from alcohol, heart failure, epilepsy, or a combination of all these.

As a poet, and short story writer as well, he wrote about the feelings he experienced, experienced in images born in his haunted mind. A passion for beauty and deep rooted fears for death are predominant themes throughout his works.

Annabel Lee

It was many and many a year ago,
In a kingdom by the sea,
That a maiden there lived whom you may know

By the name of Annabel Lee;
And this maiden she[1] lived with no other thought
Than to love and be loved by me.

I was a child and she was a child,
In this kingdom by the sea,
But we loved with a love that was more than love—
I and my Annabel Lee—
With a love that the winged seraphs[2] of Heaven
Coveted[3] her and me.

And this was the reason that, long ago,
In this kingdom by the sea,
A wind blew out of a cloud, chilling
My beautiful Annabel Lee;
So that her highborn kinsmen came
And bore her away from me,
To shut her up in a sepulchre[4]
In this kingdom by the sea.

The angels, not half so happy in Heaven,
Went envying her and me—
Yes!—that was the reason (as all men know,
In this kingdom by the sea)
That the wind came out of the cloud by night,
Chilling and killing my Annabel Lee.

But our love it was stronger by far than the love
Of those who were older than we—
Of many far wiser than we—
And neither the angels in Heaven above,
Nor the demons under the sea,
Can ever dissever[5] my soul from the soul
Of the beautiful Annabel Lee.

For the moon never beams, without bringing me dreams
Of the beautiful Annabel Lee;
And the stars never rise, but I see the bright eyes[6]

Of the beautiful Annabel Lee;
And so, all the night-tide,[7] I lie down by the side
Of my darling—my darling—my life and my bride,
In the sepulchre there by the sea—
In her tomb by the sounding sea.

Notes

[1] this maiden she: Poe uses two subjects in order to maintain the rhythm, just as he does in line 27 "our love it was…"

[2] seraphs: the 6-winged angels standing in the presence of God.

[3] covet: desire eagerly; envy very much.

[4] sepulchre: tomb; grave.

[5] dissever: sever; separate; disunite.

[6] the stars never... but I see…: the stars never rise without my seeing…

[7] night-tide: night-time.

Commentary

This bereaving poem *Annabel Lee* was published in January 1850, three months after his beloved wife Virginia Clemm died of tuberculosis. The coherent layout of the poem is quite clear. First, the poet looks back into the distant past to a time "in a kingdom by the sea", where he and his lover Annabel Lee lived and loved. They were both very young but their love was so great that even "the winged seraphs of Heaven", the highest rank of angels, envied them for it. And then death came to Annabel Lee, and her kinsmen carried her away to her grave. The poet attributes her death to the envious angels, and he vows that no power can separate her soul from his. He remembers her always and even sleeps by the side of her tomb every night thereafter for a long time. The theme of the poem centers on the death of a beautiful woman and the timelessness of genuine love. Their love remains alive and eternal because their souls are forever inseparably united as one.

It is important to note that quite a few poetic writing skills are used in this poem. The very opening of the poem—"It was many and many a year ago"—suggests a tale told many times, since many of the oldest legends tell the story of two young lovers separated by fate of families. Poe also uses the following unusual words for the more common words, such as "maiden" for "girl", "seraph" for "angel", "kinsmen" for "relatives", "dissever" for "separate", and "sepulchre" for "tomb" so as to achieve more poetic effect. The mood of the poem changes from the quiet mournful beginning, becoming slowly more emphatic as the angels are blamed, and rising to a high point of defiance. Poe insistently uses repetition to achieve emphatic effect. The girl's name and the phrase "in this kingdom by the sea" become refrains and are repeated like the insistent tolling of the sound of church-bells at a funeral.

This solemn beat reflects a basic anapestic rhythm which becomes increasingly stronger and more pronounced like a drumbeat as the poem reaches its emotional climax. In a certain sense, Poe's poems are meant to be spoken and heard in a solemn, eloquent manner.

Questions and Exercises

1. What kinds of poetic skills does the poet use to convey to the reader the message of the timelessness of love?
2. Study the poem and see how the poet successfully brings a realistic as well as supernatural note into the poem. Explain the literary elements and rhetorical devices that Poe has used to create this effect.

Henry Wadsworth Longfellow

Henry Wadsworth Longfellow (1807—1882) was one of the best-known American poets during the 19th century. He was popular because of his high-mindedness and the gentleness, sweetness and purity of his poetry. However, his style and subjects were conventional, especially in comparison with Whitman or other more modern writers. Nevertheless, he was a milestone in the development of American poetry, and many of his works, though accused of didacticism by many intellectuals in the West, are inspiring in our view.

It is Longfellow's shorter poems that have made him the America's well-known poet. Of these perhaps the most popular are: *A Psalm of Life, The Children's Hour,* and *The Village Blacksmith.* He died on March 24, 1882. Although buried in America his bust was placed in the Poets' Corner of Westminster Abbey in England.

Longfellow was not as typically American as many authors of the United States have been. Long years of study and foreign travel made him a world citizen. He once said, "Nationality is a good thing to a certain extent, but universality is better." His works are highly spiritual, and his poems are filled with melody and the charm of meter. The following poem is "what the heart of the young man said to the psalmist". The psalmist here may refer to Longfellow himself or the writer of Ecclesiastes.

A Psalm of Life

Tell me not, in mournful numbers[1]
　　Life is but an empty dream! —
For the soul is dead that slumbers,
　　And things are not what they seem.

Life is real! Life is earnest!

And the grave is not its goal;
Dust thou art, to dust returnest,[2]
Was not spoken of the soul.

Not enjoyment, and not sorrow,
Is our destined end or way;
But to act, that each tomorrow
Find us farther than today.

Art is long, and Time is fleeting,
And our hearts, though stout and brave,
Still, like muffled drums, are beating
Funeral marches to the grave.

In the world's broad field of battle,
In the bivouac[3] of Life,
Be not like dumb, driven cattle!
Be a hero in the strife!

Trust no Future, howe'er pleasant!
Let the dead Past bury its dead!
Act—act in the living Present
Heart within, and God o'erhead!

Lives of great men all remind us
We can make our lives sublime,
And, departing, leave behind us
Footprints on the sands of time;[4]

Footprints, that perhaps another,
Sailing o'er life's solemn main,[5]
A forlorn and shipwrecked brother,
Seeing, shall take heart[6] again.

Let us, then, be up and doing,
With a heart for any fate;
Still achieving, still[7] pursuing;
Learn to labor and to wait.

Notes

[1] numbers: metrical feet; verses.

[2] Dust thou art, to dust returnest: This is a quotation from Genesis, III. 19. God said, "For dust thou art, and unto dust shalt thou return" before He drove Adam and Eve from Eden. This line bears the meaning that human beings are certain to die.

[3] bivouac: a soldiers' camp without tents or other cover.

[4] the sands of time: time, as measured by sand in an hourglass.

[5] main: (poetic) sea.

[6] heart: courage.

[7] still: (poetic) always, ever, constantly.

Commentary

A Psalm of Life was published in the *Knickerbocker Magazine* in October 1838. It also appeared in Longfellow's first published collection *Voices of the Night* in 1839. In nine quatrains of alternately rhymed trochaic tetrameters, this popular didactic poem stresses the importance of a full and sincere activity in making the most of life's brief span, rather than yielding to the moody feelings of vain regret or dejection.

Questions and Exercises

1. Which lines in this poem impress you most? And what useful enlightenment can you obtain from the poem?
2. Write a short essay entitled *My Outlook on Life* by comparing your ideas with Longfellow's.

Walt Whitman

Walt Whitman (1819—1892) was the poet of America and American democracy. Whitman's great contribution to American literature is his use of free verse, which has no regular meter, rhyme, or line length. His poetry depends on natural rhythms in speech and the counterpoint of stressed and unstressed syllables. He is regarded as one of the great innovators in American literature, in both content and form of his poetry.

His world-famous *Leaves of Grass* gave America its first genuine epic poem. Its publication in 1855 marked the birth of truly American poetry, and changed Whitman from a conventional, undistinguished man of letters into one of America's most original poets. From then on Whitman made lifelong efforts to expand the book by weaving his extraordinary insights and rich, varied experience of American life into his monumental poetry. Its first edition of 1855 only collected 12 poems and the deathbed edition of 1892 consisted of 401 poems. The book *Leaves of Grass* has been praised as "Democratic Bible" and as the "American Epic". The title itself is symbolic. The grass is seen everywhere. It is most plain-looking and humble, often unnoticed and trodden underfoot. But it is full of vitality, and will never die out. The same is true of the people. What is more, the themes of *Leaves of Grass* are also multiple. The ideas Whitman expresses in it are democratic ones, including his singing of science, labor, nature, liberty, equality, and fraternity. Apart from his celebration of an ideal democratic society, he also mercilessly attacked the corruption that was growing severe in American society, especially after the Civil War. He loved the common people, and always enjoyed living among them.

I Hear America Singing

I hear America singing, the varied carols[1] I hear,
Those of mechanics, each one singing his[2] as it should be blithe[3] and strong,
The carpenter singing his as he measures his plank or beam,
The mason singing his as he makes ready for work, or leaves off work,
The boatman singing what belongs to him in his boat, the deckhand singing on the steamboat deck,
The shoemaker singing as he sits on his bench, the hatter singing as he stands,
The wood-cutter's song, the ploughboy's on his way in the morning, or at noon intermission or at sundown,
The delicious singing of the mother, or of the young wife at work, or of the girl sewing or washing,
Each singing what belongs to him or her and to none else,[4]
The day what belongs to the day[5], at night the party of young fellows, robust, friendly,
Singing with open mouths their strong melodious songs.

Notes

[1] varied carols: a wide variety of joyful songs.
[2] his: his own song.
[3] blithe: merry and light-hearted.
[4] Each singing what belongs to him or her and to none else: Everyone is singing his or her own song instead of others' to express his or her own feelings.
[5] The day what belongs to the day: The day is singing a song that belongs to the day.

Commentary

This whole poem forms a conceptual metaphor in which Walt Whitman displays to readers an exhilarating picture of the United States: a group of proud and healthy American laborers from all walks of life are singing their own songs while working—the mechanic, the carpenter, the mason, the boatman, the deckhand, the shoemaker, the hatter, the wood-cutter, the ploughboy, the mother, the young wife, and the girl, they are all singing songs that belong to themselves. All these songs are melodiously mingled together to form a pleasant grand chorus in praise of the promising America and the American Dream. From cities to the countryside, from the sea to the land, everywhere is prevailed with merry songs.

Questions and Exercises

1. Find out examples to illustrate how the total effect of the poem is achieved, especially through the use of parallelism and repetition.
2. What kind of image does the poet wish to establish in the reader's mind about American workers? To whom does each song belong? Are the people literally singing songs? How should we interpret "singing" figuratively?

O Captain! My Captain![1]

O Captain! My Captain! Our fearful trip[2] is done,
The ship has weather'd every rack,[3] the prize[4] we sought is won,
The port is near, the bells I hear, the people all exulting,
While follow eyes the steady keel, the vessel grim and daring; [5]
    But O heart! heart! heart!
        O the bleeding drops of red,
            Where on the deck my Captain lies,
                Fallen cold and dead.

O Captain! My Captain! Rise up and hear the bells;
Rise up—for you the flag is flung—for you the bugle trills, [6]
For you bouquets and ribbon'd wreaths—for you the shores a-crowding,
For you they call, the swaying mass, their eager faces turning;
Here Captain! Dear father!
    This arm beneath your head!
        It is some dream that on the deck,
            You've fallen cold and dead.

My Captain does not answer, his lips are pale and still,
My father does not feel my arm, he has no pulse nor will,
The ship is anchor'd safe and sound, its voyage closed and done,

From fearful trip the victor ship comes in with object won:
Exult O shores, and ring O bells!
But I with mournful tread, [7]
Walk the deck my Captain lies,
Fallen cold and dead.

Notes

[1] My Captain: referring to President Abraham Lincoln who was assassinated on April 14, 1865, in the Ford Theatre, Washington, D.C. This poem was written as part of the Memories of President Lincoln.

[2] fearful trip: Here the poet is comparing the American Civil War to a fearful trip.

[3] weather'd every rack: come through all the strong storms and trials.

[4] the prize: the abolition of the Negro slavery system.

[5] While follow eyes the steady keel, the vessel grim and daring: While eyes are following the course of the steady-moving keel, the ship becomes solemn and stately magnificent. keel: the timber or steel structure on which the ship is built.

[6] trills: plays with a shaky and vibrating sound.

[7] tread: lingering pace with sad steps.

Commentary

O Captain! My Captain! is one of the most popular poems by Whitman, in which America is compared to a ship, with President Abraham Lincoln as her captain. As a strong supporter for the abolition of the slavery, Whitman wrote this poem of elegy as part of the Memories for the death of President Lincoln who was assassinated on April 14, 1865, in the Ford Theatre, Washington, D. C. On the one hand, cheerful people on the shores are waiting for the return of the victor ship. On the other hand, the sad narrator on the deck, with tears on his face, is looking at the father-like, but dead captain. The theme of the poem can be found in the famous saying that "freedom is not free"—to acquire anything valuable we have to pay a price, even including our lives. With three conventional octet stanzas rhyming *aabbcded* and a traditional metrical pattern of iambus, this closed form of poetry appears more solemn, rather effective, and quite appropriate for the subject of this elegiac poem.

Questions and Exercises

1. Analyze the function of the traditional rhythm and rhyme in the poem and explain how they are appropriately used for the subject of the poem.
2. This poem is obviously written in the form of an allegory. What is the overall connotative meaning in this poem?

Emily Dickinson

Emily Dickinson (1830—1886) was a shy New England recluse, who wrote nearly 1,800 poems in her lifetime, and has come to be regarded as a chief poet, as great as Whitman, in the late 19th century. In theme and technique, her poetry was American, but unlike Whitman, she explores the inner life of individuals in her poetry.

As a young girl she finished her education at South Hadley Female Academy. After graduation she lived quietly at her father's home until she was twenty-four years old in 1854. She remained single to the end of her life, but her life was profoundly affected by two men, Benjamin Newton and Charles Wadsworth. The former was a lawyer, who introduced her to inspiring books and encouraged her to display her talent in verse. The latter was her "dearest earthly friend" who was a married clergyman; however, nothing came of the affair between them. Then she returned to her native home in Amherst. And it was at this time that she began to dress entirely in white, avoided strangers, and only kept communication with a number of intimates through letters and notes. This marked the beginning of the strange years of her retirement. Her existence has seemed sad to many people, but reading her life in her letters one actually finds that she was quite happy and peaceful to live alone. She died at Amherst on May 16, 1886.

Although Dickinson lived in the flood of the romantic revolution, she seems to have nothing in common with the leading writers of the time. She appears to be wholly original, taking the stuff of her poetry merely from her personal experiences. She just expressed what she felt about love, nature, friendship, death, and immortality, and developed her own poetic form with many peculiar features. In addition to such characteristics as the abundant use of dashes, irregular punctuation and capitalization quite typical of her own, her mode of expression is characterized by clear-cut and delicately original imagery, precise diction, complex rhythms, and fragmentary and mysteriously strange metrical patterns.

67

Success is counted sweetest
By those who ne'er succeed.
To comprehend a nectar[1]
Requires sorest need.

Not one of all the purple host[2]

Who took the Flag to-day[3]
Can tell the definition,
So clear, of victory,

As he,[4] defeated, dying,
On whose forbidden ear[5]
The distant strains of triumph[6]
Burst agonized and clear!

Notes

[1] nectar: the drink of the gods; any delicious or inspiring beverage.

[2] the purple host: the royal army. "purple" is an archaic word for army, referring to a soldier's wound received in battle. The color is traditionally a royal color, hence, it is a victorious one here.

[3] Who took the Flag to-day: Who won the victory today.

[4] Can tell the definition, / So clear, of victory, / As he: Can give a definition of victory as clear as one...

[5] forbidden ear: ear that has lost the capacity of hearing.

[6] strains of triumph: songs or music of victory.

Commentary

Those who have not achieved success may think success is precious because they have an intense need for it. The poet cites one specific kind of success—victory in battlefield when the soldier hears the sounds of victory just before he dies. In the last awareness before death, the dying soldier understands the true meaning of success for which he is sacrificing his precious life. Real success, then, is a profound realization of the heavy price one pays. It is an inward feeling rather than public acclaim or material gain. Hence, success can be determined only by oneself.

Question and Exercises

1. According to the poem, who can understand success most? What sort of feelings does the poet show toward the victor and the defeated?
2. Do you agree or disagree with the poet's observation about success and human nature expressed in this poem? Why or why not?
3. Write a short essay in terms of your understanding about success and failure, compared with Emily Dickinson's.

712

Because I could not stop for Death—
He kindly stopped for me—
The Carriage held but just Ourselves—
And Immortality.[1]

We slowly drove—He knew no haste
And I had put away
My labor and my leisure too,
For His Civility—

We passed the School, where Children strove
At Recess—in the Ring—
We passed the Fields of Gazing Grain[2]—
We passed the Setting Sun—

Or rather—He passed Us—
The Dews drew quivering and chill—
For only Gossamer, my Gown—
My Tippet—only Tulle[3]—

We paused before a House that seemed
A Swelling of the Ground—
The Roof was scarcely visible—
The Cornice[4]— in the Mound—

Since then—'tis Centuries—and yet
Feels shorter than the Day
I first surmised the Horses' Heads
Were toward Eternity.[5]

Notes

[1] The Carriage held but just Ourselves—And Immortality: The Carriage had three people in it. They were the speaker of the poem, Death, and Immortality as the chaperone.

[2] Gazing Grain: the grain that has kernels like gazing eyes.

[3] The Dews drew quivering…only Tulle: The morning dews made me feel cold and

trembling, because the clothes I wore were just a thin light silk dress, and my shoulder scarf was just of a thin net-like fabric.

[4] Cornice: the molded and projecting horizontal part that crowns an architectural composition such as a gate or door. Here it refers to the cover of the coffin.

[5] I first surmised the Horses' Heads / Were toward Eternity: For the first time I guessed that our carriage was heading toward the future life of the dead world.

Commentary

The poem is a dramatic representation of the passage from this world of the living to the afterlife. The event is a metaphorical *use* of an activity familiar enough to people of the 19th century—a formal but friendly drive in a carriage in the country of a gentleman and his intended lady. The gentleman in question, however, is Death himself, and the lady is an imagined persona of the poet. She is looking back upon how life had been before she came, and her memories are infused with the subtle tensions of one not completely at rest.

In the first two lines the persona is too busy and too contented as she lives her life to stop for the gentleman's call, but through his kindness and consideration, she is compelled at last to go with him. In the third line, the dramatic scene is set in the carriage. The situation is one of intimacy—the Carriage held but just Ourselves. He has called on her as a beau and, like a true gentleman, he has included a chaperone, Immortality. The seemingly disparate elements of "children", "Gazing Grain" and "Setting Sun" are transferred to these parts of the world. In addition, the three elements summarize the progress and passage of a lifetime, alluding to the three states of youth, maturity and old age, the cycle of day from morning to evening, and even a suggestion of seasonal progression from spring through ripening to decline.

The mood of intimacy created in the carriage is ironically suffocating. In its depiction of Death on one hand as the courtly suitor and on the other as the deceitful seducer, the poem reflects a basic ambiguity about death and immortality. Is death a release from a lifetime of work and suffering? Is it the gateway to a lasting peace in paradise? Or is it simply a cold destruction of life itself? All these questions are left for readers to think about.

Questions and Exercises

1. How many people are there in the carriage? What kind of journey are they making?
2. When the landscape changes continuously as their carriage passed "the School", "the Fields" and "the Setting Sun", what stages of life can these images remind us of?
3. Write an essay to explain whether the poet's attitude toward life and death is positive or negative, then present your own idea about this cycle of life and death.

Robert Frost

Robert Frost (1874—1963) is now firmly established as one of the undisputed masters of modern American poetry and is the best-known and most readily welcome New England poet today.

Frost did many different things in his life to make a living. He was once a school teacher, a shoemaker, a mill worker, a farmer, and a newspaper reporter, but he continued to keep up a lively interest in literature. Frost is a New England poet by temperament and subject matter, and maintains the conservatism and restraint of the old New England personality. The subjects of his poems often deal with life characteristic of this part of the country. He loves the quiet countryside and hills there and continued to use the traditional metrical forms for some of his work.

An important contribution Frost had made to English literature is that he revolutionized blank verse—his poems often sound so much like conversation. Thus, he seemed to believe that his poems gain their special effects from a combination of speech informality and the formality of meter. In fact, Frost, a master of blank verse, had composed most of his narrative poems in it.

The central theme of his works is to assert that the human beings are related to each other through maintaining a proper balance between a fruitful affection and a self-respecting, self-reliant independence. Frost sees people as essentially lonely and yet constantly dependent on the affection and support of others. He thinks that there exists some uncertainty in life for everyone of us, and that to care for each other is what we human beings really need.

The Road Not Taken

Two roads diverged in a yellow wood,
And sorry I could not travel both.
And be one traveler, long I stood
And looked down one as far as I could
To where it bent in the undergrowth;

Then took the other, as just as fair,[1]
And having perhaps the better claim,
Because it was grassy and wanted wear;[2]
Though as for that the passing there

Had worn them really about the same,

And both that morning equally lay
In leaves no step had trodden black.
Oh, I kept the first for another day!
Yet knowing how way leads on to way,
I doubted if I should ever come back.

I shall be telling this with a sigh
Somewhere ages and ages hence:
Two roads diverged in a wood, and I—
I took the one less traveled by,
And that has made all the difference.

Notes

[1] Then took the other, as just as fair: Then I took the other road, which is as proper as it is fair (both proper and fair).

[2] wanted wear: lacked wear; was not quite worn because few travelers had trodden it.

Commentary

The setting of this poem is in some woods, but in fact, the place where it occurs can really be anywhere and at any time. The poem seems to be about the poet, walking in the woods in autumn, choosing which road he should follow on his walk. It may also represent a moment in anyone's life where an arduous problematic choice has to be made. Frost turns this universal dilemma into poetry of gentle yet firm understanding. We must make a decision. We must decide which way to go. Actually, sometimes we even feel painful because we have to give up one desirable thing at the expense of another. Then, whatever the outcome, one must accept the consequences of one's choice since it is impossible to go back and have another chance to choose otherwise. In the poem, the poet hesitates for a long time, wondering which road to take, because they are both pretty. In the end, he follows the one which seems to have fewer travelers on it. Symbolically, the speaker chooses to follow an unusual, solitary life; here Frost perhaps was speaking of his choice to become a poet rather than some commoner profession. The poem is written in classic five-line stanzas (quintet), with the rhyme scheme of *abaab*.

Questions and Exercises

1. What does the speaker say about the two roads? What is the symbolic meaning of the two roads in the poem?

2. Why did the poet choose the road that is less traveled by? What does this symbolize?
3. Different interpretations make good literature so much of a pleasure to read. What does the speaker conclude about his choice? And what choices in your own life have made a difference in the course it has taken?

Stopping by Woods on a Snowy Evening

Whose woods[1] these are I think I know.
His house is in the village though;
He will not see me stopping here
To watch his woods fill up with snow.

My little horse must think it queer
To stop without a farmhouse near
Between the woods and frozen lake
The darkest evening of the year.

He gives his harness bells a shake
To ask if there is some mistake.
The only other sound's the sweep
Of easy wind[2] and downy flake. [3]

The woods are lovely, dark and deep,
But I have promises to keep,
And miles to go before I sleep, [4]
And miles to go before I sleep.

Notes

[1] woods: The word "woods" here may stand for nature in general.
[2] easy wind: gentle breeze; light wind.
[3] downy flake: soft and fluffy pieces of snow.
[4] sleep: death at the end of one's life, or simply a rest at night.

Commentary

Stopping by Woods on a Snowy Evening deals with a dilemma between choosing the unknown mysterious nature and the earthly routine life. The rhyme scheme is a complex pattern of interlocking stanzas: *aaba, bbcb, ccdc, dddd.*

This poem focuses on two possibilities in the whole course of life: stopping to indulge oneself in the beauty of nature, or moving on to return to the active world of work and responsibility. A man passing by a dark woods stops because the beauty of the woods in the darkness appeals him. Nevertheless, he feels a pressure to move on, to return to his responsibilities and obligations. The repeated line may goes beyond its literal meaning and invites readers to interpret "sleep" as the final sleep of death. Once we make this interpretive leap, we can consider "miles to go" as perhaps the time the speaker has left to live, and "promises" as the obligation he must fulfill before he dies. His stopping to look at the falling snow can be interpreted as a temporary retreat from such responsibilities or as a desire to escape from them. It can also be argued that the poem represents a moment of relaxation from the demanding journey of life, an almost aesthetic enjoyment and appreciation of natural beauty which is wholesome and restorative against the chaotic existence of modern man.

Questions and Exercises

1. What is your understanding of "promises to keep" in *Stopping by Woods on a Snowy Evening*?
2. What are the literal and literary meanings of this poem respectively? Try to figure out the central theme of the poem, and then state out your personal response about such a theme.

Part 3

A Guide to Appreciating English Drama

1 Nature of Drama

The term "drama" refers to an art form that is written down by a dramatist in prose or verse dialogue and is primarily intended for theatrical performance. Meanwhile the term "play" mainly refers to a piece of dramatic work performed for the audience in the theater. Therefore, the two terms "drama" and "play" are closely related to each other. Because of this dual nature, playwrights can present their experience more vividly and more profoundly than through other forms of literature. Drama differs essentially from fiction and poetry in that the dramatist's intention is fulfilled, not by people reading his work, but by its presentation to the audience by his collaborators (the play's director, actors and theater staff) using theatrical devices (spectacle, music, and the like).

A drama is usually organized in the form of acts and scenes. An act is the main part into which a drama is divided; it usually consists of several scenes. A scene usually begins whenever the time or place of the action changes. A drama includes two important elements: dialogue (lines that the characters speak), and stage directions (instructions that tell actors how to say their lines and how to move on the stage.) The stage directions appear in brackets "[ ]"or in *italics*. As a result, a printed drama is not yet a completed work of art; rather, it is a blueprint for a production; the finished product of it is a presentation on a stage before an audience.

As readers, there are several ways to make a play come to life. We must: (1) place ourselves in the theater; (2) imagine ourselves among the real theater audience; (3) carefully note and imaginatively respond to the stage directions to evoke in our mind the particulars of the setting, the lighting of each scene, the costumes, physical appearance, and the gestures of the performers. Only in so doing can we effectively visualize the scenes and hear the sound of the story in our mind's eye.

2 Main Elements of Drama

A drama should mainly consist of the following six elements: plot, character, dialogue, staging, music, and theme.

2.1 Plot

Plot is the structure of a play's action, the things that happen in the play and the ways in which those incidents connect. Any plot of a drama must have conflict; the two sides, or the pros and cons of the conflict are usually represented by the protagonist and the antagonist in the play. The protagonist may be one person or many, and the antagonist may be a person, a group, or a social force.

Most drama is structured on the five-part plan of *exposition, rising action (complication), climax, falling action (anticlimax),* and *denouement* (*resolution*). This applies to comedy as well as to tragedy (See the diagram below). Unlike a novel, which can be of almost any length, a play has to be economical, presenting events in a short span of time that in reality would develop over a longer period. For this reason, a play should in theory deal with one main subject, and the scene should not be moved abruptly from place to place.

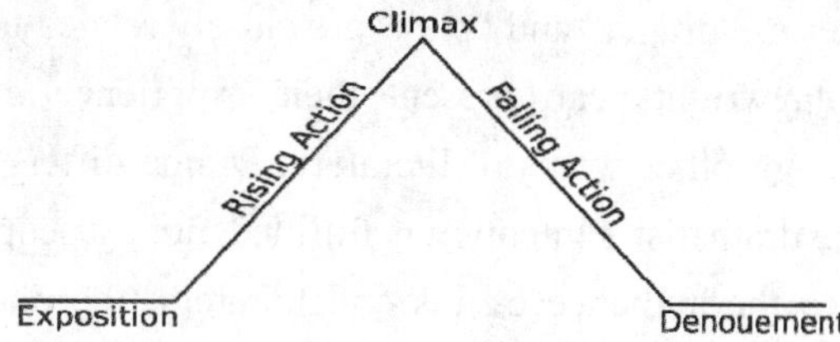

The first thing the dramatist has to do is to establish the setting by means of exposition which should be revealed clearly and slowly enough for the audience to get the necessary information. Then the playwright prepares the audience for future developments through rising action (complication) to push the conflict with more depth and wider breadth. Finally, the complication proceeds through the rising action to its climax, the most crucial turning point of the play. After the climax, there is the falling action—nothing new can be added—any high point in the story hereafter becomes anticlimactic. Things fall into place, and the play heads toward its conclusion (denouement).

2.2 Character

Character is an essentially important element of drama for the fact that plot is character in action. Just as the dramatist has to tell his story economically, he must be just as economical in depicting his characters. Characters in a play must be quickly introduced to the audience and become familiar within a short time. Characters may be depicted as great people (as in classical drama), or as ordinary people, as is more usually the case in modern drama.

According to different criteria, characters can also be divided into round characters, flat characters, dynamic characters and static characters. The round (three dimensional) characters who are neither wholly good nor wholly evil, but wholly human, are certainly the most convincing and rich characters. The minor roles of most plays tend to be flat, that is, one-dimensional, or stereotyped characters. Characters who change and develop as the play progresses are called dynamic ones as opposed to the flat characters whose personal traits remain unchanged throughout the play.

Character may be portrayed in four ways. First, a character is delineated by appearance. The actor's physical qualities give an immediate impression to the audience, which is why many modern playwrights have described the character's appearance in considerable detail. Second, a character is revealed by speech, as the kind of language employed by the characters, their manner of speaking, and their tone of voice, all signify something about their personalities. Third, a character is established by action, because a character's external actions will supply us with clues to his or her inner motivations. Fourth, a character may be revealed by what others say about him or her. Often, dramatists use other characters' comment as a way to reveal the truth about an absent character.

2.3 Dialogue

The medium of drama is dialogue—the words spoken by the actors. Ezra Pound, the modern American poet, once described drama as "persons moving about on a stage using words"—in short, people talking, either in verse or in prose. Listening to their talk we can hear identifiable, individual voices. So dramatists use dialogues to advance the plot and delineate characters.

However, what is important is that dialogues in drama must be clear since the language must be immediately understood by the audience in the theater. In addition, the dialogue should be interesting to capture the spirit of life, and the diction must be appropriate for the character and the situation. Therefore dramatists aim at appropriateness, rather than abstract beauty, of the language used. Then, the language of drama must be dynamic, as it is a means of articulating the conflicting motivations. Last but not the least, good dialogues must be suited for oral expression in drama.

2.4 Staging

By staging we have in mind the spectacle a play presents in performance. In other words, staging refers to all of the specific visual aspects of a play—scenery, lighting, costume, make-up, and the movement of the actors.

From the 17th century to the 19th century, an elaborate use of enormous and complicated settings was employed on the stage. The realistic and naturalistic movements in the late 19th century gave spectacle a new importance, believing that the environment could serve as a conditioning force in determining behavior. Hence spectacle began to assume an organic role in the theater, as a means of reinforcing theme, providing psychological and physical environment, and creating atmosphere for the play.

2.5 Sound effect

Sound effect refers to all of the auditory aspect of a play, including music, the tonal pattern of the spoken words, and various common sounds such as door slams, storming, wind howling, weapons firing, cars driving by, and the like. Many modern playwrights had a keen sensitivity for the expressiveness of sound to enhance the mood of their plays.

2.6 Theme

Theme refers to the reasoning aspect of drama. In addition to the rationale of individual characters, a play's theme summarizes the moral and indicates the symbolic meaning of the play as a whole. A play may convey various interpretations to an audience. Dramatists do not usually make an explicit statement of their themes, unless their purpose is didactic. Unlike the medieval writers, most of the modern playwrights do not supply clear-cut solutions to the problems they raise in their plays. Their purposes are to provoke thought of the audience rather than to persuade them to adopt a ready-made answer to life.

As readers, we reach for a theme as a way of organizing our responses to a play. It is often helpful to try to express the theme of a play in a carefully worded sentence or two. But at the same time, we should also be aware that any summary statement of a complex work of art is bound to be limited and limiting, because chances are very high that a play may quite often include more than one theme. Perhaps we can best approach consideration of a play's theme by noting the dialogues and actions of its characters, who frequently represent conflicting ideals, values and viewpoints.

3 How to Read Drama

3.1 Determine the setting

When we begin to read a play, the first thing we must do is to familiarize ourselves with its setting and circumstances. Look at the description of the location at the beginning, and we will discover when and where the story takes place.

After learning when and where the play occurs, we should try to create in our minds our own "stage set" as we begin to read. Try to make our own blueprint of what the stage set would look like: the placement of the walls, the doors, the furniture, etc. In this way we can visualize where characters enter and exit the set and where they are located during specific scenes.

Stage directions can also help us to summon up another vital dimension of the play in performance: its "sound". Just as you should try to picture the particular actor, you must also try to "hear" the music, the natural sounds, and even the inflection of voice that the playwright has imagined for the play.

3.2 Familiarize the cast

The next step of reading a play is to familiarize yourself with the cast, a list of characters at the beginning of a printed play. Look at this list carefully to see who the characters are: their age, sex, occupation, and their relationship to one another. You will really get to know the characters by seeing them in action once the play unfolds, but before you begin, it is helpful to know who they are and how they relate to one another. After you are well into the play, you should consider what strikes you most about various characters—humorous, cunning, evil, noble, humane, or vulnerable.

Different characters have different functions in the play. The main character is often referred to as the protagonist. The one with whom the protagonist is in conflict is the antagonist. The minor characters, often called foils, are often interacted with the protagonist.

3.3 Follow the action

Usually the first scene of a play should be the key to what is to follow. It should introduce you to the tone of the play—whether serious or comic—and to the characters and the main action. If the chief characters do not appear in the opening scene, they will probably be mentioned, talked about, or foreshadowed. Their appearance in later scenes will be prepared for in advance.

As you move on into the play, all the things we have spoken of should be kept in mind: the kind of theater in which the play is presented; the stage set; the setting of the action; the tendencies of the characters and their interplay with each other. Observe, as you progress to read, what information is revealed. Which characters seem to be the "good guys"? Which are the "bad guys", the villains, the unjust ones, or the selfish ones?

In a struggle between two or more people, which character appears to have the upper hand? How does the power shift during the course of the play? At the same time, you should note what is happening in the play, that is, what action is unfolding. Take note of who enters and who exits and when a certain action occurs so that you will not get lost in the process of reading the play.

3.4 Identify the theme

Pause somewhere along the way of reading—perhaps at the end of an act, or simply when the thought strikes you—to reflect on the possible *theme* of the play. What does the play seem to be concerned about, in terms of ideas, moral values, and philosophical considerations? Different characters stand for different ideas and represent various sides of a moral confrontation. Perhaps the play is dealing with honor and duty to his nation, or piety to the gods. Perhaps it concerns a contest of good against evil. Perhaps it takes up the subject of injustice. If it is a comedy, it may simply be dealing with human pretensions and pomposity. Once you think you have identified the theme or themes of the play, observe how the playwright develops this aspect as the action unfolds.

3.5 Reach a conclusion

As the play approaches its end, think back on what you have experienced. Try to describe how you felt as you were reading and how you feel at present now that you are finished with the play. Has the play entertained you? Has it given you a new perspective? Finally, what in the play has exerted the strongest impact on your emotion? Perhaps there are certain aspects of the play that confused you or that you did not quite understand. If so, you might reread those sections and discuss them with your friends and your instructor. Ideally, in the end, you should have obtained not only a reading experience, but an imagined theater experience about the whole play.

4 Categories of Drama

Some plays evoke laughter, others tears. Some are comic, others tragic, still others a mixture of both. The comic view celebrates life and affirms it; it is typically joyous and festive. The tragic view highlights life's sorrows; it is typically brooding and solemn. Tragic plays end unhappily, often with the death of the hero; comedies usually end happily, often with a celebration.

Sometimes we are told on the title page what kind of play we are reading: a tragedy, a comedy, a farce, or a history. This information can often help us understand the basis on which we are supposed to experience the play to be read. If it is a serious play, we should expect to take a sober, thoughtful outlook at the events. If it is a comedy, we know that we are meant to laugh and not to take the characters or the incidents very seriously. If it is a farce, we understand that there will be wild excitement and that both the characters and the plot will be highly exaggerated.

4.1 Tragedy

Tragedy is not what many of us think it is—a sad play with an unhappy ending. It is a drama dealing with serious themes ending in the suffering or death of one or more of the principal characters. The action in tragedy is significant and serious, and it is often the protagonists' fatal mistake they have made that causes the tragedy; the tragic characters suffer intensely and perhaps die, having exhausted all the possibilities of their life.

Traditionally, a tragedy is defined as a play that involves serious action of universal significance and has important moral and philosophical implications. The hero or heroine is usually a person of royal or noble blood—or some other exceptional character—who suffers a tragic fate. The play usually ends unhappily.

Thus, we can see that tragedy is an assertion of the greatness of humanity. It shows our ability to rise to heights of human dignity in the face of an opposing force which we ourselves know will finally destroy us. Protagonists of tragedy may make a glaring mistake or even commit some evil deed, knowingly or unknowingly, and suffer from curses upon themselves and their family for several generations afterwards. Tragedy retains its great charm for the audience mainly due to the following reasons.

First, in the minds of the audience, tragic protagonists are great people. There is no escape for the tragic protagonists. They are doomed, and we watch in awe as they move toward that doom. Without hope of rescue, the tragic protagonists, whatever foul deeds they may have done and whatever human foolishness they may have displayed, rise to the height in strength, courage, and defiance.

Then, tragedy does not deal with the incidental catastrophe which can be avoided; it tackles the inevitable. It is not saddening and depressing in the sense of a fatal accident or some destructive catastrophe. Tragedy is positive and optimistic in its view of the heights human beings can reach. So, there is considerable distinction between the tragic protagonist and the religious or revolutionary martyr. The martyr suffers and dies for a particular cause, making the suffering and death worth the pain. But in tragedy, with the death of the central figure, tears of compassion rather than sadness may be shed. There can be profound emotional involvement, but there remains the fundamental optimism at the end of a good tragedy. By the end, when tranquility has been restored, the audience has gone through a kind of spiritual purification. They realized how great human beings can be when facing the inevitable tragic occasions.

Next, tragic heroes come from among the audience. Instead of originally being a certain noble figure from a royal or noble family, the protagonist in tragedy in modern drama may be a little man or a little woman, but in no sense a little person. The protagonist has suffers tragedy because of an innate tragic flaw, whether pride, arrogance, vanity, or whatever, that lead to his/her final doom.

Finally, the audiences are inextricably engaged in a constant thread of irony throughout a tragedy. They are quite aware of what is going to happen, or why it is happening, while the character concerned remains in ignorance. The harder the protagonist tries to avoid the disaster, the faster it arrives. In this sense, tragedy is a kind of real art; and those who believe they have created tragedy may merely end up writing a sad play with an unhappy ending, which is by no means a tragedy at all.

4.2 Comedy

The term "comedy" was Greek in origin. The primitive festival from which comedy grew was a happy one, marked by jokes and laughter. Today, comedy is a term broadly applied to a light, humorous play with a happy ending.

As for comedy, a wide range of plays fall under this heading; but usually a comedy is a play that is light in tone, is designed to amuse and provoke laughter, is concerned with issues tending not to be serious, and has a happy ending. The most sophisticated kinds of comedy—intellectual comedy and comedy of manner—stress wit, satire, and ideas.

Traditionally, comedy is often considered inferior to tragedy in insight and power. However, in some cases, the comic greatness is as great as that of tragedy. The romantic comedies of Shakespeare and the penetrating social comedies of Bernard Shaw are such examples. Great comedies also provide an insight into the nature of human condition and enhance our understanding of life. Comedy strives to make us laugh at humanity's vices and follies. Comedy frequently exaggerates or distorts the defects of human nature to achieve the desired effects.

Another distinct feature of comedy is the heavy reliance on stock characters and stereotype situations. The playwrights poke fun at various recognizable human traits, and the audience, in turn, can immediately sense these characters' essential personal qualities. At the opposite end of the genre of comedy is *farce,* a light humorous play full of silly things happening. The playwright of a farce often emphasizes plot twists and exaggerated characters.

4.3 Tragicomedy

Tragicomedy is a genre of drama with bits of comedy added into a tragedy. It is like a sweet-and-sour sauce and a mixture of serious and comic elements. In such plays, the action, serious in theme and in subject matter, seems to be leading to a tragic disaster until an unexpected and often arbitrary turn in events brings about a happy ending. This sort of play is not so much a union of tragedy and comedy. So it lacks the awe we associate with tragedy and the fun we associate with comedy.

In the 20th century the term tragicomedy has acquired a new meaning and the form has become thoroughly respectable. Indeed, many of the best plays of the 20th century are described not as tragedies or comedies but as tragicomedies—distinctive fusion (not merely mixture) of tragedy and comedy. Eugene O'Neill, for example, wrote a hilarious comedy *Ah, Wilderness!* and a somber tragedy *Long Day's Journey into Night,* set in the same place and based on the same experience of his own youth. The general theme is human beings' severe sufferings, but the techniques adopted are those of comedy: with the characters saying funny things.

4.4 Domestic drama and melodrama

Two other types of drama that should be mentioned here are *domestic drama* and *melodrama. Domestic drama* expresses and focuses on the realistic everyday lives of middle or lower classes. According to the *English Communications Syllabus*, domestic drama refers to a dramatic story containing an emphasis on its characters' intimate relationships and their responses to the unfolding events in their lives. The characters, their lives, and the events that occur within the play are usually classified as "ordinary" events, lives, and characters. Domestic drama does, however, take the approach in which it concerns people much like ourselves, taken from the lower and middle classes of society, who struggle with everyday problems such as poverty, sickness, crime, and family strife. One scholar suggests that domestic drama takes up possibly one third of the plays being written.

Melodrama is a type of play that is full of sudden events, unusually strong feelings, and exaggerated characters. It emphasizes emotional effects such as fear, suspense, moral judgment, and often pits good characters against evil ones to achieve its ends. It is usually based around having the same character traits, e.g. a hero (always the fearless one), heroine (the love of the hero, usually the one that the hero saves), villain (usually likes the heroine too) and villain's sidekick (typically gets in the way of the villain).

Both *domestic drama* and *melodrama* were common stage plays in early 19th century, usually romantic and sensational in plot and incident, in which songs and music were interspersed. But later, the musical element gradually ceased to be an essential feature, and now both the two names denote dramatic plays that are characterized by sensational incidents and violent appeals to the emotions, yet mostly with happy endings.

In discussing genres and categories of drama, it is important for us to remember that these are just convenient guides for understanding drama rather than ironclad divisions. They help readers, and audience as well, appreciate what the playwright, director, and performers are trying to do in accomplishing the desired effects.

Questions and Exercises

1. What main elements should we take into consideration when we read drama? What are your effective approaches to read a written text of drama?
2. What are the three most important categories of English drama? What are the dramatist's writing purpose of each category respectively?
3. Though tragedy deals with miserable happenings of mankind, we can obtain even more powerful enlightenments from reading tragedies. What are the general causes for tragedies anyway? Discuss in class why many people prefer reading tragedies.

Selected Readings of English Drama

William Shakespeare

William Shakespeare (1564—1616) is regarded as the greatest English playwright and poet in the history of English literature. He has been universally acknowledged to be the summit of the English Renaissance, and one of the greatest playwrights the world over.

Shakespeare's plays are divided into three groups—comedies, histories, and tragedies. Most of the comedies are romantic fantasies, designed to delight and amuse their audiences. The histories illustrate the moral lessons to be learned from the crimes of ambitious and treacherous leaders of state. The tragedies deal with death, morality, and destruction and show how the breaking of a moral law inevitably leads to disaster.

Julius Caesar begins with the events of the year 44 B.C., after Caesar, the great Roman general at the time, already endowed with the dictatorship, had returned to Rome from a successful campaign in Spain, and when there are fears that he will allow himself to be crowned the king. Distrust of Caesar's ambition gives rise to a conspiracy against him among Roman lovers of freedom, notably Cassius and Casca; they win over to their cause Brutus, who reluctantly joins them from a sense of duty to the republic. Caesar is slain by the conspirators in the senate house. Antony, Caesar's friend, stirs the people to fury against the conspirators by a skilful speech at Caesar's funeral. Octavius, nephew of Julius Caesar, Antony, and Lepidus, united as triumvirs, oppose the forces raised by Brutus and Cassius. Brutus and Cassius are defeated at the battle of Philippi (42 B.C.), and kill themselves.

Shakespeare dealt with an old topic in Roman history, but he approached the topic from a new angle. Instead of paying attention to the historical framework of the event, he allowed himself much freedom in the handling of the subject. In other words, Shakespeare was more concerned with its political implications and its moral impact on the audience. Shakespeare did not attempt to explain the cause of the tragedy, so the ambiguities embedded in the play puzzled many readers, making it one of the most difficult of Shakespeare's plays to assess and interpret.

Julius Caesar

Act 3, Scene 2

Rome. The Forum.

Enter Brutus and Cassius, and a throng of Citizens.

CITIZENS: We will be satisfied! Let us be satisfied!

BRUTUS: Then follow me and give me audience, friends.
Cassius, go you into the other street
And part the numbers.[1]
Those that will hear me speak, let'em stay here;
Those that will follow Cassius, go with him;
And public reasons[2] shall be rendered
Of Caesar's death.

FIRST CITIZEN: I will hear Brutus speak.

SECOND CITIZEN: I will hear Cassius and compare their reasons,
When severally we hear them rendered.

Exit Cassius, with some Citizens.

Brutus goes into the pulpit.

THIRD CITIZEN: The noble Brutus is ascended. Silence!

BRUTUS: Be patient till the last.

Romans, countrymen, and lovers! Hear me for my cause,[3] and be silent, that you may hear. Believe me for mine honor, and have respect to mine honor, that you may believe. Censure[4] me in your wisdom, and awake your senses, that you may the better judge. If there be any in this assembly, any dear friend of Caesar's, to him I say that Brutus' love to Caesar was no less than his. If then that friend demand why Brutus rose against Caesar, this is my answer: Not that I loved Caesar less, but that I loved Rome more. Had you rather Caesar were living and die all slaves, than that Caesar were dead to live all freemen? As Caesar loved me, I weep for him; as he was fortunate,[5] I rejoice at it; as he was valiant, I honor him; but as he was ambitious, I slew him. There is tears for his love, joy for his fortune, honor for his valor, and death for his ambition. Who is here so base that would be a bondman? If any, speak, for him have I offended. Who is here so rude[6] that would not be a Roman? If any, speak, for him have I offended. Who is here so vile that will not love his country? If any, speak, for him have I offended. I pause for a reply.

ALL: None, Brutus, none.

BRUTUS: Then none have I offended. I have done no more to Caesar than you shall do to Brutus. The question[7] of his death is enrolled in the Capitol, his glory not extenuated, wherein he was worthy, nor his offenses enforced, for which he suffered death.

Enter Antony and others, with Caesar's body.

Here comes his body, mourned by Mark Antony, who, though he had no hand in his death, shall receive the benefit of his dying, a place in the commonwealth,[8] as which of you shall not? With this I depart—that, as I slew my best lover for the good of Rome, I have the same dagger for myself, when it shall please my country to need my death.

ALL: Live, Brutus, live, live!

FIRST CITIZEN: Bring him with triumph home unto his house.

SECOND CITIZEN: Give him a statue with his ancestors.

THIRD CITIZEN: Let him be Caesar.

FOURTH CITIZEN: Caesar's better parts[9]
Shall be crown'd in Brutus.

FIRST CITIZEN: We'll bring him to his house with shouts and clamors.

BRUTUS: My countrymen—

SECOND CITIZEN: Peace! Silence! Brutus speaks.

FIRST CITIZEN: Peace, ho!

BRUTUS: Good countrymen, let me depart alone,
And, for my sake, stay here with Antony.
Do grace to Caesar's corpse, and grace his speech
Tending to[10] Caesar's glories, which Mark Antony,
By our permission, is allow'd to make.
I do entreat you, not a man depart,
Save I alone, till Antony have spoke.

Exit.

FIRST CITIZEN: Stay, ho, and let us hear Mark Antony.

THIRD CITIZEN: Let him go up into the public chair;[11]
We'll hear him. Noble Antony, go up.

ANTONY: For Brutus' sake, I am beholding[12] to you.

Goes into the pulpit.

FOURTH CITIZEN: What does he say of Brutus?

THIRD CITIZEN: He says, for Brutus' sake,
He finds himself beholding to us all.

FOURTH CITIZEN: 'Twere best he speak no harm of Brutus here.

FIRST CITIZEN: This Caesar was a tyrant.

THIRD CITIZEN: Nay, that's certain.
We are blest that Rome is rid of him.

SECOND CITIZEN: Peace! Let us hear what Antony can say.

ANTONY: You gentle Romans—

ALL: Peace, ho! Let us hear him.

ANTONY: Friends, Romans, countrymen, lend me your ears!
I come to bury Caesar, not to praise him.
The evil that men do lives after them,
The good is oft interred with their bones;
So let it be with Caesar. The noble Brutus
Hath told you Caesar was ambitious;
If it were so, it was a grievous fault,
And grievously hath Caesar answer'd it.
Here, under leave of[13] Brutus and the rest—
For Brutus is an honorable man;
So are they all, all honorable men—
Come I to speak in Caesar's funeral.
He was my friend, faithful and just to me;
But Brutus says he was ambitious,
And Brutus is an honorable man.
He hath brought many captives home to Rome,
Whose ransoms did the general coffers[14] fill.
Did this in Caesar seem ambitious?
When that the poor have cried, Caesar hath wept;
Ambition should be made of sterner stuff:
Yet Brutus says he was ambitious,
And Brutus is an honorable man.
You all did see that on the Lupercal[15]
I thrice presented him a kingly crown,
Which he did thrice refuse. Was this ambition?
Yet Brutus says he was ambitious,
And sure he is an honorable man.
I speak not to disprove what Brutus spoke,
But here I am to speak what I do know.
You all did love him once, not without cause;
What cause withholds you then to mourn for him?
O judgement, thou art fled to brutish beasts,
And men have lost their reason. Bear with me;
My heart is in the coffin there with Caesar,
And I must pause till it come back to me.

FIRST CITIZEN: Methinks there is much reason in his sayings.

SECOND CITIZEN: If thou consider rightly of the matter,
Caesar has had great wrong.

THIRD CITIZEN: Has he, masters?

I fear there will a worse come in his place.
FOURTH CITIZEN: Mark'd ye his words?[16] He would not take the crown;
Therefore 'tis certain he was not ambitious.
FIRST CITIZEN: If it be found so, some will dear abide it.[17]
SECOND CITIZEN: Poor soul, his eyes are red as fire with weeping.
THIRD CITIZEN: There's not a nobler man in Rome than Antony.
FOURTH CITIZEN: Now mark him, he begins again to speak.
ANTONY: But yesterday the word of Caesar might
Have stood against[18] the world. Now lies he there,
And none so poor to do him reverence.
O masters! If I were disposed to stir
Your hearts and minds to mutiny and rage,
I should do Brutus wrong and Cassius wrong,
Who, you all know, are honorable men.
I will not do them wrong; I rather choose
To wrong the dead, to wrong myself and you,
Than I will wrong such honorable men.
But here's a parchment[19] with the seal of Caesar;
I found it in his closet, 'tis his will.
Let but the commons hear this testament—
Which, pardon me, I do not mean to read—
And they would go and kiss dead Caesar's wounds
And dip their napkins[20] in his sacred blood,
Yea, beg a hair of him for memory,
And, dying, mention it within their wills,
Bequeathing it as a rich legacy
Unto their issue.[21]
FOURTH CITIZEN: We'll hear the will. Read it, Mark Antony.
ALL: The will, the will! We will hear Caesar's will.
ANTONY: Have patience, gentle friends, I must not read it;
It is not meet you know how Caesar loved you.
You are not wood, you are not stones, but men;
And, being men, hearing the will of Caesar,
It will inflame you, it will make you mad.
'Tis good you know not that you are his heirs,
For if you should, O, what would come of it!
FOURTH CITIZEN: Read the will; we'll hear it, Antony.
You shall read us the will, Caesar's will.
ANTONY: Will you be patient? Will you stay awhile?

I have o'ershot[22] myself to tell you of it.
I fear I wrong the honorable men
Whose daggers have stabb'd Caesar; I do fear it.

FOURTH CITIZEN: They were traitors. Honorable men!

ALL: The will! The testament!

SECOND CITIZEN: They were villains, murderers. The will!
Read the will!

ANTONY: You will compel me then to read the will?
Then make a ring about the corpse of Caesar,
And let me show you him that made the will.
Shall I descend? And will you give me leave?

ALL: Come down.

SECOND CITIZEN: Descend.

He comes down from the pulpit.

THIRD CITIZEN: You shall have leave.

FOURTH CITIZEN: A ring, stand round.

FIRST CITIZEN: Stand from the hearse, stand from the body.

SECOND CITIZEN: Room for Antony, most noble Antony.

ANTONY: Nay, press not so upon me, stand far off.

ALL: Stand back; room, bear back!

ANTONY: If you have tears, prepare to shed them now.
You all do know this mantle.[23] I remember
The first time ever Caesar put it on;
'Twas on a summer's evening, in his tent,
That day he overcame the Nervii.[24]
Look, in this place ran Cassius' dagger through;
See what a rent the envious[25] Casca made;
Through this the well-beloved Brutus stabb'd;
And as he pluck'd his cursed steel away,
Mark how the blood of Caesar follow'd it,
As rushing out of doors, to be resolved[26]
If Brutus so unkindly[27] knock'd, or no;
For Brutus, as you know, was Caesar's angel.
Judge, O you gods, how dearly Caesar loved him!
This was the most unkindest cut[28] of all;
For when the noble Caesar saw him stab,
Ingratitude,[29] more strong than traitors' arms,
Quite vanquish'd him. Then burst his mighty heart,
And, in his mantle muffling up his face,

Even at the base of Pompey's statue,
Which all the while ran blood,[30] great Caesar fell.
O, what a fall was there, my countrymen!
Then I, and you, and all of us fell down,
Whilst bloody treason flourish'd[31] over us.
O, now you weep, and I perceive you feel
The dint[32] of pity. These are gracious drops.
Kind souls, what weep you when you but behold
Our Caesar's vesture wounded? Look you here,
Here is himself, marr'd,[33] as you see, with traitors.

FIRST CITIZEN: O piteous spectacle!
SECOND CITIZEN: O noble Caesar!
THIRD CITIZEN: O woeful day!
FOURTH CITIZEN: O traitors! villains!
FIRST CITIZEN: O most bloody sight!
SECOND CITIZEN: We will be revenged.
ALL: Revenge! About![34] Seek! Burn! Fire! Kill!
Slay! Let not a traitor live!
ANTONY: Stay, countrymen.
FIRST CITIZEN: Peace there! Hear the noble Antony.
SECOND CITIZEN: We'll hear him, we'll follow him, we'll die with him.
ANTONY: Good friends, sweet friends, let me not stir you up
To such a sudden flood of mutiny.[35]
They that have done this deed are honorable.
What private griefs they have, alas, I know not,
That made them do it. They are wise and honorable,
And will, no doubt, with reasons answer you.
I come not, friends, to steal away your hearts.
I am no orator, as Brutus is;
But, as you know me all, a plain blunt man,
That love my friend, and that they know full well
That gave me public leave[36] to speak of him.
For I have neither wit, nor words, nor worth,
Action, nor utterance, nor the power of speech,[37]
To stir men's blood. I only speak right on;[38]
I tell you that which you yourselves do know;
Show you sweet Caesar's wounds, poor dumb mouths,
And bid them speak for me. But were I Brutus,
And Brutus Antony, there were an Antony

Would ruffle up[39] your spirits and put a tongue
In every wound of Caesar that should move
The stones of Rome to rise and mutiny.

ALL: We'll mutiny.

FIRST CITIZEN: We'll burn the house of Brutus.

THIRD CITIZEN: Away, then! Come, seek the conspirators.

ANTONY: Yet hear me, countrymen; yet hear me speak.

ALL: Peace, ho! Hear Antony, most noble Antony!

ANTONY: Why, friends, you go to do you know not what.
Wherein [40] hath Caesar thus deserved your loves?
Alas, you know not; I must tell you then.
You have forgot the will I told you of.

ALL: Most true, the will! Let's stay and hear the will.

ANTONY: Here is the will, and under Caesar's seal.
To every Roman citizen he gives,
To every several[41] man, seventy-five drachmas.[42]

SECOND CITIZEN: Most noble Caesar! We'll revenge his death.

THIRD CITIZEN: O royal[43] Caesar!

ANTONY: Hear me with patience.

ALL: Peace, ho!

ANTONY: Moreover, he hath left you all his walks,[44]
His private arbors,[45] and new-planted orchards,
On this side Tiber; he hath left them you,
And to your heirs forever—common pleasures,[46]
To walk abroad[47] and recreate yourselves.
Here was a Caesar! When comes such another?

FIRST CITIZEN: Never, never. Come, away, away!
We'll burn his body in the holy place[48]
And with the brands[49] fire the traitors' houses.
Take up the body.

SECOND CITIZEN: Go fetch fire.

THIRD CITIZEN: Pluck[50] down benches.

FOURTH CITIZEN: Pluck down forms, windows, anything.

Exeunt Citizens with the body.

ANTONY: Now let it work. Mischief, thou art afoot,[51]
Take thou what course thou wilt.

Enter a Servant.

How now, fellow?

SERVANT: Sir, Octavius is already come to Rome.

ANTONY: Where is he?

SERVANT: He and Lepidus are at Caesar's house.

ANTONY: And thither will I straight to visit him.
He comes upon a wish.[52] Fortune[53] is merry,
And in this mood will give us anything.

SERVANT: I heard him say Brutus and Cassius
Are rid [54] like madmen through the gates of Rome.

ANTONY: Belike they had some notice of the people,
How I had moved them.[55] Bring me to Octavius.

Exeunt.

Notes

[1] part the numbers: divide the crowd.

[2] public reasons: reasons concerning the public good.

[3] for my cause: for the sake of the cause I represent.

[4] censure: judge.

[5] fortunate: successful (in war).

[6] rude: uncivilized.

[7] question: reasons.

[8] a place in the commonwealth: the right to live in a free republic.

[9] parts: qualities.

[10] tending to: referring to.

[11] public chair: orator's platform.

[12] beholding: indebted; very grateful.

[13] under leave of: with permission from.

[14] general coffers: public treasury.

[15] Lupercal: on the feast of Lupercal. Feb. 15 was a feast day in honor of Lupercus, protector of flocks and herds, to ensure the animals fertility in the spring.

[16] Mark'd ye: Have you heard…?

[17] If it be…abide it: If it can be proved so, some people will pay dearly for it.

[18] stood against: overcome the opposition of.

[19] parchment: document.

[20] napkins: handkerchiefs.

[21] issue: children.

[22] o'ershot: go too far.

[23] mantle: cloak.

[24] Nervii: the most war-like of the Gallic tribes, whom Caesar conquered in 57 B.C.; he himself fought valiantly in the battle, and his victory was celebrated with more than usual rejoicing in Rome.

[25] envious: malicious.
[26] be resolved: make sure.
[27] unkindly: both cruelly and unnaturally.
[28] unkindest cut: the wound that hurt most.
[29] ingratitude: the blow struck by Brutus's ingratitude.
[30] Which all the while ran blood: Caesar's blood was pouring out all over the statue, so that it seemed as though the statue was bleeding.
[31] flourish'd: triumphed.
[32] dint: blow.
[33] marr'd: mutilated.
[34] About: set about doing it.
[35] flood of mutiny: wave of violence.
[36] public leave: permission to speak in public.
[37] neither wit…power of speech: wit: intelligence; worth: authority; action: gesture; utterance: elocution; power of speech: rhetoric.
[38] right on: directly.
[39] ruffle up: stir.
[40] wherein: in what way.
[41] several: individual.
[42] drachmas: silver coins in ancient Greece.
[43] royal: generous.
[44] walks: gardens.
[45] private arbors: summer houses.
[46] common pleasures: public pleasure gardens.
[47] abroad: in the open air.
[48] holy place: the Forum, the center of religious as well as political life in Rome.
[49] brands: burning wood from the funeral pyre.
[50] pluck: pull.
[51] afoot: begun.
[52] upon a wish: just as I wished.
[53] Fortune : the goddess of Fortune.
[54] Are rid: have ridden.
[55] Belike…them: Probably they had got some warning about how I have influenced the citizens.

Commentary

In this play, we see very little of Julius Caesar himself, but we hear a lot about him—Mark Antony praises him; Brutus loves him; Cassius hates him; and the Roman citizens change in their feelings towards him from admiration to dislike, then back again to respect and love. Caesar is murdered at the beginning of Act 3, and you may at first think it odd that the hero should vanish from the stage before the play is half-finished. But although the man is dead, his spirit lives on. It is present in the minds of those who murdered him, and of those who seek to avenge the murder.

The two speeches made after Caesar's death, one by Brutus and the other by Antonio, are specimens of great oration. In Act 3, Scene 2, the citizens demand to know why Caesar was murdered, and Brutus addresses them in prose, trying to present a reasoned argument to justify the murder. He tells them that he loved Caesar, but that he loved freedom even more. This answer satisfies the people, and they are ready to accept Brutus in Caesar's place.

Antony's speech is delivered in verse form; there is no attempt to produce logical argument. His oration—with its repetitions, rhetorical questions, ironies, and open display of emotion—is aimed at the hearts, rather than the heads, of the people. We see the citizens in the process of changing their minds every time that Antony makes a well-calculated pause in his speech. Antony takes care with his references to the conspirators: his first allusion to them as "honourable men" seems quite straightforward, but with each repetition the phrase gathers irony. It is a citizen, not Antony himself, who finally gives words to Antony's meaning: "They were traitors. Honourable men!" Antony cannot be faulted for his understanding of the psychology of crowds, and he easily achieves his desired end. He displays Caesar's body, and points to the many wounds. The citizens are provoked to the point of mutiny, and after Antony has read Caesar's will they riot, threatening the lives of the conspirators.

Questions and Exercises

1. What kind of rhetorical methods do both Brutus and Antony adopt in order to convince their audience? Which one do you like better? Give your reasons.
2. Act out the orations of Brutus and Antony in Act 3, Scene 2.

Hamlet, Prince of Denmark

(*Excerpt from* Act 3, Scene 1)

Hamlet:

To be, or not to be:[1] that is the question:[2]
Whether 'tis nobler in the mind to suffer
The slings and arrows of outrageous[3] fortune,
Or to take arms against a sea of troubles,[4]
And by opposing end them?[5] To die: to sleep;
No more;[6] and by a sleep to say we end
The heart-ache and the thousand natural shocks

That flesh is heir to, 'tis a consummation[7]
Devoutly to be wish'd. To die, to sleep;
To sleep: perchance to dream: ay, there's the rub;[8]
For in that sleep of death what dreams may come
When we have shuffled off[9] this mortal coil,[10]
Must give us pause:[11] there's the respect
That makes calamity of so long life;[12]
For who would bear the whips and scorns of time,[13]
The oppressor's wrong, the proud man's contumely,
The pangs of despised[14] love, the law's delay,
The insolence of office and the spurns[15]
That patient merit of the unworthy takes,[16]
When he himself might his quietus make[17]
With a bare bodkin?[18] Who would fardels bear,[19]
To grunt and sweat under a weary life,
But that[20] the dread of something after death,
The undiscover'd country from whose bourn[21]
No traveller returns, puzzles the will
And makes us rather bear those ills we have
Than fly to others that we know not of?
Thus conscience[22] does make cowards of us all;
And thus the native hue of resolution
Is sicklied o'er with the pale cast of thought,[23]
And enterprises of great pitch and moment[24]
With this regard[25] their currents turn awry,
And lose the name of action.[26]

Notes

[1] To be, or not to be: To live, or to die.

[2] the question: Hamlet expands in the next four lines by debating with himself which is the more honourable course—patiently to endure earthly misfortunes, or boldly to oppose them.

[3] outrageous: willful, very offensive, immoral.

[4] to take...troubles: The metaphor of fighting with human weapons against the superhuman force of the sea is an apt expression of Hamlet's sense of futility.

[5] by opposing end them: put an end to one's troubles by fighting against them rather than stoically enduring them.

[6] No more: That is all.

[7] consummation: final ending.

[8] rub: In the game of bowls, "rub" is anything that impedes the course of the bowl.

[9] shuffled off: got free from.

[10] this mortal coil: this whole business of earthly living.

[11] give us pause: make us stop to think. The subject of must give is "what dreams may come".

[12] there's the respect…of so long life: That's why misfortune goes on for so long.

[13] time: this temporal world.

[14] despised: unvalued.

[15] the spurns: scornful rejection or contemptuous refusal.

[16] That patient merit of the unworthy takes: The worthy person patiently receives the contemptuous scorns from the unworthy people.

[17] his quietus make: settle his final bill; get rid of the worldly sufferings.

[18] with a bare bodkin: with a mere short dagger.

[19] fardels bear: endure these burdens.

[20] but that: unless.

[21] bourn: frontier; boundary.

[22] conscience: awareness of our present situation; moral understanding.

[23] the native... thought: the natural colour of courage which is blood-red grows pale with too much thinking.

[24] enterprises of great pitch and moment: undertakings of vital importance.

[25] with this regard: on this account; because of such deliberation.

[26] lose the name of action: lose the honour that comes from action.

Commentary

In Shakespeare's play *Hamlet, Prince of Demark*, Old Hamlet, king of Denmark, is recently dead, and his brother Claudius has assumed the throne and married his widow Gertrude. Young Hamlet, returning from University at Wittenberg, learns from the ghost of his father that Claudius murdered him by pouring poison into his ear, and is commanded to avenge the murder without injuring Gertrude. Hamlet tells his friend Horatio and the guard Marcellus that he intends to feign madness, and swears them to secrecy. Immediately after his famous soliloquy of deliberation, he begins to repudiate Ophelia, whom he has loved while spied on by Claudius and Ophelia's father Polonius. He welcomes a troupe of visiting players, and arranges a performance of a play about fratricide, which Claudius breaks off, in apparently guilty and fearful fury, when the player appears to murder his uncle by pouring poison into his ear. Hamlet refrains from killing Claudius while he is at prayer, but stabs through the arras in his mother's bedroom, and mistakenly kills the old counsellor Polonius. Claudius sends Hamlet to England with sealed orders that he be killed on arrival. Hamlet outwits him, however, by returning to Denmark. During Hamlet's absence Ophelia has gone mad with grief from Hamlet's rejection of her and her father's death, and is found drowned. Her brother Laertes, having returned from France, determines to avenge his sister's death. Hamlet and Laertes meet in the graveyard where Ophelia is to be buried, and fight in her grave. Claudius arranges a fencing match between Hamlet and Laertes, giving the latter a poisoned sword; an exchange of weapons results in the deaths of both combatants. Gertrude has drunk a poisoned cup intended for her son, and the dying Hamlet has finally succeeded in killing Claudius.

Hamlet's speech "To be, or not to be" is famous mostly because it seems to be governed by reason rather than by frenzied emotion. Able to do little for completing his plan of revenge, Hamlet sparks an internal philosophical debate on the advantages and disadvantages of existence, and meditates whether or not it is right to get rid of the worldly troubles by ending one's own life. Hamlet asks the universal question for all dejected souls—is it nobler to live miserably or to end one's sorrows with a single stroke? He knows that the answer would be undoubtedly "yes" if death were just like a dreamless sleep. Yet, the "rub" Hamlet faces is the fear of what may come into our dreams, that is, the "dread of something after death".

It is said not without reason that the key-note of Hamlet's character is melancholy, and there can be no Hamlet without melancholy. But his melancholy is not the negative, over-subtle, fruitless kind. He seems to understand that his mere revenge upon his uncle would in no way solve the troubles that upset him. Revenge is easy, but it is not personal revenge that he seeks. Hamlet is a man of the Renaissance. The murder of his father and his uncle's usurpation brings him to the understanding that "The time is out of joint", and awakens him to the realization of a great responsibility, the reformation of the world as a whole. What Hamlet actually wishes to achieve will be to expose the roots of evil and to establish a reign of real justice.

Questions and Exercises

1. Why does sleep appear to be so fearful for Hamlet even though it can put an end to the numerous headaches in our life? Why would most people prefer to bear all the sufferings in life rather than choose death as a means to end them?
2. What stylistic methods are employed in the soliloquy? Rewrite this part in prose form.
3. Act out this dramatic monologue in class as if you did it on a stage.

Oscar Wilde

Oscar Wilde (1854—1900) was born in Dublin, Ireland, in 1854, went first to Trinity College, Dublin, majoring in classical studies, and then to Oxford, from which he graduated in 1878. Oscar Wilde's life story was as extraordinary as his literary career. His mother, Lady Jane Francesca Wilde, was a poet and journalist who wrote under the pen name of Sperenza. His father, Sir William Wilde, was an Irish antiquarian, gifted writer, and distinguished physician. Young Oscar settled down in London, and then visited Italy and Greece. Soon he established himself both as a writer and as a spokesman for the school of "Art for Art's Sake".

Wilde's reputation in the theater world began in 1892 with *Lady Windermere's Fan* (1892). In the years that followed he came out with a brilliant series of comedies of manners that combined polished social drama with sparklingly witty dialogue. After *A Woman of No Importance* (1893) and *An Ideal Husband* (1895), his best play *The Importance of Being Earnest* was produced in 1895 and hailed as the first modern comedy in English literature. The plot is extremely well-knit, but all about events of the most improbable and trivial significance in daily life. What Wilde took the London stage by storm with is his witty, epigrammatic style, insolent ease of utterance, and suave urbanity. With the production of these plays, Wilde reached the peak of his career.

Despite his theatrical triumph on the London stage, Wilde's personal life was much talked about and criticized by the English people of his time. His intimate association with Alfred Douglas brought about his tragic downfall. When Douglas' father charged Wilde with homosexuality in 1895, he was sentenced to two years of hard labor for the crime of sodomy. After his release from prison in 1897, Wilde left England and wandered around Europe for the last three years of his life. In 1900, he died of cerebral meningitis in a cheap Paris hotel at the age of 46.

The Importance of Being Earnest is Oscar Wilde's most successful play. According to some critics, few comedies of the English stage have as much wit and elegance. The plot is by no means complicated: Two young ladies love two gentlemen. These two gentlemen, for their respective reasons, have to invent false identities for themselves, otherwise they will not be able to get the ladies' love. One misunderstanding after another occurs, and what the audience gets is one surprise after another. The ending is very conventional: all the misunderstandings have been cleared up and the four lovers become two couples. The significance of the play lies in its jeering at the Victorian values, most of all, the idea of the so-called "earnestness".

The Importance of Being Earnest

(*Excerpt from* Act 1)

Jack: Charming day it has been, Miss Fairfax.

Gwendolen: Pray don't talk to me about the weather, Mr. Worthing. Whenever people talk to me about the weather, I always feel quite certain that they mean something else.

And that makes me so nervous.

Jack: I do mean something else.

Gwendolen: I thought so. In fact, I am never wrong.

Jack: And I would like to be allowed to take advantage of Lady Bracknell's temporary absence...

Gwendolen: I would certainly advise you to do so. Mamma has a way of coming back suddenly into a room that I have often had to speak to her about.

Jack: [*nervously*] Miss Fairfax, ever since I met you I have admired you more than any girl... I have ever met since... I met you.

Gwendolen: Yes, I am quite well aware of the fact. And I often wish that in public, at any rate, you had been more demonstrative. For me you have always had an irresistible fascination. Even before I met you I was far from indifferent to you. [*Jack looks at her in amazement.*] We live, as I hope you know, Mr. Worthing, in an age of ideals. The fact is constantly mentioned in the more expensive monthly magazines, and has reached the provincial pulpits,[1] I am told; and my ideal has always been to love some one of the name of Ernest. There is something in that name that inspires absolute confidence. The moment Algernon first mentioned to me that he had a friend called Ernest, I knew I was destined to love you.

Jack: You really love me, Gwendolen?

Gwendolen: Passionately!

Jack: Darling! You don't know how happy you've made me.

Gwendolen: My own Ernest!

Jack: But you don't really mean to say that you couldn't love me if my name wasn't Ernest?

Gwendolen: But your name is Ernest.

Jack: Yes, I know it is. But supposing it was something else? Do you mean to say you couldn't love me then?

Gwendolen: [*glibly*] Ah! that is clearly a metaphysical speculation,[2] and like most metaphysical speculations has very little reference at all to the actual facts of real life, as we know them.

Jack: Personally, darling, to speak quite candidly, I don't much care about the name of Ernest... I don't think the name suits me at all.

Gwendolen: It suits you perfectly. It is a divine name. It has a music of its own. It produces vibrations.

Jack: Well, really, Gwendolen, I must say that I think there are lots of other much nicer names. I think Jack, for instance, a charming name.

Gwendolen: Jack?... No, there is very little music in the name Jack, if any at all, indeed.

It does not thrill. It produces absolutely no vibrations... I have known several Jacks, and they all, without exception, were more than usually plain. Besides, Jack is a notorious domesticity[3] for John! And I pity any woman who is married to a man called John. She would probably never be allowed to know the entrancing[4] pleasure of a single moment's solitude. The only really safe name is Ernest

Jack: Gwendolen, I must get christened at once—I mean we must get married at once. There is no time to be lost.

Gwendolen: Married, Mr. Worthing?

Jack: [*astounded*] Well...surely. You know that I love you, and you led me to believe, Miss Fairfax, that you were not absolutely indifferent to me.

Gwendolen: I adore you. But you haven't proposed to me yet. Nothing has been said at all about marriage. The subject has not even been touched on.

Jack: Well...may I propose to you now?

Gwendolen: I think it would be an admirable opportunity. And to spare you any possible disappointment, Mr. Worthing, I think it only fair to tell you quite frankly before-hand that I am fully determined to accept you.

Jack: Gwendolen!

Gwendolen: Yes, Mr. Worthing, what have you got to say to me?

Jack: You know what I have got to say to you.

Gwendolen: Yes, but you don't say it.

Jack: Gwendolen, will you marry me? [*goes on his knees*]

Gwendolen: Of course I will, darling. How long you have been about it! I am afraid you have had very little experience in how to propose.

Jack: My own one, I have never loved any one in the world but you.

Gwendolen: Yes, but men often propose for practice. I know my brother Gerald does. All my girl-friends tell me so. What wonderfully blue eyes you have, Ernest! They are quite, quite, blue. I hope you will always look at me just like that, especially when there are other people present. [*Enter Lady Bracknell.*]

Lady Bracknell: Mr. Worthing! Rise, sir, from this semi-recumbent posture. It is most indecorous.[5]

Gwendolen: Mamma! [*He tries to rise; she restrains him.*] I must beg you to retire. This is no place for you. Besides, Mr. Worthing has not quite finished yet.

Lady Bracknell: Finished what, may I ask?

Gwendolen: I am engaged to Mr. Worthing, mamma. [*They rise together.*]

Lady Bracknell: Pardon me, you are not engaged to any one. When you do become engaged to some one, I, or your father, should his health permit him, will inform you of the fact. An engagement should come on a young girl as a surprise, pleasant or unpleasant, as the case may be. It is hardly a matter that she could be allowed to arrange for herself... And now I have a few questions to put to you, Mr. Worthing.

While I am making these inquiries, you, Gwendolen, will wait for me below in the carriage.

Gwendolen: [*reproachfully*] Mamma!

Lady Bracknell: In the carriage, Gwendolen! [*Gwendolen goes to the door. She and Jack blow kisses to each other behind Lady Bracknell's back. Lady Bracknell looks vaguely about as if she could not understand what the noise was. Finally turns round.*] Gwendolen, the carriage!

Gwendolen: Yes, mamma. [*goes out, looking back at Jack*]

Lady Bracknell: [*sitting down*] You can take a seat, Mr. Worthing. [*looks in her pocket for note-book and pencil*]

Jack: Thank you, Lady Bracknell, I prefer standing.

Lady Bracknell: [*pencil and note-book in hand*] I feel bound to tell you that you are not down on my list of eligible[6] young men, although I have the same list as the dear Duchess of Bolton has. We work together, in fact. However, I am quite ready to enter your name, should your answers be what a really affectionate mother requires. Do you smoke?

Jack: Well, yes, I must admit I smoke.

Lady Bracknell: I am glad to hear it. A man should always have an occupation of some kind. There are far too many idle men in London as it is. How old are you?

Jack: Twenty-nine.

Lady Bracknell: A very good age to be married at. I have always been of opinion that a man who desires to get married should know either everything or nothing. Which do you know?

Jack: [*after some hesitation*] I know nothing, Lady Bracknell.

Lady Bracknell: I am pleased to hear it. I do not approve of anything that tampers with[7] natural ignorance. Ignorance is like a delicate exotic fruit; touch it and the bloom is gone. The whole theory of modern education is radically unsound. Fortunately in England, at any rate, education produces no effect whatsoever. If it did, it would prove a serious danger to the upper classes, and probably lead to acts of violence in Grosvenor Square. What is your income?

Jack: Between seven and eight thousand a year.

Lady Bracknell: [*makes a note in her book*] In land, or in investments?

Jack: In investments, chiefly.

Lady Bracknell: That is satisfactory. What between the duties expected of one during one's lifetime, and the duties exacted from[8] one after one's death, land has ceased to be either a profit or a pleasure. It gives one position, and prevents one from keeping it up. That's all that can be said about land.

Jack: I have a country house with some land, of course, attached to it, about fifteen hundred acres, I believe; but I don't depend on that for my real income. In fact, as far as I can make out, the poachers are the only people who make anything out of it.

Lady Bracknell: A country house! How many bedrooms? Well, that point can be cleared up afterwards. You have a town house, I hope? A girl with a simple, unspoiled nature, like Gwendolen, could hardly be expected to reside in the country.

Jack: Well, I own a house in Belgrave Square, but it is let by the year to Lady Bloxham. Of course, I can get it back whenever I like, at six months' notice.

Lady Bracknell: Lady Bloxham? I don't know her.

Jack: Oh, she goes about very little. She is a lady considerably advanced in years.

Lady Bracknell: Ah, nowadays that is no guarantee of respectability of character. What number in Belgrave Square?

Jack: 149.

Lady Bracknell: [*shaking her head*] The unfashionable side. I thought there was something. However, that could easily be altered.

Jack: Do you mean the fashion, or the side?

Lady Bracknell: [*sternly*] Both, if necessary, I presume. What are your politics?

Jack: Well, I am afraid I really have none. I am a Liberal Unionist.

Lady Bracknell: Oh, they count as Tories. They dine with us. Or come in the evening, at any rate. Now to minor matters. Are your parents living?

Jack: I have lost both my parents.

Lady Bracknell: To lose one parent, Mr. Worthing, may be regarded as a misfortune; to lose both looks like carelessness. Who was your father? He was evidently a man of some wealth. Was he born in what the Radical papers call the purple of commerce,[9] or did he rise from the ranks of the aristocracy?

Jack: I am afraid I really don't know. The fact is, Lady Bracknell, I said I had lost my parents. It would be nearer the truth to say that my parents seem to have lost me... I don't actually know who I am by birth. I was... well, I was found.

Lady Bracknell: Found!

Jack: The late Mr. Thomas Cardew, an old gentleman of a very charitable and kindly disposition, found me, and gave me the name of Worthing, because he happened to have a first-class ticket for Worthing in his pocket at the time. Worthing is a place in Sussex. It is a seaside resort.

Lady Bracknell: Where did the charitable gentleman who had a first-class ticket for this seaside resort find you?

Jack: [*gravely*] In a hand-bag.

Lady Bracknell: A hand-bag?

Jack: [*very seriously*] Yes, Lady Bracknell. I was in a hand-bag—a somewhat large, black leather hand-bag, with handles to it—an ordinary hand-bag in fact.

Lady Bracknell: In what locality did this Mr. James, or Thomas, Cardew come across this ordinary hand-bag?

Jack: In the cloak-room at Victoria Station. It was given to him in mistake for his own.

Lady Bracknell: The cloak-room at Victoria Station?

Jack: Yes. The Brighton line.

Lady Bracknell: The line is immaterial.[10] Mr. Worthing, I confess I feel somewhat bewildered by what you have just told me. To be born, or at any rate bred, in a hand-bag, whether it had handles or not, seems to me to display a contempt for the ordinary decencies of family life that reminds one of the worst excesses of the French Revolution. And I presume you know what that unfortunate movement led to? As for the particular locality in which the hand-bag was found, a cloak-room at a railway station might serve to conceal a social indiscretion—has probably, indeed, been used for that purpose before now—but it could hardly be regarded as an assured basis for a recognized position in good society.

Jack: May I ask you then what you would advise me to do? I need hardly say I would do anything in the world to ensure Gwendolen's happiness.

Lady Bracknell: I would strongly advise you, Mr. Worthing, to try and acquire some relations as soon as possible, and to make a definite effort to produce at any rate one parent, of either sex, before the season is quite over.

Jack: Well, I don't see how I could possibly manage to do that. I can produce the hand-bag at any moment. It is in my dressing-room at home. I really think that should satisfy you, Lady Bracknell.

Lady Bracknell: Me, sir! What has it to do with me? You can hardly imagine that I and Lord Bracknell would dream of allowing our only daughter—a girl brought up with the utmost care—to marry into a cloak-room, and form an alliance with a parcel? Good morning, Mr. Worthing!

[*Lady Bracknell sweeps out in majestic indignation.*]

Jack: Good morning! [*Algernon, from the other room, strikes up*[11] *the Wedding March. Jack looks perfectly furious, and goes to the door.*] For goodness' sake don't play that ghastly tune, Algy. How idiotic you are!

[*The music stops, and Algernon enters cheerily.*]

Notes

[1] provincial pulpits: religious teachings in local churches.

[2] a metaphysical speculation: an abstract opinion based on a guessing process.

[3] a notorious domesticity: bad-famed liking for home life.

[4] entrancing: delightful; wonderful.

[5] semi-recumbent posture: half-kneeling or half standing manner of the body; indecorous: in bad taste or not in accordance with good manners.

[6] eligible: suitable (to be chosen as a would-be husband).

[7] tampers with: unnaturally pretend to have.
[8] exacted from: demanded the payment from.
[9] the purple of commerce: splendid wealth of being a businessman.
[10] immaterial: unimportant.
[11] strikes up: begins to act out.

Commentary

The above excerpt from Act 1 of *The Importance of Being Earnest* describes Jack's proposing to Gwendolen, daughter to Lady Bracknell, and the mother's arrogant interrogation of the young man. John Worthing (Jack), a rich young country squire, invents a very useful young brother called Ernest living in London, in order that he may be able to go up to town to seek pleasure as often as he likes. So his name is Jack in the country and Ernest in town. And this gives rise to a series of misunderstandings and comic scenes. Note the wit, humor, and satire in the highly comic dialogues, and the effective exposure of the haughtiness and snobbishness of Lady Bracknell, a female specimen of the English aristocratic-bourgeois class.

Questions and Exercises

1. How do you understand the title of the play? What is your impression of Gwendolen? What are the most striking traits in Lady Bracknell's character?
2. Act out this part of the play in groups in class, as if you were actually performing on the stage.

George Bernard Shaw

George Bernard Shaw (1856—1950) was born in Dublin, Ireland. He attended some schools, but he hated them and declared that he learned absolutely nothing in schools. When he was twenty years old, he moved to London, where he acquired much knowledge through self education. In 1891, he was deeply moved by Ibsen's play *A Doll's House* and determined to embark on drama writing.

He joined several literary and political societies, notably the Fabian society. This society preached the belief of constitutional and evolutionary socialism. He was a freethinker, a supporter of women's rights, and an advocate of equality of income, the abolition of private property. He also campaigned as a writer for the simplification of spelling and punctuation and the reform of the English alphabet. He was a well-known journalist and public speaker when his first play *The Widower's Houses* (1893) was published. Other plays followed: *Arms and the Man* (1898), *The Chocolate Soldier, You*

Never Can Tell (1898), *Mrs. Warren's Profession* (1898), *The Devil's Disciple* (1901), and *Caesar and Cleopatra* (1901), *Major Barbara* (1905), *Pygmalion* (1913), *Saint Joan* (1923), *The Apple Cart* (1929).

Shaw, a prolific writer, wrote 51 plays, most of which have become classical and frequently put on the stage. Like Ibsen, Shaw regarded plays as a means to an end, and this end is not just to bring pleasure to the audience, but to attack the various evils in the bourgeois world and the very foundations of capitalism. Shaw was awarded the Nobel Prize for Literature in 1925. He died at the age of 94 on November 2, 1950.

Social criticism characterizes almost all his fifty-one plays. He introduced to the stage such subjects as slum poverty, prostitution, war, religion, family disturbances, health, and economics—previously confined to political meetings, the courts, or the pulpit. Shaw's plays aimed at the minds of playgoers rather than at their emotions and physical sensations. He always raised questions in his works and demanded the audience to think about these questions themselves. No one before him had raised so many social questions on the stage, and his significant exposure of the capitalist society places him among the most important representatives of critical realism in modern English drama.

Pygmalion

(ACT III Excerpt)

THE PARLOR-MAID: [*opening the door*] Miss Doolittle. [*She withdraws.*]

HIGGINS: [*rising hastily and running to Mrs. Higgins*] Here she is, mother. [*He stands on tiptoe and makes signs over his mother's head to Eliza to indicate to her which lady is her hostess.*]

Eliza, who is exquisitely dressed, produces an impression of such remarkable distinction and beauty as she enters that they all rise, quite fluttered. Guided by Higgins's signals, she comes to Mrs. Higgins with studied grace.[1]

LIZA: [*speaking with pedantic correctness of pronunciation and great beauty of tone*] How do you do, Mrs. Higgins? [*She gasps slightly in making sure of the H in Higgins,*[2] *but is quite successful.*] Mr. Higgins told me I might come.

MRS. HIGGINS: [*cordially*] Quite right: I'm very glad indeed to see you.

PICKERING: How do you do, Miss Doolittle?

LIZA: [*shaking hands with him*] Colonel Pickering, is it not?

MRS. EYNSFORD HILL: I feel sure we have met before, Miss Doolittle. I remember your eyes.

LIZA: How do you do? [*She sits down on the ottoman gracefully in the place just left vacant by Higgins.*]

MRS. EYNSFORD HILL: [*introducing*] My daughter Clara.

LIZA: How do you do?

CLARA: [*impulsively*] How do you do? [*She sits down on the ottoman beside Eliza, devouring her with her eyes.*]

FREDDY: [*coming to their side of the ottoman*] I've certainly had the pleasure.[3]

MRS. EYNSFORD HILL: [*introducing*] My son Freddy.

LIZA: How do you do?

Freddy bows and sits down in the Elizabethan chair, infatuated.

HIGGINS: [*suddenly*] By George, yes: it all comes back to me! [*They stare at him.*] Covent Garden! [*lamentably*] What a damned thing![4]

MRS. HIGGINS: Henry, please! [*He is about to sit on the edge of the table.*] Don't sit on my writing-table: you'll break it.

HIGGINS: [*sulkily*] Sorry.

He goes to the divan, stumbling into the fender and over the fire-irons on his way; extricating himself with muttered imprecations; and finishing his disastrous journey by throwing himself so impatiently on the divan that he almost breaks it. Mrs. Higgins looks at him, but controls herself and says nothing.

A long and painful pause ensues.

MRS. HIGGINS: [*at last, conversationally*[5]] Will it rain, do you think?

LIZA: The shallow depression in the west of these islands is likely to move slowly in an easterly direction. There are no indications of any great change in the barometrical situation.[6]

FREDDY: Ha! ha! how awfully funny!

LIZA: What is wrong with that, young man? I bet I got it right.

FREDDY: Killing![7]

MRS. EYNSFORD HILL: I'm sure I hope it won't turn cold. There's so much influenza about. It runs right through our whole family regularly every spring.

LIZA: [*darkly*] My aunt died of influenza: so they said.

MRS. EYNSFORD HILL: [*clicks her tongue sympathetically*]!!!

LIZA: [*in the same tragic tone*] But it's my belief they done the old woman in.[8]

MRS. HIGGINS: [*puzzled*] Done her in?

LIZA: Y-e-e-e-es, Lord love you! Why should she die of influenza? She come through diphtheria right enough the year before. I saw her with my own eyes. Fairly blue with it, she was. They all thought she was dead; but my father he kept ladling gin down her throat til she came to so sudden that she bit the bowl off the spoon.[9]

MRS. EYNSFORD HILL: [*startled*] Dear me!

LIZA: [*piling up the indictment*[10]] What call[11] would a woman with that strength in her have to die of influenza? What become of her new straw hat that should have come to me? Somebody pinched it; and what I say is, them as pinched it done her in.[12]

MRS. EYNSFORD HILL: What does doing her in mean?

HIGGINS: [*hastily*] Oh, that's the new small talk.[13] To do a person in means to kill them.

MRS. EYNSFORD HILL: [*to Eliza, horrified*] You surely don't believe that your aunt was killed?

LIZA: Do I not! Them she lived with[14] would have killed her for a hat-pin, let alone a hat.

MRS. EYNSFORD HILL: But it cant have been right for your father to pour spirits[15] down her throat like that. It might have killed her.

LIZA: Not her. Gin was mother's milk to her. Besides, he'd poured so much down his own throat that he knew the good of it.

MRS. EYNSFORD HILL: Do you mean that he drank?

LIZA: Drank! My word! Something chronic.[16]

MRS. EYNSFORD HILL: How dreadful for you!

LIZA: Not a bit. It never did him no harm[17] what I could see. But then he did not keep it up regular.[18] [*cheerfully*] On the burst, as you might say, from time to time.[19] And always more agreeable when he had a drop in. When he was out of work, my mother used to give him fourpence and tell him to go out and not come back until he'd drunk himself cheerful and loving-like. There's lots of women has to make their husbands drunk to make them fit to live with.[20] [*now quite at her ease*] You see, it's like this. If a man has a bit of a conscience, it always takes him when he's sober; and then it makes him low-spirited. A drop of booze just takes that off and makes him happy. [*to Freddy, who is in convulsions of suppressed laughter*] Here! What are you sniggering at?

FREDDY: The new small talk. You do it so awfully well.

LIZA: If I was doing it proper, what was you laughing at?[21] [*to Higgins*] Have I said anything I oughtn't?

MRS. HIGGINS: [*interposing*] Not at all, Miss Doolittle.

LIZA: Well, that's a mercy,[22] anyhow. [*expansively*[23]] What I always say is—

HIGGINS: [*rising and looking at his watch*] Ahem!

LIZA: [*looking round at him; taking the hint; and rising*] Well: I must go. [*They all rise. Freddy goes to the door.*] So pleased to have met you.[24] Good-bye. [*She shakes hands with Mrs. Higgins.*]

MRS. HIGGINS: Good-bye.

LIZA: Good-bye, Colonel Pickering.

PICKERING: Good-bye, Miss Doolittle. [*They shake hands.*]

LIZA: [*nodding to the others*] Good-bye, all.

FREDDY: [*opening the door for her*] Are you walking across the Park, Miss Doolittle? If so—

LIZA: Walk! Not bloody likely.[25] [*sensation*] I am going in a taxi. [*She goes out.*]

Pickering gasps and sits down. Freddy goes out on the balcony to catch another glimpse of Eliza.

MRS. EYNSFORD HILL: [*suffering from shock*] Well, I really cant get used to the new ways.

CLARA: [*throwing herself discontentedly into the Elizabethan chair*] Oh, it's all right, mamma, quite right. People will think we never go anywhere or see anybody if you are so old-fashioned.

MRS. EYNSFORD HILL: I daresay I am very old-fashioned; but I do hope you won't begin using that expression, Clara. I have got accustomed to hear you talking about men as rotters, and calling everything filthy and beastly; though I do think it horrible and unlady-like. But this last[26] is really too much. Don't you think so, Colonel Pickering?

PICKERING: Dont ask me. Ive been away in India for several years; and manners have changed so much that I sometimes dont know whether Im at a respectable dinner-table or in a ship's forecastle. (注意：Don't, I've 这些词中省去"'"是萧伯纳故意的改革)

CLARA: It's all a matter of habit. There's no right or wrong in it. Nobody means anything by it. And it's so quaint, and gives such a smart emphasis to things that are not in themselves very witty. I find the new small talk delightful and quite innocent.

MRS. EYNSFORD HILL: [*rising*] Well, after that, I think it's time for us to go.

Notes

[1] studied grace: deliberately planned elegant manner.

[2] She gasps slightly in making sure of the H in Higgins: The sound [h] in London accent is not pronounced.

[3] I've certainly had the pleasure: I've certainly had the pleasure of meeting you.

[4] By George… What a damned thing: By God, I suddenly remember where we met. … It's such a boring thing to see you again.

[5] conversationally: for the sake of conversation.

[6] The shallow depression in the west of these islands…any great change in the barometrical situation: Liza is speaking in a very pedantic way about the weather condition just like a weatherman. these islands: the British Isles.

[7] Killing: Extremely funny.

[8] they done the old woman in: (nonstandard dialect) they killed the old lady. done: did.

[9] Why should she die of influenza? …she bit the bowl off the spoon: Liza uses a lot of nonstandard London dialect here. come: came. Fairly blue with it, she was: She was fairly blue with it. My father he: My father.

[10] piling up the indictment: accumulating more and more excitement.

[11] call: reason; cause.

[12] them as pinched it done her in: they that pinched it did her in.

[13] the new small talk: casual conversation for social intercourses. The opposite phrase is "large talk", which refers to formal business talk.

[14] Them she lived with: Those with whom she lived.

[15] spirits: alcohol.

[16] Something chronic: (London dialect) Very terrible, meaning it is his old habit to drink a lot.

[17] It never did him no harm: It did him no harm.

[18] regular: regularly.

[19] On the burst, as you might say, from time to time: Drinking a lot on unexpected occasions.

[20] There's lots of women has to make their husbands drunk to make them fit to live with: (nonstandard English) There are lots of women who have to make their husbands drunk to make them fit to live with.

[21] If I was doing it proper, what was you laughing at: If I was doing it properly, what were you laughing at?

[22] That's a mercy: thank God.

[23] expansively: increasingly excited.

[24] So pleased to have met you: Now she has resumed to use the graceful language that Higgins had taught her.

[25] Not bloody likely: Absolutely impossible. In upper class English, "bloody" is a very mean word to use.

[26] this last: this last expression. The word "bloody" is so horrifying that Mrs. Eynsford Hill does not want to repeat it.

Commentary

The original story of Pygmalion is drawn from Ovid's Greek mythology *Metamorphoses*. Pygmalion, the king of Cyprus and a sculptor as well, who mistrusted the virtue of women, and devoted most of his time to his art of sculpture. One day he created a statue of a woman with ivory and named her as Galatea. The sculptor loved his own creation so much that prayed to the goddess Aphrodite to give him a wife who resembled the statue. The goddess brought the statue itself to life. He finally marries the statue.

George Bernard Shaw used this mythology for his play *Pygmalion,* which was made into a musical in 1956 and a successful film version in 1964, both called *My Fair Lady*. Shaw's *Pygmalion* is a comedy about a phonetics expert who attempts to make a lady out of an uneducated Cockney flower-girl. Prof. Higgins tutors a poor Cockney flower girl, Eliza Doolittle, how to speak and behave like an upper-class lady. She originally belonged to the lower class. But at the moment she was accepted by the upper class, she felt on top of the world. Yet, Prof. Higgins' behaviors almost let her go back to the Hell, because she was still a neglected flower girl in Higgins' eye and was never respected. Unlike the Cyprus king who finally married his creation, Eliza decides to leave Higgins to keep her own independence. Just as Eliza said about herself, "The difference between a flower girl and a lady is not what she behaves but how she's treated."

Act III takes place during Mrs. Higgins' at-home party. Her son Henry shows up suddenly and explains to her that he wants to experiment on a common flower girl to see whether she can behave well like an upper-class lady. Eliza makes quite an impact on everyone with her studied grace and pedantic speech. Everything promises to go well until Mrs. Eynsford brings up the subject of influenza, which causes Eliza to launch into the topic of her own aunt, who supposedly died of influenza. In her over-shot excitement, her old accent, along with shocking facts such as her aunt's and father's alcoholism, slip out. From Eliza's first debut and debacle, we are shown an additional lesson that just speaking correctly is not enough to pass a flower girl off as a duchess.

Questions and Exercises

1. What is the Pygmalion myth? In what significant ways, and with what effect, has Shaw transformed that myth in his play?
2. It has been said that *Pygmalion* is not a play about turning a flower girl into a duchess, but one about turning a woman into a human being. Do you agree?
3. While Eliza Doolittle is being remade, Victorian society itself can be said to be unmade. How does Shaw reveal the pruderies, hypocrisies, and inconsistencies of this higher society to which the curbstone flower girl aspires? Do Shaw's sympathies lie with the lower class or upper class?

Eugene O'Neill

Eugene O'Neill (1888—1953) was the son of a celebrated romantic actor in a traveling theatre company, best known for his role as the Count of Monte Cristo. Eugene happened to be born in New York while his father was performing there. He spent his childhood on trains, in hotels or backstage in theatres. In 1906 he entered Princeton University, but he only stayed there for one year. He left it in order to start what he called his "real-education", i.e. experiences of life. He became a seaman, and for five years he traveled all over the world, doing all sorts of hard jobs in many different countries. All the time, he observed and learned about the life of rough, uneducated workers, brooding about the various ironies which fate played in their lives.

O'Neill is unquestionably America's greatest playwright, and received the Nobel Prize for Literature in 1936. He was the first American playwright to regard drama as serious literature and the first one to write tragedies consistently. He saw the theatre as a place to present profound ideas.

O'Neill wrote forty-five plays which were highly experimental in form and style, combining together literary theories of symbolism, naturalism and expressionism. He had a great influence on later American playwrights, and on those of other countries. Next to Shakespeare and Shaw, O'Neill's plays are the most widely translated and produced in the world. About twenty of O'Neill's plays are considered as major works, the best of which include *The Emperor Jones* (1920), *The Hairy Ape* (1922), *Desire Under the Elms* (1924), *Long Day's Journey Into Night* (1956).

He wrote on many subjects and in a wide variety of styles. His plays ranged from one act long to eleven acts long, the latter having to be presented throughout a whole afternoon and evening, with a break for dinner.

The Hairy Ape

Scene 7

Nearly a month later. An I. W. W. local[1] *near the waterfront, showing the interior of a front room on the ground floor, and the street outside. Moonlight on the narrow street, buildings massed in black shadow. The interior of the room, which is general assembly room, office, and reading room, resembles some dingy settlement boys' club. A desk and high stool are in one corner. A table with papers, stacks of pamphlets, chairs about it, is at center. The whole is decidedly cheap and commonplace and unmysterious as a room could well be. The Secretary is perched on the stool making entries in a large ledger. An eye shade casts his face into shadows.*[2] *Eight or ten men, longshoremen, iron workers, and the like, are grouped about the table. Two are playing checkers. One is writing a letter. Most of them are smoking pipes. A big signboard is on the wall at the rear, "Industrial Workers of the World—Local No. 57."*

Yank comes down the street outside. He is dressed as in Scene 5. He moves cautiously, mysteriously. He comes to a point opposite the door; tiptoes softly up to it, listens, is impressed by the silence within, knocks carefully, as if he were guessing at the password to some secret rite. Listens. No answer. Knocks again a bit louder. No answer. Knocks impatiently, much louder.

Secretary: [*turning around on his stool*] What the hell is that—someone knocking? [*shouts*] Come in, why don't you? [*All the men in the room look up.* Yank *opens the door slowly, gingerly, as if afraid of an ambush. He looks around for secret doors, mystery, is taken aback by the commonplaceness of the room and the men in it, thinks he may have gotten in the wrong place, then sees the* *signboard on the wall and is reassured.*]

Yank: [*blurts out*] Hello.

Men: [*reservedly*] Hello.

Yank: [*more easily*] I tought I'd bumped into de wrong dump.[3]

Secretary: [*scrutinizing him carefully*] Maybe you have. Are you a member?

Yank: Naw, not yet. Dat's[4] what I come for—to join.

Secretary: That's easy. What's your job—longshore?

Yank: Naw. Fireman—stoker on de liners.

Secretary: [*with satisfaction*] Welcome to our city. Glad to know you people are waking up at last. We haven't got many members in your line.

Yank: Naw. Dey're all dead to de woild.[5]

Secretary: Well, you can help to wake 'em. What's your name? I'll make out your card.

Yank: [*confused*] Name? Lemme tink.[6]

Secretary: [*sharply*] Don't you know your own name?

Yank: Sure, but I been just Yank for so long—Bob, dat's it—Bob Smith.

Secretary: [*writing*] Robert Smith. [*fills out the rest of card*] Here you are. Cost you half a dollar.

Yank: Is dat all—four bits?[7] Dat's easy. [*gives the Secretary the money*]

Secretary: [*throwing it in drawer*] Thanks. Well, make yourself at home. No introductions needed. There's literature on the table. Take some of those pamphlets with you to distribute aboard ship. They may bring results. Sow the seed, only go about it right. Don't get caught and fired. We got plenty out of work. What we need is men who can hold their jobs—and work for us at the same time.

Yank: Sure. [*But he still stands, embarrassed and uneasy.*]

Secretary: [*looking at him—curiously*] What did you knock for? Think we had a coon [8] in uniform to open doors?

Yank: Naw. I tought it was locked—and dat yuh'd wanter give me the once-over trou a peep-hole or somep'n to see if I was right.[9]

Secretary: [*alert and suspicious but with an easy laugh*] Think we were running a crap game?[10] That door is never locked. What put that in your nut?

Yank: [*with a knowing grin, convinced that this is all camouflage, a part of the secrecy*] Dis burg is full of bulls, ain't it? [11]

Secretary: [*sharply*] What have the cops got to do with us? We're breaking no laws.

Yank: [*with a knowing wink*] Sure. Youse wouldn't for woilds.[12] Sure. I'm wise to dat.

Secretary: You seem to be wise to a lot of stuff none of us knows about.

Yank: [*with another wink*] Aw, dat's aw right, see. [*Then made a bit resentful by the suspicious glances from all sides.*] Aw, can it! Youse needn't put me trou de toid degree.[13] Can't youse see I belong? Sure! I'm reg'lar. I'll stick, get me? I'll shoot de woiks for youse. Dat's why I wanted to join in.

Secretary: [*breezily, feeling him out*[14]] That's the right spirit. Only are you sure you understand what you've joined? It's all plain and above board; still, some guys get a wrong slant on us. [*sharply*] What's your notion of the purpose of the I.W.W.?

Yank: Aw, I know all about it.

Secretary: [*sarcastically*] Well, give us some of your valuable information.

Yank: [*cunningly*] I know enough not to speak outa my toin. [15] [*then resentfully again*] Aw, say! I'm reg'lar. I'm wise to de game. I know yuh got to watch your step wit a stranger. For all youse know, I might be a plain-clothes dick, or somep'n, dat's what yuh're tinkin', huh? Aw, forget it! I belong, see? Ask any guy down to de docks if I don't.

Secretary: Who said you didn't?

Yank: After I'm 'nitiated, I'll show yuh.

Secretary: [*astounded*] Initiated? There's no initiation.

Yank: [*disappointed*] Ain't there no password—no grip[16] nor nothin'?

Secretary: What'd you think this is—the Elks—or the Black Hand?[17]

Yank: De Elks, hell! De Black Hand, dey're a lot of yellow backstickin' Ginees.[18] Naw. Dis is a man's gang, ain't it?

Secretary: You said it! That's why we stand on our two feet in the open.[19] We got no secrets.

Yank: [*surprised but admiringly*] Yuh mean to say yuh always run wide open—like dis?

Secretary: Exactly.

Yank: Den yuh sure got your noive wit youse! [20]

Secretary: [*sharply*] Just what was it made you want to join us? Come out with that straight.

Yank: Yuh call me? Well, I got noive, too! Here's my hand. Yuh wanter blow tings up, don't yuh? Well, dat's me! I belong!

Secretary: [*with pretended carelessness*] You mean change the unequal conditions of society by legitimate direct action—or with dynamite?

Yank: Dynamite! Blow it often de oith—steel—all de cages—all de factories, steamers, buildings, jails—de Steel Trust and all dat makes it go.[21]

Secretary: So—that's your idea, eh? And did you have any special job in that line you wanted to propose to us? [*He makes a sign to the men, who get up cautiously one by one and group behind Yank.*]

Yank: [*boldly*] Sure, I'll come out wit it. I'll show youse I'm one of de gang. Dere's dat millionaire guy, Douglas—

Secretary: President of the Steel Trust, you mean? Do you want to assassinate him?

Yank: Naw, dat don't get yuh nothin'. I mean blow up de factory, de woiks, where he makes de steel. Dat's what I'm after—to blow up de steel, knock all de steel in de woild up to de moon. Dat'll fix tings! [*eagerly, with a touch of bravado*] I'll do it by me lonesome! I'll show yuh! Tell me where his woiks is, how to git there, all de dope.[22] Gimme de stuff, de old butter—and watch me do de rest![23] Watch de smoke and see it move! I don't give a damn if dey nab me—long as it's done! I'll soive life for it—and give 'em de laugh![24] [*half to himself*] And I'll write her a letter and tell her de hairy ape done it. Dat'll square tings.[25]

Secretary: [*stepping away from Yank*] Very interesting. [*He gives a signal. The men, huskies all, throw themselves on Yank and before he knows it they have his legs and arms pinioned. But he is too flabbergasted to make a struggle, anyway. They feel him over for weapons.*]

Man: No gat, no knife. Shall we give him what's what and put the boots to him?[26]

Secretary: No. He isn't worth the trouble we'd get into. He's too stupid. [*He comes closer and laughs mockingly in Yank's face*] Ho-ho! By God, this is the biggest joke they've put up on us yet. Hey, you Joke! Who sent you—Burns or Pinkerton?[27] No, by God, you're such a bonehead I'll bet you're in the Secret Service! Well, you dirty spy, you rotten agent provocator, you can go back and tell whatever skunk is paying you blood-money for betraying your brothers that he's wasting his coin. You couldn't catch a cold.[28] And tell him that all he'll ever get on us, or ever has got, is just his own sneaking plots that he's framed up to put us in jail. We are what our manifesto says we are, neither more nor less—and we'll give him a copy of that any time he calls. And as for you—[*He glares scornfully at Yank, who is sunk in an oblivious stupor.*] Oh, hell, what's the use of talking? You're a brainless ape.

Yank: [*aroused by the word to fierce but futile struggles*] What's dat, yuh Sheeny bum, yuh![29]

Secretary: Throw him out, boys. [*In spite of his struggles, this is done with gusto and eclat. Propelled by several parting kicks, Yank lands sprawling in the middle of the narrow cobbled street. With a growl he starts to get up and storm the closed door, but stops bewildered by the confusion in his brain, pathetically impotent. He sits there, brooding, in as near to the attitude of Rodin's "The Thinker"*[30] *as he can get in his position.*]

Yank: [*bitterly*] So dem boids[31] don't tink I belong, neider. Aw, to hell wit 'em! Dey're in de wrong pew—de same old bull—soapboxes and Salvation Army[32]—no guts! Cut out an hour often de job a day and make me happy! Gimme a dollar more a day and make me happy! Tree square a day, and cauliflowers in de front yard—ekal rights[33]—a woman and kids—a lousy vote—and I'm all fixed for Jesus, huh? Aw, hell! What does dat get yuh? Dis ting's in your inside, but it ain't your belly. Feedin' your face—sinkers and coffee—dat don't touch it.[34] It's way down—at de bottom. Yuh can't grab it, and yuh can't stop it. It moves, and everyting moves. It stops and de whole woild stops. Dat's me now—I don't tick,[35]see? —I'm a busted Ingersoll[36], dat's what. Steel was me, and I owned de woild. Now I ain't steel, and de woild owns me. Aw, hell! I can't see—it's all dark, get me? It's all wrong! [*He turns a bitter mocking face up like an ape gibbering at the moon.*] Say, youse up dere, Man in de Moon, yuh look so wise, gimme de answer, huh? Slip me de inside dope, de information right from de stable—where do I get off at, huh?

A Policeman: [*who has come up the street in time to hear this last—with grim humor*] You'll get off at the station, you boob, if you don't get up out of that and keep movin'.

Yank: [*looking up at him—with a hard, bitter laugh*] Sure. Lock me up! Put me in a cage! Dat's de on'y answer yuh know. G'wan, lock me up![37]

Policeman: What you been doin'?

Yank: Enuf to gimme life for![38] I was born, see? Sure, dat's de charge. Write it in de blotter. I was born, get me!

Policeman: [*jocosely*] God pity your old woman! [*then matter-of-fact*] But I've no time for kidding. You're soused. I'd run you in but it's too long a walk to the station. Come on now, get up, or I'll fan your ears with this club. Beat it now! [*He hauls* Yank *to his feet.*]

Yank: [*in a vague mocking tone*] Say, where do I go from here?

Policeman: [*giving him a push—with a grin, indifferently*] Go to hell.

CURTAIN

Notes

[1] An I.W.W. local: A local branch of the Industrial Workers of the World.

[2] An eye shade casts his face into shadows: His face is covered in shadows with something worn on the head above the eyes to keep out light.

[3] I tought I'd bumped into de wrong dump: I thought I'd come into the wrong place.

[4] Dat's: That's.

[5] Naw. Dey're all dead to de woild: No. They are all numb and insensitive to this world.

[6] Lemme tink: Let me think.

[7] four bits: four coins of 12.5 cents.

[8] coon: nigger.

[9] dat yuh'd wanter give me the once-over trou a peep-hole or somep'n to see if I was right: that you'd want to give me the quick glance through a peep-hole or something to see if I was a good man.

[10] a crap game: gambling game.

[11] Dis burg is full of bulls, ain't it: This city is full of policemen, isn't it?

[12] Youse wouldn't for woilds: You would never on earth break laws.

[13] Youse needn't put me trou de toid degree: You needn't cross-examine me. Toid degree: third degree—the rough treatment of a prisoner by the police in order to obtain information or a statement of guilt.

[14] feeling him out: testing or sounding out; trying to find out his opinion or real intention.

[15] speak outa my toin: speak out my real intention. toin: turn.

[16] grip: signaling gesture of the hand.

[17] the Elks, the Black Hand: the names of two underworld organizations.

[18] dey're a lot of yellow backstickin' Ginees: they are a group of cowardly Italians.

[19] stand on our two feet in the open: are honest and open to the public without any secrets.

[20] Den yuh sure got your noive wit youse: Then you sure got your courage with you! noive: nerve.

[21] Blow it often de oith…and all dat makes it go: Blow it off the earth—steel mills—all the iron cages—all the factories, steamers, buildings, jails—the Steel Trust and all that makes it go.

[22] dope: information.

[23] Gimme de stuff, de old butter—and watch me do de rest: Just give me the things needed and the explosives, and then watch me do the rest.

[24] I'll soive life for it—and give 'em de laugh: I'm willing to stay in jail all my life to show my scorn at them by so doing. soive: serve.

[25] Dat'll square tings: That will even my revenge.

[26] Shall we give him what's what and put the boots to him: Shall we just teach him a lesson, and kick him out?

[27] Burns or Pinkerton: the names of private detectives.

[28] You couldn't catch a cold: you can get nothing from it.

[29] yuh Sheeny bum: you Jewish rascal.

[30] Rodin's *"The Thinker"*: (French: "Le Penseur") one of Auguste Rodin's famous bronze sculptures, which depicts a man in sober meditation battling with a powerful internal struggle.

[31] dem boids: those boys (guys).

[32] Salvation Army: The Salvation Army, an international movement, is an evangelical part of the universal Christian Church. At the heart of every Salvation Army program is a practical hand of assistance for the poor.

[33] Tree square a day, and cauliflowers in de front yard—ekal rights: Three square meals a day, and plant some cauliflowers in the front yard—equal rights.

[34] Dis ting's in your inside, but it ain't your belly. Feedin' your face—sinkers and coffee—dat don't touch it: The whole business is in your heart, it isn't in your belly. Feeding you on the surface by supplying you with fried dough and coffee—that has nothing to do with it.

[35] tick: complain.

[36] busted Ingersoll: worthless Ingersoll, who was once an American lawyer, orator, and

an advocator of agnosticism.

[37] G'wan, lock me up: Go on and put me into prison!

[38] Enuf to gimme life for: Enough to give me a life sentence.

Commentary

O'Neill's great purpose was to try and discover the root of human desires and frustrations. He wanted contemporary American drama to achieve the power of ancient Greek tragedies. Most of the characters in his plays are seeking meaning and purpose in their lives, some through love, some through religion, and some through revenge, but all met disappointment. *The Hairy Ape* with its eight scenes is very illustrative of this theme.

Scene 1 takes place deep inside a large passenger ship where the firemen who stoke the ship's engines with coal. Their living space is so low that they cannot stand up straight and their posture is ape-like. Yank, the hero, is bitter about the cruel conditions of the workers, but he tells them to be proud of their work, and glorifies himself as a man of steel, strength and muscle.

Scene 2 takes place on the passenger deck. There are two women: Mildred, aged 20, is a delicate, pale, pretty girl in a white dress, who appears discontented and disdainful; her aunt is a fat, rich old lady who is pompous and proud. The women are quarrelling. Mildred wishes to help the poor, and is interested to learn about the lives of the ship's workers. She has received permission from the officers to visit the engine room. Her aunt accuses her of being frivolous and insincere.

Scene 3 takes places in the ship's "stoke-hole". The men are doing a back-breaking job by shoveling coal amid noise and heat. The men are dumbfounded when Mildred appears in her white dress. Yank delivers a furious, murderous speech against the boss before he sees her. Mildred is shocked by the brutal, half-naked man. She calls Yank a hairy ape and begs the officers to take her away.

Scene 4 takes place in the firemen's living quarters. The men think that the officers have treated them as monkeys in a zoo instead of giving them the dignity of honest workers. They accuse Yank of falling in love with Mildred, just to tease him. He boasts that he will show her who is superior, but he really wants revenge.

Scene 5 takes place in a fashionable part of New York, on a Sunday. Yank and a comrade, dirty and unshaven, look at the shops and compare the wealth with their own lives. A crowd of rich people come out of a church, and discuss the sermon which has been against radicals. Yank insults them. The police come; they beat and arrest him.

Scene 6 is in a prison on an island. Yank, still suffering from the beating, is behind bars, like an aged animal. He considers himself innocent. He learns from other prisoners that Mildred's grandfather is a big capitalist of the steel industry, famous for suppressing labor unions. Yank swears revenge and tries to break out of the prison, but the guards come with water hoses to prevent him.

In Scene 7, Yank tries to join the labor union named the Industrial Workers of the World (I. W. W.) in order to bomb the capitalist steel magnate for revenge. The union officials think he is mad and throw him out on the street. Yank feels bitter and confused.

In Scene 8, Yank goes to the zoo at night. He talks to the gorilla and agrees that they are brothers. In his sympathy for the caged animal, he sets it free. But the great hairy ape kills him mercilessly.

The main character Yank initially attempts to seek meaning and purpose in his life. Unable to realize his dream, he strives to take revenge on the upper class oppressors, but with the result of complete disappointment. The tone of this play is very pessimistic, leaving the hero without any illusion or hope for life.

Questions and Exercises

1. Yank assumes more than once the posture of Rodin's "The Thinker" in the play. What does it have to do with the play's motif and tone? What are the major images and symbols employed in the play to dramatize the theme?
2. Why do you think the play is subtitled "A Comedy of Ancient and Modern Life in Eight Scenes"? Write a short essay about the importance of identity as a human being.

Arthur Miller

Arthur Miller (1915—2005) was born in a middle class Jewish family in New York. He finished high school during the Depression when his father's small business failed and the family suddenly became poor. After leaving high school, Miller started a series of jobs—as a truck driver, a crewman on a tanker, a waiter, and in an auto-parts warehouse at a wage of 15 dollars a week. While working, he saw the injustices of the capitalist system and the hardships of the workers.

As a playwright, Arthur Miller was regarded as a titan of American theater and was revered for works that spoke for the common man. Miller's personal life, including a stormy marriage to sex symbol Marilyn Monroe, often captivated America.

In 1949 he won a Pulitzer Prize with his masterpiece *Death of a Salesman* and achieved an international reputation. It is the story of a traveling salesman—a metaphor for American society—who chooses popularity and getting rich as the false goals for his life and is finally driven to suicide. Miller believes that the common man is the tragic hero of modern times. Critics early linked him with the Ibsenite "problem play".

Death of a Salesman

[*The knocking is heard again. He takes a few steps away from her, and she vanishes into the wing. The light follows him, and now he is facing young* BIFF, *who carries a suitcase.* BIFF *steps toward him. The music is gone.*]

Biff: Why didn't you answer?

Willy: Biff! What are you doing in Boston?

Biff: Why didn't you answer! I've been knocking for five minutes, I called you on the phone—

Willy: I just heard you. I was in the bathroom and had the door shut. Did anything happen home?

Biff: Dad—I let you down.

Willy: What do you mean?

Biff: Dad...

Willy: Biff, what's this about? [*putting his arm around* BIFF] Come on, let's go downstairs and get you a malted.[1]

Biff: Dad, I flunked math.

Willy: Not for the term?

Biff: The term. I haven't got enough credits to graduate.

Willy: You mean to say Bernard wouldn't give you the answers?

Biff: He did, he tried, but I only got a sixty-one.

Willy: And they wouldn't give you four points?

Biff: Birnbaum refused absolutely. I begged him. Pop, but he won't give me those points. You gotta talk to him before they close the school. Because if he saw the kind of man you are, and you just talked to him in your way, I'm sure he'd come through for me. The class came right before practice, see, and I didn't go enough. Would you talk to him? He'd like you, Pop. You know the way you could talk.

Willy: You're on.[2] We'll drive right back.

Biff: Oh, Dad, good work! I'm sure he'll change it for you!

Willy: Go downstairs and tell the clerk I'm checkin' out.[3] Go right down.

Biff: Yes, sir! See, the reason he hates me. Pop—one day he was late for class so I got up at the blackboard and imitated him. I crossed my eyes and talked with a lithe.

Willy: [*laughing*] You did? The kids like it?

Biff: They nearly died laughing!

Willy: Yeah? What'd you do?

Biff: The thquare root of thixthy twee is... [WILLY *bursts out laughing;* BIFF *joins him.*] And in the middle of it he walked in! [WILLY *laughs and* THE WOMAN *joins in offstage.*]

Willy: [*without hesitation*] Hurry downstairs and—

Biff: Somebody in there?

Willy: No, that was next door. [The WOMAN *laughs offstage*.]

Biff: Somebody got in your bathroom!

Willy: No, it's the next room, there's a party—

The Woman: [*Enters, laughing. She lisps this.*] Can I come in? There's something in the bathtub, Willy, and it's moving!

[WILLY *looks at* BIFF, *who is staring open-mouthed and horrified at* THE WOMAN.]

Willy: Ah—you better go back to your room. They must be finished painting by now. They're painting her room so I let her take a shower here. Go back, go back... [*He pushes her.*]

The Woman: [*resisting*] But I've got to get dressed, Willy, I can't—

Willy: Get out of here! Go back, go back... [*suddenly striving for the ordinary*] This is Miss Francis, Biff, she's a buyer. They're painting her room. Go back, Miss Francis, go back...

The Woman: But my clothes, I can't go out naked in the hall!

Willy: [*pushing her off stage*] Get outa here! Go back, go back!

[BIFF *slowly sits down on his suitcase as the argument continues off-stage.*]

The Woman: Where's my stockings? You promised me stockings, Willy!

Willy: I have no stockings here!

The Woman: You had two boxes of size nine sheers for me, and I want them!

Willy: Here, for God's sake, will you get outa here!

The Woman: [*enters holding a box of stockings*] I just hope there's nobody in the hall. That's all I hope. [*to* BIFF] Are you football or baseball?

Biff: Football.

The Woman: [*angry, humiliated*] That's me too. G'night. [*She snatches her clothes from* WILLY, *and walks out.*]

Willy: [*after a pause*] Well, better get going. I want to get to the school first thing in the morning. Get my suits out of the closet. I'll get my valise. [BIFF *doesn't move.*] What's the matter? [BIFF *remains motionless, tears falling.*] She's a buyer. Buys for J. H. Simmons. She lives down the hall—they're painting. You don't imagine—[*He breaks off. After a pause.*] Now listen, pal, she's just a buyer. She sees merchandise in her room and they have to keep it looking just so... [*Pause. Assuming command.*] All right, get my suits. [BIFF *doesn't move.*] Now stop crying and do as I say. I gave you an order. Biff, I gave you an order! Is that what you do when I give you an order? How dare you cry? [*putting his arm around* BIFF] Now look, Biff, when you grow up you'll understand about these things. You mustn't—you mustn't over-emphasize a thing like this. I'll see Birnbaum first thing in the morning.

Biff: Never mind.

Willy: [*getting down beside* BIFF] Never mind! He's going to give you those points. I'll see to it.

Biff: He wouldn't listen to you.

Willy: He certainly will listen to me. You need those points for the U. of Virginia.

Biff: I'm not going there.

Willy: Heh? If I can't get him to change that mark you'll make it up in Summer school. You've got all summer to—

Biff: [*his weeping breaking from him*] Dad...

Willy: [*infected by it*] Oh, my boy...

Biff: Dad...

Willy: She's nothing to me. Biff, I was lonely, I was terribly lonely.

Biff: You—you gave her Mama's stockings! [*His tears break through and he rises to go.*]

Willy: [*grabbing for* BIFF] I gave you an order!

Biff: Don't touch me, you—liar!

Willy: Apologize for that!

Biff: You fake! You phony little fake![4] You fake! [*Overcome, he turns quickly and weeping fully goes out with his suitcase.* WILLY *is left on the floor on his knees.*]

Willy: I gave you an order! Biff, come back here or I'll beat you! Come back here! I'll whip you! [STANLEY *comes quickly in from the right and stands in front of* WILLY.]

Willy: [*shouts at* STANLEY]: I gave you an order...

Stanley: Hey, let's pick it up, pick it up, Mr Loman. [*He helps* WILLY *to his feet.*] Your boys left with the chippies. They said they'll see you home.

[*A second waiter watches some distance away.*]

Willy: But we were supposed to have dinner together. [*Music is heard,* WILLY*'s theme.*]

Stanley: Can you make it?

Willy: I'll—sure, I can make it. [*Suddenly concerned about his clothes*.] Do I—I look all right?

Stanley: Sure, you look all right. [*He flicks a speck off* WILLY's *lapel.*]

Willy: Here—here's a dollar.

Stanley: Oh, your son paid me. It's all right.

Willy: [*putting it in* Stanley's *hand*] No, take it. You're a good boy.

Stanley: Oh, no, you don't have to...

Willy: Here—here's some more. I don't need it any more. [*after a slight pause*] Tell me—is there a seed store in the neighborhood?

Stanley: Seeds? You mean like to plant? [*As* WILLY *turns,* STANLEY *slips the money back into his jacket pocket.*]

Willy: Yes. Carrots, peas...

Stanley: Well, there's hardware stores on Sixth Avenue, but it may be too late now.

Willy: [*anxiously*] Oh, I'd better hurry. I've got to get some seeds. [*He starts off to the* *right.*] I've got to get some seeds, right away. Nothing's planted. I don't have a thing in the ground. [WILLY *hurries out as the light goes down.* STANLEY *moves over to the right after him, watches him off. The other waiter has been staring at* WILLY.]

Stanley: [*to the waiter*] Well, whatta you looking at?

[*The waiter picks up the chairs and moves off right.* STANLEY *takes the table and follows him. The light fades on this area. There is a long pause, the sound of the flute coming over. The light gradually rises on the kitchen, which is empty.* HAPPY *appears at the door of the house, followed by* BIFF. HAPPY *is carrying a large bunch of long-stemmed roses. He enters the kitchen, looks around for* LINDA. *Not seeing her, he turns to* BIFF, *who is just outside the house door, and makes a gesture with his hands, indicating "Not here, I guess". He looks into the living-room and freezes. Inside,* LINDA, *unseen, is seated,* Willy's *coat on her lap. She rises ominously and quietly moves toward* HAPPY, *who backs up into the kitchen, afraid.*]

Happy: Hey, what're you doing up? [LINDA *says nothing but moves toward him implacably.*] Where's Pop? [*He keeps backing to the right, and now* LINDA *is in full view in the doorway to the living room.*] Is he sleeping?

Linda: Where were you?

Happy: [*trying to laugh it off*] We met two girls, Mom, very fine types. Here, we brought you some flowers. [*Offering them to her.*] Put them in your room, Mom.

[*She knocks them to the floor at* BIFF'*s feet. He has now come inside and closed the door behind him. She stares at* BIFF, *silently.*]

Happy: Now what'd you do that for? Mom, I want you to have some flowers—

Linda: [*cutting* HAPPY *off, violently to* BIFF] Don' t you care whether he lives or dies?

Happy: [*going to the stairs*] Come upstairs, Biff.

Biff: [*with a flare of disgust, to* HAPPY] Go away from me! [*to* LINDA] What do you mean, lives or dies? Nobody's dying around here, pal.

Linda: Get out of my sight! Get out of here!

Biff: I wanna see the boss.

Linda: You're not going near him!

Biff: Where is he? [*He moves into the living-room and* LINDA *follows.*]

Linda: [*shouting after* BIFF] You invite him to dinner. He looks forward to it all day—[BIFF *appears in his parents' bedroom, looks around, and exits.*]—and then you desert him there. There's no stranger you'd do that to!

Happy: Why? He had a swell time with us. Listen, when I—[LINDA *comes back into the kitchen.*]—desert him I hope I don't outlive the day!

Linda: Get out of here!

Happy: Now look, Mom...

Linda: Did you have to go to women tonight? You and your lousy rotten whores!

[BIFF *re-enters the kitchen.*]

Happy: Mom, all we did was follow Biff around trying to cheer him up! [*to* BIFF] Boy, what a night you gave me!

Linda: Get out of here, both of you, and don't come back! I don't want you tormenting him any more. Go on now, get your things together! [*to* BIFF You can sleep in his apartment. [*She starts to pick up the flowers and stops herself.*] Pick up this stuff, I'm not your maid any more. Pick it up, you bum,[5] you! [HAPPY *turns his back to her in refusal.* BIFF *slowly moves over and gets down on his knees, picking up the flowers.*]

Linda: You're a pair of animals! Not one, not another living soul would have had the cruelty to walk out on that man in a restaurant!

Biff: [*not looking at her*] Is that what he said?

Linda: He didn't have to say anything. He was so humiliated he nearly limped when he came in.

Happy: But, Mom, he had a great time with us—

Biff: [*cutting him off violently*] Shut up! [*Without another word,* HAPPY *goes upstairs.*]

Linda: You! You didn't even go in to see if he was all right!

Biff: [*still on the floor in front of* LINDA, *the flowers in his hand: with self-loathing*] No. Didn't. Didn't do a damned thing. How do you like that, heh? Left him babbling in a toilet.

Linda: You louse. You...

Biff: Now you hit it on the nose! [*He gets up, throws the flowers in the wastebasket.*] The scum of the earth, and you're looking at him!

Linda: Get out of here!

Biff: I gotta talk to the boss. Mom. Where is he?

Linda: You're not going near him. Get out of this house!

Biff: [*with absolute assurance, determination*] No. We're gonna have an abrupt conversation, him and me.

Linda: You're not talking to him! [*Hammering is heard from outside the house, off right.* BIFF *turns toward the noise.*]

Linda: [*suddenly pleading*] Will you please leave him alone?

Biff: What's he doing out there?

Linda: He's planting the garden!

Biff: [*quietly*] Now? Oh, my God! [BIFF *moves outside,* LINDA *following. The light dies down on them and comes up on the center of the apron as* WILLY *walks into it. He is carrying a flashlight, a hoe, and a handful of seed packets. He raps the top of the hoe sharply to fix it firmly, and then moves to the left, measuring off the distance with his foot. He holds the flashlight to look at the seed packets, reading off the instructions. He is in the blue of night.*]

Willy: Carrots... quarter-inch apart. Rows... one-foot rows. [*He measures it off.*] One foot. [*He puts down a package and measures off.*] Beets. [*He puts down another package,* *and measures again.*] Lettuce. [*He reads the package, puts it down.*] One foot—[*He breaks off as* BEN *appears at the right and moves slowly down to him.*] What a proposition, ts, ts. Terrific, terrific. 'Cause she's suffered, Ben, the woman has suffered. You understand me? A man can't go out the way he came in, Ben, a man has got to add up to something. You can't, you can't—[BEN *moves toward him as though to interrupt.*] You gotta consider, now. Don't answer so quick. Remember, it's a guaranteed twenty-thousand-dollar proposition. Now look, Ben, I want you to go through the ins and outs[6] of this thing with me. I've got nobody to talk to, Ben, and the woman has suffered, you hear me?

Ben: [*standing still, considering*] What's the proposition?

Willy: It's twenty thousand dollars on the barrelhead.[7] Guaranteed, gilt-edged, you understand?

Ben: You don't want to make a fool of yourself. They might not honor the policy.[8]

Willy: How can they dare refuse? Didn't I work like a coolie to meet every premium on the nose? And now they don't pay off! Impossible!

Ben: It's called a cowardly thing, William.

Willy: Why? Does it take more guts to stand here the rest of my life ringing up a zero? [9]

Ben: [*yielding*] That's a point, William. [*He moves, thinking, turns.*] And twenty thousand—that is something one can feel with the hand, it is there.

Willy: [*now assured, with rising power*] Oh, Ben, that's the whole beauty of it! I see it like a diamond, shining in the dark, hard and rough, that I can pick up and touch in my hand. Not like—like an appointment! This would not be another damned-fool appointment, Ben, and it changes all the aspects. Because he thinks I'm nothing, see, and so he spites me. But the funeral—[*straightening up*] Ben, that funeral will be massive! They'll come from Maine, Massachusetts, Vermont, New Hampshire! All the old-timers with the strange license plates—that boy will be thunderstruck, Ben, because he never realized—I am known! Rhode Island, New York, New Jersey—I am known, Ben, and he'll see it with his eyes once and for all. He'll see what I am, Ben! He's in for a shock, that boy!

Ben: [*coming down to the edge of the garden*] He'll call you a coward.

Willy: [*suddenly fearful*] No, that would be terrible.

Ben: Yes. And a damned fool.

Willy: No, no, he mustn't, I won't have that! [*He is broken and desperate.*]

Ben: He'll hate you, William. [*The gay music of the boys is heard.*]

Willy: Oh, Ben, how do we get back to all the great times? Used to be so full of light, and comradeship, the sleigh-riding in winter, and the ruddiness on his cheeks. And always some kind of good news coming up, always something nice coming up ahead. And never even let me carry the valises in the house, and simonizing,[10] simonizing that little red car! Why, why can't I give him something and not have him hate me?

Ben: Let me think about it. [*He glances at his watch.*] I still have a little time. Remarkable proposition, but you've got to be sure you're not making a fool of yourself. [BEN *drifts off upstage and goes out of sight. Biff comes down from the left.*]

Willy: [*suddenly conscious of* BIFF, *turns and looks up at him, then begins picking up the packages of seeds in confusion*] Where the hell is that seed? [*indignantly*] You can't see nothing out here! They boxed in the whole goddam neighborhood!

Biff: There are people all around here. Don't you realize that?

Willy: I'm busy. Don't bother me.

Biff: [*taking the hoe from* WILLY] I'm saying good-bye to you, Pop. [WILLY *looks at him, silent, unable to move.*] I'm not coming back any more.

Willy: You're not going to see Oliver tomorrow?

Biff: I've got no appointment, Dad.

Willy: He put his arm around you, and you've got no appointment?

Biff: Pop, get this now, will you? Everytime I've left it's been a fight that sent me out of here. Today I realized something about myself and I tried to explain it to you and I—I think I'm just not smart enough to make any sense out of it for you. To hell with whose fault it is or anything like that. [*He takes* WILLY's *arm.*] Let's just wrap it up, heh? Come on in, we'll tell Mom. [*He gently tries to pull* WILLY to *left.*]

Willy: [*frozen, immobile, with guilt in his voice*] No, I don't want to see her.

Biff: Come on! [*He pulls again, and* WILLY tries *to pull away*.]

Willy: [*highly nervous*] No, no, I don't want to see her.

Biff: [*tries* to *look into* WILLY's *face, as if to find the answer there*] Why don't you want to see her?

Willy: [*more harshly now*] Don't bother me, will you?

Biff: What do you mean, you don't want to see her? You don't want them calling you yellow, do you? This isn't your fault; it's me, I'm a bum. Now come inside! [WILLY *strains to get away.*] Did you hear what I said to you?

[WILLY *pulls away and quickly goes by himself into the house. Biff follows.*]

Linda: [*to* WILLY] Did you plant, dear?

Biff: [*at the door, to* LINDA] All right, we had it out. I'm going and I'm not writing any more.

Linda: [*going to* WILLY *in the kitchen*] I think that's the best way, dear. 'Cause there's no use drawing it out, you'll just *never* get along. [WILLY *doesn't respond.*]

Biff: People ask where I am and what I'm doing, you don't know, and you don't care. That way it'll be off your mind and you can start brightening up again. All right? That clears it, doesn't it? [WILLY *is silent, and* BIFF *goes to him.*] You gonna wish me luck, scout! [*He extends his hand.*] What do you say?

Linda: Shake his hand, Willy.

Willy: [*turning to her, seething with hurt*] There's no necessity to mention the pen[11] at all, y'know.

Biff: [*gently*] I've got no appointment, Dad.

Willy: [*erupting fiercely*] He put his arm around... ?

Biff: Dad, you're never going to see what I am, so what's the use of arguing? If I strike oil[12] I'll send you a check. Meantime forget I'm alive.

Willy: [*to* LINDA] Spite, see?

Biff: Shake hands. Dad.

Willy: Not my hand.

Biff: I was hoping not go this way.

Willy: Well, this is the way you're going. Good-bye. [BIFF *looks at him a moment, then turns sharply and goes to the stairs.*]

Willy: [*stops him*] May you rot in hell if you leave this house!

Biff: [*turning*] Exactly what is it that you want from me?

Willy: I want you to know, on the train, in the mountains, in the valleys, wherever you go, that you cut down your life for spite![13]

Biff: No, no.

Willy: Spite, spite, is the word of your undoing! And when you're down and out, remember what did it. When you're rotting somewhere beside the railroad tracks, remember, and don't you dare blame it on me!

Biff: I'm not blaming it on you!

Willy: I won't take the rap for this, you hear? [HAPPY *comes down the stairs and stands on the bottom step, watching.*]

Biff: That's just what I'm telling you!

Willy: [*sinking into a chair at the table, with full accusation*] You're trying to put a knife in me—don't think I don't know what you're doing!

Biff: All right, phony! Then let's lay it on the line. [*He whips the rubber tube*[14] *out of his pocket and puts it on the table.*]

Happy: You crazy—

Linda: Biff! [*She moves to grab the hose, but* BIFF *holds it down with his hand.*]

Biff: Leave it there! Don't move it!

Willy: [*not looking at it*] What is that?

Biff: You know goddam well what that is.

Willy: [*caged, wanting to escape*] I never saw that.

Biff: You saw it. The mice didn't bring it into the cellar! What is this supposed to do, make a hero out of you? This supposed to make me sorry for you?

Willy: Never heard of it.

Biff: There'll be no pity for you, you hear it? No pity!

Willy: [*to* LINDA] You hear the spite!

Biff: No, you're going to hear the truth—what you are and what I am!

Linda: Stop it!

Willy: Spite!

Happy: [*coming down toward* BIFF] You cut it now!

Biff: [*to* HAPPY] The man don't know who we are! The man is gonna know! [*To* WILLY]—We never told the truth for ten minutes in this house!

Happy: We always told the truth!

Biff: [*turning on him*] You big blow, are you the assistant buyer? You're one of the two assistants to the assistant, aren't you?

Happy: Well, I'm practically—

Biff: You're practically full of it! We all are! And I'm through with it. [*to* WILLY] Now hear this, Willy, this is me.

Willy: I know you!

Biff: You know why I had no address for three months? I stole a suit in Kansas City and I was in jail. [*to* LINDA, *who is sobbing*] Stop crying. I'm through with it.

[LINDA *turns away from them, her hands covering her face.*]

Willy: I suppose that's my fault!

Biff: I stole myself out of every good job since high school!

Willy: And whose fault is that?

Biff: And I never got anywhere because you blew me so full of hot air I could never stand taking orders from anybody! That's whose fault it is!

Willy: I hear that!

Linda: Don't, Biff!

Biff: It's goddam time you heard that! I had to be boss big shot in two weeks and I'm through with it!

Willy: Then hang yourself! For spite, hang yourself!

Biff: No! Nobody's hanging himself, Willy! I ran down eleven flights with a pen in my hand today. And suddenly I stopped, you hear me? And in the middle of that office building, do you hear this? I stopped in the middle of that building and I saw—the sky. I saw the things that I love in this world. The work and the food and time to sit and smoke. And I looked at the pen and said to myself, what the hell am I grabbing this for? Why am I trying to become what I don't want to be? What am I doing in an office, making a contemptuous, begging fool of myself, when all I want is out there, waiting for me the minute I say I know who I am! Why can't I say that, Willy? [*He tries to make* WILLY *face him, but* WILLY *pulls away and moves to the left.*]

Willy: [*with hatred, threateningly*] The door of your life is wide open!

Biff: Pop! I'm a dime a dozen,[15] and so are you!

Willy: [*turning on him now in an uncontrolled outburst*] I am not a dime a dozen! I am Willy Loman, and you are Biff Loman! [BIFF *starts for* WILLY, *but is blocked by* HAPPY. *In his fury,* BIFF *seems on the verge of attacking his father.*]

Biff: I am not a leader of men, Willy, and neither are you. You were never anything but a hard-working drummer who landed in the ash-can like all the rest of them! I'm one dollar an hour, Willy! I tried seven states and couldn't raise it. A buck an hour! Do you gather my meaning? I'm not bringing home any prizes any more, and you're going to stop waiting for me to bring them home!

Willy: [*directly to* BIFF] You vengeful, spiteful mut!

[BIFF *breaks from* HAPPY. WILLY, *in fright, starts up the stairs.* BIFF *grabs him.*]

Biff: [at *the peak of his fury*] Pop, I'm nothing! I'm nothing! Pop. Can't you understand that? There's no spite in it any more, I'm just what I am, that's all.

[BIFF's *fury has spent itself, and he breaks down, sobbing, holding on to* WILLY, *who dumbly fumbles for* BIFF's face.]

Willy: [*astonished*] What're you doing? What're you doing? [*to* LINDA] Why is he crying?

Biff: [*crying, broken*] Will you let me go, for Christ's sake? Will you take that phony dream and burn it before something happens? [*Struggling to contain himself, he pulls away and moves to the stairs.*] I'll go in the morning. Put him—put him to bed. [*Exhausted,* BIFF *moves up the stairs to his room.*]

Willy: [*after a long pause, astonished, elevated*] Isn't that—isn't that remarkable? Biff—he likes me!

Linda: He loves you, Willy!

Happy: [*deeply moved*] Always did, Pop.

Willy: Oh, Biff. [*staring wildly*] He cried! Cried to me. [*He is choking with his love, and now cries out his promise.*] That boy—that boy is going to be magnificent!

[BEN *appears in the light just outside the kitchen.*]

Ben: Yes, outstanding, with twenty thousand behind him.

Linda: [*sensing the racing of his mind, fearfully, carefully*] Now come to bed, Willy. It's all settled now.

Willy: [*finding it difficult not to rush out of the house*] Yes, we'll sleep. Come on. Go to sleep, Hap.

Ben: And it does take a great kind of a man to crack the jungle. [*In accents of dread,* BEN'*s idyllic music starts up.*]

Happy: [*his arm around* LINDA] I'm getting married. Pop, don't forget it. I'm changing everything. I'm gonna run that department before the year is up. You'll see. Mom. [*He kisses her.*]

Ben: The jungle is dark but full of diamonds, Willy.

[WILLY *turns, moves, listening to* BEN.]

Linda: Be good. You're both good boys, just act that way, that's all.

Happy: Night, Pop. [*He goes upstairs.*]

Linda: [*to* WILLY] Come, dear.

Ben: [*with greater force*] One must go in to fetch a diamond out.

Willy: [*to* LINDA, *as he moves slowly along the edge of the kitchen, toward the door*] I just want to get settled down, Linda. Let me sit alone for a little.

Linda: [*almost uttering her fear*] I want you upstairs.

Willy: [*taking her in his arms*] In a few minutes, Linda. I couldn't sleep right now. Go on, you look awful tired. [*He kisses her.*]

Ben: Not like an appointment at all. A diamond is rough and hard to the touch.

Willy: Go on now. I'll be right up.

Linda: I think this is the only way, Willy.

Willy: Sure, it's the best thing.

Ben: Best thing!

Willy: The only way. Everything is gonna be—go on, kid, get to bed. You look so tired.

Linda: Come right up.

Willy: Two minutes.

[LINDA *goes into the living-room, then reappears in her bedroom.* WILLY *moves just outside the kitchen door.*]

Willy: Loves me. [*wonderingly*] Always loved me. Isn't that a remarkable thing? Ben, he'll worship me for it!

Ben: [*with promise*] It's dark there, but full of diamonds.

Willy: Can you imagine that magnificence with twenty thousand dollars in his pocket?

Linda: [*calling from her room*] Willy! Come up!

Willy: [*calling into the kitchen*] Yes! Yes. Coming! It's very smart, you realize that, don't you, sweetheart? Even Ben sees it. I gotta go, baby. 'Bye! 'Bye! [*going over to* BEN, *almost dancing*] Imagine? When the mail comes he'll be ahead of Bernard again!

Ben: A perfect proposition all around.

Willy: Did you see how he cried to me? Oh, if I could kiss him, Ben!

Ben: Time, William, time!

Willy: Oh, Ben, I always knew one way or another we were gonna make it. Biff and I!

Ben: [*looking at his watch*] The boat. We'll be late. [*He moves slowly off into the darkness.*]

Willy: [*elegiacally, turning to the house*] Now when you kick off, boy, I want a seventy-yard boot, and get right down the field under the ball, and when you hit, hit low and hit hard, because it's important, boy. [*He swings around and faces the audience.*] There's all kinds of important people in the stands, and the first thing you know... [*Suddenly realizing he is alone.*] Ben! Ben, where do I... ? [*He makes a sudden movement of search.*] Ben, how do I... ?

Linda: [*calling*] Willy, you coming up?

Willy: [*uttering a gasp of fear, whirling about as if to quiet her*] Sh! [*He turns around as if to find his way; sounds, faces, voices, seem to be swarming in upon him and he flicks at them, crying,* 'Sh! Sh!' *Suddenly music, faint and high, stops him. It rises in intensity, almost to an unbearable scream. He goes up and down on his toes, and rushes off* *around the house.*] Shhh!

Linda: Willy? [*There is no answer.* LINDA *waits.* BIFF *gets up off his bed. He is still in his clothes.* HAPPY *sits up.* BIFF *stands listening.*]

Linda: [*with real fear*] Willy, answer me! Willy!

[*There is the sound of a car starting and moving away at full speed.*]

Linda: No!

Biff: [*crushing down the stairs*] Pop!

[*As the car speeds off, the music crashes down in a frenzy of sound, which becomes the soft pulsation of a single cello string.* BIFF *slowly returns to his bedroom. He and* HAPPY *gravely don their jackets.* LINDA *slowly walks out of her room. The music has developed into a dead march. The leaves of day are appearing over everything.* CHARLEY *and* BERNARD, *somberly dressed, appear and knock on the kitchen door.* BIFF *and* HAPPY *slowly descend the stairs to the kitchen as* CHARLEY *and* BERNARD *enter. All stop a moment when* LINDA, *in clothes of mourning, bearing a little bunch of roses, comes through the draped doorway into the kitchen. She goes to* CHARLEY *and takes his arm. Now all move toward the audience, through the wall-line of the kitchen. At the limit of the apron,* LINDA *lays down the flowers, kneels, and sits back on her heels. All stare down at the grave.*]

Notes

[1] malted: malted milk.

[2] You're on: You've convinced me.

[3] I'm checkin' out: I'm leaving the hotel after paying the bill.

[4] You phony little fake: You insincere little false guy.

[5] bum: habitual beggar or loafer.

[6] the ins and outs: the inner difficulties when something is looked at in detail.

[7] It's twenty thousand dollars on the barrelhead: I can get twenty thousand dollars from the insurance company after I hang myself to death.

[8] They might not honor the policy: They might not keep the agreement by paying the check.

[9] ringing up a zero: paying the insurance premium just to get nothing.

[10] simonizing: making the car shining by putting wax on it.

[11] the pen: in the appointment Biff stole the pen from the boss.

[12] strike oil: have good luck in making money.

[13] you cut down your life for spite: you would ruin your life due to your desire of showing contempt.

[14] the rubber tube: the rubber hose with which Willy tried to commit suicide by inhaling gas from the heater.

[15] a dime a dozen: very cheap, here it means very ordinary and common, not important.

Commentary

The play *Death of a Salesman*, written in two long acts, is a tragedy of Willy Loman, a common salesman who sells his life in order to realize his American Dream. Willy believes that a well-liked and personally-attractive man in business will obtain the material comforts offered by modern American life. His blind faith leads to his rapid psychological decline when he finally cannot cope with the disparity between the dream and reality. In fact, Willy has not succeeded well. Aged over 60, he is still in debt and furthermore, he is now too old for his job. His old buyers have retired, methods of selling have changed, and the new buyers either ridicule him or do not know him.

Willy's idol is his elder brother, Ben, who, as a young man, went into the African jungle and returned with a wealth of diamonds—fulfilling the American dream of "getting rich quick", no matter how risky or unscrupulous the means. Brother Ben is dead when the play takes place, but his ghost still urges Willy to pursue wealth. Willy alone can see and speak to Ben's ghost, so his family thinks that he talks to himself and is losing his mind. Willy has a loving, admiring wife, Linda, who always agrees with him, praises him and encourages him to be optimistic even when there is little cause for optimism since a realistic attitude would be better.

They have two sons, both over 30, both unmarried, and both living at home. Willy educated his boys to be popular and successful rather than to work hard. He even permitted them to be dishonest. His greatest hopes were for Biff, the elder son, who was a dazzling football star in high school at the expense of his studies. Biff never became a success in life. He saw the falseness of his father's dreams and went to the West. Yet, he comes home with no money, and Willy believes that Biff is deliberately courting failure out of spite, trying to deprive his father of a successful son to be proud of. Father and son argue and cannot see eye to eye. The younger son, Happy, followed his father's footsteps into business, but he is merely a boaster. He is extravagant with his small salary and keeps no money to help his parents. His main interest in life is chasing women.

With his hope destroyed and in order to earn insurance money for Biff, Willy commits suicide by roaring off in his car to make the final profit—selling his life.

Questions and Exercises

1. What are the causes that make Willy commit suicide? What role does Ben play in Willy's final decision to kill himself for the insurance money?
2. Willy is the victim of the "massive dreams" in the United States at the time. Write a short essay entitled "The Disillusionment of Illusive Dreams" in light of the dominant theme of *Death of a Salesman*.

Part 4

A Guide to Appreciating English Fiction

1 Introduction

1.1 Essence of fiction

Telling stories must have begun very early in human history. Most people have learned how narratives are structured even before they know how to read. Once children can tell a story, they also know how to exaggerate, add or delete details, rearrange events, and bend some facts. In other words, they know how to fictionalize a narrative to achieve a desired effect. This kind of informal or personal narrative is similar in many ways to the more structured literary fiction to be discussed in this part of the book.

A work of fiction is a narrative that originates in the imagination of the author. Sometimes the stories are "true", but more often they are not. Some fiction—historical or autobiographical fiction, for example—may focus on real people and the plot may be grounded in actual events, but the way characters interact and how the plot unfolds are the author's own invention. The purposes of fiction are mainly for entertainment, instruction, and aesthetic pleasure of the reader.

In an inclusive sense, fiction is any literary narrative, whether in prose or verse. In a narrower sense, fiction denotes only narratives that are written in prose and sometimes it is used simply as a synonym for novel. Fictional writings in prose form can usually be divided, according to their lengths, into novels, novelettes, and short stories.

1.2 Novel and novelette

A novel refers to a narrative in prose form of considerable length and complexity that deals with human experiences. The novel as an extended narrative is distinguished from the short story and the novelette, as it has a greater variety of characters, deeper complication of plot, ampler development of setting, and more sustained exploration of the characters' motives than do the shorter, more concentrated modes. A novelette refers to a narrative of fiction intermediate in length and complexity between a novel and a short story. According to a definition suggested by E. M. Forster, a novel or a novelette should at least contain 50,000 words.

The English writer Daniel Defoe is commonly given credit for writing the first novel in 1719. His *Robinson Crusoe* is an episodic narrative similar to a picaresque but unified by a single setting as well as by a central character. By the 19th century, the novel reached a high point in its development, replacing other kinds of extended narratives. Writers such as George Eliot, Charles Dickens, William Thackeray, and Charlotte and Emily Brontë appealed to this desire by creating large fictional worlds of the Victorian society. From these roots, the novel as a literary genre continued to develop throughout the 20th century and into the present.

1.3 Short story

While the novel or novelette is an extended piece of narrative fiction, the short story is limited in length and scope. Unlike the novelist, the short story writer cannot devote a great deal of space to developing a highly complex plot or a large number of characters. As a result, the short story usually develops only one character in depth. By concentrating on a single incident, the short story writer mostly develops the character by showing his or her responses to the events. In order to reveal the story's theme clearly, many contemporary short story writers often make his character experience an *epiphany*, a moment of illumination in which something hidden or not explicitly understood becomes immediately clear, usually at the end of the story.

Short stories as a literary genre has a long history all over the world. Some of the most ancient short stories include the fables of the Greek writer Aesop, the retellings by the Roman writer Ovid, and *The Arabian Nights* in Asia. The Biblical stories of Cain and Abel are well-known short stories in the Middle Ages. In 18th-century England, Joseph Addison and Sir Richard Steele published many short stories in the magazine *The Spectator*. The short story as a distinct literary genre came in the 19th century, whose representatives include Balzac and Maupassant in France, Chekhov in Russia, Sir Walter Scott in England, Washington Irving, Edgar Allan Poe, and Nathaniel Hawthorne in the United States.

In addition, novelists such as Milton, Dickens, Hardy, D. H. Lawrence and many others also wrote short stories. Since 1900, enormous short stories have been published every year. Some of the most important short stories in English are those by 20th-century Irish writers. Foremost among them is James Joyce. His collection of short stories, *Dubliners* (1914), contains painfully truthful representations of life in his country. Combining naturalism with symbolism, his stories achieved world acclaim as a modern model of form.

As a form of literature, the short story has flourished in the United States at the turn of the 20th century. Mark Twain is famous for sarcasm and humor; O. Henry is famed for his surprise endings; Sherwood Anderson with his *Winesburg, Ohio*, (1919) has proved that absence of plot could enhance portrayal of characters.

The more recent American short-story writers include Flannery O'Connor, with her passionate moral concern. John Cheever and John Updike, who are noted for their dispassionate stories about the ironies of northern suburban life, were among the most eminent short story writers after the Second World War.

2 Chief Elements of Fiction

To appreciate fiction, we have to get ourselves familiar with such elements as plot, character, setting, point of view, style, tone, symbolism, theme, so on and so forth.

2.1 Plot

Plot refers to what happens in a story, so it is the first and most obvious element of a novel. In a well-plotted story, everything is related, and nothing is irrelevant. Unlike life, which is random and unpredictable, the fictional story is usually shaped by an organic chain of events, one leading inevitably to another in a series of rising actions to a moment of crisis—the climax. For the reader, the plot is the structural element with unity, coherence, and logic. For the writer, the plot is the guiding principle of selection and arrangement of events. (See *Part 3 A Guide to Appreciating English Drama* 2.1)

(1) Conflict

The first concept concerning plot is the conflict, which refers to a struggle between two opposing forces or characters in literary works. Most essentially, a conflict is the opposition of two people. They may fight, argue, or help each other. Then a conflict may exist between two larger groups of people, between an individual and larger forces, such as natural objects, ideas, modes of behavior, public opinion, and the like. The existence of difficult choices within an individual's mind (a character vs. himself) is another kind of conflict widely used in fiction.

Conflict can be external or internal. External conflict may take the form of a basic opposition between man and nature as in Ernest Hemingway's *The Old Man and the Sea* or between man and society as in Theodore Dreiser's *An American Tragedy.* It may also take the form of an opposition among characters (between protagonist and antagonist). Internal conflict, on the other hand, focuses on two or more elements contesting within the a character's own mind. The dilemma of Hamlet's monologue "To be or not to be, that is the question" is a good example of internal conflict. Some internal conflicts, in fact, are never made explicit enough and must be drawn out by the reader from what the characters do or say as the plot unfolds.

(2) Five stages of plot development

The traditional plot development of a story usually consists of five stages. Exposition, complication, climax, falling action, resolution.

(A) Exposition is the beginning section in which the author provides the necessary background information, sets the scene, establishes the situation, and dates the action. It usually introduces the characters and the conflict, or at least the potential for conflict.

(B) Complication, also known as the rising action, develops and intensifies the conflict with the advancement of the plot.

(C) Climax, or crisis, is that moment at which the plot reaches its point of greatest emotional intensity; it is the turning point of the plot, directly followed by some falling action and the resolution.

(D) Falling action comes when the crisis has been reached, the tension subsides and the plot moves toward its conclusion.

(E) Resolution, also called the conclusion or the denouement, refers to the outcome of the conflicts.

(3) Ordering of plot

(A) Chronological order. It is the customary way of ordering the plot. The writer presents the plot chronologically, that is, in the order of their occurrence in time. However, it is important to recognize that, even within plots that are mainly chronological, the temporal sequence is often deliberately broken for the sake of emphasis and effect. After having captured the reader, the author may go backward to the beginning, and then forward again to the middle or to the end of the story. (See *flashback* below.) In still other cases, the chronology of the plot may shift forward in time in order to establish suspense. (See *foreshadowing* below.)

(B) Flashback. Sometimes the writer may interrupt the action in a flashback in order to describe crucial events that occurred earlier. The flashback is one form of exposition, the process of giving the reader necessary background information that actually took place at some earlier period of time. Flashbacks provide us the information that would otherwise be unavailable and thus increase our knowledge and understanding of the present situation.

(C) Foreshadowing. The writer will usually add coherence to the plot by signaling to the reader in advance the outcome of the action. These hints are known as foreshadowing.

2.2 Two major types of characters

The term "character" applies to any individuals—animals, things, or natural forces, appearing in a literary work. No writer can present an entire life story of a protagonist nor can each character in a story get equal importance for development. Some grow to be full and alive, and others remain shadowy. Mainly, characters fall into two major types.

(1) Round characters undergo change

The basic trait of round characters is that the authors present enough detail to render them full, lifelike, and memorable. Round characters represent a number of qualities, and are complex multidimensional characters of considerable intellectual and emotional depth. A complementary quality about round characters is that they are dynamic, that is, they are able to recognize, change with, and adjust to different circumstances. Such changes may be shown in their action, their acceptance of the need for making changes, and their ability to discover unrecognized truths. Major characters (protagonists, heroes, heroines) in fiction are usually round characters, and it is just because of such complexity of the characters that most of us become fascinated.

Because a round character usually plays a major role in a story, he/she is often called the hero or heroine. When some major characters are not necessarily heroic, so it is preferable to use the more neutral term protagonist, which means the "first character". The protagonist is the major or central character of the plot; his opponent, the character against whom the protagonist struggles or contends, is the antagonist.

(2) Flat characters stay the same

They represent a single characteristic, trait, or idea, or at most a very limited number of such qualities. Flat characters are also referred to as *type characters, stock characters,* or *one-dimensional characters*. They have much in common with the kind of *stock characters* who appear again and again in certain types of literary works.

The terms *round* and *flat* do not automatically imply value judgments. Each kind of character has its particular functions. Even when they are minor characters, as they usually are, flat characters are often convenient devices to draw out and help us to understand the personalities of the main characters.

To understand fiction better, we have to know two more terms resulting from *round* and *flat characters.* The protagonist is usually round and easy enough to identify: he or she is the essential character without whom there will be no plot. It is the protagonist's fate on which the attention of the reader is focused. Yet, the antagonist can be somewhat more difficult to identify, especially when he is not a human being, as is the case with the marlin that challenges the courage and endurance of the old fisherman Santiago in Ernest Hemingway's *The Old Man and the Sea.* In fact, the antagonist may not be a living creature at all, but rather the hostile social or natural environment with which the protagonist is forced to fight against.

2.3 Methods of characterization

Characterization means the creation of imaginary persons so that they seem lifelike. It refers to the personality a character displays; also it is the means by which the writer reveals that personality. There are two fundamental methods of characterization: direct characterization and indirect characterization.

(1) Direct characterization

Direct characterization relies on direct exposition and comment on the character made by the author through the use of names and description of appearance.

Names are often used to provide essential clues in characterization. Some characters are given names that suggest their dominant traits. This is especially true to allegorical writings of symbolism. For example, Angel in *Tess,* one who is supposed to save Tess' soul; Pearl in *The Scarlet Letter,* her mother Hester Prynne's only cherished hope; and Hester sounds like Hestier, Zeus' sister in Greek mythology, who is a very beautiful goddess.

In fiction, details of appearance (clothes and looks) often provide essential clues to characters. Details of dress may offer clues to background, occupation, and economic and social status. Details of physical appearance can help to identify a character's age and the general state of his physical and emotional health: whether the character is strong or weak, happy or sad, calm or restless.

Most customarily, in direct characterization, the author interrupts the narrative and expresses himself directly, through comments on the personality of the characters, including the thoughts and feelings in the character's minds. By so doing the author asserts full control over characterization and tells us exactly what our attitude toward that character should be.

(2) Indirect characterization

The other method of characterization is the indirect method of showing. In so doing, the author steps aside to allow the characters to reveal themselves directly through their own dialogues and actions instead of being directed by the writer.

Showing the character through speaking is a very common method of characterization. The task of establishing character through dialogue is not a simple one. Some characters are careful and guarded in what they say: they speak only indirectly, and we must infer what they actually mean from their words. Others are more frank: they tell us exactly what they think. For this reason the reader must be prepared to analyze dialogues in a number of different aspects: the identity of the speaker; the occasion; what is being said; the identity of the addresser and the addressee; the speaker's tone, stress, and dialect.

Although determining the reliability of characters can be difficult, most authors provide clues. One can also test reliability by looking at the character's subsequent conduct or action to see if what he does somehow contradicts what he says.

It is true that one's behavior is a logical and even necessary extension of one's psychology and personality. So the only essential and definitive method of depicting character is through *action*. A small gesture or an insignificant facial expression usually carries with it less significance than some larger and overt act. But this is not always the case. Very often some small and involuntary action, due to its spontaneous and unconscious quality, tells us more about a character's inner life. One helpful way to identify the importance of a behavior is on the basis of motive that lies behind the underlying causes. If we are successful in doing so, we may safely assume that we have made some important discoveries about the character. However, telling and showing in many cases, are not mutually exclusive. Most authors employ a combination of the two.

(3) Presenting the characters' motivation

Because round characters, in particular, are complex, and are not always easy to understand. They may act differently in similar situations, just as real people do. They wrestle with decisions, resist temptation, make mistakes, ask questions, search for answers, hope and dream, rejoice and despair. What is important is not whether we approve of a character's actions but whether those actions are *plausible*—whether the actions make sense in light of what we know about the character. We need to see a character's motivation—the reasons behind his or her behavior—or we will not believe or accept that behavior. Therefore, by presenting the characters' motivation can also be important for characterization.

For instance, in John Updike's *A & P*, given Sammy's age, his dissatisfaction with his job, and his desire to impress the young woman whom he calls Queenie, the decision he makes at the end of the story is perfectly plausible. Without having established his motivation, Updike could not have expected readers to accept Sammy's actions. Even when readers get to know a character, they still are not able to predict how a complex, round character will behave in a given situation; only a flat character is predictable. The tension that develops as readers wait to see how a character will act or react, and thus how a story's conflict will be resolved, is what holds readers' interest and keeps them involved as a story's action unfolds.

2.4 Setting

In its narrow sense, setting is the place and time of the work, but broadly it includes the total environment of the fiction. Setting, therefore, refers to such factors as the physical locale that frames the action, the time of day or year, the climatic conditions, and the historical period during which the action takes place.

Setting has the basic function to help the reader visualize the action of the work and thus adds credibility and authenticity to the characters. There are two main types of setting, and they also function differently.

(1) Natural environment

The setting for a great number of stories is, of course, the out-of-doors. Nature herself is seen as a force that shapes action and therefore directs the lives of the characters. The open road may be a place where one person seeks flight. A lake may be the place where one person literally rescues another. Bushes may furnish places of concealment, while a mountaintop is a spot to protect occupants from being attacked by the outside world. In short, nature is one of the major forces governing the circumstances of characters.

(2) Manufactured environment

Manufactured things can always reflect the people related to them. A richly decorated house shows the expensive tastes and resources of the characters owning it. A few cracks in the plaster of the wall may show the character declining in fortune or power. Ugly and dilapidated surroundings may show weariness, negligence, or even hostility of the characters living in them.

(3) Main functions of setting

Setting usually has five functions in a work of literature.

(A) Setting as a background for action. Everything happens somewhere. For this reason, fiction requires a setting or background of some kind. Sometimes this background is extensive and highly developed. In other cases, setting is so slight that it can be dealt with in a single sentence or just inferred from a dialogue and action.

(B) Setting as an antagonist. Often, the forces of nature function as a causal agent or antagonist, helping to establish conflict or to determine the outcome of events.

(C) Setting as a means to create a proper atmosphere. Many authors use settings as a means of stimulating the reader's expectations and establishing an appropriate state of mind for the events to come.

(D) Setting as a means to reveal the personality of a character. Very often the way in which a character perceives or reacts to the setting will tell the reader more about the personality of character and his or her state of mind.

(E) Setting as a means to reinforce theme. Setting can also be used as a means of reinforcing and clarifying the theme of a story.

2.5 Point of view

A story must have a storyteller: a narrative voice, real or implied, that presents the story to the reader. When we talk about narrative voice, we are talking about point of view—the position from which the story is told. It governs the reader's access to the story and determines just how much he can know at any given moment about what is taking place. The point of view is so crucial that, once having been chosen, it will shape the way in which everything else is presented and perceived, including plot, characters, and setting. If we change the point of view, we will change the story. To have a better understanding of point of view, we should have an understanding of the following general concepts.

(1) Omniscient point of view

In the omniscient point of view, the author self tells the whole story. He or she assumes complete knowledge of the characters' actions and thoughts, and can thus move at will from one place to another, one time to another, one character to another, and can even speak his or her own views directly to the reader as the plot progresses. Examples are Hawthorne's *The Scarlet Letter,* and Hardy's *Tess of the D'Urbervilles.*

(2) Limited omniscient point of view

When the limited omniscient position is used, the author still narrates the story but restricts his or her revelation—and therefore our knowledge—of the thoughts of all but one character. This character may be either a main or peripheral character. A good example is Jane Austen's *Pride and Prejudice.*

(3) Objective point of view

In the objective position, the author is more restricted than in any other. Though the author is the narrator, he or she refuses to enter the minds of any of the characters. The writer sees them as we would in real life. This point of view is sometimes called "dramatic" because we see the characters as we would the characters in a play. We learn about them from what they say and do, how they look, and what other characters say about them. But we don't learn what they think unless they tell us. This point of view is the least common of all. The typical examples are Hemingway's *Hills Like White Elephant* and *The Killers.*

(4) First-person point of view

In the first-person position, the author is even more restricted—letting one of the characters tell the story, eliminating the author as narrator. This character-narrator may be a major character who is at the center of events or a minor character who does not participate but simply observes the action. Examples of first-person narrator are Charles Dickens's *Great Expectations*, Mark Twain's *Huckleberry Finn*, F. Scott Fitzgerald's *The Great Gatsby,* and Charlotte Brontë's *Jane Eyre.*

(5) Second-person point of view

Although a second-person narration (in which the narrator tells a listener what he or she has done, using the personal pronoun "you") is possible, it is rare because in effect the second person actually requires a first-person voice. This viewpoint requires also that the listener be the character who has lived through the narration. Thus a parent might be telling a child what the child did during infancy. Or a doctor might tell a patient with amnesia about what occurred when his memory was gone, or a lawyer may present a story of a crime directly to the accused criminal by way of accusation. In practice, the second-person point of view is of only passing use in most fiction.

(6) Third-person point of view

If the narrator is not introduced as a character, and if everything in the work is described in the third person, the author is using the third-person point of view.

When the author wishes to be the all-knowing narrator, not limited by time, place, or character, but free to roam and comment at will, he is using the third-person omniscient point of view, in which the narrator is evidently the author self who sees all, knows all, and tells all. This intrusive narrator not only reports and comments, but also evaluates the actions and motives of the characters, and sometimes expresses personal views about human life in general.

However, the omniscient narrator may also choose to be unintrusive (alternative terms are impersonal or objective). Such a narrator, for the most part, just describes, reports, or shows the action in dramatic scenes without introducing his own comments or judgments.

(7) Stream of consciousness

Later writers, such as James Joyce, Virginia Woolf, and William Faulkner, developed the unintrusive third-person technique into stream of consciousness, a narrative method of modern fiction to describe the unbroken flow of perceptions, thoughts, feelings, random associations, and expectations in the waking mind. It is a mode of narration to reproduce the continuous flow of a character's mental process without the narrator's intervention. It is mainly conducted in the form of interior monologue in which the author does not interrupt as a describer, guide or commentator. The author's main task is to give an exact presentation of the process of the character's consciousness.

2.6 Theme

(1) A full understanding of theme

The theme is what the author has to say. It is the central and dominating idea in a story. Therefore, the theme is the central statement about life that unifies and controls the total work. When we talk about theme, we should always bear in mind the following points.

(A) Theme is not the issue, or problem, or subject that the writer deals with, but rather the comment or statement the author makes about that subject matter. Theme in literature, whether it takes the form of a brief and meaningful insight or a comprehensive vision of life, is the author's way of communicating and sharing perceptions or feelings with his readers or, as is often the case, the author's way of probing and exploring the puzzling questions of human existence, most of which do not yield neat, tidy, or universally acceptable answers.

(B) A theme does not exist as an intellectual abstraction that an author adds to the work like icing on a cake; it is originated from the interplay of the various elements of the work and is organically related to the work's total structure and texture.

(C) The theme may be less fully developed in some works of fiction than in others. This is especially the case of detective, gothic, and adventure fiction, where the author wants primarily to entertain by producing mystification or engaging the reader in a series of exciting and fast-moving incidents. Works of this type, in fact, often do not have a demonstrable theme at all.

(D) It is entirely possible that intelligent readers will differ, at times radically, on just what the theme of a given work is. Differences of opinion are perfectly acceptable as long as the interpretation being offered is reasonably derived from the facts of the story.

(E) The theme of a given work need not be in agreement with the reader's particular beliefs and values. The idea or ideas that an author expresses are closely related to his or her values, or "value system". We readers are under no obligation to accept the story's theme as it is presented to us, especially if we believe that it violates the truth of our own experience. But we must remember that although literature is full of ideas that may strike us as unpleasant, controversial, or simply wrongheaded, literary sophistication should warn us against dismissing them out of hand. Many stories survive, in part at least, because of the fresh and challenging ideas and insights they offer. Such ideas and insights have the power to liberate our minds and our imaginations, and consequently, cause us to reflect critically about our own values, beliefs, and assumptions.

(2) Ways to identify theme

When we attempt to identify the theme of a novel we are trying to formulate in our own words the statement about life or human experience that is made by the total work. The task requires us to analyze a number of elements in their relation to one another and to the work as a whole. To identify theme is valuable because it forces us to understand the various aspects of the work that we had previously ignored or undervalued.

Because different kinds of works will yield different themes in different ways, there is no *one* correct approach to identifying themes. The following suggestions, however, may prove helpful.

(A) Avoid confusing a work's theme with its subject. Theme is the abstract, generalized statement that the work makes about a concrete subject or situation. Although an idea may be expressed in a phrase or single word, yet gaining a full understanding of ideas about a work will be difficult unless they can be put in complete sentences. Thus, "love for human beings" may be an idea, but it is not an assertion about anything, and therefore it is not a theme. In dealing with Lawrence's *Lady Chatterley's Lover*, for example, little is accomplished with the statement that the story is about the love between a man and a woman. It is much more helpful to see Lawrence's story as expressing the idea that the harmonious love of a man and a woman is so essential that one may be saved or destroyed in an age of modern civilization.

(B) Be sure that the theme does the work full justice. There is always the danger of failing to discover its total significance or overstating the theme beyond the story, and thus making the work appear more universally applicable than it is. Authors, like all intelligent people, know that most of the really important questions about human experience do not yield up easy, formulistic answers. As readers, we must be careful not to credit literary works with solutions and answers where such issues are only being explored or where only tentative answers are being proposed.

(C) Testify whether the theme we propose is fully supported by all of the work's elements. If our statement of the theme leaves certain elements or facts unexplained, or if those elements and details fail to confirm our statement, then unless the work itself is flawed, chances are high that we have been only partially successful in our identification of the theme. If we want to be successful to find out the real theme, we have to be open-minded and objective, and not just to pay attention to some rather than all the elements of the work or, what is worse, to read into them what simply is not there, commonly known as the heresy of interpretation.

(D) Be alert that the title a writer gives the work often suggests a particular emphasis for the reader's attention. Just as the title of a work sometimes serves to identify the work's protagonist, it may also provide clues about theme. For example, Joseph Conrad's *Heart of Darkness* refers not only to the uncharted center of Africa, the "dark" continent, but to the capacity for evil and corruption that exists in the human heart. However, it is more common that the writer gives the book a name simply to attract our attention instead of furnishing us with a theme.

2.7 Tone

Tone refers to the methods by which writers convey attitudes toward the subject matter, characters, or audience. For this reason, tone and attitude are often closely mingled together. The distinction lies in the fact that tone refers not to attitudes but to those techniques of presentation that reveal these attitudes. Word choice and sentence structure help to create the tone of a work, which may be intimate or distant, bitter or affectionate, straightforward or cautious, supportive or critical, respectful or disdainful.

In literature, the term tone is made up of many elements in addition to what we actually say: the speed, pitch, and loudness of speech, the degree of enthusiasm, facial expressions, posture, and the distance kept between the addresser and addressee.

In appreciating a novel, we infer the author's tone through close and careful study of the various elements within the work, including plot, character, setting, point of view, and style. No matter how hard an author tries to conceal his or her feelings, his tone can be inferred by the choices he or she makes in the process of presenting the material. Consequently, if we are careful enough, it is not that difficult to get the tone and the underlying attitudes of the novel.

2.8 Irony

To determine the tone or attitude of a writer in a novel, we need to know something about the term "irony". In Greek comedy the character called the *eiron* was a dissembler, who characteristically spoke in understatement and deliberately pretended to be less intelligent than he was, yet triumphed over the *alazon*—the self-deceiving and stupid braggart. Now the term "irony" still has the root sense of hiding what is actually the case, not, however, in order to deceive, but to achieve special rhetorical or artistic effects. In literature, irony is a mode of ambiguous or indirect expression. There are three major types of irony:

verbal irony, situational irony, and dramatic irony.

(1) Verbal irony

It is a statement in which one thing is said and another is meant. When we say that a woman is handsome and clever, we may mean she is too bossy or manly and too clever to be pleasant. In a verbal irony, the implication of a speaker differs sharply, and often oppositely, from the meaning that is superficially expressed. A typical instance of irony is the famed sentence with which Jane Austen opens *Pride and Prejudice*: "It is a truth universally acknowledged that a single man in possession of a good fortune must be in want of a wife." Part of the ironic implication is that a single woman is in want of a rich husband. Sometimes the use of irony by Alexander Pope and other masters is very complicated, which is why many literary ironists are misinterpreted and sometimes (like Daniel Defoe and Jonathan Swift in the 18th century) get into serious trouble with the dull-witted authorities. So following the great ironists like Plato, Swift, Austen, or Henry James is a test of skill and intelligence in reading between the lines.

(2) Structural irony

The author introduces a structural feature that serves to sustain a double meaning and evaluation throughout the work. One common literary device of this sort is the invention of a naïve hero, or else a naïve narrator or spokesman, whose naivety and simplicity leads him to persist in putting an interpretation on affairs which the knowing reader is called on to alter and correct. One example of the naïve spokesman is Swift's well-meaning economist who writes the "Modest Proposal" to convert children of the oppressed and poverty-stricken Irish into a financial asset. Swift's stubbornly credulous Gulliver is yet another good case in point.

(3) Dramatic irony

This is a special kind of situational irony in which a character perceives a situation in a limited way while the audience, including other characters, may see it in greater perspective. The character therefore is able to understand things in only one way while the larger audience can perceive two or more. Writers of Greek tragedy, who based their plots on legends whose outcome was already known to their audience, made frequent use of this device. Examples of dramatic irony are the scenes in William Shakespeare's *Twelfth Night*, *King Lear,* F. S. Fitzgerald's innocent Jay Gatsby, and Thomas Hardy's Mayor of Casterbridge.

(4) Cosmic irony

It is attributed to literary works in which a fate is represented as though deliberately manipulating events so as to lead the protagonist to false hopes, only to frustrate and mock them. Cosmic irony is also called *situational irony*, or *irony of situation,* referring to conditions that transcend and overpower human capacities. In other words, the fate of man is governed by cosmic laws. These forces may be psychological, social, political, or environmental. Such kind of situational irony connected with a pessimistic or fatalistic view of life is sometimes also called *irony of fate*. This favorite structural device is often used by Thomas Hardy. In his *Tess of the D'Urbervilles,* the heroine, having lost her virtue because of her innocence, then loses her happiness because of her honesty, finds it again only by murder, and having been briefly happy, is hanged.

2.9 Style

One of the qualities that gives a work of literature its individual personality is its style, the way in which the writer uses language, selecting and arranging words to say what he or she wants to say. In other words, style is made up of an author's choice and arrangement of diction to convey both a theme and the author's individuality. Elements of style include subject, diction, and structure.

(1) Subject

This refers to the topic of a literary work, the experience or idea being written about. Modern authors have responded to the rapid expansion of human knowledge by exploring new topics for literature, for example, the effects of technology on life or the working of the human mind.

(2) Diction

It is the author's use of appropriate words to convey a particular meaning. The choice of words should be suitable for the situation and subject being written about and should also be able to reflect the author's personality. Modern authors have experimented with diction to create startling effects. Some may use technical scientific language; and others may sacrifice meaning and use words purely for their sound.

(3) Structure

It is the framework or general plan of a piece of literature. The structure of an essay is its outline, or the scheme of its thesis statement and topic sentences. The structure of a short story is its plot and the arrangement of events in the plot. An example of a modern innovation in structure is the stream-of-consciousness story, which dispenses with plot and imitates the continuous flow of human thought.

3 How to Read Fiction?

While you read more fictional works, you will begin naturally paying careful attention to the above-discussed literary elements in fiction, such as plot, character, setting, point of view, style, tone, symbol, allegory, and theme. By looking at these elements you will be able to understand and appreciate the story more fully.

The following brief guidelines in the form of questions are designed to help you appreciate stories effectively. Be alert to ask yourself these questions while reading, you can surely gain a better understanding of the fictional works selected in this book.

3.1 Look at the plot

How do the all the events in the story relate to one another?
How are they related to the story as a whole?
What conflicts occur in the story?
How are these conflicts developed or resolved?
Does the story include any noteworthy plot devices, such as flashbacks or foreshadowing?

3.2 Analyze the characters

Who are the protagonists? And who are the antagonists?
What are the characters' most striking traits?
How do these individuals interact with one another?
What motivates them to take certain actions?
Are the characters fully developed, or are they stereotypes whose sole purpose is to express a single trait or to move the plot along?

3.3 Identify the setting

At what time period and in what geographic location does the action of the story occur?
How does the setting affect the characters of the story?
How does it determine the relationships among the characters?
How does the setting affect the plot?
Does the setting create a mood or atmosphere for the story?
In what way does the setting reinforce the central ideas that the story examines?

3.4 Examine the narrative point of view

What person(s) is/are telling the story?
Is the story told in the first person or in the third person?
Does the narrator see from various perspectives, or is the story restricted to the perspective of one person?
Is the narrator a major character telling his or her own story or a minor character who witnesses events in the story?
How much does the narrator know about the development of the events?
Does the narrator present an accurate picture of events?
Does the narrator understand the full significance of the story he or she is telling?

3.5 Analyze the style, tone, and language

Does the writer make any unusual use of diction or syntax?
Does the writer use imaginative figures of speech? What are the patterns of imagery?

What styles or levels of speech are associated with particular characters?
What words or phrases are repeated throughout the work?
Is the story's style plain or elaborate?
Does the narrator's tone reveal his or her attitude toward characters or events?
Are there any discrepancies between the narrator's attitude and the attitude of the author?
Is the tone of the story playful, humorous, ironic, satirical, serious, solemn, bitter, formal, or informal—or does the tone suggest some other attitude?

3.6 Focus on symbolism and allegory

Does the author use any objects or ideas symbolically?
What characters or objects in the story are part of an allegorical framework?
How does an object establish its symbolic or allegorical significance in the story?
Does the same object have different meanings at different places in the story?
Are the symbols or allegorical figures conventional or unusual?
At what points in the story do symbols or allegorical figures appear?

3.7 Identify the themes

What is the central theme? And what other themes are explored?
How is this central idea or concept expressed in the work?
What elements of the story develop the central theme?
How do character, plot, setting, point of view, and symbols reinforce the central theme?
How does the title of the story contribute to readers' understanding of the central theme?

In the process of reading, try to refer to the above list of questions to assist yourself for better comprehension of the work. Of course, you may not answer all the questions listed here; sometimes it will turn out quite helpful even if you can just refer to some of them.

Questions and Exercises

1. What are the main elements to take into account when we read a work of fiction?
2. *Theme* refers to the reasoning aspect of a piece of literature. What should be the most important ways to figure out the dominant theme of a work of fiction?
3. What does irony refer to in literature? Discuss in class how writers use irony to reveal his or her attitude in their works?

Selected Readings of English Fiction

Jonathan Swift

Jonathan Swift (1667—1745) was born in Dublin. His father died before he was born. His family was very poor, and he was compelled to accept help from relatives. He once studied at Dublin University. After graduation, he worked as a secretary for a distant relative, Sir William Temple, a diplomat and a writer of some fame. He read and studied widely, and after his relation with Temple grew unbearable, he left and worked in a little church in Ireland. There, Swift wrote a number of articles and pamphlets which brought him into notice as a satirist of the age. Among his satirical works were *A Tale of a Tub* (1697), *The Battle of the Books* (1697), and *A Modest Proposal* (1729). For several years, he was one of the most important figures in London. The Whigs feared the lash of his satire; the Tories feared to lose his support. But much to his disappointment, his dream to become a bishopric in England was disillusioned. Instead, the Tories offered him the position of a dean at St. Patrick's Cathedral in Dublin, which he accepted bitterly. With his return to Ireland began the last act of his tragic life. There he wrote his best-known literary work *Gulliver's Travels* (1726), which is a satire on the whole English society of the early 18th century. During the last years of his life Swift suffered from a brain disease and died in 1745.

Swift is a talented writer whose simple, direct, and highly effective style won him enormous reputation. His writings are characteristic by satirical vehemence and poetic elegance in the English language. *Gulliver's Travels* is a satire on every aspect of the English society in the early 18th century, including politics, religion, justice and military. Artistically, *Gulliver's Travels* is both a fantasy and a realistic work of fiction. Though the four voyages are full of illusions to contemporary events, the satire was mainly intended as an allegorical and fierce attack on universal human follies and social evils. Swift once wrote of himself, "His satire points at no defect, / But what all mortals may correct."

Gulliver's Travels

Chapter IV

[*Mildendo*[1] *the metropolis of Lilliput, described, together with the emperor's palace.*

A conversation between the author and a principal secretary, concerning the affairs of that empire. The author's offers to serve the emperor in his wars.]

The first request I made, after I had obtained my liberty, was, that I might have license to see Mildendo, the metropolis; which the emperor easily granted me, but with a special charge to do no hurt either to the inhabitants or their houses. The people had notice, by proclamation, of my design to visit the town. The wall which encompassed it is two feet and a half high, and at least eleven inches broad, so that a coach and horses may be driven very safely round it; and it is flanked with strong towers at ten feet distance. I stepped over the great western gate, and passed very gently, and sidling through the two principal streets, only in my short waistcoat, for fear of damaging the roofs and eaves of the houses with the skirts of my coat. I walked with the utmost circumspection, to avoid treading on any stragglers who might remain in the streets, although the orders were very strict, that all people should keep in their houses, at their own peril. The garret windows and tops of houses were so crowded with spectators, that I thought in all my travels I had not seen a more populous place. The city is an exact square, each side of the wall being five hundred feet long. The two great streets, which run across and divide it into four quarters, are five feet wide. The lanes and alleys, which I could not enter, but only view them as I passed, are from twelve to eighteen inches. The town is capable of holding five hundred thousand souls;[2] the houses are from three to five stories; the shops and markets well provided.

The emperor's palace is in the centre of the city where the two great streets meet. It is enclosed by a wall of two feet high, and twenty feet distance from the buildings. I had his majesty's permission to step over this wall; and, the space being so wide between that and the palace, I could easily view it on every side. The outward court is a square of forty feet, and includes two other courts: in the inmost are the royal apartments, which I was very desirous to see, but found it extremely difficult; for the great gates, from one square into another, were but eighteen inches high, and seven inches wide. Now the buildings of the outer court were at least five feet high, and it was impossible for me to stride over them without infinite damage to the pile, though the walls were strongly built of hewn stone, and four inches thick. At the same time the emperor had a great desire that I should see the magnificence of his palace; but this I was not able to do till three days after, which I spent in cutting down with my knife some of the largest trees in the royal park, about a hundred yards distant from the city. Of these trees I made two stools, each about three feet high, and strong enough to bear my weight. The people having received notice a second time, I went again through the city to the palace with my two stools in my hands. When I came to the side of the outer court, I stood upon one stool, and took the other in my hand; this I lifted over the roof, and gently set it down on the space between the first and second court, which was eight feet wide. I then stepped over the building very conveniently from one stool to the other, and drew up the first after me with a hooked stick. By this contrivance I got into the inmost court; and, lying down upon my side, I applied my face to the windows of the middle stories, which were left open on purpose, and discovered the most splendid apartments that can be imagined. There I saw the empress and the young princes, in their several lodgings, with their chief attendants about them. Her imperial majesty was pleased to smile very graciously upon me,[3] and gave me out of the window her hand to kiss.

But I shall not anticipate the reader with further descriptions of this kind,[4] because I reserve them for a greater work, which is now almost ready for the press; containing a general description of this empire, from its first erection, through along series of princes; with a particular account of their wars and politics, laws, learning, and religion; their plants and animals; their peculiar manners and customs, with other matters very curious and useful; my chief design at present being only to relate such events and transactions as happened to the public or to myself during a residence of about nine months in that empire.

One morning, about a fortnight after I had obtained my liberty, Reldresal, principal secretary (as they style him) for private affairs, came to my house attended only by one servant. He ordered his coach to wait at a distance, and desired I would give him an hour's audience; which I readily consented to, on account of his quality and personal merits, as well as of the many good offices he had done me during my solicitations at court. I offered to lie down that he might the more conveniently reach my ear, but he chose rather to let me hold him in my hand during our conversation. He began with compliments on my liberty; said "he might pretend to some merit in it;"[5] but, however, added, "that if it had not been for the present situation of things at court, perhaps I might not have obtained it so soon. For, said he, as flourishing a condition as we may appear to be in to foreigners, we labor under two mighty evils: a violent faction at home, and the danger of an invasion, by a most potent enemy, from abroad. As to the first, you are to understand, that for about seventy moons[6] past there have been two struggling parties in this empire, under the names of Tramecksan and Slamecksan,[7] from the high and low heels of their shoes, by which they distinguish themselves.

It is alleged, indeed, that the high heels are most agreeable to our ancient constitution; but, however this be, his majesty has determined to make use only of low heels[8] in the administration of the government, and all offices in the gift of the crown, as you cannot but observe; and particularly that his majesty's imperial heels are lower at least by a Drurr than any of his court (*Drurr* is a measure about the fourteenth part of an inch). The animosities between these two parties run so high, that they will neither eat, nor drink, nor talk with each other. We compute the Tramecksan, or high heels, to exceed us in number; but the power is wholly on our side. We apprehend his imperial highness, the heir to the crown, to have some tendency towards the high heels;[9] at least we can plainly discover that one of his heels is higher than the other, which gives him a hobble in his gait. Now, in the midst of these intestine disquiets, we are threatened with an invasion from the island of Blefuscu, which is the other great empire of the universe, almost as large and powerful as this of his majesty. For as to what we have heard you affirm, that there are other kingdoms and states in the world inhabited by human creatures as large as yourself, our philosophers are in much doubt, and would rather conjecture that you dropped from the moon, or one of the stars; because it is certain, that a hundred mortals of your bulk would in a short time destroy all the fruits and cattle of his majesty's dominions: besides, our histories of six thousand moons make no mention of any other regions than the two great empires of Lilliput and Blefuscu. Which two mighty powers have, as I was going to tell you, been engaged in a most obstinate war for six-and-thirty moons past.[10] It began upon the following occasion. It is allowed on all hands, that the primitive way of breaking eggs, before we eat them, was upon the larger end; but his present majesty's grandfather,[11] while he was a boy, going to eat an egg, and breaking it according to the ancient practice, happened to cut one of his fingers. Whereupon the emperor his father published an edict, commanding all his subjects, upon great penalties, to break the smaller end of their eggs. The people so highly resented this law, that our histories tell us, there have been six rebellions raised on that account; wherein one emperor lost his life, and another his crown.[12] These civil commotions were constantly fomented by the monarchs of Blefuscu; and when they were quelled, the exiles always fled for refuge to that empire. It is computed that eleven thousand persons have at several times suffered death, rather than submit to break their eggs at the smaller end. Many hundred large volumes have been published upon this controversy: but the books of the Big-Endians have been long forbidden, and the whole party rendered incapable by law of holding employments. During the course of these troubles, the emperors of Blefuscu did frequently expostulate by their ambassadors, accusing us of making a schism in religion, by offending against a fundamental doctrine of our great prophet Lustrog, in the fifty-fourth chapter of the Blundecral (which is their Alcoran).[13] This, however, is thought to be a mere strain upon the text; for the words are these: that all true believers break their eggs at the convenient end; and which is the convenient end, seems, in my humble opinion to be left to every man's conscience, or at least in the power of the chief magistrate to determine. Now, the Big-endian exiles have found so much credit in the emperor of Blefuscu's court, and so much private assistance and encouragement from their party here at home, that a bloody war has been carried on between the two empires for six-and-thirty moons, with various success; during which time we have lost forty capital ships, and a much greater number of smaller vessels, together with thirty thousand of our best seamen and soldiers; and the damage received by the enemy is reckoned to be somewhat greater than ours. However, they have now equipped a numerous fleet, and are just preparing to make a descent upon us; and his imperial majesty, placing great confidence in your valor and strength, has commanded me to lay this account of his affairs before you.

I desired the secretary to present my humble duty to the emperor; and to let him know, "that I thought it would not become me, who was a foreigner, to interfere with parties; but I was ready, with the hazard of my life, to defend his person and state against all invaders."

Notes

[1] Mildendo: an anagram of London.

[2] five hundred thousand souls: The population of London in 1700 has been estimated at 550,000.

[3] Her imperial majesty...upon me: This is perhaps an allusion to Queen Anne's inclination towards the Tories.

[4] anticipate the reader…of this kind: tell the reader beforehand what he can read later.

[5] pretend to some merit in it: claim some credit or worth for my liberty; he claimed that he had made some contribution in releasing me.

[6] about seventy moons: If Lilliputian "moons" can indicate years, this implies that party strife originated in the Civil War, which ended 74 years before 1725 (when Swift was writing his first version of *Gulliver's Travels*).

[7] Tramecksan and Slamecksan: the High Church party (Tories), and Low Church party (Whigs).

[8] his Majesty has determined to make use only of low heels: George I favored the Whigs.

[9] tendency towards the High-Heels: George II, then Prince of Wales, favored the Tories.

[10] six-and-thirty moons: England was at war with France from 1689 (35 years before 1725) until 1697 (War of the League of Augsburg), and again 1701—1713 (War of the Spanish Succession).

[11] grandfather: presumably Henry VIII, who cut his finger (felt injured at not being allowed to marry Anne Boleyn) because he approached his egg (symbol of Easter, and so of Christianity) from the larger end (the Catholic Church). To soothe his childish irritation, his father (Henry himself in his adult capacity of King) commanded his subjects to approach their eggs from the smaller end (the Church of England). Thus Big-Endians are Catholics, Small-Endians Anglicans.

[12] one emperor…and another: Charles I…and James II.

[13] Alcoran: the Koran.

Commentary

Gulliver's Travels, Swift's masterpiece, records the four voyages of Lemuel Gulliver, and his adventures in four astounding countries. The first one tells of his voyage and shipwreck in Lilliput, where the inhabitants are about as tall as man's thumbs, and all their acts and motives are on the same dwarfish scale. The two great parties, the Littleendians and Bigendians, who have plunged the country into civil war over the momentous question of whether an egg should be broken on its big or on its little end, are satires on the politics at the time.

In the second voyage Gulliver is abandoned in Brobdingnag, where the inhabitants are giants, and everything is done upon an enormous scale. When Gulliver tells about his own people and their ambitions and wars and conquests, the giants can only wonder that such great venom could exist in such little insects.

In the third voyage Gulliver continues his adventures in Laputa, which is a satire upon all the scientists and philosophers. Laputa is a flying island, held up in the air by a loadstone; and all the professors of the famous academy there are of the same airy constitution.

In the fourth voyage the merciless satire is carried out to its logical conclusion. This brings us to the land of the Houyhnhnms, in which horses, superior and intelligent creatures, are the ruling animals. All our interest, however, is centered on the Yahoos, a frightful race, having the form and appearance of man, but living in unspeakable degradation.

Chapter IV of *Gulliver's Travels* tells of Gulliver's early experience in Lilliput after he is captured by the Lilliputians after the shipwreck. From a principal secretary, Gulliver is informed of the affairs of that empire. The satire becomes obvious when we find that there is a violent faction between two struggling parties in the empire, a reference to the Whigs and the Tories at the time. There is civil strife between Lilliput and the neighboring empire of Blefuscu due to a quarrel between the two ways of breaking eggs, whether upon the larger end or upon the smaller one. Swift uses plain and straightforward language to describe the smallness of the Lilliputians not only in appearance but also in everything they do and say, which helps emphasize their ridiculous actions.

Questions and Exercises

1. In this chapter, Swift describes the smallness of the Lilliputians. What does this "smallness" imply in the author's satire of the aristocratic bourgeois society of the time?
2. What is the cause of the civil strife and war between Lilliput and the neighboring

empire of Blefuscu? What is the target of the author's satire?

3. What are some elements of the society that Swift exposes as ridiculous in *Gulliver's Travels*? Is the satire "gentle" or "violent"?

Charles Dickens

Charles Dickens (1812—1870) is undoubtedly regarded as the greatest representative of the English critical realism. He was born at Portsmouth, where his father was a clerk in the Navy Pay Office. In 1821 the Dickens family moved to a poor quarter in London. The old Mr. Dickens was heavily in debt and did not know which way to turn for money. The few possessions they had were sold one by one, but things still went from bad to worse. Finally Mr. Dickens was taken to the Marshalsea Prison, London, for debt. Shortly afterwards Mrs. Dickens and the younger children went to the prison, too, to join the father.

Meanwhile the 12-year-old Charles, weak and sensitive, was sent to work in an underground cellar at a blacking factory in the East End of London. He was lonely and hungry. At the age of 15, Dickens left school for good and became a lawyers clerk. After work, he learned shorthand and visited the British Museum Library, filling up the gaps in his education by self reading.

The rest of his life is a story of work, and work without rest. He followed up the triumph of *Pickwick Papers* with a quick succession of outstanding novels in which he masterly depicted the life of contemporary English society. From 1838 to 1841 appeared *Oliver Twist*, *Nicholas Nickleby*, *The Old Curiosity Shop*, *Dombey and Son*, *David Copperfield*, *Hard Times*, *Little Dorrit*, *A Tale of Two Cities*, *Great Expectations,* and so on. His energy was almost boundless, but his use of it was so prodigal that he died, worn out, at the age of 58.

Oliver Twist

The room in which the boys were fed, was a large stone hall, with a copper at one end: out of which the master, dressed in an apron for the purpose,[1] and assisted by one or two women, ladled the gruel at mealtimes. Of this festive composition[2] each boy had one porringer, and no more—except on occasions of great public rejoicing,[3] when he had two ounces and a quarter of bread besides.

The bowls never wanted washing. The boys polished them with their spoons till they shone again; and when they had performed this operation (which never took very long, the spoons being nearly as large as the bowls), they would sit staring at the copper, with such eager eyes, as if they could have devoured the very bricks of which it was composed; employing themselves, meanwhile, in sucking their fingers most assiduously, with the view of catching up any stray splashes of gruel[4] that might have been cast thereon. Boys have generally excellent appetites.

Oliver Twist and his companions suffered the tortures of slow starvation for three months: at last they got so voracious and wild with hunger, that one boy, who was tall for his age, and hadn't been used to that sort of thing[5] (for his father had kept a small cook-shop), hinted darkly to his companions, that unless he had another basin of gruel per diem,[6] he was afraid he might some night happen to eat the boy who slept next him, who happened to be a weakly youth of tender age. He had a wild, hungry eye; and they implicitly believed him. A council was held; lots were cast who should walk up to the master after supper that evening, and ask for more; and it fell to Oliver Twist.[7]

The evening arrived; the boys took their places. The master, in his cook's uniform, stationed himself at the copper; his pauper assistants ranged themselves behind him; the gruel was served out; and a long grace was said over the short commons.[8] The gruel disappeared; the boys whispered each other, and winked at Oliver; while his next neighbours nudged him. Child as he was, he was desperate with hunger, and reckless with misery. He rose from the table; and advancing to the master, basin and spoon in hand, said, somewhat alarmed at his own temerity:

"Please, sir, I want some more."

The master was a fat, healthy man; but he turned very pale. He gazed in stupefied astonishment on the small rebel for some seconds, and then clung for support to the copper. The assistants were paralyzed with wonder; the boys with fear.

"What!" said the master at length, in a faint voice.

"Please, sir," replied Oliver, "I want some more."

The master aimed a blow at Oliver's head with the ladle; pinioned him in his arm;[9] and shrieked aloud for the beadle.

The board were sitting in solemn conclave,[10] when Mr. Bumble[11] rushed into the room in great excitement, and addressing the gentleman in the high chair, said,

"Mr. Limbkins,[12] I beg your pardon, sir! Oliver Twist has asked for more!"

There was a general start. Horror was depicted on every countenance.

"For MORE!" said Mr. Limbkins. "Compose yourself, Bumble, and answer me distinctly. Do I understand that he asked for more, after he had eaten the supper allotted by the dietary?"

"He did, sir," replied Bumble.

"That boy will be hung," said the gentleman in the white waistcoat. "I know that boy will be hung."

Nobody controverted the prophetic gentleman's opinion. An animated discussion took place. Oliver was ordered into instant confinement; and a bill was next morning pasted on the outside of the gate, offering a reward of five pounds to anybody who would take Oliver Twist off the hands of the parish.[13] In other words, five pounds and Oliver Twist were offered to any man or woman who wanted an apprentice to any trade, business, or calling.

"I never was more convinced of anything in my life," said the gentleman in the white waistcoat, as he knocked at the gate and read the bill next morning: "I never was more convinced of anything in my life, than I am that that boy will come to be hung."

As I purpose to show in the sequel whether the white waist-coated gentleman was right or not, I should perhaps mar the interest of this narrative (supposing it to possess any at all), if I ventured to hint just yet, whether the life of Oliver Twist had this violent termination or no.[14]

Notes

[1] for the purpose: for the purpose of starting the meal.

[2] festive composition: (humorously used) the mixture of various leftovers from a sumptuous banquet.

[3] occasions of great public rejoicing: occasions of exhilarating public festivities.

[4] with the view of catching up any stray splashes of gruel: with the hope of catching sight of some splashing of porridge.

[5] that sort of thing: the torture of slow starvation.

[6] per diem: (Latin) each day.

[7] it fell to Oliver Twist: The lot was cast to Oliver Twist.

[8] a long grace was said over the short commons: There were long prayers to be said before each meal which just took a brief duration of time.

[9] pinioned him in his arms: seized the boy tightly by binding his arms at the back.

[10] The board...conclave: The parish board of directors were having a secret meeting.

[11] Mr. Bumble: the beadle, a servant of the church.

[12] Mr. Limbkins: the director of the parish board.

[13] take Oliver Twist off the hands of the parish: get rid of Oliver Twist from the orphanage which was run by the parish.

[14] As I purpose...termination or no: This paragraph is the writer's own remark about the incident.

Commentary

Oliver Twist, written in 1837—1938, tells the story of an orphan boy, whose adventures provide a description of the lower depths of London. Oliver Twist is of unknown parentage. He is born in a workhouse and brought up under cruel conditions. The tyrant at whose hands he especially suffers is Bumble, the parish beadle. After serving an unhappy apprenticeship to an undertaker, he runs away to London, where he falls into the hands of a gang of thieves. The head of the gang is old Fagin, and the other chief members are the burglar Bill Sikes, his mistress Nancy, and the artful Dodger, a young pickpocket. They make every effort to force Oliver into being a thief. After a succession of miserable sufferings, he is rescued by a relative of his, and is finally able to live a normal life.

In the preface to the novel, Dickens proclaims himself a realist, and he does appear as such in his novel *Oliver Twist*. He makes his readers aware of the inhumanity of city life under capitalism. The first eleven chapters provide a most bitter and thoroughgoing exposure of the terrible conditions in the English workhouse of the time and the cruel treatment of a poor orphan by all sorts of philanthropists. The famous scene in Chapter II selected here, in which Oliver is beaten up and punished merely because he ventures to ask for an extra portion of gruel to alleviate his intolerable hunger, is only one of the many details to show the extreme brutality and corruption of the oppressors and their agents. Scenes like this abound in this novel, from which we can see the great critical realist Charles Dickens voicing the helpless sufferings of the poor and oppressed of his time.

Questions and Exercises

1. What do you think happened in workhouses during the reign of Queen Victoria?
2. There is a lot of humor in Dickens' writing. Can you just find some examples in this part to show the writer's sense of humor?
3. Irony is a rather important technique in writing fiction. Try to find out where the irony lies in this chapter and tell what kind of irony Dickens is employing here.

Jane Austen

Jane Austen (1775—1817) was the youngest daughter of George Austen, rector of the village of Steventon in Hampshire. She received a good education at home. She lived an uneventful life amid the provincial surroundings of the South, and never married throughout her life.

Jane Austen started writing at an early age. Her main novels include: *Sense and Sensibility* (1811), *Pride and Prejudice* (1813), *Mansfield Park* (1814), *Emma* (1816), and *Persuasion* (1818). In her works she never touched upon the class conflicts of her time, and restricted her subject matter to a narrow range of society and events: a quiet and prosperous, middle-class circle in provincial surroundings. However, she treated this material with such subtlety of observation, depth of psychological penetration and delicacy of touch that she is ranked among the best of English novelists.

Her works show a wealth of character studies, and abound in wit, humor and charm. *Pride and Prejudice* is the most popular of her novels. The characters are remarkably portrayed and come to life under her pen: the long-winded match-making mother; the sycophantic clergyman; the clever and quick-minded Elizabeth whose prejudice is matched with Darcy's pride; the empty-headed and flirtatious Kitty and Lidia; the modest, earnest, and unselfish Jane; and the good-natured Mr. Bennet whose dry humor adds poignancy to the novel. It is not without reason to say that Jane Austen is credited with having brought the English novel to its maturity.

Pride and Prejudice

Chapter 56

One morning, about a week after Bingley's engagement with Jane had been formed, as he and the females of the family were sitting together in the dining room, their attention was suddenly drawn to the window, by the sound of a carriage; and they perceived a chaise and four driving up the lawn. It was too early in the morning for visitors, and besides, the equipage did not answer to that of any of their neighbours. The horses were posted;[1] and neither the carriage, nor the livery of the servant who preceded it, were familiar to them. As it was certain, however, that somebody was coming, Bingley instantly prevailed on Miss Bennet to avoid the confinement of such an intrusion, and walk away with him into the shrubbery. They both set off, and the conjectures of the remaining three continued, though with little satisfaction, till the door was thrown open and their visitor entered. It was Lady Catherine de Bourgh.

They were of course all intending to be surprised; but their astonishment was beyond their expectation; and on the part of Mrs. Bennet and Kitty, though she was perfectly unknown to them, even inferior to[2] what Elizabeth felt.

She entered the room with an air more than usually ungracious, made no other reply to Elizabeth's salutation than a slight inclination of the head, and sat down without saying a word. Elizabeth had mentioned her name to her mother on her ladyship's entrance, though no request of introduction had been made.

Mrs. Bennet all amazement, though flattered by having a guest of such high importance, received her with the utmost politeness. After sitting for a moment in silence, she said very stiffly to Elizabeth,

"I hope you are well, Miss Bennet. That lady, I suppose, is your mother."

Elizabeth replied very concisely that she was.

"And that I suppose is one of your sisters."

"Yes, madam," said Mrs. Bennet, delighted to speak to a Lady Catherine. "She is my youngest girl but one. My youngest of all is lately married, and my eldest is somewhere about the grounds, walking with a young man who, I believe, will soon become a part of the family."

"You have a very small park here," returned Lady Catherine after a short silence.

"It is nothing in comparison of Rosings,[3] my lady, I dare say; but I assure you it is much larger than Sir William Lucas's."

"This must be a most inconvenient sitting room for the evening, in summer; the windows are full west."

Mrs. Bennet assured her that they never sat there after dinner, and then added,

"May I take the liberty of asking your ladyship whether you left Mr. and Mrs. Collins well."

"Yes, very well. I saw them the night before last."

Elizabeth now expected that she would produce a letter for her from Charlotte, as it seemed the only probable motive for her calling. But no letter appeared, and she was completely puzzled.

Mrs. Bennet, with great civility, begged her ladyship to take some refreshment; but Lady Catherine very resolutely, and not very politely, declined eating any thing; and then, rising up, said to Elizabeth,

"Miss Bennet, there seemed to be a prettyish kind of a little wilderness on one side of your lawn. I should be glad to take a turn in it, if you will favour me with your company."

"Go, my dear," cried her mother, "and shew her ladyship about the different walks. I think she will be pleased with the hermitage."

Elizabeth obeyed, and running into her own room for her parasol, attended her noble guest down stairs. As they passed through the hall, Lady Catherine opened the doors into the dining-parlour and drawing-room, and pronouncing them, after a short survey, to be decent looking rooms, walked on.

Her carriage remained at the door, and Elizabeth saw that her waiting-woman was in it. They proceeded in silence along the gravel walk that led to the copse; Elizabeth was determined to make no effort for conversation with a woman who was now more than usually insolent and disagreeable.

"How could I ever think her like her nephew?" said she, as she looked in her face.

As soon as they entered the copse, Lady Catherine began in the following manner:

"You can be at no loss, Miss Bennet, to understand the reason of my journey hither. Your own heart, your own conscience, must tell you why I come."

Elizabeth looked with unaffected astonishment.

"Indeed, you are mistaken, Madam. I have not been at all able to account for the honour of seeing you here."

"Miss Bennet," replied her ladyship, in an angry tone, "you ought to know, that I am not to be trifled with. But however insincere *you* may choose to be, you shall not find *me* so. My character has ever been celebrated for its sincerity and frankness, and in a cause of such moment[4] as this, I shall certainly not depart from it. A report of a most alarming nature reached me two days ago. I was told that not only your sister was on the point of being most advantageously married, but that *you*, that Miss Elizabeth Bennet, would, in all likelihood, be soon afterwards united to my nephew, my own nephew, Mr. Darcy. Though I *know* it must be a scandalous falsehood, though I would not injure him so much as to suppose the truth of it possible, I instantly resolved on setting off for this place, that I might make my sentiments known to you."

"If you believed it impossible to be true," said Elizabeth, colouring with astonishment and disdain, "I wonder you took the trouble of coming so far. What could your ladyship propose by it?"

"At once to insist upon having such a report universally contradicted."[5]

"Your coming to Longbourn, to see me and my family," said Elizabeth coolly, "will be rather a confirmation of it; if, indeed, such a report is in existence."

"If! Do you then pretend to be ignorant of it? Has it not been industriously circulated by yourselves? Do you not know that such a report is spread abroad?"

"I never heard that it was."

"And can you likewise declare, that there is no *foundation* for it?"

"I do not pretend to possess equal frankness with your ladyship. *You* may ask questions which *I* shall not choose to answer."

"This is not to be borne.[6] Miss Bennet, I insist on being satisfied. Has he, has my nephew, made you an offer of marriage?"

"Your ladyship has declared it to be impossible."

"It ought to be so; it must be so, while he retains the use of his reason. But *your* arts and allurements may, in a moment of infatuation, have made him forget what he owes to himself and to all his family. You may have drawn him in."

"If I have, I shall be the last person to confess it."

"Miss Bennet, do you know who I am? I have not been accustomed to such language as this. I am almost the nearest relation he has in the world, and am entitled to know all his dearest concerns."

"But you are not entitled to know *mine*; nor will such behaviour as this, ever induce me to be explicit."

"Let me be rightly understood. This match, to which you have the presumption to aspire, can never take place. No, never. Mr. Darcy is engaged to *my daughter*. Now what have you to say?"

"Only this; that if he is so, you can have no reason to suppose he will make an offer to me."

Lady Catherine hesitated for a moment, and then replied,

"The engagement between them is of a peculiar kind. From their infancy, they have been intended for each other. It was the favourite wish of *his* mother, as well as of hers. While in their cradles, we planned the union: and now, at the moment when the wishes of both sisters[7] would be accomplished in their marriage, to be prevented by a young woman of inferior birth, of no importance in the world, and wholly unallied to the family! Do you pay no regard to the wishes of his friends? To his tacit engagement with Miss De Bourgh? Are you lost to every feeling of propriety and delicacy?[8] Have you not heard me say that from his earliest hours he was destined for his cousin?"

"Yes, and I had heard it before. But what is that to me? If there is no other objection to my marrying your nephew, I shall certainly not be kept from it by knowing that his mother and aunt wished him to marry Miss De Bourgh. You both did as much as you could in planning the marriage. Its completion depended on others. If Mr. Darcy is neither by honour nor inclination confined to his cousin, why is not he to make another choice? And if I am that choice, why may not I accept him?"

"Because honour, decorum, prudence, nay, interest, forbid it. Yes, Miss Bennet, interest; for do not expect to be noticed by his family or friends, if you willfully act against the inclinations of all. You will be censured, slighted, and despised, by every one connected with him. Your alliance will be a disgrace; your name will never even be mentioned by any of us."

"These are heavy misfortunes," replied Elizabeth. "But the wife of Mr. Darcy must have such extraordinary sources of happiness necessarily attached to her situation, that she could, upon the whole, have no cause to repine."[9]

"Obstinate, headstrong girl! I am ashamed of you! Is this your gratitude for my attentions to you last spring? Is nothing due to me on that score?[10] Let us sit down. You are to understand, Miss Bennet, that I came here with the determined resolution of carrying my purpose; nor will I be dissuaded from it. I have not been used to submit to any person's whims. I have not been in the habit of brooking disappointment."

"*That* will make your ladyship's situation at present more pitiable; but it will have no effect on *me*."

"I will not be interrupted. Hear me in silence. My daughter and my nephew are formed for each other. They are descended, on the maternal side, from the same noble line; and, on the father's, from respectable, honourable, and ancient—though untitled—families. Their fortune on both sides is splendid. They are destined for each other by the voice of every member of their respective houses; and what is to divide them? The upstart pretensions[11] of a young woman without family, connections, or fortune. Is this to be endured! But it must not, shall not be. If you were sensible of your own good, you would not wish to quit the sphere in which you have been brought up."

"In marrying your nephew, I should not consider myself as quitting that sphere. He is a gentleman; I am a gentleman's daughter; so far we are equal."

"True. You *are* a gentleman's daughter. But who was your mother? Who are your uncles and aunts? Do not imagine me ignorant of their condition."

"Whatever my connections may be," said Elizabeth, "if your nephew does not object to them, they can be nothing to *you*."

"Tell me once for all, are you engaged to him?"

Though Elizabeth would not, for the mere purpose of obliging Lady Catherine, have answered this question, she could not but say, after a moment's deliberation,

"I am not."

Lady Catherine seemed pleased.

"And will you promise me, never to enter into such an engagement?"

"I will make no promise of the kind."

"Miss Bennet I am shocked and astonished. I expected to find a more reasonable young woman. But do not deceive yourself into a belief that I will ever recede. I shall not go away till you have given me the assurance I require."

"And I certainly never shall give it. I am not to be intimidated into anything so wholly unreasonable. Your ladyship wants Mr. Darcy to marry your daughter; but would my giving you the wished-for promise make their marriage at all more probable? Supposing him to be attached to me, would my refusing to accept his hand make him wish to bestow it on his cousin? Allow me to say, Lady Catherine, that the arguments with which you have supported this extraordinary application[12] have been as frivolous as the application was ill-judged. You have widely mistaken my character, if you think I can be worked on by such persuasions as these. How far your nephew might approve of your interference in *his* affairs, I cannot tell; but you have certainly no right to concern yourself in mine. I must beg, therefore, to be importuned no farther on the subject."

"Not so hasty, if you please. I have by no means done. To all the objections I have already urged, I have still another to add. I am no stranger to the particulars of your youngest sister's infamous elopement. I know it all; that the young man's marrying her was a patched-up business,[13] at the expense of your father and uncles. And is *such* a girl to be my nephew's sister? Is *her* husband, is the son of his late father's steward, to be his brother? Heaven and earth!—of what are you thinking? Are the shades of Pemberley[14] to be thus polluted?"

"You can *now* have nothing farther to say," she resentfully answered. "You have insulted me in every possible method. I must beg to return to the house."

And she rose as she spoke. Lady Catherine rose also, and they turned back. Her ladyship was highly incensed.

"You have no regard, then, for the honour and credit of my nephew! Unfeeling, selfish girl! Do you not consider that a connection with you must disgrace him in the eyes of everybody?"

"Lady Catherine, I have nothing farther to say. You know my sentiments."

"You are then resolved to have him?"

"I have said no such thing. I am only resolved to act in that manner, which will, in my own opinion, constitute my happiness, without reference to you, or to any person so wholly unconnected with me."

"It is well. You refuse, then, to oblige me. You refuse to obey the claims of duty, honour, and gratitude. You are determined to ruin him in the opinion of all his friends, and make him the contempt of the world."

"Neither duty, nor honour, nor gratitude," replied Elizabeth, "have any possible claim on me, in the present instance. No principle of either would be violated by my marriage with Mr. Darcy. And with regard to the resentment of his family, or the indignation of the world, if the former were excited by his marrying me, it would not give me one moment's concern—and the world in general would have too much sense to join in the scorn."

"And this is your real opinion! This is your final resolve! Very well. I shall now know how to act. Do not imagine, Miss Bennet, that your ambition will ever be gratified. I came to try you. I hoped to find you reasonable; but, depend upon it, I will carry my point."

In this manner Lady Catherine talked on, till they were at the door of the carriage, when, turning hastily round, she added, "I take no leave of you,[15] Miss Bennet. I send no compliments to your mother. You deserve no such attention. I am most seriously displeased."

Elizabeth made no answer; and without attempting to persuade her ladyship to return into the house, walked quietly into it herself. She heard the carriage drive away as she proceeded up stairs. Her mother impatiently met her at the door of the dressing-room, to ask why Lady Catherine would not come in again and rest herself.

"She did not choose it," said her daughter, "she would go."

"She is a very fine-looking woman! and her calling here was prodigiously civil! for she only came, I suppose, to tell us the Collinses were well. She is on her road somewhere, I dare say, and so, passing through Meryton,[16] thought she might as well call on you. I suppose she had nothing particular to say to you, Lizzy?"

Elizabeth was forced to give into a little falsehood here; for to acknowledge the substance of their conversation was impossible.

Notes

[1] posted: hired from an inn, implying the guest comes from afar.

[2] inferior to: not as much as.

[3] Rosings: name of Lady Catherine's House.

[4] a cause of such moment: such an important event.

[5] having such a report universally contradicted: having this news publicly denied.

[6] borne: endured; tolerated.

[7] both sisters: Lady Catherine and Darcy's mother.

[8] propriety and delicacy: conventional appropriateness and gracious subtlety.

[9] no cause to repine: no reason for dissatisfaction.

[10] Is nothing due to me on that score: In spring that year, Elizabeth went to Lady Catherine's home as a guest and was warmly entertained. That is why the latter thought she should be politely treated by Elizabeth.

[11] upstart pretensions: aspiring wishful thinking.

[12] application: request.

[13] a patched-up business: a matter that was rescued or put right with money.

[14] the shades of Pemberley: the graceful scenery of Darcy's manor.

[15] take no leave of you: say no good-bye to you.

[16] Meryton: name of the district where the Bannets live.

Commentary

The plot of *Pride and Prejudice* evolves mainly around the Bennet family at Longbourn near London. Mr. and Mrs. Bennet have five grown-up daughters. The marriage prospects of the girls are Mrs. Bonnet's chief concern in life, since under the law of the time the family estate will, on Mr. Bennet's death, pass on to his nearest male relation. At the opening of the novel, Mr. Charles Bingley, a rich bachelor, takes Netherfied Park, an estate near Longbourn, and brings there his friend, Mr. Fitzwilliam Darcy. Bingley falls in love with Jane, the eldest Bennet girl. Darcy is attracted to her next sister, the lively and witty Elizabeth, but offends her by his supercilious behavior. Thus Darcy's pride is pitted against Elizabeth's prejudice. He proposes to her but is rejected. Darcy's pride of status is founded on social prejudice, while Elizabeth's prejudice against him is rooted in pride of her own quick perceptions. Thus, Darcy, having been brought up in such a way that he scorns all those outside his own social circle, must overcome his own prejudice in order to win Elizabeth's heart and get her as his wife. After many twists and turns, however, things are cleared up, and the two couples are happily united. One important theme of the novel is that both pride and prejudice are bound to prevent people from reasoning objectively.

In Chapter 56, Austen vividly narrates Lady Catherine's intervention between the relationship of Elizabeth and Darcy. Their conversation is one of the most brilliant and dramatic scenes in the whole book. On hearing that her nephew Darcy is pursuing Elizabeth, Lady Catherine is violently outraged. She deliberately comes to Elizabeth for obstruction. Lady Catherine is aggressively arrogant, while Elizabeth refutes her calmly with bravery, and wins a complete victory at the end.

Elizabeth, the most intelligent and quick-witted protagonist in the story, is one of the most well-known female characters in English literature. Her admirable qualities are numerous—she is lovely, clever, and, in terms of making dialogues, she converses as brilliantly as anyone. Her honesty, virtue, and lively wit enable her to rise above the nonsense and bad behavior that pervade her spiteful society. She becomes the idealized type of new heroine that was not common in previous English literature.

Questions and Exercises

1. Try to make a character analysis and see what main characteristics of Elizabeth and Lady Catherine are respectively revealed in Chapter 56.
2. Read the whole novel to get at least the overall gist of the story, and then discuss what moral lessons can be drawn from the main characters' marriages in the story.

Emily Brontë

Emily Brontë (1818—1848) is one of the famous literary Brontë sisters. When she was two years old, her father, an Irish clergyman, moved the family to the remote village of Haworth set in the bleak moors in Yorkshire. The moorland scenery played a significant part in the lives of the Brontë sisters and nurtured their imagination.

Emily's only novel *Wuthering Heights* was published in 1847, two months after the appearance of Charlotte's *Jane Eyre,* which was immediately and hugely successful. On the contrary, the dark, brooding, strange yet powerful *Wuthering Heights* did not fare well at the time of its publication. It was only after Emily's death that it was re-assessed and became widely recognized as a masterpiece in English literature. Soon after the publication of her novel, Emily's health began to deteriorate rapidly. In 1848 she died of tuberculosis.

The story of *Wuthering Heights* is narrated by Lockwood, temporary tenant of Thrushcross Grange, who at the opening of the novel stumbles into the violent world of Wuthering Heights, the home of his landlord Heathcliff. The narration is taken up by the housekeeper, Nelly Dean, who had been witness of the interlocked destinies of the original owners of the Heights, the Earnshaw family, and of the Grange, the Linton family. Gradually the novel brings the reader back to the origins of the hatred. Mr. Earnshaw brings home from Liverpool the strange child Heathcliff. As he grows up, he brings love, jealousy, hatred, and revenge into the two families. To ruin other people's happiness does not bring him real comfort. Heathcliff eventually destroys himself.

Wuthering Heights belongs to the tradition of Gothic novels. The setting is often in a remote soil, actions take place in ruined, deserted places, and the novel usually pursues the creation of a grotesque atmosphere through depiction of a rather bizarre and terrifying natural environment. There were steep hills and precipitous slopes stretching far and deep. Ridges stood high like some giants on the landscape. Leafless trees stood on bare rocks and strong winds howled across the moor.

Wuthering Heights

Chapter 15

Another week over—and I[1] am so many days nearer health, and spring! I have now heard all my neighbour's history, at different sittings, as the housekeeper[2] could spare time from more important occupations. I'll continue it in her own words, only a little condensed. She is, on the whole, a very fair narrator, and I don't think I could improve her style.

In the evening, she said, the evening of my visit to the Heights, I knew, as well as if I saw him, that Mr. Heathcliff was about the place; and I shunned going out, because I still carried his letter in my pocket, and didn't want to be threatened or teased any more. I had made up my mind not to give it till my master went somewhere, as I could not guess how its receipt would affect Catherine. The consequence was, that it did not reach her before the lapse of three days. The fourth was Sunday, and I brought it into her room after the family were gone to church. There was a manservant left to keep the house with me, and we generally made a practice of locking the doors during the hours of service;[3] but on that occasion the weather was so warm and pleasant that I set them wide open, and, to fulfill my engagement, as I knew who would be coming, I told my companion that the mistress wished very much for some oranges, and he must run over to the village and get a few, to be paid for on the morrow. He departed, and I went upstairs.

Mrs. Linton[4] sat in a loose, white dress, with a light shawl over her shoulders, in the recess of the open window, as usual. Her thick, long hair had been partly removed at the beginning of her illness, and now she wore it simply combed in its natural tresses over her temples and neck. Her appearance was altered, as I had told Heathcliff; but when she was calm, there seemed unearthly beauty in the change. The flash of her eyes had been succeeded by a dreamy and melancholy softness; they no longer gave the impression of looking at the objects around her: they appeared always to gaze beyond, and far beyond—you would have said out of this world. Then the paleness of her face—its haggard aspect having vanished as she recovered flesh—and the peculiar expression arising from her mental state, though painfully suggestive of their causes, added to the touching interest which she awakened; and—invariably to me, I know, and to any person who saw her, I should think—refuted more tangible proofs of convalescence, and stamped her as one doomed to decay.

A book lay spread on the sill before her, and the scarcely perceptible wind fluttered its leaves at intervals. I believe Linton had laid it there: for she never endeavoured to divert herself with reading, or occupation of any kind, and he would spend many an hour in trying to entice her attention to some subject which had formerly been her amusement. She was conscious of his aim, and in her better moods endured his efforts placidly, only showing their uselessness by now and then suppressing a wearied sigh, and checking him at last with the saddest of smiles and kisses. At other times, she would turn petulantly away, and hide her face in her hands, or even push him off angrily; and then he took care to let her alone, for he was certain of doing no good.

Gimmerton chapel bells were still ringing; and the full, mellow flow of the beck in the valley came soothingly on the ear. It was a sweet substitute for the yet absent murmur of the summer foliage, which drowned that music about the Grange when the trees were in leaf. At Wuthering Heights it always sounded on quiet days following a great thaw or a season of steady rain. And of Wuthering Heights Catherine was thinking as she listened: that is, if she thought or listened at all; but she had the vague, distant look I mentioned before, which expressed no recognition of material things either by ear or eye.

"There's a letter for you, Mrs. Linton," I said, gently inserting it in one hand that rested on her knee. "You must read it immediately, because it wants an answer. Shall I break the seal?" "Yes," she answered, without altering the direction of her eyes. I opened it—it was very short. "Now," I continued, "read it." She drew away her hand, and let it fall. I replaced it in her lap, and stood waiting till it should please her to glance down; but that movement was so long delayed that at last I resumed:

"Must I read it, ma'am? It is from Mr. Heathcliff."

There was a start and a troubled gleam of recollection, and a struggle to arrange her ideas. She lifted the letter, and seemed to peruse it; and when she came to the signature she sighed: yet still I found she had not gathered its import, for, upon my desiring to hear her reply, she merely pointed to the name, and gazed at me with mournful and questioning eagerness.

"Well, he wishes to see you," said I, guessing her need of an interpreter. "He's in the garden by this time, and impatient to know what answer I shall bring."

As I spoke, I observed a large dog lying on the sunny grass beneath raise its ears as if about to bark, and then smoothing them back, announce, by a wag of the tail, that someone approached whom it did not consider a stranger. Mrs. Linton bent forward, and listened breathlessly. The minute after a step traversed the hall; the open house was too tempting for Heathcliff to resist walking in: most likely he supposed that I was inclined to shirk my promise, and so resolved to trust to his own audacity. With straining eagerness Catherine gazed towards the entrance of her chamber. He did not hit the right room directly, she motioned me to admit him, but he found it out ere I could reach the door, and in a stride or two was at her side, and had her grasped in his arms.

He neither spoke nor loosed his hold for some five minutes, during which period he bestowed more kisses than ever he gave in his life before, I dare say: but then my mistress had kissed him first, and I plainly saw that he could hardly bear, for downright agony, to look into her face! The same conviction had stricken him as me, from the instant he beheld her, that there was no prospect of ultimate recovery there—she was fated, sure to die.

"Oh, Cathy! Oh, my life! how can I bear it?" was the first sentence he uttered, in a tone that did not seek to disguise his despair. And now he stared at her so earnestly that I thought the very intensity of his gaze would bring tears into his eyes; but they burned with anguish: they did not melt.

"What now?" said Catherine, leaning back, and returning his look with a suddenly clouded brow: her humor was a mere vane for constantly varying caprices. "You and Edgar have broken my heart, Heathcliff! And you both came to bewail the deed to me, as if you were the people to be pitied! I shall not pity you, not I. You have killed me—and thriven on it, I think. How strong you are! How many years do you mean to live after I am gone?"

Heathcliff had knelt on one knee to embrace her; he attempted to rise, but she seized his hair, and kept him down.

"I wish I could hold you," she continued bitterly, "till we were both dead! I shouldn't care what you suffered. I care nothing for your sufferings. Why shouldn't you suffer? I do! Will you forget me? Will you be happy when I am in the earth? Will you say twenty years hence, 'That's the grave of Catherine Earnshaw. I loved her long ago, and was wretched to lose her; but it is past. I've loved many others since: my children are dearer to me than she was; and at death, I shall not rejoice that I am going to her: I shall be sorry that I must leave them!' Will you say so, Heathcliff?"

"Don't torture me till I am as mad as yourself," cried he, wrenching his head free, and grinding his teeth.

The two, to a cool spectator, made a strange and fearful picture. Well might Catherine deem that heaven would be a land of exile to her, unless with her mortal body she cast away her moral character also. Her present countenance had a wild vindictiveness in its white cheek, and a bloodless lip and scintillating eye; and she retained in her closed fingers a portion of the locks she had been grasping. As to her companion, while raising himself with one hand, he had taken her arm with the other; and so inadequate was his stock of gentleness to the requirements of her condition, that on his letting go I saw four distinct impressions left blue in the colourless skin.

"Are you possessed with a devil," he pursued savagely, "to talk in that manner to me when you are dying? Do you reflect that all those words will be branded on my memory, and eating deeper eternally after you have left me? You know you lie to say I have killed you: and, Catherine, you know that I could as soon forget you as my existence! Is it not sufficient for your infernal selfishness, that while you are at peace I shall writhe in the torments of hell?"

"I shall not be at peace," moaned Catherine, recalled to a sense of physical weakness by the violent, unequal throbbing of her heart, which beat visibly and audibly under this excess of agitation. She said nothing further till the paroxysm was over; then she continued, more kindly—

"I'm not wishing you greater torment than I have, Heathcliff. I only wish us never to be parted: and should a word of mine distress you hereafter, think I feel the same distress underground, and for my own sake, forgive me! Come here and kneel down again! You never harmed me in your life. Nay, if you nurse anger, that will be worse to remember than my harsh words! Won't you come here again? Do!"

Heathcliff went to the back of her chair, and leant over, but not so far as to let her see his face, which was livid with emotion. She bent round to look at him; he would not permit it: turning abruptly, he walked to the fireplace, where he stood, silent, with his back towards us. Mrs. Linton's glance followed him suspiciously: every movement woke a new sentiment in her. After a pause and a prolonged gaze, she resumed; addressing me in accents of indignant disappointment—

"Oh, you see, Nelly, he would not relent a moment to keep me out of the grave. *That* is how I'm loved! Well, never mind. That is not *my* Heathcliff. I shall love mine yet; and take him with me: he's in my soul. And," added she, musingly, "the thing that irks me most in this shattered prison, after all. I'm tired, tired of being enclosed here. I'm wearying to escape into that glorious world,[5] and to be always there: not seeing it dimly through tears, and yearning for it through the walls of an aching heart; but really with it, and in it. Nelly, you think you are better and more fortunate than I; in full health and strength: you are sorry for me—very soon that will be altered. I shall be sorry for *you.* I shall be incomparably beyond and above you all. I *wonder* he won't be near me!" She went on to herself. "I thought he wished it. Heathcliff, dear! you should not be sullen now. Do come to me, Heathcliff."

In her eagerness she rose and supported herself on the arm of the chair. At that earnest appeal he turned to her, looking absolutely desperate. His eyes, wide and wet, at last flashed fiercely on her; his breast heaved convulsively. An instant they held asunder,[6] and then how they met I hardly saw, but Catherine made a spring, and he caught her, and they were locked in an embrace from which I thought my mistress would never be released alive: in fact, to my eyes, she seemed directly insensible. He flung himself into the nearest seat, and on my approaching hurriedly to ascertain if she had fainted, he gnashed at me, and foamed like a mad dog, and gathered her to him with greedy jealousy. I did not feel as if I were in the company of a creature of my own species: it appeared that he would not understand, though I spoke to him; so I stood off, and held my tongue, in great perplexity.

A movement of Catherine's relieved me a little presently: she put up her hand to clasp his neck, and bring her cheek to his as he held her; while he, in return, covering her with frantic caresses, said wildly—

"You teach me now how cruel you've been—cruel and false. Why did you despise me? Why did you betray your own heart, Cathy? I have not one word of comfort. You deserve this. You have killed yourself. Yes, you may kiss me, and cry; and ring out my kisses and tears: they'll blight you—they'll damn you. You loved me—then what *right* had you to leave me? What right—answer me—for the poor fancy you felt for Linton? Because misery and degradation, and death, and nothing that God or Satan could inflict would have parted us, *you*, of your own will, did it. I have not broken your heart—*you* have broken it; and in breaking it, you have broken mine. So much the worse for me, that I am strong. Do I want to live? What kind of living will it be when you—oh, God! would *you* like to live with your soul in the grave?"

"Let me alone. Let me alone," sobbed Catherine. "If I have done wrong, I'm dying for it. It is enough! You left me too: but I won't upbraid you! I forgive you. Forgive me!"

"It is hard to forgive, and to look at those eyes, and feel those wasted hands," he answered. "Kiss me again; and don't let me see your eyes! I forgive what you have done to me. I love *my* murderer—but *yours*! How can I?"

They were silent—their faces hid against each other, and washed by each other's tears. At least, I suppose the weeping was on both sides; as it seemed Heathcliff *could* weep on a great occasion like this.

I grew very uncomfortable, meanwhile; for the afternoon wore fast away, the man whom I had sent off returned from his errand, and I could distinguish, by the shine of the westering sun up the valley, a concourse thickening outside Gimmerton chapel porch.

"Service is over," I announced. "My master will be here in half an hour."

Heathcliff groaned a curse, and strained Catherine closer: she never moved.

Ere long I perceived a group of the servants passing up the road towards the kitchen wing. Mr. Linton was not far behind; he opened the gate himself and sauntered slowly up, probably enjoying the lovely afternoon that breathed as soft as summer.

"Now he is here," I exclaimed. "For Heaven's sake, hurry down! You'll not meet anyone on the front stairs. Do be quick; and stay among the trees till he is fairly in."

"I must go, Cathy," said Heathcliff, seeking to extricate himself from his companion's arms. "But if I live, I'll see you again before you are asleep. I won't stray five yards from your window."

"You must not go!" she answered, holding him as firmly as her strength allowed. "You shall not, I tell you."

"For one hour," he pleaded earnestly.

"Not for one minute," she replied.

"I *must*—Linton will be up immediately," persisted the alarmed intruder.

He would have risen, and unfixed her fingers by the act—she clung fast, gasping: there was mad resolution in her face.

"No!" she shrieked. "Oh, don't, don't go. It is the last time! Edgar will not hurt us. Heathcliff, I shall die! I shall die!"

"Damn the fool! There he is," cried Heathcliff, sinking back into his seat. "Hush, my darling! Hush, hush, Catherine! I'll stay. If he shot me so, I'd expire with a blessing on my lips."

And there they were fast again.[7] I heard my master mounting the stairs—the cold sweat ran from my forehead: I was horrified.

"Are you going to listen to her ravings?" I said passionately. "She does not know what she says. Will you ruin her, because she has not wit to help herself? Get up! You could be free instantly. That is the most diabolical deed that ever you did. We are all done for—master, mistress, and servant.

I wrung my hands, and cried out; Mr. Linton hastened his step at the noise. In the midst of my agitation, I was sincerely glad to observe that Catherine's arms had fallen relaxed, and her head hung down.

"She's fainted or dead," I thought: "so much the better. Far better that she should be dead, than lingering a burden and a misery-maker to all about her."

Edgar sprang to his unbidden guest, blanched with astonishment and rage. What he meant to do, I cannot tell; however, the other stopped all demonstrations, at once, by placing the lifeless looking form[8] in his arms.

"Look there!" he said; "unless you be a fiend, help her first—then you shall speak to me!"

He walked into the parlour, and sat down. Mr. Linton summoned me, and with great difficulty, and after resorting to many means, we managed to restore her to sensation; but she was all bewildered; she sighed, and moaned, and knew nobody. Edgar, in his anxiety for her, forgot her hated friend. I did not. I went, at the earliest opportunity, and besought him to depart; affirming that Catherine was better, and he should hear from me in the morning how she passed the night.

"I shall not refuse to go out of doors," he answered; "but I shall stay in the garden: and, Nelly, mind you keep your word to morrow. I shall be under those larch trees. Mind! or I pay another visit, whether Linton be in or not.

He sent a rapid glance through the half-open door of the chamber, and, ascertaining that what I stated was apparently true, delivered the house of his luckless presence.

Notes

[1] I: Lockwood, a guest at Thrushcross Grange, to whom Nelly is telling the story.

[2] the housekeeper: Nelly Dean.

[3] service: ceremony of worship.

[4] Mrs. Linton: Catherine.

[5] that glorious world: the world of the dead.

[6] hold asunder: hold away from each other.

[7] they were fast again: they held firmly again.

[8] the lifeless looking form: the dying Catherine.

Commentary

Wuthering Heights thoroughly examines the dark side of human nature. It displays that human passion can be both constructive and destructive. In the novel, various human weaknesses are exposed: Catherine is selfish, Edgar weak, Heathcliff savage, Isabella ill-tempered, and Cathy willful. Their weaknesses generate fearful consequences that nearly destroy every character in the novel. But Emily did not condemn the characters. She narrated the story with impartial compassion. The writer seemed to emphasize that it was fate that drove them together, and under a special environment human love becomes a source of tragic disaster.

Critics have commented that the darkly powerful figure of Heathcliff bears much resemblance to Satanic / Byronic hero. Chapter 15 is one of the climactic chapters of the novel. As Catherine and Heathcliff meet for the last time, their love seems to have been torn from their living flesh, and appears as primal and savage as the moors themselves. Here, love is shown to be able to overcome the boundary between life and death.

Questions and Exercises

1. What is the main plot of the whole novel? What causes the tragic ending of the love between Heathcliff and Catherine? Would it have been possible, under the circumstances, for the victimized lovers to find a way out?
2. Is Heathcliff's revenge upon the Earnshaw and Linton families justifiable? What is the author's attitude toward Heathcliff, judging from the final futility of the revenge?
3. What are the respective personalities of Heathcliff, Catherine, Hindley, and Edgar? Suppose you were one of them, what would you choose to do in their juxtaposed situations?

Thomas Hardy

Thomas Hardy (1840—1928), novelist and poet, is one of the representatives of English critical realism at the turn of the 19th century. He was born in Dorset, a southern county of England, which he called Wessex in his books. His father, a builder himself, wanted him to become a builder. At the age of 22, Hardy went to London, where he studied architecture for five years but at the same time also became interested in literature and philosophy. On his return to his native countryside in 1867, Hardy worked as an architect for several years. His first attempt at literature proved successful. So he gave up architecture and made literature his profession.

Hardy's principal works are the Wessex Novels, i.e., the novels describing the characters and environment of his native countryside. They include *Under the Greenwood Tree* (1872), *Far from the Madding Crowd* (1874), *The Return of the Native* (1878), *The Mayor of Casterbridge* (1886), *Tess of the D'Urbervilles* (1891) and *Jude the Obscure* (1896).

These novels have for their setting the agricultural region of the southern counties of England. He truthfully depicts the impoverishment and decay of small farmers who became hired field hands and roamed the country in search of seasonal jobs. These laborers were mercilessly exploited by the rich landowners. The author was pained to see the deterioration of the patriarchal mode of life in rural England, which was one of the reasons accounting for the growing pessimistic mood that runs throughout his novels. According to his pessimistic philosophy, mankind is subjected to the rule of some hostile mysterious fate, bringing misfortune into human life. Strong elements of naturalism, combined with a tendency towards symbolism are the main features of his novels.

Among his famous novels, *Tess of the D'Urbervilles* and *Jude the Obscure* could be regarded as the summit of his realism. But both novels were given a hostile reception by the bourgeois public. The malicious criticism which they incurred discouraged the author to such an extent that he ceased writing novels altogether. At the end of the nineties, almost at the age of sixty, Hardy turned entirely to poetry.

Tess of the D'Urbervilles, a Pure Woman Faithfully Portrayed, tells the tragic life story of a beautiful country girl, Tess Durbeyfield. Tess is the daughter of a poor villager who at the beginning of the novel, discovers that he is the descendent of the ancient family of the D'Urbervilles. So Tess is encouraged by her parents to seek out the old noble family. Yet, she is seduced by Alec D'Urberville, the son of a rich merchant who has bought his title into the class of gentry. Tess gives birth to an illegitimate child, thus scandalizing the narrow-minded people around her. The child dies soon after its birth, and she is considered a sinful woman. Trying to build a new life for herself, she leaves home and works at a distant farm as a dairymaid. There she meets Angel Clare, a clergyman's son. The young couple fall in love and are engaged to each other. On their wedding night, Tess confesses to Angel her affair with Alec. Angel, himself also a sinner, who has had some affair with a bad woman, casts her off. Soon he leaves for Brazil. Misfortune and hardship come upon poor Tess and her family. Her father dies and the whole family members are threatened with starvation.

Now Alec has become a preacher, still rich and still influential. Tess has made some pathetic appeals to Angel Clare to come back from abroad but in vain, and Alec tells her that Clare will never come back and presses his attentions upon her. She is driven to accept his protection and lives with him. Clare, returning from Brazil and feeling regretted for his harshness to Tess, finds her in such a bad situation. Maddened by this second wrong done her by Alec, she murders him in a fit of despair. After hiding with

Clare in a forest for a short time, Tess falls into the claws of law. Fateful circumstances and tragic coincidences abound in the book, and the whole story is filled with a feeling of dismal foreboding and doom.

Tess of the D'Urbervilles

Chapter 11

The twain[1] cantered along for some time without speech, Tess as she clung to him still panting in her triumph, yet in other respects dubious. She had perceived that the horse was not the spirited one he sometimes rode, and felt no alarm on that score, though her seat was precarious enough despite her tight hold of him. She begged him to slow the animal to a walk, which Alec accordingly did.

"Neatly done, was it not, dear Tess?" he said by and by.

"Yes!" said she. "To be much obliged to you."

"And are you?"

She did not reply.

"Tess, why do you always dislike my kissing you?"

"I suppose—because I don't love you."

"You are quite sure?"

"I am angry with you sometimes!"

"Ah, I half feared as much." Nevertheless, Alec did not object to that confession. He knew that anything was better than frigidity. "Why haven't you told me when I have made you angry?"

"You know very well why. Because I cannot help myself here."

"I haven't offended you often by love-making?"

"You have sometimes."

"How many times?"

"You know as well as I—too many times."

"Every time I have tried."

She was silent, and the horse ambled along for a considerable distance, till a faint luminous fog, which had hung in the hollows all the evening, became general and enveloped them. It seemed to hold the moonlight in suspension, rendering it more pervasive than in clear air. Whether on this account, or from absentmindedness, or from sleepiness, she did not perceive that they had long ago passed the point at which the lane to Trantridge branched from the highway, and that her conductor had not taken the Trantridge track.

She was inexpressibly weary. She had risen at five o'clock every morning of that week, had been on foot the whole of each day and on this evening had in addition walked the three miles to Chaseborough, waited three hours for her neighbours without eating or drinking, her impatience to start them preventing either; she had then walked a mile of the way home, and had undergone the excitement of the quarrel, till, with the slow progress of their steed, it was now nearly one o'clock. Only once, however, was she overcome by actual drowsiness. In that moment of oblivion her head sank gently against him.

D'Urberville stopped the horse, withdrew his feet from the stirrups, turned sideways on the saddle, and enclosed her waist with his arm to support her.

This immediately put her on the defensive, and with one of those sudden impulses of reprisal to which she was liable she gave him a little push from her. In his ticklish position he nearly lost his balance and only just avoided rolling over into the road, the horse, though a powerful one, being fortunately the quietest he rode.

"That is devilish unkind!" he said. "I mean no harm—only to keep you from falling."

She pondered suspiciously; till, thinking that this might after all be true, she relented, and said quite humbly, "I beg your pardon, sir."

"I won't pardon you unless you show some confidence in me. Good God!" he burst out, "what am I, to be repulsed so by a mere chit like you? For near three mortal months have you trifled with my feelings, eluded me, and snubbed me; and I won't stand it!"

"I'll leave you to-morrow, sir."

"No, you will not leave me to-morrow! Will you, I ask once more, show your belief in me by letting me clasp you with my arm? Come, between us two and nobody else, now. We know each other well; and you know that I love you, and think you the prettiest girl in the world, which you are. Mayn't I treat you as a lover?"

She drew a quick pettish breath of objection, writhing uneasily on her seat, looked far ahead, and murmured, "I don't know—I wish—how can I say yes or no when—"

He settled the matter by clasping his arm round her as he desired, and Tess expressed no further negative. Thus they sidled slowly onward till it struck her they had been advancing for an unconscionable time—far longer than was usually occupied by the short journey from Chaseborough, even at this walking pace, and that they were no longer on hard road, but in a mere trackway.

"Why, where be we?" she exclaimed.

"Passing by a wood."

"A wood—what wood? Surely we are quite out of the road?"

"A bit of The Chase—the oldest wood in England. It is a lovely night, and why should we not prolong our ride a little?"

"How could you be so treacherous!" said Tess, between archness and real dismay, and getting rid of his arm by pulling open his fingers one by one, though at the risk of slipping off herself. "Just when I've been putting such trust in you, and obliging you to please you, because I thought I had wronged you by that push! Please set me down, and let me walk home."

"You cannot walk home, darling, even if the air were clear. We are miles away from Trantridge, if I must tell you, and in this growing fog you might wander for hours among these trees."

"Never mind that," she coaxed. "Put me down, I beg you. I don't mind where it is; only let me get down, sir, please!"

"Very well, then, I will—on one condition. Having brought you here to this out-of-the-way place, I feel myself responsible for your safe-conduct home, whatever you may yourself feel about it. As to your getting to Trantridge without assistance, it is quite impossible; for, to tell the truth, dear, owing to this fog, which so disguises everything, I don't quite know where we are myself. Now, if you will promise to wait beside the horse while I walk through the bushes till I come to some road or house, and ascertain exactly our whereabouts, I'll deposit you here willingly. When I come back I'll give you full directions, and if you insist upon walking you may; or you may ride—at your pleasure."

She accepted these terms, and slid off on the near side, though not till he had stolen a cursory kiss. He sprang down on the other side.

"I suppose I must hold the horse?" said she.

"Oh no; it's not necessary," replied Alec, patting the panting creature. "He's had enough of it for to-night."

He turned the horse's head into the bushes, hitched him on to a bough, and made a sort of couch or nest for her in the deep mass of dead leaves.

"Now, you sit there," he said. "The leaves have not got damp as yet. Just give an eye to the horse—it will be quite sufficient."

He took a few steps away from her, but, returning, said, "By the bye,[2] Tess, your father has a new cob to-day. Somebody gave it to him."

"Somebody? You!"

D'Urberville nodded.

"O how very good of you that is!" she exclaimed, with a painful sense of the awkwardness of having to thank him just then.

"And the children have some toys."

"I didn't know—you ever sent them anything!" she murmured, much moved. "I almost wish you had not—yes, I almost wish it!"

"Why, dear?"

"It—hampers me so."

"Tessy—don't you love me ever so little now?"

"I'm grateful," she reluctantly admitted. "But I fear I do not—" The sudden vision of his passion for herself as a factor in this result so distressed her that, beginning with one slow tear, and then following with another, she wept outright.

"Don't cry, dear, dear one! Now sit down here, and wait till I come." She passively sat down amid the leaves he had heaped, and shivered slightly. "Are you cold?" he asked.

"Not very—a little."

He touched her with his fingers, which sank into her as into down. "You have only that puffy muslin dress on—how's that?"

"It's my best summer one. 'Twas very warm when I started, and I didn't know I was going to ride, and that it would be night."

"Nights grow chilly in September. Let me see." He pulled off a light overcoat that he had worn, and put it round her tenderly. "That's it—now you'll feel warmer," he continued. "Now, my pretty, rest there; I shall soon be back again."

Having buttoned the overcoat round her shoulders he plunged into the webs of vapour which by this time formed veils between the trees. She could hear the rustling of the branches as he ascended the adjoining slope, till his movements were no louder than the hopping of a bird, and finally died away. With the setting of the moon the pale light lessened, and Tess became invisible as she fell into reverie upon the leaves where he had left her.

In the meantime Alec D'Urberville had pushed on up the slope to clear his genuine doubt as to the quarter of The Chase they were in. He had, in fact, ridden quite at random for over an hour, taking any turning that came to hand[3] in order to prolong companionship with her, and giving far more attention to Tess's moonlit person than to any wayside object. A little rest for the jaded animal[4] being desirable, he did not hasten his search for landmarks. A clamber over the hill into the adjoining vale brought him to the fence of a highway whose contours he recognized, which settled the question of their whereabouts. D'Urberville thereupon turned back; but by this time the moon had quite gone down, and partly on account of the fog The Chase was wrapped in thick darkness, although morning was not far off. He was obliged to advance with outstretched hands to avoid contact with the boughs, and discovered that to hit the exact spot from which he had started was at first entirely beyond him. Roaming up and down, round and round, he at length heard a slight movement of the horse close at hand; and the sleeve of his overcoat unexpectedly caught his foot.

"Tess!" said D'Urberville.

There was no answer. The obscurity was now so great that he could see absolutely nothing but a pale nebulousness at his feet, which represented the white muslin figure he had left upon the dead leaves. Everything else was blackness alike. D'Urberville stooped; and heard a gentle regular breathing. He knelt and bent lower, till her breath warmed his face, and in a moment his cheek was in contact with hers. She was sleeping soundly, and upon her eyelashes there lingered tears.

Darkness and silence ruled everywhere around. Above them rose the primeval yews and oaks of The Chase, in which were poised gentle roosting birds in their last nap; and about them stole the hopping rabbits and hares. But, might some say, where was Tess's guardian angel? where was the providence of her simple faith? Perhaps, like that other god of whom the ironical Tishbite spoke, he was talking, or he was pursuing, or he was in a journey, or he was sleeping and not to be awaked.[5]

Why it was that upon this beautiful feminine tissue, sensitive as gossamer, and practically blank as snow as yet, there should have been traced such a coarse pattern as it was doomed to receive; why so often the coarse appropriates the finer thus, the wrong man the woman, the wrong woman the man, many thousand years of analytical philosophy have failed to explain to our sense of order. One may, indeed, admit the possibility of a retribution lurking in the present catastrophe. Doubtless some of Tess D'Urberville's mailed ancestors rollicking home from a fray had dealt the same measure even more ruthlessly towards peasant girls of their time. But though to visit the sins of the fathers upon the children[6] may be a morality good enough for divinities, it is scorned by average human nature; and it therefore does not mend the matter.

As Tess's own people down in those retreats are never tired of saying among each other in their fatalistic way: "It was to be." There lay the pity of it. An immeasurable social chasm was to divide our heroine's personality thereafter from that previous self of hers who stepped from her mother's door to try her fortune at Trantridge poultry-farm.

Notes

[1] The twain: (arch.) The two. Here it refers to Tess and Alec.

[2] By the bye: (*informal and becoming rare*) By the way.

[3] to hand: within reach.

[4] jaded animal: tired-out horse.

[5] he was sleeping and not to be awaked: cf. I Kings XVIII: 27: Elijah mocked them, and said, "Cry aloud: for he is a god; either he is talking, or he is pursuing, or he is in a journey, or peradventure he sleepeth, and must be awaked."

[6] to visit the sins of the fathers upon the children: cf. Exodus XX: 5: "I the Lord thy God am a jealous God, visiting the iniquity of the fathers upon the children unto the third and fourth generation of them that hate me."

Commentary

Tess of the D'Urbervilles tells the tragic life story of a beautiful country girl, brave, hard-working, sweet-natured and innocent. The selected Chapter 11 depicts the seduction of Tess by Alec when she has worked hard and long hours all week as a family maid in his home. For the first time she realizes that Alec's willingness to help her and her family is his hold over her. As will be seen several times in this part of the story, his provision of material aid to the impoverished family compels Tess to be grateful to him. She makes a valiant effort to be independent of him, but in the end the struggle is too much for her. In this chapter, the pure and simple Tess is deeply sympathized while sinister and selfish Alec is acutely exposed and lashed.

Questions and Exercises

1. The setting of each event in *Tess of the D'Urbervilles* is appropriate to the action taking place in it. Analyze the gloomy setting of this chapter to illustrate this device.
2. When Alec asks Tess to allow him to be her lover, she says, "I don't know—I wish—how can I say yes or no when—" What attitude does Tess reveal towards Alec?
3. Do you think Tess is to blame for her moving towards Alec's trap? Write an essay to analyze the causes for Tess's tragedy from both historical and feministic perspectives.

Oscar Wilde

Oscar Wilde (1854—1900), the great poet, satirist and playwright, is as misunderstood nowadays as he was in his own time. His personal life did not bring him happiness and fulfillment, but his art did. In his essays and lectures he expounds the theory of "art for art's sake," and his fiction is devoted to this principle as well.

With the whole life of 46 years, Wilde spent most of it in publicizing his aestheticism. The great genius created remarkable works for his readers while he was tasting bitter fruits. His tragic life testified the failure of his aestheticism. Though the Victorian age had had its revenge on one of its most talented critics, his work could never be destroyed. The following selection is one of his well-known short stories bearing apparent features of a fairy tale.

The Nightingale and the Rose

"She said that she would dance with me if I brought her red roses," cried the young Student, "but in all my garden there is no red rose."

From her nest in the oak tree the Nightingale heard him, and she looked out through the leaves and wondered.

"No red rose in all my garden!" he cried, and his beautiful eyes filled with tears. "Ah, on what little things does happiness depend! I have read all that the wise men have written, and all the secrets of philosophy are mine, yet for want of a red rose is my life made wretched."[1]

"Here at last is a true lover," said the Nightingale. "Night after night have I sung of him, though I knew him not: night after night have I told his story to the stars and now I see him. His hair is dark as the hyacinth—blossom, and his lips are red as the rose of his desire; but passion has made his face like pale ivory, and sorrow has set her seal upon his brow."

"The Prince gives a ball to-morrow night," murmured the young Student, "and my love will be of the company. If I bring her a red rose she will dance with me till dawn. If I bring her a red rose, I should hold her in my arms, and she will lean her head upon my shoulder, and her hand will be clasped in mine. But there is no red rose in my garden, so I shall sit lonely, and she will pass me by. She will have no heed of me, and my heart will break."

"Here, indeed, is the true lover," said the Nightingale. "What I sing of, he suffers: what is joy to me, to him is pain. Surely love is a wonderful thing. It is more precious than emeralds, and dearer than fine opals.[2] Pearls and pomegranates cannot buy it, nor is it set forth in the market-place. It may not be purchased of the merchants, nor can it be weighed out in the balance for gold."

"The musicians will sit in their gallery," said the young Student, "and play upon their stringed instruments, and my love will dance to the sound of the harp and the violin.[3] She will dance so lightly that her feet will not touch the floor, and the courtiers in their gay dresses will throng round her. But with me she will not dance, for I have no red rose to give her," and he flung himself down on the grass, and buried his face in his hands, and wept.

"Why is he weeping?" asked a little Green Lizard, as he ran past him with his tail in the air.

"Why, indeed?" said a Butterfly, who was fluttering about after a sunbeam.

"Why, indeed?" whispered a Daisy to his neighbour, in a soft, low voice.

"He is weeping for a red rose," said the Nightingale.

"For a red rose?" they cried: "how very ridiculous!" and the little Lizard, who was something of a cynic, laughed outright.[4]

But the Nightingale understood the secret of the Student's sorrow, and she sat silent in the oak-tree, and thought about the mystery of Love.

Suddenly she spread her brown wings for flight, and soared into the air. She passed through the grove like a shadow and like a shadow she sailed across the garden.

In the center of the grass-plot was standing a beautiful Rose-tree, and when she saw it she flew over to it, and lit upon a spray.

"Give me a red rose," she cried, "and I will sing you my sweetest song."

But the Tree shook its head.

"My roses are white," it answered; "as white as the foam of the sea, and whiter than the snow upon the mountain. But go to my brother who grows round the old sun-dial, and perhaps he will give you what you want."

So the Nightingale flew over to the Rose-tree that was growing round the old sun-dial.

"Give me a red rose," she cried, "and I will sing you my sweetest song."

But the Tree shook its head.

"My roses are yellow," it answered; "as yellow as the hair of the mermaiden[5] who sits upon an amber throne, and yellower than the daffodil that blooms in the meadow before the mower comes with his scythe. But go to my brother who grows beneath the Student's window, and perhaps he will give you what you want."

So the Nightingale flew over to the Rose-tree that was growing beneath the Student's window.

"Give me a red rose," she cried, "and I will sing you my sweetest song."

But the Tree shook its head.

"My roses are red," it answered, "as red as the feet of the dove, and redder than the great fans of coral[6] that wave and wave in the ocean-cavern. But the winter has chilled my veins, and the frost has nipped[7] my buds, and the storm has broken my branches, and I shall have no roses at all this year."

"One red rose is all I want," cried the Nightingale, "only one red rose! Is there no way by which I can get it?"

"There is a way," answered the Tree; "but it is so terrible that I dare not tell it to you."

"Tell it to me," said the Nightingale, "I am not afraid."

"If you want a red rose," said the Tree, "you must build it out of music by moonlight, and stain it with your own heart's blood. You must sing to me with your breast against a thorn. All night long you must sing to me, and the thorn must pierce your heart, and your life-blood must flow into veins, and become mine."

"Death is a great price to pay for a red rose," cried the Nightingale, "and Life is very dear to all. It is pleasant to sit in the green wood, and to watch the Sun in his chariot of gold, and the Moon in her chariot of pearl. Sweet is the scent of the hawthorn, and sweet are the bluebells that hide in the valley, and the heather that blows on the hill. Yet love is better than Life, and what is the heart of a bird compared to the heart of a man?"

So she spread her brown wings for flight, and soared into the air. She swept over the garden like a shadow, and like a shadow she sailed through the grove.

The young Student was still lying on the grass, where she had left him, and the tears were not yet dry in his beautiful eyes.

"Be happy," cried the Nightingale, "be happy; you shall have your red rose. I will build it out of music by moonlight, and stain it with my own heart's blood. All that I ask of you in return is that you will be a true lover, for Love is wiser than Philosophy, though he is wise, and mightier than Power, though he is mighty. Flame-coloured are his wings, and coloured like flame is his body. His lips are sweet as honey, and his breath is like frankincense."

The Student looked up from the grass, and listened, but he could not understand what the Nightingale was saying to him, for he only knew the things that are written down in books.

But the Oak-tree understood, and felt sad, for he was very fond of the little Nightingale, who had built her nest in his branches.

"Sing me one last song," he whispered; "I shall feel lonely when you are gone."

So the Nightingale sang to the Oak-tree, and her voice was like water bubbling from a silver jar.

When she had finished her song, the Student got up, and pulled a note-book and a lead-pencil out of his pocket.

"She had form," he said to himself, as he walked away through the grove—"that cannot be denied to her; but has she got feeling? I am afraid not. In fact, she is like most artists; she is all style without any sincerity.[8] She would not sacrifice herself for others. She thinks merely of music, and everybody knows that the arts are selfish. Still, it must be admitted that she has some beautiful notes in her voice. What a pity it is that they do not mean anything, or do any practical good!" And he went into his room, and lay down on his little pallet-bed, and began to think of his love; and, after a time, he fell asleep.

And when the moon shone in the heavens the Nightingale flew to the Rose-tree, and set her breast against the thorn. All night long she sang, with her breast against the thorn, and the cold crystal Moon leaned down and listened. All night long she sang, and the thorn went deeper and deeper into her breast, and her life-blood ebbed away from her.

She sang first of the birth of love in the heart of a boy and a girl. And on the topmost spray [9] of the Rose-tree there blossomed a marvelous rose, petal following petal, as song followed song. Pale was it, at first, as the mist that hangs over the river—pale as the feet of the morning, and silver as the wings of the dawn. As the shadow of a rose in a mirror of silver, as the shadow of a rose in a water-pool, so was the rose that blossomed on the topmost spray of the Tree.

But the Tree cried to the Nightingale to press closer against the thorn. "Press closer, little Nightingale," cried the Tree, "or the Day will come before the rose is finished."

So the Nightingale pressed closer against the thorn, and louder and louder grew her song, for she sang of the birth of passion in the soul of a man and a maid.

And a delicate flush of pink came into the leaves of the rose, like the flush in the face of the bridegroom when he kisses the lips of the bride. But the thorn had not yet reached her heart, so the rose's heart remained white, for only a Nightingale's heart's blood can crimson the heart of a rose.

And the Tree cried to the Nightingale to press closer against the thorn. "Press closer, little Nightingale," cried the Tree, "or the Day will come before the rose is finished."

So the Nightingale pressed closer against the thorn, and the thorn touched her heart, and a fierce pang of pain shot through her. Bitter, bitter was the pain, and wilder and wilder grew her song, for she sang of the Love that is perfected by Death, of the Love that dies not in the tomb.[10]

And the marvelous rose became crimson, like the rose of the eastern sky. Crimson was the girdle of petals,[11] and crimson as a ruby was the heart.

But the Nightingale's voice grew fainter, and her little wings began to beat, and a film came over her eyes. Fainter and fainter grew her song, and she felt something choking her in her throat.

Then she gave one last burst of music. The white Moon heard it, and she forgot the dawn, and lingered on in the sky. The red rose heard it, and it trembled all over with ecstasy, and opened its petals to the cold morning air. Echo bore it to her purple cavern in the hills, and woke the sleeping shepherds from their dreams. It floated through the reeds of the river, and they carried its message to the sea.

"Look, look!" cried the Tree, "the rose is finished now;" but the Nightingale made no answer, for she was lying dead in the long grass, with the thorn in her heart.

And at noon the Student opened his window and looked out.

"Why, what a wonderful piece of luck!" He cried; "here is a red rose! I have never seen any rose like it in all my life. It is so beautiful that I am sure it has a long Latin name;" and he leaned down and plucked it.

Then he put on his hat, and ran up to the Professor's house with the rose in his hand.

The daughter of the Professor was sitting in the doorway winding blue silk on a reel, and her little dog was lying at her feet.

"You said that you would dance with me if I brought you a red rose," cried the Student. "Here is the reddest rose in all the world. You will wear it to-night next your heart, and as we dance together it will tell you how I love you."

But he girl frowned.

"I am afraid it will not go with my dress," she answered; "and, besides, the Chamberlain's[12] nephew had sent me some real jewels, and everybody knows that jewels cost far more than flowers."

"Well, upon my word, you are very ungrateful," said the Student angrily; and he threw the rose onto he street, where it fell into the gutter, and a cartwheel went over it.

"Ungrateful!" said the girl. "I tell you what, you are very rude; and, after all, who are you? Only a Student. Why, I don't believe you have even got silver buckles to your shoes as the Chamberlain's nephew has;" and she got up from her chair and went into the house.

"What a silly thing Love is!" said the Student as he walked away. "It is not half as useful as Logic, for it does not prove anything, and it is always telling one of things that are not going to happen, and making one believe things that are not true. In fact, it is quite unpractical, and, as in this age to be practical is everything, I shall go back to Philosophy and study Metaphysics."[13]

So he returned to his room and pulled out a great dusty book, and began to read.

Notes

[1] I have read all that the wise men have written…my life made wretched: We all know that Oscar Wilde believed in art for art's sake. To him, the only purpose of the artist is art, not religion, or science, or interest. He who paints or writes only for financial return, or to propagandize political and economic interests can only arouse feelings of disgust. Therefore the author keeps poking fun at the student, the professor, the dusty heavy books, logic, philosophy, intellect, and metaphysics. This theory of art has been under much criticism. Many people believe that the artist cannot be detached from human life. His artistic works, being part of his human activities, must necessarily be guided by his sense of moral responsibility, his ideal and his view of what is true, good, and beautiful.

[2] emeralds…opals: different kinds of gems or precious stones, including ruby, diamond, emerald, sapphire, opal, jade, etc.

[3] dance to the sound of the harp and the violin: dance according to the sound of the harp and the violin.

[4] something of a cynic, laughed outright: "something of a cynic" means a cynic without fully deserving the name. A cynic is a person who believes that everybody is motivated by his selfishness. laughed outright: burst out laughing.

[5] mermaiden: also mermaid, a fabled creature of the sea with the head and upper body of a woman and the tail of a fish.

[6] redder than the great fans of coral: Notice the metaphor "fan", which refers to anything resembling a fan.

[7] nipped: checked or stopped the growth of.

[8] She had form…she is all style without any sincerity: "Form" is the design, pattern, or structure as opposed to the substance. The Student's comment on the Nightingale's music reminds us of Oscar Wilde's contemporaries' criticisms of his

works.

[9] spray: a small branch bearing buds, flowers or berries.

[10] She sang of the Love…that dies not in the tomb: She sang of the love that grows and grows until they die, and of the love that will live in eternity.

[11] the girdle of petals: girdle originally refers to a belt or something like a belt worn at the waist. Here it means a band of red color round the middle of the petals.

[12] the Chamberlain: the official who manages the household for the King.

[13] Metaphysics: the branch of philosophy that systematically investigates the nature of first principles and problems of ultimate reality.

Commentary

This story is written in the form of a fairy tale—stories in which fairies play a part or which contain other supernatural or magical elements such as imaginary persons, animals and inanimate objects. These stories are mainly for children. But the best fairy tales are also valuable for grown-ups to read for their veiled comments on life. In some other cases, readers are continually reminded of the author who is often the chief actor in the story. *The Nightingale and the Rose* serves as a good example. A young Student seemed to be madly in love. He felt sad because he could not find a Red Rose in the whole garden for his love. The Nightingale was so moved by his love that she was determined to help him. But the only way to get a Red Rose in the cold winter was for the Nightingale to build it out of her music and to stain it with her heart's blood.

In this touching story, the Red Rose has a symbolic meaning. It stands for true love, which comes only from one's heart, and it is more precious than one's life. But as we can see in the story, the Student does not really understand what love is, nor does the daughter of the Professor, the Lizard, the Daisy, and the Butterfly. The only character who truly understands love and values love, and is ready to sacrifice her life for love is the Nightingale.

From what we know about Oscar Wilde, we have reason to believe that when he wrote the part about the Nightingale who sang song after song with her breast pressed harder and harder against the thorn to produce a Red Rose, he probably was talking about himself who wrote story after story for his love of mankind. And the Student's comment about the Nightingale's music that it had form but no feelings also reminded us of the author' critics who denounced his works and labeled him as an art-for-art's-sake writer.

Questions and Exercises

1. The Rose obviously serves as an important symbol in this story. What does it symbolize? Why does the author make it so difficult to procure? Give your explanation.

2. What do you think Oscar Wilde is trying to say in this fairy tale in light of the fact that he has been criticized for his belief in "art for art's sake"?
3. Write a short essay by making comment on the varied attitudes of all the characters in this story towards love.

James Joyce

James Joyce (1882—1941) was born in Dublin into a Catholic family, but he renounced the Christian faith during his last year at school. Although he took no part in the Irish nationalist movement and left Ireland in 1904 to live and work abroad for the rest of his life, he never forgot his motherland, the setting for all his fiction is his hometown in Dublin, the capital of Ireland.

His first important work was a collection of fifteen short stories entitled *Dubliners*, which was published in 1914 after passing from publisher to publisher for eight years. Just because of the depressing description of the Irish national spirit, the book was published after numerous hassles from publishers and almost a decade after they were written. The Dubliners portrayed in these short stories are usually grimy and miserable and indecent individuals. They are generally the sensitive or young ones, and the world is often seen as foolish, futile and unpleasant.

His novel, *A Portrait of the Artist as a Young Man* (1916), is largely autobiographical. It related his experiences from infancy to early manhood, and described how he discovered his career as an artist.

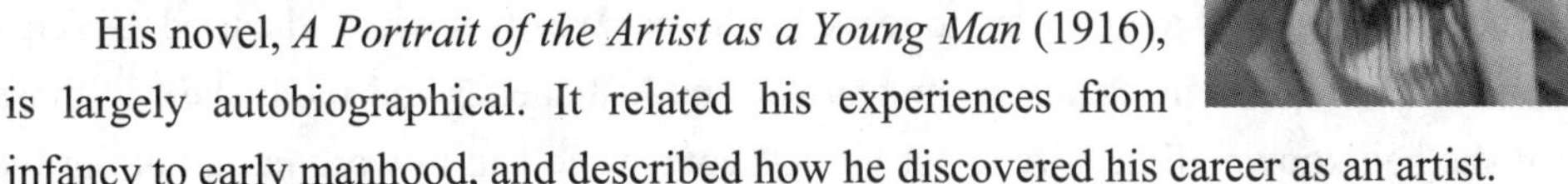

Ulysses (1922) is generally acknowledged to be his masterpiece and a typical example of stream of consciousness technique. The novel deals with the events of one day in Dublin in June, 1904. His last novel, *Finnegans Wake* (1939), took him fourteen years to finish and he claimed it to be his masterpiece. Joyce caused an uproar of opposition during his lifetime, but today he is recognized as a master of the technique of stream of consciousness in fiction. Although he is not the inventor, he perfected it through lifelong effort to reveal the inner mental state of his characters.

Eveline

She sat at the window watching the evening invade the avenue. Her head was leaned against the window curtains, and in her nostrils was the odor of dusty cretonne. She was tired.

Few people passed. The man out of the last house passed on his way home; she heard his footsteps clacking along the concrete pavement and afterwards crunching on the cinder path before the new red houses. One time there used to be a field there in which they used to play every evening with other people's children. Then a man from Belfast bought the field and built houses in it—not like their little brown houses, but bright brick houses with shining roofs. The children of the avenue used to play together in that field—the Devines, the Waters, the Dunns, little Keogh the cripple, she and her brothers and sisters. Ernest,[1] however, never played: he was too grown up. Her father used often to hunt them in out of the field with his blackthorn stick; but usually little Keogh used to keep *nix* and call out when he saw her father coming. Still they seemed to have been rather happy then. Her father was not so bad then; and besides, her mother was alive. That was a long time ago; she and her brothers and sisters were all grown up; her mother was dead. Tizzie Dunn was dead, too, and the Waters had gone back to England. Everything changes. Now she was going to go away like the others, to leave her home.

Home! She looked round the room, reviewing all its familiar objects which she had dusted once a week for so many years, wondering where on earth all the dust came from. Perhaps she would never see again those familiar objects from which she had never dreamed of being divided. And yet during all those years she had never found out the name of the priest whose yellowing photograph hung on the wall above the broken harmonium beside the colored print of the promises made to Blessed Margaret Mary Alacoque. He had been a school friend of her father. Whenever he showed the photograph to a visitor her father used to pass it with a casual word: "He is in Melbourne now."[2]

She had consented to go away, to leave her home. Was that wise? She tried to weigh each side of the question. In her home anyway she had shelter and food; she had those whom she had known all her life about her. Of course she had to work hard, both in the house and at business. What would they say of her in the Stores when they found out that she had run away with a fellow? Say she was a fool, perhaps; and her place would be filled up by advertisement. Miss Gavan would be glad. She had always had an edge on her, especially whenever there were people listening.

"Miss Hill, don't you see these ladies are waiting?"

"Look lively, Miss Hill, please."

She would not cry many tears at leaving the Stores.

But in her new home, in a distant unknown country, it would not be like that. Then she would be married—she, Eveline. People would treat her with respect then. She would not be treated as her mother had been. Even now, though she was over nineteen, she sometimes felt herself in danger of her father's violence. She knew it was that that had given her the palpitations. When they were growing up he had never gone for her, like he used to go for Harry and Ernest, because she was a girl; but latterly he had begun to threaten her and say what he would do to her only for her dead mother's sake. And now she had nobody to protect her, Ernest was dead and Harry, who was in the church decorating business, was nearly always down somewhere in the country. Besides, the invariable squabble for money on Saturday nights had begun to weary her unspeakably. She always gave her entire wages—seven shillings—and Harry always sent up what he could, but the trouble was to get any money from her father. He said she used to squander the money, that she had no head, that he wasn't going to give her his hard-earned money to throw about the streets, and much more, for he was usually fairly bad on Saturday night. In the end he would give her the money and ask her had she any intention of buying Sunday's dinner. Then she had to rush out as quickly as she could and do her marketing, holding her black leather purse tightly in her hand as she elbowed her way through the crowds and returning home late under her load of provisions. She had hard work to keep the house together and to see that the two young children who had been left to her charge went to school regularly and got their meals regularly. It was hard work—a hard life—but now that she was about to leave it she did not find it a wholly undesirable life.

She was about to explore another life with Frank. Frank was very kind, manly, open-hearted. She was to go away with him by the night-boat to be his wife and to live with him in Buenos Aires, where he had a home waiting for her. How well she remembered the first time she had seen him; he was lodging in a house on the main road where she used to visit. It seemed a few weeks ago. He was standing at the gate, his peaked cap pushed back on his head and his hair tumbled forward over a face of bronze. Then they had come to know each other. He used to meet her outside the Stores every evening and see her home. He took her to see *The Bohemian Girl*[3] and she felt elated as she sat in an unaccustomed part of the theatre with him. He was awfully fond of music and sang a little. People knew that they were courting, and, when he sang about the lass that loves a sailor, she always felt pleasantly confused. He used to call her Poppens[4] out of fun. First of all it had been an excitement for her to have a fellow and then she had begun to like him. He had tales of distant countries. He had started as a deck boy at a pound a month on a ship of the Allan Line[5] going out to Canada. He told her the names of the ships he had been on and the names of the different services. He had sailed through the Straits of Magellan and he told her stories of the terrible Patagonians.[6] He had fallen on his feet in Buenos Aires, he said, and had come over to the old country just for a holiday. Of course, her father had found out the affair and had forbidden her to have anything to say to him.

"I know these sailor chaps," he said.

One day he had quarreled with Frank, and after that she had to meet her lover secretly.

The evening deepened in the avenue. The white of two letters in her lap grew indistinct. One was to Harry; the other was to her father. Ernest had been her favorite, but she liked Harry too. Her father was becoming old lately, she noticed; he would miss her. Sometimes he could be very nice. Not long before, when she had been laid up for a day, he had read her out a ghost story and made toast for her at the fire. Another day, when their mother was alive, they had all gone for a picnic to the Hill of Howth. She remembered her father putting on her mother's bonnet to make the children laugh.

Her time was running out, but she continued to sit by the window, leaning her head against the window curtain, inhaling the odor of dusty cretonne. Down far in the avenue she could hear a street organ playing. She knew the air. Strange that it should come that very night to remind her of the promise to her mother, her promise to keep the home together as long as she could. She remembered the last night of her mother's illness; she was again in the close, dark room at the other side of the hall and outside she heard a melancholy air of Italy. The organ-player had been ordered to go away and given sixpence. She remembered her father strutting back into the sick-room saying:

"Damned Italians! Coming over here!"[7]

As she mused the pitiful vision of her mother's life laid its spell on the very quick of her being—that life of commonplace sacrifices closing in final craziness. She trembled as she heard again her mother's voice saying constantly with foolish insistence:

"`Derevaun Seraun! Derevaun Seraun!"[8]

She stood up in a sudden impulse of terror. Escape! She must escape![9] Frank would save her. He would give her life, perhaps love, too. But she wanted to live. Why should she be unhappy? She had a right to happiness. Frank would take her in his arms, fold her in his arms. He would save her.

She stood among the swaying crowd in the station at the North Wall. He held her hand and she knew that he was speaking to her, saying something about the passage over and over again. The station was full of soldiers with brown baggages. Through the wide doors of the sheds she caught a glimpse of the black mass of the boat, lying in beside the quay wall, with illumined portholes. She answered nothing. She felt her cheek pale and cold and, out of a maze of distress, she prayed to God to direct her, to show her what was her duty. The boat blew a long mournful whistle into the mist. If she went, tomorrow she would be on the sea with Frank, steaming towards Buenos Aires. Their passage had been booked. Could she still draw back after all he had done for her? Her distress awoke a nausea in her body and she kept moving her lips in silent fervent prayer.

A bell clanged upon her heart. She felt him seize her hand: "Come!"

All the seas of the world tumbled about her heart. He was drawing her into them: he would drown her. She gripped with both hands at the iron railing.

"Come!"

No! No! No! It was impossible. Her hands clutched the iron in frenzy. Amid the seas[10] she sent a cry of anguish.

"Eveline! Evvy!"

He rushed beyond the barrier and called to her to follow. He was shouted at to go on, but he still called to her. She set her white face to him, passive, like a helpless animal. Her eyes gave him no sign of love or farewell or recognition.

Notes

[1] Ernest: Eveline's brother.

[2] He is in Melbourne now: People left Ireland, even the priest.

[3] *The Bohemian Girl*: an opera composed by the Irish composer Michael William Balfe (1808—1870).

[4] Poppens: female swans.

[5] the Allan line: the Allan Shipping Company.

[6] the terrible Patagonians: Patagonia is in the extreme southern tip of South America. There were horrible stories brought back by early white sailors, describing the native tribal people there as cannibals.

[7] Damned Italians! Coming over here: The father's attitude towards the Italians indicated the narrow-mindedness of the Irish that Joyce resented.

[8] Derevaun Seraun! Derevaun Seraun: Gaelic for "The end of pleasure is pain".

[9] escape: The central theme of the story is the desire to escape and the inability of action, which, to Joyce, is symbolic of the situation of Ireland at his own time.

[10] Amid the seas: Tumbled about her heart; amid tense mental struggle.

Commentary

Eveline, a nineteen-year-old girl, struggles with poverty and the difficulties of supporting her family. She lives a dull and boring life with her irritable father. She works very hard, both at a store and at home, and she is planning to leave Ireland forever. Her means of escape is a sailor named Frank, who promises her a new life in Buenos Aires. Frank treats her with great tenderness and entertains her with stories about his travels around the world. Still, she sympathizes with her father and regrets the idea of leaving him in his old age. She remembers her mother's death, when she promised her to keep the home together as long as she could. At the end, however, she is too paralyzed and too frightened to leave Dublin. Just before the ship leaves, she gives up and finds herself without enough courage to pursue the freedom she had long desired in the outside world. Although set in Dublin and focused upon the theme of paralysis, *Eveline* turns out to be a short story interconnected by symbols and moods. The paralysis of the soul of Dubliners is evidently revealed through this story. Eveline, her father, and her lover Frank are just a few of such samples.

Questions and Exercises

1. Why should Eveline's father forbid her to see Frank?
2. What was Eveline's dilemma about leaving home? Make some comment on whether Eveline should leave her home or not. (Think about her relations with her family and Frank.) What moral lessons should we learn from Eveline's tragedy?
3. Write a short passage about the central theme of the story entitled "Dilemma of the Irish Reflected from Eveline".

Katherine Mansfield

Katherine Mansfield (1888—1923), an outstanding British short story writer, was born in Wellington, New Zealand. She studied at Queens College, London, where she met and later married John Middleton Murray, a famous critic, and also D. H. Lawrence. After years of ill-health and struggle as a freelance writer and reviewer, she achieved success with *Bliss and Other Stories* (1920) and *The Garden Party* (1922). Critics praised her for capturing the essence of Chekhov's art for stories by emphasizing breath-taking atmosphere and actual life rather than exciting plot. She was also well known for her refreshing originality and sensitiveness to beauty. Just as she won world fame, however, her health grew worse; she died early of tuberculosis at the age of thirty-five.

A Dill Pickle[1]

And then, after six years, she saw him again. He was seated at one of those little bamboo tables decorated with a Japanese vase of paper daffodils.[2] There was a tall plate of fruit in front of him, and very carefully, in a way she recognized immediately as his "special" way, he was peeling an orange.

He must have felt that shock of recognition in her for he looked up and met her eyes. Incredible! He didn't know her! She smiled; he frowned. She came towards him. He closed his eyes an instant, but opening them his face lit up as though he had struck a match in a dark room. He laid down the orange and pushed back his chair, and she took her little warm hand out of her muff and give it to him.

"Vera!" he exclaimed. "How strange. Really, for a moment I didn't know you. Won't you sit down? You've had lunch? Won't you have some coffee?"

She hesitated, but of course she meant to.

"Yes, I'd like to have some coffee." And she sat down opposite him.

"You've changed. You've changed very much," he said, staring at her with that eager, lighted look. "You look so well. I've never seen you look so well before."

"Really?" She raised her veil and unbuttoned her high fur collar. "I don't feel very well. I can't bear the weather, you know."

"Ah, no. You hate the cold..."

"Loathe it." She shuddered. "And the worst of it is that the older one grows..."

He interrupted her. "Excuse me," and tapped on the table for the waitress. "Please bring some coffee and cream." To her: "You are sure you won't eat anything? Some fruit, perhaps. The fruit here is very good."

"No, thanks. Nothing."

"Then that's settled." And smiling just a hint too broadly he took up the orange again. "You were saying—the old one grows—"

"The colder," she laughed. But she was thinking how well she remembered that trick of his—the trick of interrupting her—and of how it used to exasperate her six years ago. She used to feel then as though he, quite suddenly, in the middle of what she was saying, put his hand over her lips, turned from her, attended to something different, and then took his hand away, and with the same slightly too broad smile, gave her his attention again. ... Now we are ready. That is settled.

"The colder!" He echoed her words, laughing too. "Ah, ah. You still say the same things. And there is another thing about you that is not changed at all—your beautiful voice—your beautiful way of speaking." Now he was very grave; he leaned towards her, and she smelled the warm, stinging scent of the orange peel. "You have only to say one word and I would know your voice among all other voices. I don't know what it is—I've often wondered—that makes your voice such a haunting memory... Do you remember that first afternoon we spent together at Kew Gardens? You were so surprised because I didn't know the names of any flowers. I am still just as ignorant for all your telling me. But whenever it is very fine and warm, and I see some bright colors—it's awfully strange—I hear your voice saying: 'Geranium,[3] marigold[4] and verbena.[5]' And I feel those three words are all I recall of some forgotten, heavenly language... You remember that afternoon?"

"Oh, yes, very well." She drew a long, soft breath, as though the paper daffodils between them were almost too sweet to bear. Yet, what had remained in her mind of that particular afternoon was an absurd scene over the tea table. A great many people taking tea in a Chinese pagoda, and he behaving like a maniac about the wasps—waving them away, flapping at them with his straw hat, serious and infuriated out of all proportion to the occasion. How delighted the sniggering tea drinkers had been. And how she had suffered.

But now, as he spoke, that memory faded. His was the truer. Yes, it had been a wonderful afternoon, full of geranium and marigold and verbena, and—warm sunshine. Her thoughts lingered over the last two words as though she sang them. In the warmth, as it were, another memory unfolded. She saw herself sitting on a lawn. He lay beside her, and suddenly, after a long silence, he rolled over and put his head in her lap.

"I wish," he said, in a low, troubled voice, "I wish that I had taken poison and were about to die—here now!"

At that moment a little girl in a white dress, holding a long, dripping water lily, dodged from behind a bush, stared at them, and dodged back again. But he did not see. She leaned over her.

"Ah, why do you say that? I could not say that."

But he gave a kind of soft moan, and taking her hand he held it to his cheek.

"Because I know I am going to love you too much—far too much. And I shall suffer so terribly, Vera, because you never, never will love me."

He was certainly far better looking now than he had been then. He had lost all that dreamy vagueness and indecision. Now he had the air of a man who has found his place in life, and fills it with a confidence and an assurance which was, to say the least, impressive. He must have made money, too. His clothes were admirable, and at that moment he pulled a Russian cigarette case out of his pocket.

"Won't you smoke?"

"Yes, I will." She hovered over them, "They look very good."

"I think they are. I get them made for me by a little man in St. James's Street. I don't smoke very much. I'm not like you—but when I do, they must be delicious, very fresh cigarettes. Smoking isn't a habit with me; it's a luxury—like perfume. Are you still so fond of perfume? Ah, when I was in Russia..."

She broke in: "You've really been to Russia?"

"Oh, yes. I was there for over a year. Have you forgotten how we used to talk of going there?"

"No, I've not forgotten."

He gave a strange half laugh and leaned back in his chair. "Isn't it curious? I have really carried out all those journeys that we planned. Yes, I have been to all those places that we talked of, and stayed in them long enough to—as you used to say, 'air oneself in them'. In fact, I have spent the last three years of my life traveling all the time. Spain, Corsica,[6] Siberia,[7] Russia, Egypt. The only country left is China, and I mean to go there, too, when the war is over."

As he spoke, so lightly, tapping the end of his cigarette against the ashtray, she felt the strange beast that had slumbered so long within her bosom stir, stretch itself, yawn, prick up its ears, and suddenly bound to its feet, and fix its longing, hungry stare upon those far away places. But all she said was, smiling gently: "How I envy you."

He accepted that. "It has been," he said, "very wonderful—especially Russia. Russia was all that we had imagined, and far, far more. I even spent some days on a river boat on the Volga.[8] Do you remember that boatman's song that you used to play?"

"Yes." It began to play in her mind as she spoke.

"Do you ever play it now?"

"No, I've no piano."

He was amazed at that. "But what has become of your beautiful piano?"

She made a little grimace. "Sold. Ages ago."

"But you were so fond of music," he wondered.

"I've no time for it now," said she.

He let it go at that. "That river life," he went on, "is something quite special. After a day or two you cannot realize that you have ever known another. And it is not necessary to know the language—the life of the boat creates a bond between you and the people that's more than sufficient. You eat with them, pass the day with them, and in the evening there is the endless singing."

She shivered, hearing the boatman's song break out again loud and tragic, and seeing the boat floating on the darkening river with melancholy trees on either side... Yes, I should like that," said she, stroking her muff.

"You'd like almost everything about Russian life," he said warmly. "It's so informal, so impulsive, so free without question. And the peasants are so splendid. They are such human beings—yes, that is it. Even the man who drives your carriage has—has some real part in what is happening. I remember the evening a party of us, two friends of mine and the wife of one of them, went for a picnic by the Black Sea.[9] We took supper and champagne and ate and drank on the grass. And while we were eating the coachman came up. "Have a dill pickle," he said. He wanted to share with us. That seemed to me so right, so—you know what I mean?"

And she seemed at that moment to be sitting on the grass beside the mysteriously Black Sea, black as velvet, and rippling against the banks in silent, velvet waves. She saw the carriage drawn up to one side of the road, and the little group on the grass, their faces and hands white in the moonlight. She saw the pale dress of the woman outspread and her folded parasol, lying on the grass like a huge pearl crochet hook. Apart from them, with his supper in a cloth on his knees, sat the coachman. "Have a dill pickle," said he, and although she was not certain what a dill pickle was, she saw the greenish glass jar with a red chili like a parrot's beak glimmering through. She sucked in her cheeks; the dill pickle was terribly sour...

"Yes, I know perfectly what you mean," she said.

In the pause that followed they looked at each other. In the past when they looked at each other like that they had felt such a boundless understanding between them that their souls had, as it were, put their arms round each other and dropped into the same sea, content to be drowned, like mournful lovers. But now, the surprising thing was that it was he who held back. He who said: "What a marvelous listener you are. When you look at me with those wild eyes I feel that I could tell you things that I would never breathe to another human being."

Was there just a hint of mockery in his voice or was it her fancy? She could not be sure.

"Before I met you," he said, "I had never spoken of myself to anybody. How well I remember one night the night that I brought you the little Christmas tree, telling you all about my childhood. And of how I was so miserable that I ran away and lived under a cart for two days without being discovered. And you listened, and your eyes shone, and I felt that you had even made the little Christmas tree listen too, as in a fairy story."

But of that evening she had remembered a little pot of caviar.[10] It had cost seven and sixpence. He could not get over it. Think of it—a tiny jar like that costing seven and sixpence. While she ate it he watched her, delighted and shocked.

"No, really, that is eating money. You could not get seven shillings into a little pot that size. Only think of the profit they must make..." And he had begun some immensely complicated calculations...

But now good-bye to the caviar. The Christmas tree was on the table, and the little boy lay under the cart with his head pillowed on the yard dog. "The dog was called Bosun," she cried delightedly.

But he did not follow. "Which dog? Had you a dog? I don't remember a dog at all."

"No, no. I mean the yard dog when you were a little boy." He laughed and snapped the cigarette case to.

"Was he? Do you know I had forgotten that? It seems such ages ago, I cannot believe that it is only six years. After I had recognized you today—I had to take such a leap—I had to take a leap over my whole life to get back to that time. I was such a kid then." He drummed on the table. "I've often thought how I must have bored you. And now I understand so perfectly why you wrote to me as you did—although at the time that letter nearly finished my life. I found it again the other day, and I couldn't help laughing as I read it. It was so clever—such a true picture of me." He glanced up. "You're not going?"

She had buttoned her collar again and drawn her veil.

"Yes, I am afraid I must," she said, and managed a smile. Now she knew that he had been mocking.

"Ah, no, please," he pleaded. "Don't go just for a moment," and he caught up one of her gloves from the table and clutched at it as if that would hold her. "I see so few people to talk to nowadays, that I have turned into a sort of barbarian," he said. "Have I said something to hurt you?"

"Not a bit," she lied. But as she watched him draw her glove through his fingers, gently, gently, her anger really did die down, and besides, at the moment he looked more like himself of six years ago...

"What I really wanted then," he said softly, "was to be a sort of carpet—to make myself into a sort of carpet for you to walk on so that you need not be hurt by the sharp stones and the mud that you hated so. It was nothing more positive than that—nothing more selfish. Only I did desire, eventually, to turn into a magic carpet and carry you away to all those lands you longed to see."

As he spoke she lifted her head as though she drank something; the strange beast in her bosom began to purr...

"I felt that you were more lonely than anybody else in the world," he went on, "yet, perhaps, that you were the only person in the world who was really, truly alive. Born out of your time," he murmured, stroking the glove, "fated."

Ah, God! What had she done! How had she dared to throw away her happiness like this. This was the only man who had ever understood her. Was it too late? Could it be too late? She was that glove that he held in his fingers...

"And then the fact that you had no friends and never had made friends with people. How I understood that, for neither had I. Is it just the same now?"

"Yes," she breathed. "Just the same. I am as alone as ever."

"So am I," he laughed gently, "just the same."

Suddenly with a quick gesture he handed her back the glove and scraped his chair on the floor. "But what seemed to me so mysterious then is perfectly plain to me now. And to you, too, of course... It simply was that we were such egoists, so self-engrossed, so wrapped up in ourselves that we hadn't a corner in our hearts for anybody else. Do you know," he cried, naïve and hearty, and dreadfully like another side of that old self again, "I began studying a Mind System when I was in Russia, and I found that we were not peculiar at all. It's quite a well known form of... "

She had gone. He sat there, thunder-struck, astounded beyond words... And then he asked the waitress for his bill.

"But the cream has not been touched," he said. "Please do not charge me for it."

Notes

[1] dill pickle: a particular vegetable preserved in pickle, i.e. vinegar or salt water, which is flavored with dill (herb with scented leaves and seeds).

[2] daffodil: a type of yellow flower of early spring.

[3] geranium: a plant of genus Geranium, family Geraniaceae, having brightly colored

flowers and pungent-smelling leaves.

[4] marigold: any of various types of garden plant with orange or yellow flowers.

[5] verbena: type of herbaceous plant whose garden varieties have flowers of many colors.

[6] Corsica: an island in the Mediterranean, southeast of France and 80 km west of Italy, near Sardinia.

[7] Siberia: the Asiatic part extending from the Urals to the Pacific.

[8] Volga: a river (3,700 km long) of the western Russia, the longest in Europe

[9] Black Sea: an inland sea (area 436,415 sq. km.) between S.E. Europe and Asia Minor, with an outlet to the Mediterranean through the Bosporus.

[10] caviar: pickled roe of sturgeon or other large fish, eaten as a delicacy.

Commentary

This story shows the extent to which romantic love is dependent upon circumstances and the sharp clash of certain character traits at a particular time. The author Katherine Mansfield actually points up the heroine's sensitivity and the man's insensitivity to others—their feelings, their attitudes, and their inner emotions. They had been intimate lovers six years ago; but when they met again, the man seemed to have totally forgotten her though she was still extremely alert to his presence. During the whole meeting, it is actually the man who did most of the talking, paying scant attention to her change of feelings. In some sense, this story is highly feministic. Due to the man's egotism, self-centeredness and Chauvinism, the woman finally decides to leave him again, for there is no hope of restoring their lost love.

Questions and Exercises

1. What is the connotative meaning of the title?
2. What is the man doing these years? And what is the present situation of the woman? Describe the setting of their meeting six years later in your own words.
3. How clearly did the lovers understand one another six years ago? How clearly do they understand one another now?
4. In what way or ways do you think the selected story bears out the author's style of writing?

Edward Morgan Forster

Edward Morgan Forster (1879—1970), better known as E. M. Forster, was a widely read novelist in English-speaking countries in the first half of his life. Later, he was famous for his essays, short stories and literary criticism which expressed his opinions on social, political and moral attitudes in England.

In 1924, he published his masterpiece *A Passage to India.* Although this novel exposed many abuses of India under British imperialist rule, this was not Forster's main purpose. Still primarily concerned with human relationships, he posed the questions: Is any equilibrium and understanding possible between East and West? Can an Indian be truly a friend of an Englishman? The point of the novel is the subtle and profound study of the relationship between the various characters.

According to E. M. Forster, life is arbitrary and unpredictable, and a person's nature is developed through his relations with others. As a result, Forster's highest ideals were truthfulness and kindness. He felt that goodwill, common sense and a sensitive regard for individuals should be cultivated, and a constant effort to resolve conflicts through good personal relationships should be made, no matter how severe life is. He criticized social conventions and customs, particularly those remaining from the Victorian era, which tended towards narrowness, shallowness, rigidity, and coldness of English people. He interpreted all these human weaknesses as emotional immaturity.

Mr. Andrews

The souls of the dead were ascending towards the Judgment Seat and the Gate of Heaven. The world soul pressed them on every side, just as the atmosphere presses upon rising bubbles, striving to vanquish them, to break their thin envelope of personality, to mingle their virtue with its own. But they resisted, remembering their glorious individual life on earth, and hoping for an individual life to come.

Among them ascended the soul of a Mr. Andrews who, after a beneficent and honorable life, had recently deceased[1] at his house in town. He knew himself to be kind, upright and religious, and though he approached his trial with all humility, he could not be doubtful of its result. God was not now a jealous God. He would not deny salvation merely because it was expected. A righteous soul may reasonably be conscious of its own righteousness and Mr. Andrews was conscious of his.

"The way is long," said a voice, "but by pleasant converse[2] the way becomes shorter. Might I travel in your company?"

"Willingly," said Mr. Andrews. He held out his hand, and the two souls floated upwards together.

"I was slain fighting the infidel,"[3] said the other exultantly, "and I go straight to those joys of which the Prophet speaks."

"Are you not a Christian?" asked Mr. Andrews gravely.

"No, I am a Believer. But you are a Moslem, surely?"

"I am not," said Mr. Andrews. "I am a Believer."

The two souls floated upwards in silence, but did not release each other's hands; "I am broad church,"[4] he added gently. The word "broad" quavered strangely amid the interspaces.

"Relate to me your career," said the Turk at last.

"I was born of a decent middle-class family, and had my education at Winchester and Oxford. I thought of becoming a missionary, but was offered a post in the Board of Trade, which I accepted. At thirty-two I married, and had four children, two of whom have died. My wife survives me. If I had lived a little longer I should have been knighted."

"Now I will relate my career. I was never sure of my father, and my mother does not signify. I grew up in the slums of Salonika. [5] Then I joined a band and we plundered the villages of the infidel. I prospered and had three wives, all of whom survive me. Had I lived a little longer I should have had a band of my own."

"A son of mine was killed traveling in Macedonia. Perhaps you killed him."

"It is very possible."

The two souls floated upward, hand in hand. Mr. Andrews did not speak again, for he was filled with horror at the approaching tragedy. This man, so godless, so lawless, so cruel, so lustful, believed that he would be admitted into Heaven. And into what a heaven—a place full of the crude pleasures of a ruffian's life on earth! But Mr. Andrews felt neither disgust nor moral indignation. He was only conscious of an immense pity, and his own virtues confronted him not at all. He longed to save the man whose hand he held more tightly, who, he thought, was now holding more tightly on to him. And when he reached the Gate of Heaven, instead of saying, "Can I enter?" as he had intended, he cried out, "Cannot he enter?"

And at the same moment the Turk uttered the same cry. For the same spirit was working in each of them.

From the gateway a voice replied, "Both can enter." They were filled with joy and pressed forward together.

Then the voice said, "In what clothes will you enter?"

"In my best clothes," shouted the Turk, "the ones I stole." And he clad himself in a splendid turban and a waistcoat embroidered with silver, and baggy trousers, and a great belt in which were stuck pipes and pistols and knives.

"And in what clothes will you enter?" said the voice to Mr. Andrews.

Mr. Andrews thought of his best clothes, but he had no wish to wear them again. At last he remembered and said, "Robes."

"Of what color and fashion?" asked the voice.

Mr. Andrews had never thought about the matter much. He replied in hesitating tones, "White, I suppose, of some flowing soft material," and he was immediately given a garment such as he had described. "Do I wear it rightly?" he asked.

"Wear it as it pleases you," replied the voice. "What else do you desire?"

"A harp," suggested Mr. Andrews. "A small one."

A small gold harp was placed in his hand.

"And a palm[6]—no, I cannot have a palm, for it is the reward of martyrdom; my life has been tranquil and happy."

"You can have a palm if you desire it."

But Mr. Andrews refused the palm, and hurried in his white robes after the Turk, who had already entered Heaven. As he passed in at the open gate, a man, dressed like himself, passed out with gestures of despair.

"Why is he not happy?" he asked.

The voice did not reply.

"And who are all those figures, seated inside on thrones and mountains? Why are some of them terrible, and sad, and ugly?"

There was no answer. Mr. Andrews entered, and then he saw that those seated figures were all the gods who were then being worshipped on the earth. A group of souls stood round each, singing his praises. But the gods paid no heed, for they were listening to the prayers of living men, which alone brought them nourishment.

Sometimes a faith would grow weak, and then the god of that faith also drooped and dwindled and fainted for his daily portion of incense. And sometimes, owing to a revivalist movement, or to a great commemoration, or to some other cause, a faith would grow strong, and the god of that faith grow strong also. And, more frequently still, a faith would alter, so that the features of its god altered and became contradictory, and passed from ecstasy to respectability, or from mildness and universal love to the ferocity of battle. And at times a god would divide into two gods, or three, or more, each with his own ritual and precarious supply of prayer.

Mr. Andrews saw Buddha, and Vishnu, and Allah, and Jehovah, and the Elohim.[7] He saw little ugly determined gods who were worshipped by a few savages in the same way. He saw the vast shadowy outlines of the neo-Pagan Zeus. There were cruel gods, and coarse gods, and tortured gods, and, worse still, there were gods who were peevish, or deceitful, or vulgar. No aspiration of humanity was unfulfilled. There was even an intermediate state for those who wished it, and for the Christian Scientists a place where they could demonstrate that they had not died.

He did not play his harp for long, but hunted vainly for one of his dead friends. And though souls were continually entering Heaven, it still seemed curiously empty. Though he had all that he expected, he was conscious of no great happiness, no mystic contemplation of beauty, no mystic union with good. There was nothing to compare with that moment outside the gate, when he prayed that the Turk might enter and heard the Turk uttering the same prayer for him. And when at last he saw his companion, he hailed him with a cry of human joy.

The Turk was seated, in thought, and round him, by sevens, sat the virgins who are promised in the Koran.

"Oh, my dear, friend!" he called out. "Come here and we will never be parted and such as my pleasures are, they shall be yours also. Where are my other friends? Where are the men whom I love, or whom I have killed?"

"I, too, have only found you," said Mr. Andrews. He sat down by the Turk, and the virgins, who were all exactly alike, ogled them with coal black eyes.

"Though I have all that I expected," said the Turk, "I am conscious of no great happiness. There is nothing to compare with that moment outside the gate when I prayed that you might enter, and heard you uttering the same prayer for me. These virgins are as beautiful and good as I had fashioned, yet I could wish that they were better."

As he wished, the forms of the virgins became more rounded, and their eyes grew larger and blacker than before. And Mr. Andrews, by a wish similar in kind, increased the purity and softness of his garment and the glitter of his harp. For in that place their expectations were fulfilled, but not their hopes.

"I am going," said Mr. Andrews at last. "We desire infinity and we cannot imagine it. How can we expect it to be granted? I have never imagined anything infinitely good or beautiful excepting in my dreams."

"I am going with you," said the other.

Together they sought the entrance gate, and the Turk parted with his virgins and his best clothes, and Mr. Andrews cast away his robes and his harp.

"Can we depart?" they asked.

"You can both depart if you wish," said the voice, "but remember what lies outside."

As soon as they passed the gate, they felt again the pressure of the world soul. For a moment they stood hand in hand resisting it. Then they suffered it to break in upon them, and they, and all the experience they had gained, and all the love and wisdom they had generated, passed into it, and made it better.

Notes

[1] deceased: dead.

[2] converse: the opposite of something.

[3] infidel: unbeliever; someone who does not follow one's own religion.

[4] broad church: belonging to a group of the Church of England during the late 19th century who favoured greater freedom in matters of official belief.

[5] Salonika: a harbour city in Greece.
[6] palm: the leaf of the palm tree used as a sign of victory, success or honour.
[7] Buddha, and Vishnu, and Allah, and Jehovah, and the Elohim: Leading Gods of such religions as Buddhism, Hinduism, Muslim, and Christianity.

Commentary

This amusing, playful fantasy is Forster's way of expressing his opinion about religion by demonstrating his philosophy regarding human relationships. All English readers can immediately recognize the two main characters as the most conventional Christian symbols: the spirits of the dead ascending to Heaven, where they will be either admitted to Paradise or banished to Hell. But Forster continually reverses the reader's expectations by treating his characters ironically and arranging the incidents in a thoroughly untraditional manner.

Two elements in the story must be taken into consideration: the spirits of two totally different men who have died; Heaven, a place which exists only in the minds of men, and is therefore exactly what they expect it to be. The story makes two points: first, even the most opposed human beings can overcome their differences by goodwill and find happiness through unselfish friendship; and second, that religion is a delusion nurtured by ignorance and excessive individualism. Forster wishes to propose that it is better to offer one's life to the collective progress of mankind than to seek selfishly for an individual "after-life" in Heaven.

The spirits of a typically honorable middle-class Englishman and an uneducated Turkish bandit become friends on their way to Heaven. Both of them are moved by their friendship, and each fears that the other will be forbidden to enter Paradise. This unselfish caring for one another gives them great happiness. When they enter Paradise they finally realize that heaven is only a delusion invented in the minds of living men. They were far happier when they expressed their loving care for one another. So they decide to leave Heaven, to give up their own individuality and contribute the wisdom and valuable experiences of their lives for the benefit of mankind.

Questions and Exercises

1. What kind of human relationship does E. M. Forster intend to advocate through the description of the two characters in the story?
2. Does the writer believe in religion? Write a paragraph to support your interpretation about Forster's attitude toward religion.

David Herbert Lawrence

D. H. Lawrence (1885 — 1930) emerged from working-class background. His father was a miner and his mother an ex-school teacher. Dissatisfied with the drudgery of working-class life, Lawrence's mother was desperately anxious for him to acquire an education so he could rise above his origins. The fact that his mother had more education than his father caused friction in the Lawrence household. From boyhood, Lawrence was very close to his mother and, following his mother's encouragement, he studied at Nottingham University College, where he began writing short stories.

Lawrence is a writer who endeavors to lay the claims of the human heart before the reader with sharp fidelity. His works often have an intense and troubling reality as he uses symbols and poetic rhythms in his attempts to describe the indescribable. In his own time, however, he caused much controversy chiefly because of his frank, physical description of sexual passion in his last novel *Lady Chatterley's Lover*. Only after his death was his reputation solidly established as one of the greatest 20th-century English novelists.

Besides novels he also wrote poetry, travel books, essays, and short stories. Some of his finest fiction can be found in the latter genre. In 1930 Lawrence died of tuberculosis in France.

The Rocking-Horse Winner

There was a woman who was beautiful, who started with all the advantages, yet she had no luck. She married for love, and the love turned to dust. She had bonny children, yet she felt they had been thrust upon her, and she could not love them. They looked at her coldly, as if they were finding fault with her. And hurriedly she felt she must cover up some fault in herself. Yet what it was that she must cover up she never knew. Nevertheless, when her children were present, she always felt the centre of her heart go hard. This troubled her, and in her manner she was all the more gentle and anxious for her children, as if she loved them very much. Only she herself knew that at the centre of her heart was a hard little place that could not feel love, no, not for anybody. Everybody else said of her: "She is such a good mother. She adores her children." Only she herself, and her children themselves, knew it was not so. They read it in each other's eyes.

There were a boy and two little girls. They lived in a pleasant house, with a garden, and they had discreet servants, and felt themselves superior to anyone in the neighbourhood.

Although they lived in style, they felt always an anxiety in the house. There was never enough money. The mother had a small income, and the father had a small income, but not nearly enough for the social position which they had to keep up. The father went into town to some office. But though he had good prospects, these prospects never materialised. There was always the grinding sense of the shortage of money, though the style was always kept up.

At last the mother said: "I will see if I can't make something." But she did not know where to begin. She racked her brains, and tried this thing and the other, but could not find anything successful. The failure made deep lines come into her face. Her children were growing up, they would have to go to school. There must be more money, there must be more money. The father, who was always very handsome and expensive in his tastes, seemed as if he never would be able to do anything worth doing. And the mother, who had a great belief in herself, did not succeed any better, and her tastes were just as expensive.

And so the house came to be haunted by the unspoken phrase: There must be more money! There must be more money! The children could hear it all the time though nobody said it aloud. They heard it at Christmas, when the expensive and splendid toys filled the nursery.[1] Behind the shining modern rocking-horse, behind the smart doll's house, a voice would start whispering: "There must be more money! There must be more money!" And the children would stop playing, to listen for a moment. They would look into each other's eyes, to see if they had all heard. And each one saw in the eyes of the other two that they too had heard. "There must be more money! There must be more money!"

It came whispering from the springs of the still-swaying rocking-horse, and even the horse, bending his wooden, champing head, heard it. The big doll, sitting so pink and smirking in her new pram, could hear it quite plainly, and seemed to be smirking all the more self-consciously because of it. The foolish puppy, too, that took the place of the teddy-bear, he was looking so extraordinarily foolish for no other reason but that he heard the secret whisper all over the house: "There must be more money!"

Yet nobody ever said it aloud. The whisper was everywhere, and therefore no one spoke it. Just as no one ever says: "We are breathing!" in spite of the fact that breath is coming and going all the time.

"Mother," said the boy Paul one day, "Why don't we keep a car of our own? Why do we always use uncle's, or else a taxi?"

"Because we're the poor members of the family," said the mother.

"But why *are we*, Mother?"

"Well—I suppose," she said slowly and bitterly, "it's because your father has no luck."

The boy was silent for some time.

"Is luck money, mother?" he asked, rather timidly.

"No, Paul. Not quite. It's what causes you to have money."

"Oh!" said Paul vaguely. "I thought when Uncle Oscar said filthy lucker, it meant money."

"Filthy lucre[2] does mean money," said the mother. "But it's lucre, not luck."

"Oh!" said the boy. "Then what is luck, mother?"

"It's what causes you to have money. If you're lucky you have money. That's why it's better to be born lucky than rich. If you're rich, you may lose your money. But if you're lucky, you will always get more money."

"Oh! Will you? And is father not lucky?"

"Very unlucky, I should say," she said bitterly.

The boy watched her with unsure eyes.

"Why?" he asked.

"I don't know. Nobody ever knows why one person is lucky and another unlucky."

"Don't they? Nobody at all? Does nobody know?"

"Perhaps God. But He never tells."

"He ought to, then. And aren't you lucky either, mother?"

"I can't be, it I married an unlucky husband."

"But by yourself, aren't you?"

"I used to think I was, before I married. Now I think I am very unlucky indeed."

"Why?"

"Well—never mind! Perhaps I'm not really," she said.

The child looked at her to see if she meant it. But he saw, by the lines of her mouth, that she was only trying to hide something from him.

"Well, anyhow," he said stoutly, "I'm a lucky person."

"Why?" said his mother, with a sudden laugh.

He stared at her. He didn't even know why he had said it.

"God told me," he asserted, brazening it out.

"I hope He did, dear!", she said, again with a laugh, but rather bitter.

"He did, mother!"

"Excellent!" said the mother, using one of her husband's exclamations.

The boy saw she did not believe him; or rather, that she paid no attention to his assertion. This angered him somewhere, and made him want to compel her attention.

He went off by himself, vaguely, in a childish way, seeking for the clue to "luck". Absorbed, taking no heed of other people, he went about with a sort of stealth, seeking inwardly for luck. He wanted luck, he wanted it, he wanted it. When the two girls were playing dolls in the nursery, he would sit on his big rocking-horse, charging madly into space, with a frenzy that made the little girls peer at him uneasily. Wildly the horse careered, the waving dark hair of the boy tossed, his eyes had a strange glare in them. The little girls dared not speak to him.

When he had ridden to the end of his mad little journey, he climbed down and stood in front of his rocking-horse, staring fixedly into its lowered face. Its red mouth was slightly open, its big eye was wide and glassy-bright.

"Now!" he would silently command the snorting steed. "Now take me to where there is luck! Now take me!"

And he would slash the horse on the neck with the little whip he had asked Uncle Oscar for. He knew the horse could take him to where there was luck, if only he forced it. So he would mount again and start on his furious ride, hoping at last to get there.

"You'll break your horse, Paul!" said the nurse.

"He's always riding like that! I wish he'd leave off!" said his elder sister Joan.

But he only glared down on them in silence. Nurse gave him up. She could make nothing of him. Anyhow, he was growing beyond her.

One day his mother and his Uncle Oscar came in when he was on one of his furious rides. He did not speak to them.

"Hallo, you young jockey! Riding a winner?" said his uncle.

"Aren't you growing too big for a rocking-horse? You're not a very little boy any longer, you know," said his mother.

But Paul only gave a blue glare from his big, rather close-set eyes. He would speak to nobody when he was in full tilt. His mother watched him with an anxious expression on her face.

At last he suddenly stopped forcing his horse into the mechanical gallop and slid down.

"Well, I got there!" he announced fiercely, his blue eyes still flaring, and his sturdy long legs straddling apart.

"Where did you get to?" asked his mother.

"Where I wanted to go," he flared back at her.

"That's right, son!" said Uncle Oscar. "Don't you stop till you get there. What's the horse's name?"

"He doesn't have a name," said the boy.

"Gets on without all right?" asked the uncle.

"Well, he has different names. He was called Sansovino last week."

"Sansovino,[3] eh? Won the Ascot. How did you know this name?"

"He always talks about horse-races with Bassett," said Joan.

The uncle was delighted to find that his small nephew was posted with all the racing news. Bassett, the young gardener, who had been wounded in the left foot in the war and had got his present job through Oscar Cresswell, whose batman he had been, was a perfect blade of the "turf".[4] He lived in the racing events, and the small boy lived with him.

Oscar Cresswell got it all from Bassett.

"Master Paul comes and asks me, so I can't do more than tell him, sir," said Bassett, his face terribly serious, as if he were speaking of religious matters.

"And does he ever put anything on[5] a horse he fancies?"

"Well—I don't want to give him away[6]—he's a young sport, a fine sport, sir. Would you mind asking him himself? He sort of takes a pleasure in it, and perhaps he'd feel I was giving him away, sir, if you don't mind."

Bassett was serious as a church.

The uncle went back to his nephew and took him off for a ride in the car.

"Say, Paul, old man, do you ever put anything on a horse?" the uncle asked.

The boy watched the handsome man closely.

"Why, do you think I oughtn't to?" he parried.

"Not a bit of it! I thought perhaps you might give me a tip for the Lincoln."[7]

The car sped on into the country, going down to Uncle Oscar's place in Hampshire.

"Honour bright?"[8] said the nephew.

"Honour bright, son!" said the uncle.

"Well, then, Daffodil."

"Daffodil! I doubt it, sonny. What about Mirza?"

"I only know the winner," said the boy. "That's Daffodil."

"Daffodil, eh?"

There was a pause. Daffodil was an obscure horse comparatively.

"Uncle!"

"Yes, son?"

"You won't let it go any further, will you? I promised Bassett."

"Bassett be damned, old man! What's he got to do with it?"

"We're partners. We've been partners from the first. Uncle, he lent me my first five shillings, which I lost. I promised him, honour bright, it was only between me and him; only you gave me that ten-shilling note I started winning with, so I thought you were lucky. You won't let it go any further, will you?"

The boy gazed at his uncle from those big, hot, blue eyes, set rather close together. The uncle stirred and laughed uneasily.

"Right you are, son! I'll keep your tip private. How much are you putting on him?"

"All except twenty pounds,"[9] said the boy. "I keep that in reserve."

The uncle thought it a good joke.

"You keep twenty pounds in reserve, do you, you young romancer? What are you betting, then?"

"I'm betting three hundred," said the boy gravely. "But it's between you and me, Uncle Oscar! Honour bright?"

"It's between you and me all right, you young Nat Gould,"[10] he said, laughing. "But where's your three hundred?"

"Bassett keeps it for me. We're partners."

"You are, are you! And what is Bassett putting on Daffodil?"

"He won't go quite as high as I do, I expect. Perhaps he'll go a hundred and fifty."

"What, pennies?" laughed the uncle.

"Pounds," said the child, with a surprised look at his uncle. "Bassett keeps a bigger reserve than I do."

Between wonder and amusement Uncle Oscar was silent. He pursued the matter no further, but he determined to take his nephew with him to the Lincoln races.

"Now, son," he said, "I'm putting twenty on Mirza, and I'll put five on for you on any horse you fancy. What's your pick?"

"Daffodil, uncle."

"No, not the fiver on Daffodil!"

"I should if it was my own fiver," said the child.

"Good! Good! Right you are! A fiver for me and a fiver for you on Daffodil."

The child had never been to a race-meeting before, and his eyes were blue fire. He pursed his mouth tight and watched. A Frenchman just in front had put his money on Lancelot. Wild with excitement, he flayed his arms up and down, yelling "Lancelot!, Lancelot!" in his French accent.

Daffodil came in first, Lancelot second, Mirza third. The child, flushed and with eyes blazing, was curiously serene. His uncle brought him four five-pound notes, four to one.

"What am I to do with these?" he cried, waving them before the boys eyes.

"I suppose we'll talk to Bassett," said the boy. "I expect I have fifteen hundred now; and twenty in reserve; and this twenty."

His uncle studied him for some moments.

"Look here, son!" he said. "You're not serious about Bassett and that fifteen hundred, are you?"

"Yes, I am. But it's between you and me, uncle. Honour bright?"

"Honour bright all right, son! But I must talk to Bassett."

"If you'd like to be a partner, uncle, with Bassett and me, we could all be partners. Only, you'd have to promise, honour bright, uncle, not to let it go beyond us three.

Bassett and I are lucky, and you must be lucky, because it was your ten shillings I started winning with..."

Uncle Oscar took both Bassett and Paul into Richmond Park[11] for an afternoon, and there they talked.

"It's like this, you see, sir," Bassett said. "Master Paul would get me talking about racing events, spinning yarns,[12] you know, sir. And he was always keen on knowing if I'd made or if I'd lost. It's about a year since, now, that I put five shillings on Blush of Dawn for him: and we lost. Then the luck turned, with that ten shillings he had from you: that we put on Singhalese. And since that time, it's been pretty steady, all things considering. What do you say, Master Paul?"

"We're all right when we're sure," said Paul. "It's when we're not quite sure that we go down."

"Oh, but we're careful then," said Bassett.

"But when are you sure?" smiled Uncle Oscar.

"It's Master Paul, sir," said Bassett in a secret, religious voice. "It's as if he had it from heaven. Like Daffodil, now, for the Lincoln. That was as sure as eggs."[13]

"Did you put anything on Daffodil?" asked Oscar Cresswell.

"Yes, sir, I made my bit."

"And my nephew?"

Bassett was obstinately silent, looking at Paul.

"I made twelve hundred, didn't I, Bassett? I told uncle I was putting three hundred on Daffodil."

"That's right," said Bassett, nodding.

"But where's the money?" asked the uncle.

"I keep it safe locked up, sir. Master Paul he can have it any minute he likes to ask for it."

"What, fifteen hundred pounds?"

"And twenty! And forty, that is, with the twenty he made on the course."

"It's amazing!" said the uncle.

"If Master Paul offers you to be partners, sir, I would, if I were you: if you'll excuse me," said Bassett.

Oscar Cresswell thought about it.

"I'll see the money," he said.

They drove home again, and, sure enough, Bassett came round to the garden-house with fifteen hundred pounds in notes. The twenty pounds reserve was left with Joe Glee, in the Turf Commission deposit.

"You see, it's all right, uncle, when I'm sure! Then we go strong, for all we're worth, don't we, Bassett?"

"We do that, Master Paul."

"And when are you sure?" said the uncle, laughing.

"Oh, well, sometimes I'm absolutely sure, like about Daffodil," said the boy; "and sometimes I have an idea; and sometimes I haven't even an idea, have I, Bassett? Then we're careful, because we mostly go down."

"You do, do you! And when you're sure, like about Daffodil, what makes you sure, sonny?"

"Oh, well, I don't know," said the boy uneasily. "I'm sure, you know, uncle; that's all."

"It's as if he had it from heaven, sir," Bassett reiterated.

"I should say so!" said the uncle.

But he became a partner. And when the Leger[14] was coming on Paul was 'sure' about Lively Spark, which was a quite inconsiderable horse. The boy insisted on putting a thousand on the horse, Bassett went for five hundred, and Oscar Cresswell two hundred. Lively Spark came in first, and the betting had been ten to one against him. Paul had made ten thousand.

"You see," he said. "I was absolutely sure of him."

Even Oscar Cresswell had cleared two thousand.

"Look here, son," he said, "this sort of thing makes me nervous."

"It needn't, uncle! Perhaps I shan't be sure again for a long time."

"But what are you going to do with your money?" asked the uncle.

"Of course," said the boy, "I started it for mother. She said she had no luck, because father is unlucky, so I thought if I was lucky, it might stop whispering."

"What might stop whispering?"

"Our house. I hate our house for whispering."

"What does it whisper?"

"Why—why"—the boy fidgeted—"why, I don't know. But it's always short of money, you know, uncle."

"I know it, son, I know it."

"You know people send mother writs,[15] don't you, uncle?"

"I'm afraid I do," said the uncle.

"And then the house whispers, like people laughing at you behind your back. It's awful, that is! I thought if I was lucky—"

"You might stop it," added the uncle.

The boy watched him with big blue eyes, that had an uncanny cold fire in them, and he said never a word.

"Well, then!" said the uncle. "What are we doing?"

"I shouldn't like mother to know I was lucky," said the boy.

"Why not, son?"

"She'd stop me."

"I don't think she would."

"Oh!"—and the boy writhed in an odd way—"I don't want her to know, uncle."

"All right, son! We'll manage it without her knowing."

They managed it very easily. Paul, at the other's suggestion, handed over five thousand pounds to his uncle, who deposited it with the family lawyer, who was then to inform Paul's mother that a relative had put five thousand pounds into his hands, which sum was to be paid out a thousand pounds at a time, on the mother's birthday, for the next five years.

"So she'll have a birthday present of a thousand pounds for five successive years," said Uncle Oscar. "I hope it won't make it all the harder for her later."

Paul's mother had her birthday in November. The house had been 'whispering' worse than ever lately, and, even in spite of his luck, Paul could not bear up against it. He was very anxious to see the effect of the birthday letter, telling his mother about the thousand pounds.

When there were no visitors, Paul now took his meals with his parents, as he was beyond the nursery control. His mother went into town nearly every day. She had discovered that she had an odd knack of sketching furs and dress materials, so she worked secretly in the studio of a friend who was the chief 'artist' for the leading drapers. She drew the figures of ladies in furs and ladies in silk and sequins for the newspaper advertisements. This young woman artist earned several thousand pounds a year, but Paul's mother only made several hundreds, and she was again dissatisfied. She so wanted to be first in something, and she did not succeed, even in making sketches for drapery advertisements.

She was down to breakfast on the morning of her birthday. Paul watched her face as she read her letters. He knew the lawyer's letter. As his mother read it, her face hardened and became more expressionless. Then a cold, determined look came on her mouth. She hid the letter under the pile of others, and said not a word about it.

"Didn't you have anything nice in the post for your birthday, mother?" said Paul.

"Quite moderately nice," she said, her voice cold and hard and absent.

She went away to town without saying more.

But in the afternoon Uncle Oscar appeared. He said Paul's mother had had a long interview with the lawyer, asking if the whole five thousand could not be advanced at once, as she was in debt.

"What do you think, uncle?" said the boy.

"I leave it to you, son."

"Oh, let her have it, then! We can get some more with the other," said the boy.

"A bird in the hand is worth two in the bush, laddie!" said Uncle Oscar.

"But I'm sure to know for the Grand National;[16] or the Lincolnshire; or else the Derby. I'm sure to know for one of them," said Paul.

So Uncle Oscar signed the agreement, and Paul's mother touched the whole five thousand. Then something very curious happened. The voices in the house suddenly went mad, like a chorus of frogs on a spring evening. There were certain new furnishings, and Paul had a tutor. He was really going to Eton,[17] his father's school, in the following autumn. There were flowers in the winter, and a blossoming of the luxury Paul's mother had been used to. And yet the voices in the house, behind the sprays of mimosa and almond-blossom, and from under the piles of iridescent cushions, simply trilled and screamed in a sort of ecstasy: "There must be more money! Oh-h-h; there must be more money. Oh, now, now-w! Now-w-w—there must be more money!—more than ever! More than ever!"

It frightened Paul terribly. He studied away at his Latin and Greek with his tutor. But his intense hours were spent with Bassett. The Grand National had gone by: he had not 'known', and had lost a hundred pounds. Summer was at hand. He was in agony for the Lincoln. But even for the Lincoln he didn't 'know', and he lost fifty pounds. He became wild-eyed and strange, as if something were going to explode in him.

"Let it alone, son! Don't you bother about it!" urged Uncle Oscar. But it was as if the boy couldn't really hear what his uncle was saying.

"I've got to know for the Derby! I've got to know for the Derby!" the child reiterated, his big blue eyes blazing with a sort of madness.

His mother noticed how overwrought he was.

"You'd better go to the seaside. Wouldn't you like to go now to the seaside, instead of waiting? I think you'd better," she said, looking down at him anxiously, her heart curiously heavy because of him.

But the child lifted his uncanny blue eyes.

"I couldn't possibly go before the Derby, mother!" he said. "I couldn't possibly!"

"Why not?" she said, her voice becoming heavy when she was opposed. "Why not? You can still go from the seaside to see the Derby with your Uncle Oscar, if that's what you wish. No need for you to wait here. Besides, I think you care too much about these races. It's a bad sign. My family has been a gambling family, and you won't know till you grow up how much damage it has done. But it has done damage. I shall have to send Bassett away, and ask Uncle Oscar not to talk racing to you, unless you promise to be reasonable about it: go away to the seaside and forget it. You're all nerves!"

"I'll do what you like, mother, so long as you don't send me away till after the Derby," the boy said.

"Send you away from where? Just from this house?"

"Yes," he said, gazing at her.

"Why, you curious child, what makes you care about this house so much, suddenly? I never knew you loved it."

He gazed at her without speaking. He had a secret within a secret, something he had not divulged, even to Bassett or to his Uncle Oscar.

But his mother, after standing undecided and a little bit sullen for some moments, said: "Very well, then! Don't go to the seaside till after the Derby, if you don't wish it. But promise me you won't think so much about horse-racing and events as you call them!"

"Oh no," said the boy casually. "I won't think much about them, mother. You needn't worry. I wouldn't worry, mother, if I were you."

"If you were me and I were you," said his mother, "I wonder what we should do!"

"But you know you needn't worry, mother, don't you?" the boy repeated.

"I should be awfully glad to know it," she said wearily.

"Oh, well, you can, you know. I mean, you ought to know you needn't worry," he insisted.

"Ought I? Then I'll see about it," she said.

Paul's secret of secrets was his wooden horse, that which had no name. Since he was emancipated from a nurse and a nursery-governess, he had had his rocking-horse removed to his own bedroom at the top of the house.

"Surely you're too big for a rocking-horse!" his mother had remonstrated.

"Well, you see, mother, till I can have a real horse, I like to have some sort of animal about," had been his quaint answer.

"Do you feel he keeps you company?" she laughed.

"Oh yes! He's very good, he always keeps me company, when I'm there," said Paul.

So the horse, rather shabby, stood in an arrested prance in the boy's bedroom.

The Derby was drawing near, and the boy grew more and more tense. He hardly heard what was spoken to him, he was very frail, and his eyes were really uncanny. His mother had sudden strange seizures of uneasiness about him. Sometimes, for half an hour, she would feel a sudden anxiety about him that was almost anguish. She wanted to rush to him at once, and know he was safe.

Two nights before the Derby, she was at a big party in town, when one of her rushes of anxiety about her boy, her first-born, gripped her heart till she could hardly speak. She fought with the feeling, might and main, for she believed in common sense. But it was too strong. She had to leave the dance and go downstairs to telephone to the country. The children's nursery-governess was terribly surprised and startled at being rung up in the night.

"Are the children all right, Miss Wilmot?"

"Oh yes, they are quite all right."

"Master Paul? Is he all right?"

"He went to bed as right as a trivet.[18] Shall I run up and look at him?"

"No," said Paul's mother reluctantly. "No! Don't trouble. It's all right. Don't sit up. We shall be home fairly soon." She did not want her son's privacy intruded upon.

"Very good," said the governess.

It was about one o'clock when Paul's mother and father drove up to their house. All was still. Paul's mother went to her room and slipped off her white fur cloak. She had told her maid not to wait up for her. She heard her husband downstairs, mixing a whisky and soda.

And then, because of the strange anxiety at her heart, she stole upstairs to her son's room. Noiselessly she went along the upper corridor. Was there a faint noise? What was it?

She stood, with arrested muscles, outside his door, listening. There was a strange, heavy, and yet not loud noise. Her heart stood still. It was a soundless noise, yet rushing and powerful. Something huge, in violent, hushed motion. What was it? What in God's name was it? She ought to know. She felt that she knew the noise. She knew what it was.

Yet she could not place it. She couldn't say what it was. And on and on it went, like a madness.

Softly, frozen with anxiety and fear, she turned the door-handle.

The room was dark. Yet in the space near the window, she heard and saw something plunging to and fro. She gazed in fear and amazement.

Then suddenly she switched on the light, and saw her son, in his green pyjamas, madly surging on the rocking-horse. The blaze of light suddenly lit him up, as he urged the wooden horse, and lit her up, as she stood, blonde, in her dress of pale green and crystal, in the doorway.

"Paul!" she cried. "Whatever are you doing?"

"It's Malabar!" he screamed in a powerful, strange voice. "It's Malabar!"

His eyes blazed at her for one strange and senseless second, as he ceased urging his wooden horse. Then he fell with a crash to the ground, and she, all her tormented motherhood flooding upon her, rushed to gather him up.

But he was unconscious, and unconscious he remained, with some brain-fever. He talked and tossed, and his mother sat stonily by his side.

"Malabar! It's Malabar! Bassett, Bassett, I know! It's Malabar!"

So the child cried, trying to get up and urge the rocking-horse that gave him his inspiration.

"What does he mean by Malabar?" asked the heart-frozen mother.

"I don't know," said the father stonily.

"What does he mean by Malabar?" she asked her brother Oscar.

"It's one of the horses running for the Derby," was the answer.

And, in spite of himself, Oscar Cresswell spoke to Bassett, and himself put a thousand on Malabar: at fourteen to one.

The third day of the illness was critical: they were waiting for a change. The boy, with his rather long, curly hair, was tossing ceaselessly on the pillow. He neither slept nor regained consciousness, and his eyes were like blue stones. His mother sat, feeling her heart had gone, turned actually into a stone.

In the evening Oscar Cresswell did not come, but Bassett sent a message, saying could he come up for one moment, just one moment? Paul's mother was very angry at the intrusion, but on second thoughts she agreed. The boy was the same. Perhaps Bassett might bring him to consciousness.

The gardener, a shortish fellow with a little brown moustache and sharp little brown eyes, tiptoed into the room, touched his imaginary cap to Paul's mother, and stole to the bedside, staring with glittering, smallish eyes at the tossing, dying child.

"Master Paul!" he whispered. "Master Paul! Malabar came in first all right, a clean win. I did as you told me. You've made over seventy thousand pounds, you have; you've got over eighty thousand. Malabar came in all right, Master Paul."

"Malabar! Malabar! Did I say Malabar, mother? Did I say Malabar? Do you think I'm lucky, mother? I knew Malabar, didn't I? Over eighty thousand pounds! I call that lucky, don't you, mother? Over eighty thousand pounds! I knew, didn't I know I knew? Malabar came in all right. If I ride my horse till I'm sure, then I tell you, Bassett, you can go as high as you like. Did you go for all you were worth, Bassett?"

"I went a thousand on it, Master Paul."

"I never told you, mother, that if I can ride my horse, and get there, then I'm absolutely sure—oh, absolutely! Mother, did I ever tell you? I am lucky!"

"No, you never did," said his mother.

But the boy died in the night.

And even as he lay dead, his mother heard her brother's voice saying to her, "My God, Hester, you're eighty-odd thousand to the good, and a poor devil of a son to the bad. But, poor devil, poor devil, he's best gone out of a life where he rides his rocking-horse to find a winner."

Notes

[1] the nursery: the room set apart in a house for young children to play in.

[2] filthy lucre: (derogatory sense) dirty money.

[3] Sansovino, and the following Daffodil, Mirza, Lancelot, Blush of Dawn, Singhalese, Lively Spark, Malabar, are all the names of the racing horses.

[4] a perfect blade of the turf: a dashing racing horse rider.
[5] put anything on: bet any money on.
[6] give him away: reveal the secret information about him.
[7] the Lincoln: the first big race of the flat racing season.
[8] Honour bright?—Are you serious about that?
[9] All except twenty pounds: Twenty pounds sterling in 1926 was much more valuable than now, since a year's salary for a very wealthy executive manager was just 500 pounds.
[10] Nat Gould: Nathaniel Gould (1857—1919), a successful journalist and novelist, who wrote chiefly about horse racing.
[11] Richmond Park: one of London's large parks.
[12] spinning yarns: telling stories.
[13] as sure as eggs: A colloquial shortened saying for "as sure as eggs are eggs".
[14] the Leger: a horse racing meeting founded in 1776 and run in Sept. at Doncaster.
[15] writs: legal documents issued by a court or a judicial officer.
[16] the Grand National: the most famous steeplechase in the world, run in March at Aintree, near Liverpool, since 1847.
[17] Eton: the most well-known of England's public schools, founded by Henry VI in 1440.
[18] as right as a trivet: perfectly all right.

Commentary

The Rocking-Horse Winner is one of the major short stories of Lawrence. It tells a story of Paul, a small boy in a middle-class family, who perceives that there is never enough money in his family, and sets out to find a way (through gambling in a horse-race) to get money through luck. He wants to help his mother, besides, he also wants to silence the voice that haunts him at home—"There must be more money! There must be more money!"

He secretly imagines that if he rides his rocking-horse fast enough, he will somehow "know" the name of the winning horse in the next race. He finally rides his rocking-horse in his own room so furiously in order to discover the winner of the Derby that he falls into illness and dies, just as the winning horse earns his family an enormous fortune. He was overburdened to death under the great mental pressure to win in the gambling for his mother. This story reveals the horrible harm done by the endless desire for money to the soul of people, especially to the healthy development of children.

In this story, psychoanalysis, as one of Lawrence's main writing techniques, plays an important part in revealing the character's inner world.

Questions and Exercises

1. What do you think is D. H. Lawrence's attitude towards the notion of luck and happiness? And why do you think the story begins in a way as a fairy tale does?
2. How much do you know about horse racing? What does the rocking-horse symbolize?
3. How would you describe the mother's character and her relationship with her son?
4. How does *The Rocking-Horse Winner* portray the desire for material wealth? What is the tragedy of the boy?

Doris Lessing

Doris Lessing (1919—2013) was born in Persia (now Iran) on October 22, 1919 to British parents. She lived in Africa until she was thirty. In June 1995, she received an honorary degree from Harvard University. In 1996, she was on the list of nominees for the Nobel Prize for Literature and Britain's Writer's Guild Award for Fiction. In 2001, she was awarded the Prince of Asturias Prize in Literature and the David Cohen British Literature Prize. In 2007, she finally won the Nobel Prize for Literature.

Doris Lessing is very much a writer of her time, deeply involved in the changing patterns of thought and culture in the Western world. Her keenest interest is in the relationship between the black and white races in Africa, changing ways between different generations, and the position of women in society. She stands for social justice, and believes that women should be more independent and play a bigger role in improving the present society through their own influence. Her writing style is most highly developed in her short stories, and she is considered one of the best short story writers in English today.

Doris Lessing wrote novels, works of non-fiction, collections of short stories, and even one play. Her best-known books include: *The Grass Is Singing* (1950), a novel about the unequal relationships between a white farmer, his wife and their black servant in Africa; *This Was the Old Chief's Country* (1951), a collection of short stories about Africa; *The Golden Notebook* (1962), a feminist novel that explores the personal, political, and social problems of a woman writer living independently in England.

A Road to the Big City

The train left at midnight, not at six. Jansen's flare of temper at the clerk's mistake died before he turned from the counter: he did not really mind. For a week he had been with rich friends, in a vacuum of wealth,[1] politely seeing the town through their eyes. Now, for six hours, he was free to let the dry and nervous air of Johannesburg strike him direct. He went into the station buffet. It was a bare place, with shiny brown walls and tables arranged regularly. He sat before a cup of strong orange-coloured tea, and because he was in the arrested, dreamy frame of mind of the uncommitted traveller,[2] he was the spectator at a play which could not hold his attention. He was about to leave, in order to move by himself through the streets, among the people, trying to feel what they were in this city, what they had which did not exist, perhaps, in other big cities—for he believed that in every place there dwelt a daemon[3] which expressed itself through the eyes and voices of those who lived there—when he heard someone ask: Is this place free? He turned quickly, for there was a quality in the voice which could not be mistaken. Two girls stood beside him, and the one who had spoken sat down without waiting for his response: there were many empty tables in the room. She wore a tight short black dress, several brass chains, and high shiny black shoes. She was a tall broad girl with colourless hair ridged tightly round her head, but given a bright surface so that it glinted like metal. She immediately lit a cigarette and said to her companion: "Sit down for God's sake." The other girl shyly slid into the chair next to Jansen, averting her face as he gazed at her, which he could not help doing: she was so different from what he expected. Plump, childish, with dull hair bobbing in fat rolls on her neck, she wore a flowered and flounced dress and flat white sandals on bare and sunburned feet. Her face had the jolly friendliness of a little dog. Both girls showed Dutch ancestry in the broad blunt planes of cheek and forehead; both had small blue eyes, though one pair was surrounded by sandy lashes, and the other by black varnished fringes.[4]

The waitress came for an order. Jansen was too curious about the young girl to move away. "What will you have?" he asked. "Brandy," said the older one at once, "Two brandies," she added, with another impatient look at her sister—there could be no doubt that they were sisters.

"I haven't never drunk brandy," said the younger with a giggle of surprise. "Except when Mom gave me some sherry at Christmas." She blushed as the older said despairingly, half under her breath: "Oh God preserve me from it!"

"I came to Johannesburg this morning," said the little one to Jansen confidingly. "But Lilla has been here earning a living for a year."

"My God!" said Lilla again. "What did I tell you? Didn't you hear what I told you?" Then, making the best of it, she smiled professionally at Jansen and said: "Green! You wouldn't believe it if I told you. I was green when I came, but compared with Marie..." She laughed angrily.

"Have you been to Joburg before this day?" asked Marie in her confiding way.

"You are passing through," stated Lilla, with a glance at Marie. "You can tell easy if you know how to look."

"You're quite right," said Jansen.

"Leaving tomorrow, perhaps?" asked Lilla.

"Tonight," said Jansen.

Instantly Lilla's eyes left Jansen, and began to rove about her, resting on one man's face and then the next. "Midnight," said Jansen, in order to see her expression change.

"There's plenty time," she said, smiling.

"Lilla promised I could go to the bioscope,"[5] said Marie, her eyes becoming large. She looked around the station buffet, and because of her way of looking, Jansen tried to see it differently. He could. It remained for him a bare, brownish, dirty sort of place, full of badly-dressed and dull people. He felt as one does with a child whose eyes widen with terror or delight at the sight of an old woman muttering down the street, or a flowering tree. What hunched black crone from a fairy tale, what celestial tree does the child see? Marie was smiling with charmed amazement.

"Very well," said Jansen, "let's go to the flicks."

For a moment Lilla calculated, her hard blue glance[6] moving from Jansen to Marie. "You take Marie," she suggested, direct to Jansen, ignoring her sister. "She's green, but she's learning." Marie half-rose, with a terrified look. "You can't leave me," she said.

"Oh my God!" said Lilla resignedly. "Oh all right. Sit down, baby. But I've a friend to see. I told you."

"But I only just came."

"All right, all right. Sit down I said. He won't bite you."

"Where do you come from?" asked Jansen.

Marie said a name he had never heard.

"It's not far from Bloemfontein," explained Lilla.

"I went to Bloemfontein once," said Marie, offering Jansen this experience. "The bioscope there is big. Not like near home."

"What is home like?"

"But it's small," said Marie.

"What does your father do?"

"He works on the railway," Lilla said quickly.

"He's a ganger," said Marie, and Lilla rolled her eyes up and sighed.

Jansen had seen the gangers' cottages, the frail little shacks along the railway lines, miles from any place, where the washing flapped whitely on the lines over patches of garden, and the children ran out to wave to the train that passed shrieking from one wonderful fabled town to the next.

"Mom is old-fashioned," said Marie. She said the word "old-fashioned" carefully; it was not hers, but Lilla's; she was tasting it in the way she sipped at the brandy, trying it out, determined to like it. But the emotion was all her own; all the frustration of years was in her, ready to explode into joy. "She doesn't want us to be in Joburg. She says it is wrong for girls."

"Did you run away?" asked Jansen.

Wonder filled the child's face. "How did you guess I ran away?" She said, with a warm admiring smile at Lilla; "My sister sent me the money. I didn't have none at all. I was alone with Mom and Dad and my brothers are working on the copper mines."

"I see." Jansen saw the lonely girl in the little house by the railway lines, helping with the chickens and the cooking, staring hopelessly at the fashion papers, watching the trains pass, too old now to run out and wave and shout, but staring at the fortunate people at the windows with grudging envy, and reading Lilla's letters week after week: "I have a job in an office. I have a new dress. My young man said to me." He looked over the table at the two fine young South African women, with their broad and capable look, their strong bodies, their health, and he thought: Well, it happens every day. He glanced at his watch and Marie said at once: "There's time for the bioscope, isn't there?"

"You and your bioscope," said Lilla. "I'll take you tomorrow afternoon." She rose, said to Jansen in an offhand way: "Coming?" and went to the door. Jansen hesitated, then followed Marie's uncertain but friendly smile.

The three went into the street. Not far away shone a large white building with film stars kissing between thin borders of coloured shining lights. Streams of smart people went up the noble marble steps where splendid men in uniform welcomed them. Jansen, watching Marie's face, was able to see it like that. Lilla laughed and said: "We're going home, Marie. The pictures aren't anything much. There's better things to do than picture." She winked at Jansen.

They went to a two-roomed flat in a suburb. It was over a grocery store called Mac's Golden Emporium. It had tinned peaches, dried fruit, dressed dolls and rolls of cotton stuffs in the window. The flat had new furniture in it. There was a sideboard with bottles and a radio. The radio played: "Or would you like to swing on a star, carry moonbeams home in a jar, and be better off than you are..."

"I like the words," said Marie to Jansen, listening to them with soft delight. Lilla said: "Excuse me, but I have to phone my friend," and went out.

Marie said: "Have a drink." She said it carefully. She poured brandy, the tip of her tongue held between her teeth, and she spilled the water. She carried the glass to Jansen, and smiled in unconscious triumph as she set it down by him. Then she said: "Wait," and went into the bedroom. Jansen adjusted himself on the juicy upholstery of a big chair. He was annoyed to find himself here. What for? What was the good of it? He looked at himself in the glass over a sideboard. He saw a middle-aged gentleman, with a worn indulgent face, dressed in a grey suit and sitting uncomfortably in a very ugly chair. But what did Marie see when she looked at him? She came back soon, with a pair of black shiny shoes on her broad feet, and a tight red dress, and a pretty face painted over her own blunt honest face. She sat herself down opposite him, as she had seen Lilla sit, adjusting the poise of her head and shoulders. But she forgot her legs, which lay loosely in front of her, like a schoolgirl's.

"Lilla said I could wear her dresses," she said, lingering over her sister's generosity. "She said today I could live here until I earned enough to get my own flat. She said I'd soon have enough." She caught her breath. "Mom would be mad."

"I expect she would," said Jansen drily; and saw Marie react away from him. She spread her red skirts and faced him politely, waiting for him to make her evening.[7]

Lilla came in, turned her calculating, good-humored eye from her sister to Jansen, smiled, and said: "I'm going out a little. Oh, keep your hair on.[8] I'll be back soon. My friend is taking me for a walk."

The friend came in and took Lilla's arm, a large, handsome sunburned man who smiled with a good-time smile at Marie. She responded with such a passion of admiration in her eyes that Jansen understood at once what she did not see when she looked at himself. "My, my," said this young man with easy warmth to Marie. "You're a fast learner, I can see that."

"We'll be back," said Lilla to Marie. "Remember what I said." Then to Jansen, like a saleswoman: "She's not bad. Anyhow she can't get herself into any trouble here at home." The young man slipped his arm around her, and reached for a glass off the sideboard with his free hand. He poured brandy, humming with the radio: "In a shady nook, by a babbling brook..." He threw back his head, poured the brandy down, smiled broadly at Jansen and Marie, winked and said: 'Be seeing you. Don't forget to wind up the clock and put the cat out." Outside on the landing he and Lilla sang: "Carry moonbeams home in a jar, be better off than you are..." They sang their way down to the street. A car door slammed, an engine roared. Marie darted to the window, and said bitterly. "They've gone to the pictures."

"I don't think so," said Jansen. She came back, frowning, preoccupied with responsibility. "Would you like another drink?" she asked, remembering what Lilla had told her. Jansen shook his head, and sat still for a moment, weighted with inertia. [9] Then he said: "Marie, I want you to listen to me." She leaned forward dutifully, ready to listen. But this was not as she had gazed at the other man, the warm, generous, laughing, singing young man. Jansen found many words ready on his tongue, disliked them, and blurted: "Marie, I wish you'd let me send you back home tonight." Her face dulled. "No, Marie, you really must listen." She listened politely, from behind her dull resistance. He used words carefully, out of the delicacy of his compassion,[10] and saw how they faded into meaninglessness in the space between him and Marie. Then he grew brutal and desperate, because he had to reach her.[11] He said: "This sort of life isn't as much fun as it looks"; and "Thousands of girls all over the world choose the easy way because they're stupid, and afterwards they're sorry." She dropped her lids, looked at her feet in her new high shoes, and shut herself off from him. He used the words whore and prostitute; but she had never heard them except as swearwords, and did not connect them with herself. She began repeating, over and over again: "My sister's a typist; she's got a job in an office."

He said angrily: "Do you think she can afford to live like this on a typist's pay?"

"Her gentleman friend gives her things, he's generous, she told me so," said Marie doubtfully.

"How old are you, Marie?"

"Eighteen," she said, turning her broad freckled wrist, where Lilla's bracelet caught the light.

"When you're twenty-five you'll be out on the streets picking up any man you see, taking them to hotels..."

At the word "hotel" her eyes widened; he remembered she had never been in a hotel; they were something lovely on the cinema screen.

"When you're thirty you'll be an old woman."

"Lilla said she'd look after me. She promised me faithfully," said Marie, in terror at his coldness. But what he was saying meant nothing to her, nothing at all. He saw that she probably did not know what the word prostitute meant; that the things Lilla had told her meant only lessons in how to enjoy the delights of this city.

He said: "Do you know what I'm here for? Your sister expects you to take off your clothes and get into bed and..." He stopped. Her eyes were wide open, fastened on him, not in fear, but in the anxious preoccupation of a little girl who is worried she is not behaving properly. Her hands had moved to the buckle of her belt, and she was undoing it.

Jansen got up, and without speaking he gathered clothes that were obviously hers from off the furniture, from off the floor. He went into the bedroom and found a suitcase and put her things into it. "I'm putting you on to the train tonight," he said.

"My sister won't let you," she cried out. "She'll stop you."

"Your sister's a bad girl," said Jansen, and saw, to his surprise, that Marie's face showed fear at last. Those two words, "bad girl" had more effect than all his urgent lecturing.

"You shouldn't say such things," said Marie, beginning to cry. "You shouldn't never say someone's a bad girl." They were her mother's words, obviously, and had hit her hard, where she could be reached. She stood listless in the middle of the floor, weeping, making no resistance. He tucked her arm inside his, and led her downstairs. "You'll marry a nice man soon, Marie," he promised. "You won't always have to live by the railway lines."

"I don't never meet no men, except Dad," she said, beginning to tug at his arm again.

He held her tight until they were in a taxi. There she sat crouched on the edge of the seat, watching the promised city[12] sweep past. At the station, keeping a firm hold on her, he bought her a ticket and gave her five pounds, and put her into a compartment and said: "I know you hate me. One day you'll know I'm right and you'll be glad." She smiled weakly, and huddled herself into her seat, like a cold little animal, staring sadly out of the window.

He left her, running, to catch his own train which already stood waiting on the next platform.

As it drew out of the station he saw Marie waddling desperately on her tall heels along the platform, casting scared glances over her shoulder. Their eyes met; she gave him an apologetic smile, and ran on. With the pound notes clutched loosely in her hand she was struggling her way through the crowds back to the lights, the love, the joyous streets of the promised city.

Notes

[1] in a vacuum of wealth: in a relatively isolated world of material wealth.

[2] he was in the arrested, dreamy frame of mind of the uncommitted traveller: he was an absent-minded traveler without any commitment, so he was in a preoccupied, dream-like state of mind.

[3] a daemon: another way of spelling "demon". Here it means something magically powerful to control people's mind.

[4] one pair was surrounded by sandy lashes, and the other by black varnished fringes: Magie's eyes were surrounded by natural yellow lashes, while Lilla's eyes were surrounded by artificially-coated shiny lashes.

[5] go to the bioscope (flicks): go to see a movie.

[6] hard blue glance: her sexually indecent glance which is hard to understand.

[7] to make her evening: make her spend an excited evening.

[8] keep your hair on: remain calm and don't lose your temper easily.

[9] weighted with inertia: feeling depressed because of his powerless passivity.

[10] out of the delicacy of his compassion: due to his subtle feeling of sympathy for her.

[11] to reach her: to make her understand his implication.

[12] the promised city: (in the Bible) the land of Canaan promised by God to Abraham and his people. Here it refers to Johannesburg which the girls hope or believe will bring happiness or success to them.

Commentary

A Road to the Big City is the story of two sisters who admire the colourful life of a big city. The setting is the capital city of South Africa—Johannesburg—the biggest and most modern city in this country. After the elder sister Lilla comes to Johannesburg and degrades into a street girl, she sends home money to bring her younger sister Marie there too. Marie, a naïve country girl, looks childishly innocent and far from sophisticated. Her first wish after arriving is to see a movie in a big cinema. However, the first day she arrives at the "big city", she is forced by her elder sister Lilla to sell sex. Jansen, a well-traveled man who comes to Johannesburg due to a mistake in his train time-table, becomes her first "client". Being an honest person, he attempts to "rescue" Marie out of the "dirty" city. He buys her a train ticket to send her back home. But Marie gets off the train and runs back to the city as soon as Jansen leaves. Even though she knows what is in store for her in the big city, she has deliberately chosen her own fate.

The main theme of the story is obviously about the lure of life in a big city to people who live quiet, boring lives in the remote countryside. Doris Lessing illustrates in this story a world-wide problem where big differences exist between city and countryside. She also points out the willingness of people to be deluded by false values, regardless of the hazardous risks that face an innocent person like Marie.

Questions and Exercises

1. What does a big city mean to the sisters in the story? And what is a successful life for the two sisters?
2. What kind of road does Lilla choose to get into the big city? What kind of fate is waiting for Marie?
3. Why does Marie get off the train for home, running back to the city even though she understands what is in store for her?
4. Do you think what Jansen does can really solve the girls' problem? State your reasons.

Nathaniel Hawthorne

Nathaniel Hawthorne (1804—1864) was born on the fourth of July 1804 in Salem, Massachusetts. Some of his ancestors were men of prominence in the Puritan theocracy of 17th-century New England. One of them was a colonial magistrate, notorious for his part in the persecution of the Quakers, and another was a judge at the Salem Witchcraft Trial in 1692. Gradually the family fortune declined. His father, a sea captain, died in Dutch Guiana, leaving the widow and the child in misery.

With the publication of *The Scarlet Letter* in 1850, Nathaniel Hawthorne became famous as the greatest writer living then, and his reputation as a major American author has been on the increase ever since. Hawthorne was intensely aware of the misdeeds of his Puritan ancestors, and this awareness led to his understanding of evil being at the core of human life. In his mind, evil evidently exists in the human heart. Everyone seems to cover up his innermost "evil" in the way the minister in *The Scarlet Letter* tries to do with his black veil.

The Scarlet Letter

Chapter 12 The Minister's Vigil

Walking in the shadow of a dream, as it were, and perhaps actually under the influence of a species of somnambulism,[1] Mr. Dimmesdale reached the spot, where, now so long since, Hester Prynne had lived through her first hours of public ignominy. The same platform or scaffold, black and weather-stained with the storm or sunshine of seven long years, and foot-worn, too, with the tread of many culprits who had since ascended it, remained standing beneath the balcony of the meeting-house. The minister went up the steps.

It was an obscure night of early May. An unvaried pall of cloud muffled the whole expanse of sky from zenith to horizon. If the same multitude which had stood as eye-witnesses while Hester Prynne sustained her punishment could now have been summoned forth, they would have discerned no face above the platform, nor hardly the outline of a human shape, in the dark grey of the midnight. But the town was all asleep. There was no peril of discovery. The minister might stand there, if it so pleased him, until morning should redden in the east, without other risk than that the dank and chill night-air would creep into his frame, and stiffen his joints with rheumatism, and clog his throat with catarrh and cough; thereby defrauding the expectant audience of to-morrow's prayer and sermon. No eye could see him, save that ever-wakeful one which had seen him in his closet, wielding the bloody scourge.[2] Why, then, had he come hither? Was it but the mockery of penitence? A mockery, indeed, but in which his soul trifled with itself! A mockery at which angels blushed and wept, while fiends rejoiced, with jeering laughter! He had been driven hither by the impulse of that Remorse which dogged him everywhere, and whose own sister and closely linked companion was that Cowardice[3] which invariably drew him back, with her tremulous gripe, just when the other impulse had hurried him to the verge of a disclosure. Poor, miserable man! what right had infirmity like his to burden itself with crime? Crime is for the iron-nerved, who have their choice either to endure it, or, if it press too hard, to exert their fierce and savage strength for a good purpose, and fling it off at once! This feeble and most sensitive of spirits could do neither, yet continually did one thing or another, which intertwined, in the same inextricable knot, the agony of heaven-defying guilt and vain repentance.

And thus, while standing on the scaffold, in this vain show of expiation, Mr.

Dimmesdale was overcome with a great horror of mind, as if the universe were gazing at a scarlet token on his naked breast, right over his heart. On that spot, in very truth, there was, and there had long been, the gnawing and poisonous tooth of bodily pain. Without any effort of his will, or power to restrain himself, he shrieked aloud; an outcry that went pealing through the night, and was beaten back from one house to another, and reverberated from the hills in the background; as if a company of devils, detecting so much misery and terror in it, had made a plaything of the sound, and were bandying it to and fro.

"It is done!" muttered the minister, covering his face with his hands. "The whole town will awake, and hurry forth, and find me here!"

But it was not so. The shriek had perhaps sounded with a far greater power, to his own startled ears, than it actually possessed. The town did not awake; or, if it did, the drowsy slumberers mistook the cry either for something frightful in a dream, or for the noise of witches; whose voices, at that period, were often heard to pass over the settlements or lonely cottages, as they rode with Satan[4] through the air. The clergyman, therefore, hearing no symptoms of disturbance, uncovered his eyes and looked about him. At one of the chamber-windows of Governor Bellingham's mansion,[5] which stood at some distance, on the line of another street, he beheld the appearance of the old magistrate himself, with a lamp in his hand, a white night-cap on his head, and a long white gown enveloping his figure. He looked like a ghost, evoked unseasonably from the grave. The cry had evidently startled him. At another window of the same house, moreover, appeared old Mistress Hibbins,[6] the Governor's sister, also with a lamp, which, even thus far off, revealed the expression of her sour and discontented face. She thrust forth her head from the lattice, and looked anxiously upward. Beyond the shadow of a doubt, this venerable witch-lady had heard Mr. Dimmesdale's outcry, and interpreted it, with its multitudinous echoes and reverberations, as the clamour of the fiends and night-hags, with whom she was well known to make excursions into the forest.

Detecting the gleam of Governor Bellingham's lamp, the old lady quickly extinguished her own, and vanished. Possibly, she went up among the clouds. The minister saw nothing further of her motions. The magistrate, after a wary observation of the darkness—into which, nevertheless, he could see but little farther than he might into a mill-stone—retired from the window.

The minister grew comparatively calm. His eyes, however, were soon greeted by a little, glimmering light, which, at first a long way off, was approaching up the street. It threw a gleam of recognition on here a post, and there a garden-fence, and here a latticed windowpane, and there a pump, with its full trough of water, and here, again, an arched door of oak, with an iron knocker, and a rough log for the door-step. The Reverend Mr. Dimmesdale noted all these minute particulars, even while firmly convinced that the doom of his existence was stealing onward, in the footsteps which he now heard; and that the gleam of the lantern would fall upon him, in a few moments more, and reveal his long-hidden secret. As the light grew nearer, he beheld, within its illuminated circle, his brother clergyman—or, to speak more accurately, his professional father, as well as highly valued friend—the Reverend Mr. Wilson;[7] who, as Mr. Dimmesdale now conjectured, had been praying at the bedside of some dying man. And so he had. The good old minister came freshly from the death-chamber of Governor Winthrop,[8] who had passed from earth to heaven within that very hour. And now, surrounded, like the saint-like personages of olden times, with a radiant halo, that glorified him amid this gloomy night of sin- as if the departed Governor had left him an inheritance of his glory, or as if he had caught upon himself the distant shine of the celestial city, while looking thitherward to see the triumphant pilgrim pass within its gates- now, in short, good Father Wilson was moving homeward, aiding his footsteps with a lighted lantern! The glimmer of this luminary suggested the above conceits to Mr. Dimmesdale, who smiled—nay, almost laughed at them—and then wondered if he were going mad.

As the Reverend Mr. Wilson passed beside the scaffold, closely muffling his Geneva cloak[9] about him with one arm, and holding the lantern before his breast with the other, the minister could hardly restrain himself from speaking.

"A good evening to you, venerable Father Wilson! Come up hither, I pray you, and pass a pleasant hour with me!"

Good heavens! Had Mr. Dimmesdale actually spoken? For one instant, he believed that these words had passed his lips. But they were uttered only within his imagination. The venerable Father Wilson continued to step slowly onward, looking carefully at the muddy pathway before his feet, and never once turning his head toward the guilty platform. When the light of the glimmering lantern had faded quite away, the minister discovered, by the faintness which came over him, that the last few moments had been a crisis of terrible anxiety; although his mind had made an involuntary effort to relieve itself by a kind of lurid playfulness.

Shortly afterwards, the like grisly sense of the humorous again stole in among the solemn phantoms of his thought. He felt his limbs growing stiff with the unaccustomed chilliness of the night, and doubted whether he should be able to descend the steps of the scaffold. Morning would break, and find him there. The neighborhood would begin to rouse itself. The earliest riser, coming forth in the dim twilight, would perceive a vaguely defined figure aloft on the place of shame; and, half crazed betwixt alarm and curiosity, would go, knocking from door to door, summoning all the people to behold the ghost—as he needs must think it—of some defunct transgressor. A dusky tumult would flap its wings from one house to another. Then—the morning light still waxing stronger—old patriarchs would rise up in great haste, each in his flannel gown, and matronly dames, without pausing to put off their night-gear. The whole tribe of decorous personages, who had never heretofore been seen with a single hair of their heads awry, would start into public view, with the disorder of a nightmare in their aspects. Old Governor Bellingham would come grimly forth, with his King James ruff fastened askew; and Mistress Hibbins, with some twigs of the forest clinging to her skirts, and looking sourer than ever, as having hardly got a wink of sleep after her night ride;[10] and good Father Wilson, too, after spending half the night at a death-bed, and liking ill to be disturbed, thus early, out of his dreams about the glorified saints. Hither, likewise, would come the elders and deacons of Mr. Dimmesdale's church, and the young virgins who so idolized their minister, and had made a shrine for him in their white bosoms; which now, by-the-bye, in their hurry and confusion, they would scantily have given themselves time to cover with their kerchiefs. All people, in a word, would come stumbling over their thresholds, and turning up their amazed and horror-stricken visages around the scaffold. Whom would they discern there, with the red eastern light upon his brow? Whom, but the Reverend Arthur Dimmesdale, half frozen to death, overwhelmed with shame, and standing where Hester Prynne had stood!

Carried away by the grotesque horror of this picture, the minister, unawares, and to his own infinite alarm, burst into a great peal of laughter. It was immediately responded to by a light, airy, childish laugh, in which, with a thrill of the heart—but he knew not whether of exquisite pain, or pleasure as acute—he recognised the tones of little Pearl.

"Pearl! Little Pearl!" cried he, after a moment's pause; then, suppressing his voice—"Hester! Hester Prynne! Are you there?"

"Yes; it is Hester Prynne!" she replied, in a tone of surprise; and the minister heard her footsteps approaching from the sidewalk, along which she had been passing. "It is I, and my little Pearl."

"Whence come you, Hester?" asked the minister. "What sent you hither?"

"I have been watching at a death-bed," answered Hester Prynne—"at Governor Winthrop's death-bed, and have taken his measure for a robe, and am now going homeward to my dwelling."

"Come up hither, Hester, thou and little Pearl," said the Reverend Mr. Dimmesdale. "Ye have both been here before, but I was not with you. Come up hither once again, and we will stand all three together!"

She silently ascended the steps, and stood on the platform, holding little Pearl by the hand. The minister felt for the child's other hand, and took it. The moment that he did so, there came what seemed a tumultuous rush of new life, other life than his own, pouring like a torrent into his heart, and hurrying through all his veins, as if the mother and the child were communicating their vital warmth to his half-torpid system. The three formed an electric chain.

"Minister!" whispered little Pearl.

"What wouldst thou say, child?" asked Mr. Dimmesdale.

"Wilt thou stand here with mother and me, to-morrow noontide?" inquired Pearl.

"Nay; not so, my little Pearl," answered the minister; for, with the new energy of the moment, all the dread of public exposure, that had so long been the anguish of his life, had returned upon him; and he was already trembling at the conjunction in which—with a strange joy, nevertheless—he now found himself. "Not so, my child. I shall, indeed, stand with thy mother and thee one other day, but not to-morrow."

Pearl laughed, and attempted to pull away her hand. But the minister held it fast.

"A moment longer, my child!" said he.

"But wilt thou promise," asked Pearl, "to take my hand, and mother's hand, to-morrow noontide?"

"Not then, Pearl," said the minister, "but another time."

"And what other time?" persisted the child.

"At the great judgment day,[11]" whispered the minister—and, strangely enough, the sense that he was a professional teacher of the truth impelled him to answer the child so. "Then, and there, before the judgment-seat, thy mother, and thou, and I, must stand together. But the daylight of this world shall not see our meeting."

Pearl laughed again.

But, before Mr. Dimmesdale had done speaking, a light gleamed far and wide over all the muffled sky. It was doubtless caused by one of those meteors which the night-watcher may so often observe burning out to waste, in the vacant regions of the atmosphere. So powerful was its radiance, that it thoroughly illuminated the dense medium of cloud betwixt the sky and earth. The great vault brightened, like the dome of an immense lamp. It showed the familiar scene of the street, with the distinctness of mid-day, but also with the awfulness that is always imparted to familiar objects by an unaccustomed light. The wooden houses, with their jutting stories and quaint gable-peaks; the door-steps and thresholds, with the early grass springing up about them; the garden-plots, black with freshly turned earth; the wheel-track, little worn, and, even in the market-place, margined with green on either side all—were visible, but with a singularity of aspect that seemed to give another moral interpretation to the things of this world than they had ever borne before. And there stood the minister, with his hand over his heart; and Hester Prynne, with the embroidered letter glimmering on her bosom; and little Pearl, herself a symbol, and the connecting link between those two. They stood in the noon of that strange and solemn splendour, as if it were the light that is to reveal all secrets, and the daybreak that shall unite all who belong to one another.

There was witchcraft in little Pearl's eyes; and her face, as she glanced upward at the minister, wore that naughty smile which made its expression frequently so elvish. She withdrew her hand from Mr. Dimmesdale's, and pointed across the street. But he clasped both his hands over his breast, and cast his eyes towards the zenith.

Nothing was more common, in those days, than to interpret all meteoric appearances, and other natural phenomena, that occurred with less regularity than the rise and set of sun and moon, as so many revelations from a supernatural source. Thus, a blazing spear, a sword of flame, a bow, or a sheaf of arrows, seen in the midnight sky, prefigured Indian warfare. Pestilence was known to have been foreboded by a shower of crimson light. We doubt whether any marked event, for good or evil, ever befell New England, from its settlement down to Revolutionary times,[12] of which the inhabitants had not been previously warned by some spectacle of this nature. Not seldom, it had been seen by multitudes. Oftener, however, its credibility rested on the faith of some lonely eye-witness, who beheld the wonder through the colored, magnifying, and distorting medium of his imagination, and shaped it more distinctly in his afterthought. It was, indeed, a majestic idea, that the destiny of nations should be revealed, in these awful hieroglyphics, on the cope of heaven. A scroll so wide might not be deemed too expansive for Providence to write a people's doom upon. The belief was a favorite one with our forefathers, as betokening that their infant commonwealth was under a celestial guardianship of peculiar intimacy and strictness. But what shall we say, when an individual discovers a revelation, addressed to himself alone, on the same vast sheet of record! In such a case, it could only be the symptom of a highly disordered mental state, when a man, rendered morbidly self-contemplative by long, intense, and secret pain, had extended his egotism over the whole expanse of nature, until the firmament itself should appear no more than a fitting page for his soul's history and fate!

We impute it, therefore, solely to the disease in his own eye and heart, that the minister, looking upward to the zenith, beheld there the appearance of an immense letter—the letter A—marked out in lines of dull red light. Not but the meteor may have shown itself at that point, burning duskily through a veil of cloud; but with no such shape as his guilty imagination gave it; or, at least, with so little definiteness, that another's guilt might have seen another symbol in it.

There was a singular circumstance that characterized Mr. Dimmesdale's psychological state at this moment. All the time that he gazed upward to the zenith, he was, nevertheless, perfectly aware that little Pearl was pointing her finger towards old Roger Chillingworth, who stood at no great distance from the scaffold. The minister appeared to see him, with the same glance that discerned the miraculous letter. To his features, as to all other objects, the meteoric light imparted a new expression; or it might well be that the physician was not careful then, as at all other times, to hide the malevolence with which he looked upon his victim. Certainly, if the meteor kindled up the sky, and disclosed the earth, with an awfulness that admonished Hester Prynne and the clergyman of the day of judgment, then might Roger Chillingworth have passed with them for the arch-fiend, standing there with a smile and scowl, to claim his own. So vivid was the expression, or so intense the minister's perception of it, that it seemed still to remain painted on the darkness, after the meteor had vanished, with an effect as if the street and all things else were at once annihilated.

"Who is that man, Hester?" gasped Mr. Dimmesdale, overcome with terror. "I shiver at him! Dost thou know the man? I hate him, Hester!"

She remembered her oath, and was silent.

"I tell thee, my soul shivers at him!" muttered the minister again. "Who is he? Who is he? Canst thou do nothing for me? I have a nameless horror of the man!"

"Minister," said little Pearl, "I can tell thee who he is!"

"Quickly, then, child!" said the minister, bending his ear close to her lips. "Quickly! —and as low as thou canst whisper."

Pearl mumbled something into his ear, that sounded, indeed, like human language, but was only such gibberish as children may be heard amusing themselves with, by the hour together. At all events, if it involved any secret information in regard to old Roger Chillingworth, it was in a tongue unknown to the erudite clergyman, and did but increase the bewilderment of his mind. The elvish child then laughed aloud.

"Dost thou mock me now?" said the minister.

"Thou wast not bold!—thou wast not true!" answered the child. "Thou wouldst not promise to take my hand, and mother's hand, to-morrow noontide!'

"Worthy sir," answered the physician, who had now advanced to the foot of the platform. "Pious Master Dimmesdale! can this be you? Well, well, indeed! We men of study, whose heads are in our books, have need to be straitly looked after! We dream in our waking moments, and walk in our sleep. Come, good sir, and my dear friend, I pray you, let me lead you home!"

"How knewest thou that I was here?" asked the minister fearfully.

"Verily, and in good faith," answered Roger Chillingworth, "I knew nothing of the matter. I had spent the better part of the night at the bedside of the worshipful Governor Winthrop, doing what my poor skill might to give him ease. He going home to a better world, I, likewise, was on my way homeward, when this strange light shone out. Come with me, I beseech you, reverend sir; else you will be poorly able to do Sabbath[13] duty to-morrow. Aha! see now, how they trouble the brain—these books!—these books! You should study less, good sir, and take a little pastime; or these night-whimseys will grow upon you."

"I will go home with you," said Mr. Dimmesdale.

With a chill despondency, like one awaking, all nerveless, from an ugly dream, be yielded himself to the physician, and was led away.

The next day, however, being the Sabbath, he preached a discourse which was held to be the richest and most powerful, and the most replete with heavenly influences, that had ever proceeded from his lips. Souls, it is said, more souls than one, were brought to the truth by the efficacy of that sermon, and vowed within themselves to cherish a holy gratitude towards Mr. Dimmesdale throughout the long hereafter. But, as he came down the pulpit steps, the grey-bearded sexton[14] met him, holding up a black glove, which the minister recognised as his own.

"It was found," said the sexton, "this morning, on the scaffold where evil-doers are set up to public shame. Satan dropped it there, I take it, intending a scurrilous jest against your reverence. But, indeed, he was blind and foolish, as he ever and always is. A pure hand needs no glove to cover it!"

"Thank you, my good friend," said the minister gravely, but startled at heart; for, so confused was his remembrance, that he had almost brought himself to look at the events of the past night as visionary. "Yes, it seems to be my glove, indeed!"

"And, since Satan saw fit to steal it, your reverence must needs handle him without gloves, henceforward," remarked the old sexton, grimly smiling. "But did your reverence hear of the portent that was seen last night?—a great red letter in the sky—the letter A, which we interpret to stand for Angel. For, as our good Governor Winthrop was made an angel this past night, it was doubtless held fit that there should be some notice thereof!"

"No," answered the minister, "I had not heard of it."

Notes

[1] somnambulism: the action or habit of walking about while asleep.

[2] the bloody scourge: a scourge is a whip used for flogging; the previous chapter mentions that the minister plied the scourge on his shoulders pitilessly.

[3] Cowardice: "cowardice" here is regarded as the sister of remorse.

[4] Satan: the Devil.

[5] Governor Bellingham: (1592—1672) the governor of Massachusetts Bay Colony.

[6] Mistress Hibbins: Anne Bellingham Hibbins who was hung for being a witch.

[7] Mr. Wilson: the Reverend John Wilson (1588—1667), a minister who was considered a great clergyman and teacher. He was a prosecutor of Anne Hutchinson.

[8] Governor Winthrop; John Winthrop (1588—1649), the first governor of Massachusetts Bay Colony.

[9] Geneva cloak: the black cloak then worn by Calvinist ministers, its name recalling the association of John Calvin with the city of Geneva.

[10] her night ride: a witch was believed to make frequent night excursions into the forest.

[11] judgment day: (according to various religions, esp. Christianity) the day when God

will judge everyone.

[12] Revolutionary times: the American Revolution in which the North American colonies struggled to be independent of the British rule.

[13] Sabbath: a day of rest and worship by most Christian churches.

[14] sexton: a church officer or employee in charge of maintenance of the church property.

Commentary

The setting of *The Scarlet Letter* is the Puritan New England of the 17th century. An aging English scholar sends his beautiful young wife Hester Prynne to make their new home in Boston. He intends to follow her, but has been captured by the Indians and delayed for two years. When he finally comes over, he is bewildered to see his wife in pillory, holding her illicit baby in her arms, wearing a scarlet letter "A" on her breast as a lifelong sign of her sin of adultery. Determined to find out who her lover is, the old scholar disguises himself as a physician and changes his name to Roger Chillingworth. Gradually he discovers that the culprit is no other than the much-admired brilliant young clergyman, Arthur Dimmesdale. He is determined to punish the lovers spiritually. Dimmesdale is miserably tormented for his sin, and his conscience is ruthlessly preyed upon by Chillingworth. He cuts himself off from community and withers spiritually as well as physically.

Hester Prynne's response to the scarlet letter "A" is positive. She does her best to reestablish her fellowship with her neighbors on a new, honest basis, and finally proves to be a strong-minded and capable woman and wins their love and admiration. At one time she proposes to leave America for Europe with Dimmesdale, but then he refuses her. While making confession on the pillory, he dies in her arms. Hester continues her life of penance and becomes a model of endurance, goodness, courage, and victory over sin.

Chapter 12 brings the minister to the scaffold where Hester stood for punishment seven years ago. This chapter is probably the most powerful and moving part of the story, since it marks the climax of Dimmesdale's spiritual and moral crisis. The pain in his breast forced him to create an alternate way to absolution. He thought the only way for his sin to be redeemed is to stand where Hester had stood and make a frank and open declaration. Although the declaration is made at night and with the absence of his congregation, the minister is getting closer because this vigil takes place on the scaffold, rather than in his own room. What is more, his confession was finally joined by Hester and their daughter Pearl. Though the important antagonist Chillingworth also comes here in the scene, he is no longer the main threat to Dimmesdale as the latter is already doomed to his fate, and Chillingworth cannot affect the ending of events any more.

Questions and Exercises

1. What is the minister's psychological state when he is standing on the scaffold?
2. Why do you think the minister turns out to be victim of Roger Chillingworth?
3. What do you learn about Pearl from the way she talks and the way she acts in this chapter? Is the character realistic? What does she symbolize?
4. The scarlet letter "A" is rich in symbolism. What symbolic meanings does it carry in this chapter? How is the letter "A" related to the main theme of the whole novel?

Francis Scott Fitzgerald

Francis Scott Fitzgerald (1896—1940) was the most representative novelist of the 1920's. He was both a leading participant in the typically frivolous, carefree, moneymaking life of the decade and at the same time, a detached observer of it. His own life was a mirror of the times. During the twenties, he was rich and successful. When America suffered the Crash and entered the Great Depression, his fortune also failed. He died at the age of 44 just before America joined the Second World War.

Fitzgerald was very enthusiastic and excited about the new world he was living in, but lived to realize eventually that, instead of success, it was all disaster. Fitzgerald lived in the midst of the "roaring twenties"—driving fast cars, drinking hard whisky, and taking an immense delight in it. As much as he enjoyed the "roaring" of the post-war boom years, he foresaw its doom and failure.

One of the major events was his meeting Zelda Sayre in the same way as Gatsby meets Daisy. Zelda was the daughter of a judge in Montgomery, Alabama, a beautiful society girl, who told Fitzgerald that she liked him well enough but it would be too expensive for him to have her. After his discharge from the army in 1919, it became apparent that he had no means of supporting this woman. Zelda soon broke their engagement. Six months later, his novel *This Side of Paradise* had been published, and Zelda agreed to marry him now. They were married; yet throughout his life, both Fitzgerald's greatest happiness and deepest sorrow were caused by her. The Fitzgeralds lived in expensive style, and their need for money was tremendous. Here is a world of parties, similar in grandeur and extravagance to those of Gatsby's. Amid boisterous reckless merry-making, there is unmistakable anxiety over money, gloomy spiritual barrenness and a hint of decay.

The Great Gatsby

Chapter 3

There was music from my neighbor's house through the summer nights. In his blue gardens men and girls came and went like moths among the whisperings and the champagne and the stars. At high tide in the afternoon I watched his guests diving from the tower of his raft, or taking the sun on the hot sand of his beach while his two motor-boats slit the waters of the Sound,[1] drawing aquaplanes over cataracts of foam. On weekends his Rolls-Royce became an omnibus, bearing parties to and from the city between nine in the morning and long past midnight, while his station wagon scampered like a brisk yellow bug to meet all trains. And on Mondays eight servants, including an extra gardener, toiled all day with mops and scrubbing-brushes and hammers and garden-shears, repairing the ravages[2] of the night before.

Every Friday five crates of oranges and lemons arrived from a fruiterer in New York—every Monday these same oranges and lemons left his back door in a pyramid of pulpless halves. There was a machine in the kitchen which could extract the juice of two hundred oranges in half an hour if a little button was pressed two hundred times by a butler's thumb.

At least once a fortnight a corps of caterers came down with several hundred feet of canvas and enough colored lights to make a Christmas tree of Gatsby's enormous garden. On buffet tables, garnished with glistening hors-d'oeuvre,[3] spiced baked hams crowded against salads of harlequin designs and pastry pigs and turkeys bewitched to a dark gold.[4] In the main hall a bar with a real brass rail was set up, and stocked with gins and liquors and with cordials so long forgotten that most of his female guests were too young to know one from another.

By seven o'clock the orchestra has arrived, no thin five-piece affair, but a whole pitful of oboes and trombones and saxophones and viols and comets and piccolos, and low and high drums.[5] The last swimmers have come in from the beach now and are dressing upstairs; the cars from New York are parked five deep[6] in the drive, and already the halls and salons and verandas are gaudy with primary colors, and hair bobbed in strange new ways, and shawls beyond the dreams of Castile. The bar is in full swing, and floating rounds of cocktails permeate the garden outside, until the air is alive with chatter and laughter, and casual innuendo and introductions forgotten on the spot, and enthusiastic meetings between women who never knew each other's names.

The lights grow brighter as the earth lurches away from the sun, and now the orchestra is playing yellow cocktail music,[7] and the opera of voices pitches a key higher. Laughter is easier minute by minute, spilled with prodigality, tipped out at a cheerful word. The groups change more swiftly, swell with new arrivals, dissolve and form in the same breath; already there are wanderers, confident girls who weave here and there among the stouter and more stable,[8] become for a sharp, joyous moment the center of a group, and then, excited with triumph, glide on through the sea-change of faces and voices and color under the constantly changing light.

Suddenly one of these gypsies, in trembling opal, seizes a cocktail out of the air, dumps it down for courage and, moving her hands like Frisco,[9] dances out alone on the canvas platform. A momentary hush; the orchestra leader varies his rhythm obligingly for her, and there is a burst of chatter as the erroneous news goes around that she is Gilda Gray's understudy from the *Follies*.[10] The party has begun. I believe that on the first night I went to Gatsby's house I was one of the few guests who had actually been invited. People were not invited—they went there. They got into automobiles which bore them out to Long Island, and somehow they ended up at Gatsby's door. Once there they were introduced by somebody who knew Gatsby, and after that they conducted themselves according to the rules of behavior associated with an amusement park. Sometimes they came and went without having met Gatsby at all, came for the party with a simplicity of heart that was its own ticket of admission.

I had been actually invited. A chauffeur in a uniform of robin's-egg blue[11] crossed my lawn early that Saturday morning with a surprisingly formal note from his employer: the honor would be entirely Gatsby's, it said, if I would attend his "little party" that night. He had seen me several times, and had intended to call on me long before, but a peculiar combination of circumstances had prevented it—signed Jay Gatsby, in a majestic hand. Dressed up in white flannels I went over to his lawn a little while after seven, and wandered around rather ill at ease among swirls and eddies of people I didn't know—though here and there was a face I had noticed on the commuting train. I was immediately struck by the number of young Englishmen dotted about; all well dressed, all looking a little hungry, and all talking in low, earnest voices to solid and prosperous Americans. I was sure that they were selling something: bonds or insurance or automobiles. They were at least agonizingly aware of the easy money in the vicinity and convinced that it was theirs for a few words in the right key.[12]

As soon as I arrived I made an attempt to find my host, but the two or three people of whom I asked his whereabouts stared at me in such an amazed way, and denied so vehemently any knowledge of his movements, that I slunk off in the direction of the cocktail table—the only place in the garden where a single man could linger without looking purposeless and alone.

I was on my way to get roaring drunk from sheer embarrassment when Jordan Baker came out of the house and stood at the head of the marble steps, leaning a little backward and looking with contemptuous interest down into the garden. Welcome or not, I found it necessary to attach myself to someone before I should begin to address cordial remarks to the passers-by.

"Hello!" I roared, advancing towards her. My voice seemed unnaturally loud across the garden.

"I thought you might be here," she responded absently as I came up. "I remembered you lived next door to—"

She held my hand impersonally, as a promise that she'd take care of me in a minute, and gave ear to two girls in twin yellow dresses, who stopped at the foot of the steps.

"Hello!" they cried together. "Sorry you didn't win."

That was for the golf tournament. She had lost in the finals the week before.

"You don't know who we are," said one of the girls in yellow, "but we met you here about a month ago."

"You've dyed your hair since then," remarked Jordan, and I started, but the girls had moved casually on and her remark was addressed to the premature moon, produced like the supper, no doubt, out of a caterer's basket. With Jordan's slender golden arm resting in mine, we descended the steps and sauntered about the garden. A tray of cocktails floated at us through the twilight, and we sat down at a table with the two girls in yellow and three men, each one introduced to us as Mr. Mumble.

"Do you come to these parties often?" inquired Jordan of the girls beside her.

"The last one was the one I met you at," answered the girl, in an alert confident voice. She turned to her companion: "Wasn't it for you, Lucille?"

It was for Lucille, too.

"I like to come," Lucille said. "I never care what I do, so I always have a good time. When I was here last I tore my gown on a chair, and he asked me my name and address—inside of a week I got a package from Croirier's[13] with a new evening gown in it."

"Did you keep it?" asked Jordan.

"Sure I did. I was going to wear it tonight, but it was too big in the bust and had to be altered. It was gas blue and lavender beads. Two hundred and sixty-five dollars."

"There's something funny about a fellow that'll do a thing like that," said the other girl eagerly. "He doesn't want any trouble with anybody."

"Who doesn't?" I inquired.

"Gatsby. Somebody told me—"

The two girls and Jordan leaned together confidentially.

"Somebody told me they thought he killed a man once."

A thrill passed over all of us. The three Mr. Mumbles bent forward and listened eagerly.

"I don't think it's so much *that,*" argued Lucille sceptically, "it's more that he was a German spy during the war."

One of the men nodded in confirmation.

"I heard that from a man who knew all about him, grew up with him in Germany," he assured us positively.

"Oh, no," said the first girl, "it couldn't be that, because he was in the American army during the war." As our credulity switched back to her she leaned forward with enthusiasm. "You look at him sometimes when he thinks nobody's looking at him. I'll bet he killed a man."

She narrowed her eyes and shivered. Lucille shivered. We all turned and looked around for Gatsby. It was testimony to the romantic speculation he inspired that there were whispers about him from those who had found little that it was necessary to whisper about in this world.

The first supper—there would be another one after midnight—was now being served, and Jordan invited me to join her own party, who were spread around a table on the other side of the garden. There were three married couples and Jordan's escort, a persistent undergraduate given to violent innuendo, and obviously under the impression that sooner or later Jordan was going to yield him up her person[14] greater or lesser degree. Instead of rambling, this party had preserved a dignified homogeneity,[15] and assumed to itself the function of representing the staid nobility of the countryside—East Egg condescending to West Egg, and carefully on guard against its spectroscopic gaiety.

"Let's get out," whispered Jordan, after a somehow wasteful and inappropriate half-hour; "this is much too polite for me."

We got up, and she explained that we were going to find the host: I had never met him, she said, and it was making me uneasy. The undergraduate nodded in a cynical, melancholy way.

The bar, where we glanced first, was crowded, but Gatsby was not there. She couldn't find him from the top of the steps, and he wasn't on the veranda. On a chance we tried an important-looking door, and walked into a high Gothic library, paneled with carved English oak, and probably transported complete from some ruin overseas. A stout, middle-aged man, with enormous owl-eyed spectacles, was sitting somewhat drunk on the edge of a great table, staring with unsteady concentration at the shelves of books. As we entered he wheeled excitedly around and examined Jordan from head to foot.

"What do you think?" he demanded impetuously.

"About what?"

He waved his hand towards the book-shelves.

"About that. As a matter of fact you needn't bother to ascertain. I ascertained. They're real."

"The books?"

He nodded.

"Absolutely real—have pages and everything. I thought they'd be a nice durable cardboard. Matter of fact, they're absolutely real. Pages and—Here! Lemme show you."

Taking our scepticism for granted, he rushed to the bookcases and returned with Volume One of the "Stoddard Lectures".[16]

"See!" he cried triumphantly. "It's a bona-fide[17] piece of printed matter. It fooled me.

This fella's a regular Belasco. It's a triumph. What thoroughness! What realism! Knew when to stop too—didn't cut the pages.[18] But what do you want? What do you expect?"

He snatched the book from me and replaced it hastily on its shelf, muttering that if one brick was removed the whole library was liable to collapse.

"Who brought you?" he demanded. "Or did you just come? I was brought. Most people were brought."

Jordan looked at him alertly, cheerfully, without answering.

"I was brought by a woman named Roosevelt," he continued. "Mrs. Claude Roosevelt. Do you know her? I met her somewhere last night. I've been drunk for about a week now, and I thought it might sober me up to sit in a library."

Has it?

"A little bit, I think. I can't tell you yet. I've only been here an hour. Did I tell you about the books? They're real. They're—"

"You told us."

We shook hands with him gravely and went back outdoors.

There was dancing now on the canvas in the garden; old men pushing young girls backwards in eternal graceless circles, superior couples holding each other tortuously, fashionably, and keeping in the corners—and a great number of single girls dancing individualistically or relieving the orchestra for a moment of the burden of the banjo or the traps.[19] By midnight the hilarity had increased. A celebrated tenor had sung in Italian, and a notorious contralto had sung in jazz, and between the numbers[20] people were doing "stunts" all over the garden, while happy, vacuous bursts of laughter rose towards the summer sky. A pair of stage twins, who turned out to be the girls in yellow, did a baby act in costume, and champagne was served in glasses bigger than finger-bowls. The moon had risen higher, and floating in the Sound was a triangle of silver scales, trembling a little to the stiff, tinny drip of the banjoes on the lawn. I was still with Jordan Baker. We were sitting at a table with a man of about my age and a rowdy little girl, who gave way upon the slightest provocation to uncontrollable laughter. I was enjoying myself now. I had taken two finger-bowls of champagne, and the scene had changed before my eyes into something significant, elemental, and profound. At a lull in the entertainment the man looked at me and smiled.

"Your face is familiar," he said politely. Weren't you in the First Division during the war?"

"Why, yes. I was in the Twenty-eighth Infantry."

"I was in the Sixteenth until June nineteen-eighteen. I knew I'd seen you somewhere before."

We talked for a moment about some wet, gray little villages in France. Evidently he lived in this vicinity, for he told me he had just bought a hydroplane, and was going to try it out in the morning.

"Want to go with me, old sport?[21] Just near the shore along the Sound."

"What time?"

"Any time that suits you best."

It was on the tip of my tongue to ask his name when Jordan looked around and smiled.

"Having a gay time now?" she inquired.

"Much better." I turned again to my new acquaintance. "This is an unusual party for me. I haven't even seen the host. I lived over there—" I waved my hand at the invisible hedge in the distance, "and this man Gatsby sent over his chauffeur with an invitation. For a moment he looked at me as if he failed to understand.

"I'm Gatsby," he said suddenly.

"What!" I exclaimed. "Oh, I beg your pardon."

"I thought you knew, old sport. I'm afraid I'm not a very good host."

He smiled understandingly—much more than understandingly. It was one of those rare smiles with a quality of eternal reassurance in it, that you may come across four or five times in life. It faced—or seemed to face—the whole eternal world for an instant, and then concentrated on you with an irresistible prejudice in your favor. It understood you just as far as you wanted to be understood, believed in you as you would like to believe in yourself, and assured you that it had precisely the impression of you that, at your best, you hoped to convey. Precisely at that point it vanished—and I was looking at an elegant young roughneck, a year or two over thirty, whose elaborate formality of speech just missed being absurd. Some time before he introduced himself I'd got a strong impression that he was picking his words with care.

Almost at the moment when Mr. Gatsby identified himself, a butler hurried towards him with the information that Chicago was calling him on the wire. He excused himself with a small bow that included each of us in turn.

"If you want anything just ask for it, old sport," he urged me. "Excuse me. I will rejoin you later."

When he was gone I turned immediately to Jordan—constrained to assure her of my surprise. I had expected that Mr. Gatsby would be a florid and corpulent person in his middle years.

"Who is he?" I demanded. "Do you know?"

"He's just a man named Gatsby."

"Where is he from, I mean? And what does he do?"

"Now *you're* started on the subject," she answered with a wan smile. "Well, he told me once he was an Oxford man."

A dim background started to take shape behind him, but at her next remark it faded away.

"However, I don't believe it."

'Why not?"

"I don't know," she insisted, "I just don't think he went there."

Something in her tone reminded me of the other girl's "I think he killed a man," and had the effect of stimulating my curiosity. I would have accepted without question the information that Gatsby sprang from the swamps of Louisiana or from the lower East Side of New York. That was comprehensible. But young men didn't—at least in my provincial inexperience I believed they didn't—drift coolly out of nowhere and buy a palace on Long Island Sound.

"Anyhow, he gives large parties," said Jordan, changing the subject with an urban taste for the concrete. "And I like large parties. They're so intimate. At same parties there isn't any privacy."

There was the boom of a bass drum, and the voice of the orchestra leader rang out suddenly above the echolalia of the garden.

"Ladies and gentlemen," he cried, "at the request of Mr. Gatsby we are going to play for you Mr. Vladimir Tostoffs' latest work, which attracted so much attention at Carnegie Hall last May. If you read the papers, you know there was a big sensation." He smiled with jovial condescension, and added: "Some sensation!" Whereupon everybody laughed.

"The piece is known," he concluded lustily, "as Vladimir Tostoffs' *Jazz History of the World.*"

The nature of Mr. Tostoffs' composition eluded me, because just as it began my eyes fell on Gatsby, standing alone on the marble steps and looking from one group to another with approving eyes. His tanned skin was drawn attractively tight on his face and his short hair looked as though it were trimmed every day. I could see nothing sinister about him. I wondered if the fact that he was not drinking helped to set him off from his guests, for it seemed to me that he grew more correct as the fraternal hilarity increased. When the *Jazz*

History of the World was over, girls were putting their heads on men's shoulders in a puppyish, convivial way, girls were swooning backward playfully into men's arms, even into groups, knowing that someone would arrest their falls—but no one swooned backward on Gatsby, and no French bob touched Gatsby's shoulder and no singing quartets were formed with Gatsby's head for one link.

"I beg your pardon."

Gatsby's butler was suddenly standing beside us.

"Miss Baker?" he inquired. "I beg your pardon, but Mr. Gatsby would like to speak to you alone."

"With me?" she exclaimed in surprise.

"Yes, madam."

She got up slowly, raising her eyebrows at me in astonishment, and followed the butler towards the house. I noticed that she wore her evening-dress, all her dresses, like sports clothes—there was a jauntiness about her movements as if she had first learned to walk upon golf courses on clean, crisp mornings. I was alone and it was almost two. For some time confused and intriguing sounds had issued from a long, many-windowed room which overhung the terrace. Eluding Jordan's undergraduate, who was now engaged in an obstetrical conversation with two chorus girls, and who implored me to join him, I went inside.

The large room was full of people. One of the girls in yellow was playing the piano, and beside her stood a tall, red-haired young lady from a famous chorus, engaged in song. She had drunk a quantity of champagne, and during the course of her song she had decided, ineptly, that everything was very, very sad—she was not only singing, she was weeping too. Whenever there was a pause in the song she filled it with gasping, broken sobs, and then took up the lyric again in a quavering soprano. The tears coursed down her cheeks—not freely, however, for when they came into contact with her heavily beaded eyelashes they assumed an inky color, and pursued the rest of their way in slow black rivulets. A humorous suggestion was made that she sing the notes on her face, whereupon she threw up her hands, sank into a chair, and went off into a deep vinous sleep.

"She had a fight with a man who says he's her husband," explained a girl at my elbow.

I looked around. Most of the remaining women were now having fights with men said to be their husbands. Even Jordan's party, the quartet from East Egg, were rent asunder[22] by dissension. One of the men was talking with curious intensity to a young actress, and his wife, after attempting to laugh at the situation in a dignified and indifferent way, broke down entirely and resorted to flank attacks—at intervals she appeared suddenly at his side like an angry diamond, and hissed: "You promised!" into his ear.

The reluctance to go home was not confined to wayward men. The hall was at present occupied by two deplorably sober men and their highly indignant wives. The wives were sympathizing with each other in slightly raised voices.

"Whenever he sees I'm having a good time he wants to go home."

"Never heard anything so selfish in my life."

"We're always the first ones to leave."

"So are we."

"Well, we're almost the last tonight," said one of the men sheepishly. "The orchestra left half an hour ago."

In spite of the wives' agreement that such malevolence was beyond credibility, the dispute ended in a short struggle, and both wives were lifted, kicking, into the night. As I waited for my hat in the hall the door of the library opened and Jordan Baker and Gatsby came out together. He was saying some last word to her, but the eagerness in his manner tightened abruptly into formality as several people approached him to say goodbye. Jordan's party were calling impatiently to her from the porch, but she lingered for a moment to shake hands.

"I've just heard the most amazing thing," she whispered. "How long were we in there?"

"It was ... simply amazing," she repeated abstractedly. "But I swore I wouldn't tell it and here I am tantalizing you." She yawned gracefully in my face. "Please come and see me ... Phone book. Under the name of Mrs. Sigoumey Howard... My aunt..." She was hurrying off as she talked—her brown hand waved a jaunty salute as she melted into her party at the door.

Rather ashamed that on my first appearance I had stayed so late, I joined the last of Gatsby's guests, who were clustered around him. I wanted to explain that I'd hunted for him early in the evening and to apologize for not having known him in the garden.

"Don't mention it," he enjoined me eagerly. "Don't give it another thought, old sport." The familiar expression held no more familiarity than the hand which reassuringly brushed my shoulder." And don't forget we're going up in the hydroplane tomorrow morning, at nine o'clock."

Then the butler, behind his shoulder; "Philadelphia wants you on the phone, sir."

"All right, in a minute. Tell them I'll be right there... Good night."

"Good night."

"Good night." He smiled—and suddenly there seemed to be a pleasant significance in having been the last to go, as if he had desired it all the time. "Good night, old sport... Good night."

But as I walked down the steps I saw that the evening was not quite over. Fifty feet from the door a dozen headlights illuminated a bizarre and tumultuous scene. In the ditch beside the road, right side up, but violently shorn of one wheel, rested a new coup which had left Gatsby's drive not two minutes before. The sharp jut of a wall account for the detachment of the wheel, which was now getting considerable attention from half a dozen curious chauffeurs. However, as they had left their cars blocking the road, a harsh, discordant din from those in the rear had been audible for some time, and added to the already violent confusion of the scene.

A man in a long duster had dismounted from the wreck and now stood in the middle of the road, looking from the car to the tyre and from the tyre to the observers in a pleasant, puzzled way.

"See!" he explained. "It went in the ditch."

The fact was infinitely astonishing to him, and I recognized first the unusual quality of wonder, and then the man—it was the late patron of Gatsby's library.

"How'd it happen?"

He shrugged his shoulders.

"I know nothing whatever about mechanics," he said decisively.

"But how did it happen? Did you run into the wall?"

"Don't ask me," said Owl Eyes, washing his hands of the whole matter." I know very little about driving—next to nothing. It happened, and that's all I know."

"Well, if you're a poor driver you oughtn't to try driving at night."

"But I wasn't even trying," he explained indignantly," I wasn't even trying." An awed hush fell upon the bystanders.

"Do you want to commit suicide?"

"You're lucky it was just a wheel! A bad driver and not even frying!"

"You don't understand," explained the criminal," I wasn't driving. There's another man in the car."

The shock that followed this declaration found voice in a sustained "Ah-h-h!" as the door of the coupe swung slowly open. The crowd—it was now a crowd—stepped back involuntarily, and when the door had opened wide there was a ghostly pause. Then, very gradually, part by part, a pale, dangling individual stepped out of the wreck, pawing tentatively at the ground with a large uncertain dancing shoe.

Blinded by the glare of the headlights and confused by the incessant groaning of the horns, the apparition stood swaying for a moment before he perceived the man in the duster.

"Wha's matter?" he inquired calmly. "Did we run outa gas?"

"Look!"

Half a dozen fingers pointed at the amputated wheel—he stared at it for a moment, and then looked upward as though he suspected that it had dropped from the sky.

"It came off," someone explained.

He nodded.

"At first I din' notice we'd stopped."

A pause. Then, taking a long breath and straightening his shoulders, he remarked in a determined voice:

"Wonder'ff tell me where there's a gas'line station?"

At least a dozen men, some of them a little better off than he was, explained to him that wheel and car were no longer joined by any physical bond.

"Back out," he suggested after a moment. "Put her in reverse."

"But the wheel's off!"

He hesitated.

"No harm in trying," he said.

The caterwauling horns had reached a crescendo and I turned away and cut across the lawn towards home. I glanced back once. A wafer of a moon was shining over Gatsby's house, making the night fine as before, and surviving the laughter and the sound of his still glowing garden. A sudden emptiness seemed to flow now from the windows and the great doors, endowing with complete isolation the figure of the host, who stood on the porch, his hand up in a formal gesture of farewell. Reading over what I have written so far, I see I have given the impression that the events of three nights several weeks apart were all that absorbed me. On the contrary, they were merely casual events in a crowded summer, and, until much later, they absorbed me infinitely less than my personal affairs. Most of the time I worked. In the early morning the sun threw my shadow westward as I hurried down the white chasms of lower New York to the Probity Trust. I knew the other clerks and young bond-salesmen by their first names, and lunched with them in dark, crowed restaurants on little pig sausages and mashed potatoes and coffee. I even had a short affair with a girl who lived in Jersey City and worked in the accounting department, but her brother began throwing mean looks in my direction, so when she went on her vacation in July I let it blow quietly away. I took dinner usually at the Yale Club—for some reason it was the gloomiest event of my day—and then I went upstairs to the library and studied investments and securities for a conscientious hour. There were generally a few rioters around, but they never came into the library, so it was a good place to work. After that, if the night was mellow, I strolled down Madison Avenue past the old Murray Hill Hotel, and over 33rd Street to the Pennsylvania Station. I began to like New York, the racy, adventurous feel of it at night, and the satisfaction that the constant flicker of men and women and machines gives to the restless eye. I liked to walk up Fifth Avenue and pick out romantic women from the crowd and imagine that in a few minutes I was going to enter into their lives, and no one would ever know or disapprove. Sometimes, in my mind, I followed them to their apartments on the comers of hidden streets, and they turned and smiled back at me before they faded through a door into warm darkness. At the enchanted metropolitan twilight I felt a haunting loneliness sometimes, and felt it in others—poor young clerks who loitered in front of windows waiting until it was time for a solitary restaurant dinner—young clerks in the dusk, wasting the most poignant moments of night and life.

Again at eight o'clock, when the dark lanes of the Forties were lined five deep with throbbing taxicabs, bound for the theatre district, I felt a sinking in my heart. Forms leaned together in the taxis as they waited, and voices sang, and there was laughter from unheard jokes, and lighted cigarettes made unintelligible circles inside. Imagining that I, too, was hurrying towards gaiety and sharing their intimate excitement, I wished them well. For a while I lost sight of Jordan Baker, and then in midsummer I found her again. At first I was flattered to go places with her, because she was a golf champion, everyone knew her name. Then it was something more. I wasn't actually in love, but I felt a sort of tender curiosity. The bored haughty face that she turned to the world concealed something—most affectations conceal something eventually, even though they don't in the beginning—and one day I found what it was. When we were on a house-party together up in Warwick, she left a borrowed car out in the rain with the top down, and then lied about it—and suddenly I remembered the story about her that had eluded me that night at Daisy's. At her first big golf tournament there was a row that nearly reached the newspapers—a suggestion that she had moved her ball from a bad lie in the semi-final round. The thing approached the proportions of a scandal—then died away. A caddy retracted his statement, and the only other witness admitted that he might have been mistaken. The incident and the name had remained together in my mind. Jordan Baker instinctively avoided clever, shrewd men, and now I saw that this was because she felt safer on a plane where any divergence from a code would be thought impossible. She was incurably dishonest. She wasn't able to endure being at a disadvantage and, given this unwillingness, I suppose she had begun dealing in subterfuges when she was very young in order to keep that cool, insolent smile turned to the world and yet satisfy the demands of her hard, jaunty body. It made no difference to me. Dishonesty in a woman is a thing you never blame deeply—I was casually sorry, and then I forgot. It was on that same house-party that we had a curious conversation about driving a car. It started because she passed so close to some workmen that our fender flicked a button on one man's coat.

"You're a rotten driver," I protested. "Either you ought to be more careful, or you oughtn't to drive at all."

"I am careful."

"No, you're not."

"Well, other people are," she said lightly.

"What's that got to do with it?"

"They'll keep out of my way," she insisted. "It takes two to make an accident."

"Suppose you met somebody just as careless as yourself."

"I hope I never will," she answered." I hate careless people. That's why I like you."

Her gray sun-strained eyes stared straight ahead, but she had deliberately shifted our relations, and for a moment I thought I loved her. But I'm slow-thinking and full of interior rules that act as brakes on my desires, and I knew that first I had to get myself definitely out of that tangle back home. I'd been writing letters once a week and signing them: "Love, Nick," and all I could think of was how, when that certain girl played tennis, a faint moustache of perspiration appeared on her upper lip. Nevertheless there was a vague understanding that had to be tactfully broken off before I was free. Everyone suspects himself of at least one of the cardinal virtues, and this is mine: I am one of the few honest people that I have ever known.

Notes

[1] the Sound: Long Island Sound, an arm of the Atlantic Ocean between Long Island and the State of Connecticut on the mainland, just east of New York City.

[2] repairing the ravages: mending the damaged things and putting the things in order.

[3] hors-d'oeuvre: (French) a relish; a savory snack to whet the appetite before a meal.

[4] bewitched to a dark gold: baked to an unbelievably beautiful dark gold color as if by magic.

[5] no thin five-piece affair…low and high drums: not a small band composed of only five musical instruments, it was a large company of musicians. The pit is where the musicians sit, usually directly in front of the stage.

[6] parked five deep: parked one behind the other in five rows.

[7] yellow cocktail music: music designed to arouse quick, intense, and usually superficial emotional response.

[8] stouter and more stable: referring to men as stronger than women.

[9] dump it down for courage: drink it at a gulp so as to show courage; like Frisco: (slang) rapidly and vigorously; Frisco: in the manner of Frisco, a famous Spanish comic actor.

[10] the Follies: the *Ziegfeld Follies,* a satirical musical show produced by Florence Ziegfeld, very popular in the 1920s.

[11] robin's-egg blue: greenish blue.

[12] the easy money in the vicinity: the Englishmen thought they could make money easily off the rich Americans of the party; in the right key: said some appropriate and convincing words.

[13] Croirier's: an expensive women's clothing store.

[14] yield him up her person: give herself up to him.

[15] preserved a dignified homogeneity: maintained dignified manners that set them apart from others.

[16] "Stoddard Lectures": ten volumes of lectures by John Lawson Stoddard (1850－1931), a famous American public lecturer and writer.
[17] bona-fide: (Latin) genuine.
[18] didn't cut the pages: Traditionally, printers or bookbinders left the leaves of books unseparated, hence readers had to cut them open themselves.
[19] traps: (plural) percussion instruments of a dance band.
[20] numbers: songs or musical pieces in a program.
[21] old sport: (slang) a friendly casual address to a person of any age.
[22] rent asunder: torn apart.

Commentary

The story of *The Great Gatsby* is narrated by Nick Carraway, who rents a house in West Egg, a wealthy but unfashionable area populated by the new rich. His next-door neighbor is a mysterious man named Jay Gatsby, a millionaire about whom there are plenty of rumors.

Gatsby, an idealist, is a poor youth from the Midwest. He falls in love with Daisy, a wealthy girl, but is too poor to marry her. She is then married to a rich young man, Tom Buchanan. Determined to win back his lost love, Gatsby engages himself in bootlegging and other "shady" activities, thus earning enough money to buy a magnificent imitation French villa in West Egg, the poorer part in contrast to the East Egg. His extravagant lifestyle and dazzling parties every weekend are simply attempts to impress and allure Daisy to come.

Chapter 3 is remarkable for its evocation of an atmosphere of conflict and paradox. The party is crowded and yet empty. The night is beautiful but garish. The scene not only epitomizes the Jazz Age—superficiality, powerful sweetness and charm, but also represents one of the author's major themes: the paradox of his fascination with wealth and glamour and his awareness of their underlying corruption and destructive power. Gatsby tries to recapture his lost love but in vain and is finally destroyed by the influence of the wealthy people around him.

Fitzgerald dealt most skillfully with the double theme of love and money. He understood, from his own experiences, the constant need for more money will drive these men and women to unscrupulousness. Gatsby's tragedy mainly originates from his naïve and firm hold to American Dream—one might hope to satisfy every material desire and thereby to achieve happiness—which is deceptive because it proposes the satisfaction of all desire as an attainable goal, and identifies all human desire with material wealth. Consequently, the degradation of moral value and the social reality often turn out as a devastating force for his tragedy.

Questions and Exercises

1. What is the narrator's attitude toward Gatsby's summer parties? What mood is the author trying to establish in the story?
2. What kind of person do you imagine Gatsby to be? What attitude do the guests seem to have toward their host?
3. What are some of the signs that reveal the fact that the author views the party ironically?
4. What is American dream? How does Gatsby illustrate the paradox of it?

Sherwood Anderson

Sherwood Anderson (1876 – 1941) was born in the countryside of Ohio, in the Middle West. When he was still a boy, his father moved the family to an ugly factory town. His mother died when he was 14, and thereafter he was entirely on his own. He worked at many jobs—as a factory worker, a house painter, a farm hand. There young Anderson found emotional and cultural desolation; this laid the base for his later attitude of severe criticism against the "mechanization" of human beings in an industrial culture.

Sherwood Anderson was a pioneer in the short story form, whose use of plain, everyday language influenced later writers, including Ernest Hemingway and William Faulkner. In 1919 he published *Winesburg, Ohio,* the book which gave him a foremost position in contemporary American letters. Something between a novel and a collection of short stories, this work was a perfect example of Andersen's fiction. The stories abandoned traditional ideas of plot and story-telling in order simply to expose the characters who were repressed and frustrated by intolerable social and industrial systems. Instead of telling a story about actions and events, he gave psychological insights into the characters' lives through small details, building up a growing intensity of emotion until the end of the story.

The Middle West in the 1920's produced a literary movement — a great disillusionment with America along with great creativity and a brilliant literary awakening. Anderson belonged to the generation which watched America's industrialization before the First World War. He saw the deadening effect of machines on modern life and fought vigorously against standardization which robbed people of their individuality. He felt that the workers were losing their strength by giving in to machines, and he found modern industrial life degrading, humiliating and disspiriting. Anderson wrote about lonely, sad people, deformed in their characters by frustrations imposed by their societies and environment. He showed how, in their struggles, they would clutch at some aspect of truth, but adopt a narrow, rigid view of it; in trying to live according to their narrow view of truth, they are unable to understand wider truths, thus become grotesque by turning their small truths into falsehoods. But Anderson felt compassion for such emotionally frustrated people, who were the victims of modern existence.

The Egg

My father was, I am sure, intended by nature to be a cheerful, kindly man. Until he was thirty-four years old he worked as a farmhand for a man named Thomas Butterworth whose place lay near the town of Bidwell, Ohio. He had then a horse of his own, and on Saturday evenings drove into town to spend a few hours in social intercourse with other farmhands. In town he drank several glasses of beer and stood about in Ben Head's saloon—crowded on Saturday evenings with visiting farmhands. Songs were sung and glasses thumped on the bar. At ten o'clock father drove home along a lonely country road, made his horse comfortable for the night, and himself went to bed, quite happy in his position in life. He had at that time no notion of trying to rise in the world.

It was in the spring of his thirty-fifth year that father married my mother, then a country schoolteacher, and in the following spring I came wriggling and crying into the world. Something happened to the two people. They became ambitious. The American passion for getting up in the world took possession of them.[1]

It may have been that mother was responsible. Being a schoolteacher she had no doubt read books and magazines. She had, I presume, read of how Garfield, Lincoln, and other Americans[2] rose from poverty to fame and greatness, and as I lay beside her—in the days of her lying-in[3]—she may have dreamed that I would some day rule men and cities. At any rate she induced father to give up his place as a farmhand, sell his horse, and embark on an independent enterprise of his own. She was a tall silent woman with a long nose and troubled gray eyes. For herself she wanted nothing. For father and myself she was incurably ambitious.

The first venture into which the two people went turned out badly. They rented ten acres of poor stony land on Grigg's Road, eight miles from Bidwell, and launched into chicken-raising. I grew into boyhood on the place and got my first impressions of life there. From the beginning they were impressions of disaster, and if, in my turn, I am a gloomy man inclined to see the darker side of life, I attribute it to the fact that what should have been for me the happy joyous days of childhood were spent on a chicken farm.

One unversed in such matters can have no notion of the many and tragic things that can happen to a chicken. It is born out of an egg, lives for a few weeks as a tiny fluffy thing such as you will see pictured on Easter cards, then becomes hideously naked, eats quantities of corn and meal bought by the sweat of your father's brow, gets diseases called pip, cholera, and other names, stands looking with stupid eyes at the sun, becomes sick and dies. A few hens and now and then a rooster, intended to serve God's mysterious ends, struggle through to maturity. The hens lay eggs out of which come other chickens and the dreadful cycle is thus made complete. It is all unbelievably complex. Most philosophers must have been raised on chicken farms. One hopes for so much from a chicken and is so dreadfully disillusioned. Small chickens, just setting out on the journey of life, look so bright and alert and they are in fact so dreadfully stupid. They are so much like people they mix one up in one's judgments of life. If disease does not kill them, they wait until your expectations are thoroughly aroused and then walk under the wheels of a wagon—to go squashed and dead back to their maker. Vermin infest their youth, and fortunes must be spent for curative powders. In later life I have seen how a literature has been built up on the subject of fortunes to be made out of the raising of chickens. It is intended to be read by the gods who have just eaten of the tree of the knowledge of good and evil. It is a hopeful literature and declares that much may be done by simple ambitious people who own a few hens. Do not be led astray by it. It was not written for you. Go hunt for gold on the frozen hills of Alaska, put your faith in the honesty of a politician, believe if you will that the world is daily growing better and that good will triumph over evil, but do not read and believe the literature that is written concerning the hen. It was not written for you.

I, however, digress. My tale does not primarily concern itself with the hen. If correctly told it will center on the egg. For ten years my father and mother struggled to make our chicken farm pay and then they gave up their struggle and began another. They moved into the town of Bidwell, Ohio, and embarked in the restaurant business. After ten years of worry with incubators that did not hatch, and with tiny—and in their own way lovely—balls of fluff that passed on into semi-naked pullet hood and from that into dead henhood, we threw all aside and, packing our belongings on a wagon, drove down Grigg's Road toward Bidwell, a tiny caravan of hope looking for a new place from which to start on our upward journey through life.

We must have been a sad-looking lot, not, I fancy, unlike refugees fleeing from a battlefield. Mother and I walked in the road. The wagon that contained our goods had been borrowed for the day from Mr. Albert Griggs, a neighbor. Out of its side stuck the legs of cheap chairs, and at the back of the pile of beds, tables, and boxes filled with kitchen utensils was a crate of live chickens, and on top of that the baby carriage in which I had been wheeled about in my infancy. Why we stuck to the baby carriage I don't know. It was unlikely other children would be born and the wheels were broken. People who have few possessions cling tightly to those they have.[4] That is one of the facts that make life so discouraging.

Father rode on top of the wagon. He was then a baldheaded man of forty-five, a little fat, and from long association with mother and the chickens he had become habitually silent and discouraged. All during our ten years on the chicken farm he had worked as a laborer on neighboring farms and most of the money he had earned had been spent on remedies to cure chicken diseases, on Wilmer's White Wonder Cholera Cure or Professor Bidlow's Egg Producer or some other preparations that mother found advertised in the poultry papers. There were two little patches of hair on father's head just above his ears. I remember that as a child I used to sit looking at him when he had gone to sleep in a chair before the stove on Sunday afternoons in the winter. I had at that time already begun to read books and have notions of my own, and the bald path that led over the top of his head was, I fancied, some thing like a broad road, such a road as Caesar might have made on which to lead his legions out of Rome and into the wonders of an unknown world. The tufts of hair that grew above father's ears were, I thought, like forests. I fell into a half sleeping, half waking state and dreamed I was a tiny thing going along the road into a far beautiful place where there were no chicken farms and where life was a happy eggless affair.

One might write a book concerning our flight from the chicken farm into town. Mother and I walked the entire eight miles—she to be sure that nothing fell from the wagon and I to see the wonders of the world. On the seat of the wagon beside father was his greatest treasure. I will tell you of that.

On a chicken farm, where hundreds and even thousands of chickens come out of eggs, surprising things sometimes happen. Grotesques are born out of eggs as out of people. The accident does not often occur—perhaps once in a thousand births. A chicken is, you see, born that has four legs, two pairs of wings, two heads, or what not. The things do not live. They go quickly back to the hand of their maker[5] that has for a moment trembled. The fact that the poor little things could not live was one of the tragedies of life to father. He had some sort of notion that if he could but bring into henhood or roosterhood a five-legged hen or a two-headed rooster his fortune would be made. He dreamed of taking the wonder about the county fairs and of growing rich by exhibiting it to other farmhands.

At any rate, he saved all the little monstrous things that had been born on our chicken farm. They were preserved in alcohol and put each in its own glass bottle. These he had carefully put into a box, and on our journey into town it was carried on the wagon seat beside him. He drove the horses with one hand and with the other clung to the box. When we got to our destination, the box was taken down at once and the bottles removed. All during our days as keepers of a restaurant in the town of Bidwell, Ohio, the grotesques in their little glass bottles sat on a shelf back of the counter. Mother sometimes protested, but father was a rock on the subject of his treasure. The grotesques were, he declared, valuable. People, he said, liked to look at strange and wonderful things.

Did I say that we embarked in the restaurant business in the town of Bidwell, Ohio? I exaggerated a little. The town itself lay at the foot of a low hill and on the shore of a small river. The railroad did not run through the town and the station was a mile away to the north at a place called Pickleville. There had been a cider mill and pickle factory at the station, but before the time of our coming they had both gone out of business. In the morning and in the evening buses came down to the station along a road called Turner's Pike from the hotel on the main street of Bidwell. Our going to the out-of-the-way place to embark in the restaurant business was mother's idea. She talked of it for a year and then one day went off and rented an empty store building opposite the railroad station. It was her idea that the restaurant would be profitable. Traveling men, she said, would be always waiting around to take trains out of town and town people would come to the station to await incoming trains. They would come to the restaurant to buy pieces of pie and drink coffee. Now that I am older I know that she had another motive in going. She was ambitious for me. She wanted me to rise in the world, to get into a town school and become a man of the towns.

At Pickleville father and mother worked hard, as they always had done. At first there was the necessity of putting our place into shape to be a restaurant. That took a month. Father built a shelf on which he put tins of vegetables. He painted a sign on which he put his name in large red letters. Below his name was the sharp command—"EAT HERE"—that was so seldom obeyed. A showcase was bought and filled with cigars and tobacco. Mother scrubbed the floors and the walls of the room. I went to school in the town and was glad to be away from the farm, from the presence of the discouraged, sad-looking chickens. Still I was not very joyous. In the evening I walked home from school along Turner's Pike and remembered the children I had seen playing in the town school yard. A troop of little girls had gone hopping about and singing. I tried that. Down along the frozen road I went hopping solemnly on one leg. "Hippity Hop to the Barber Shop," I sang shrilly. Then I stopped and looked doubtfully about. I was afraid of being seen in my gay mood. It must have seemed to me that I was doing a thing that should not be done by one who, like myself, had been raised on a chicken farm where death was a daily visitor.

Mother decided that our restaurant should remain open at night. At ten in the evening a passenger train went north past our door followed by a local freight. The freight crew had switching to do in Pickleville, and when the work was done they came to our restaurant for hot coffee and food. Sometimes one of them ordered a fried egg. In the morning at four they resumed north-bound and again visited us. A little trade began to grow up. Mother slept at night and during the day tended the restaurant and fed our boarders while father slept. He slept in the same bed mother had occupied during the night and I went off to the town of Bidwell and to school. During the long nights, while mother and I slept, father cooked meats that were to go into sandwiches for the lunch baskets of our boarders. Then an idea in regard to getting up in the world came into his head. The American spirit took hold of him. He also became ambitious.

In the long nights when there was little to do, father had time to think. That was his undoing. He decided that he had in the past been an unsuccessful man because he had not been cheerful enough and that in the future he would adopt a cheerful outlook on life. In the early morning he came upstairs and got into bed with mother. She woke and the two talked. From my bed in the corner I listened.

It was father's idea that both he and mother should try to entertain the people who came to eat at our restaurant. I cannot now remember his words, but he gave the impression of one about to become in some obscure way a kind of public entertainer. When people, particularly young people from the town of Bidwell, came into our place, as on very rare occasions they did, bright entertaining conversation was to be made. From father's words I gathered that something of the jolly innkeeper effect[6] was to be sought. Mother must have been doubtful from the first, but she said nothing discouraging. It was father's notion that a passion for the company of himself and mother would spring up in the breasts of the younger people of the town of Bidwell. In the evening bright happy groups would come singing down Turner's Pike. They would troop shouting with joy and laughter into our place. There would be song and festivity. I do not mean to give the impression that father spoke so elaborately of the matter. He was, as I have said, an uncommunicative man. "They want some place to go. I tell you they want some place to go," he said over and over. That was as far as he got. My own imagination has filled in the blanks.

For two or three weeks this notion of father's invaded our house. We did not talk much, but in our daily lives tried earnestly to make smiles take the place of glum looks. Mother smiled at the boarders and I, catching the infection, smiled at our cat. Father became a little feverish in his anxiety to please. There was, no doubt, lurking somewhere in him, a touch of the spirit of the showman. He did not waste much of his ammunition on the railroad men he served at night, but seemed to be waiting for a young man or woman from Bidwell to come in to show what he could do. On the counter in the restaurant there was a wire basket kept always filled with eggs, and it must have been before his eyes when the idea of being entertaining was born in his brain. There was something prenatal[7] about the way eggs kept them selves connected with the development of his idea. At any rate, an egg ruined his new impulse in life.

Late one night I was awakened by a roar of anger coming from father's throat. Both mother and I sat upright in our beds. With trembling hands she lighted a lamp that stood on a table by her head. Downstairs the front door of our restaurant went shut with a bang and in a few minutes father tramped up the stairs. He held an egg in his hand and his hand trembled as though he were having a chill. There was a half-insane light in his eyes. As he stood glaring at us I was sure he intended throwing the egg at either mother or me. Then he laid it gently on the table beside the lamp and dropped on his knees beside mother's bed. He began to cry like a boy, and I, carried away by his grief, cried with him. The two of us filled the little upstairs room with our wailing voices. It is ridiculous, but of the picture we made I can remember only the fact that mother's hand continually stroked the bald path that ran across the top of his head. I have forgotten what mother said to him and how she induced him to tell her of what had happened downstairs. His explanation also has gone out of my mind. I remember only my own grief and fright and the shiny path over father's head glowing in the lamplight as he knelt by the bed.

As to what happened downstairs. For some unexplainable reason I know the story as well as though I had been a witness to my father's discomfiture. One in time gets to know many unexplainable things. On that evening young Joe Kane, son of a merchant of Bidwell, came to Pickleville to meet his father, who was expected on the ten-o'clock evening train from the South. The train was three hours late and Joe came into our place to loaf about and to wait for its arrival. The local freight train came in and the freight crew were fed. Joe was left alone in the restaurant with father.

From the moment he came into our place the Bidwell young man must have been puzzled by my father's actions. It was his notion that father was angry at him for hanging around. He noticed that the restaurant-keeper was apparently disturbed by his presence and he thought of going out. However, it began to rain and he did not fancy the long walk to town and back. He bought a five-cent cigar and ordered a cup of coffee. He had a newspaper in his pocket and took it out and began to read. "I'm waiting for the evening train. It's late," he said apologetically.

For a long time father, whom Joe Kane had never seen before, remained silently gazing at his visitor. He was no doubt suffering from an attack of stage fright. As so often happens in life he had thought so much and so often of the situation that now confronted him that he was somewhat nervous in its presence.

For one thing, he did not know what to do with his hands. He thrust one of them nervously over the counter and shook hands with Joe Kane. "How-de-do," he said. Joe Kane put his newspaper down and stared at him. Father's eyes lighted on the basket of eggs that sat on the counter and he began to talk. "Well," he began hesitatingly, "Well, you have heard of Christopher Columbus, eh?" He seemed to be angry. "That Christopher Columbus was a cheat," he declared emphatically. "He talked of making an egg stand on its end. He talked, he did, and then he went and broke the end of the egg."

My father seemed to his visitor to be beside himself at the duplicity[8] of Christopher Columbus.[9] He muttered and swore. He declared it was wrong to teach children that Christopher Columbus was a great man when, after all, he cheated at the critical moment. He had declared he would make an egg stand on end and then, when his bluff had been called, he had done a trick. Still grumbling at Columbus, father took an egg from the basket on the counter and began to walk up and down. He rolled the egg between the palms of his hands. He smiled genially. He began to mumble words regarding the effect to be produced on an egg by the electricity that comes out of the human body. He declared that, without breaking its shell and by virtue of rolling back and forth in his hands, he could stand the egg on its head. He explained that the warmth of his hands and the gentle rolling movement he gave the egg created a new center of gravity, and Joe Kane was mildly interested. "I have handled thousands of eggs," father said. "No one knows more about eggs than I do."

He stood the egg on the counter and it fell on its side. He tried the trick again and again, each time rolling the egg between the palms of his hands and saying the words regarding the wonders of electricity and the laws of gravity. When after a half hour's effort he did succeed in making the egg stand for a moment, he looked up to find that his visitor was no longer watching. By the time he had succeeded in calling Joe Kane's attention to the success of his effort, the egg had again rolled over and lay on its side.

Afire with the showman's passion and at the same time a good deal disconcerted by the failure of his first effort, father now took the bottles containing the poultry monstrosities down from their place on the shelf and began to show them to his visitor. "How would you like to have seven legs and two heads like this fellow?" he asked, exhibiting the most remarkable of his treasures. A cheerful smile played over his face. He reached over the counter and tried to slap Joe Kane on the shoulder as he had seen men do in Ben Head's saloon when he was a young farmhand and drove to town on Saturday evenings. His visitor was made a little ill by the sight of the body of the terribly deformed bird floating in the alcohol in the bottle and got up to go. Coming from behind the counter, father took hold of the young man's arm and led him back to his seat. He grew a little angry and for a moment had to turn his face away and force himself to smile. Then he put the bottles back on the shelf. In an outburst of generosity he fairly compelled Joe Kane to have a fresh cup of coffee and another cigar at his expense. Then he took a pan and filling it with vinegar, taken from a jug that sat beneath the counter, he declared himself about to do a new trick. "I will heat this egg in this pan of vinegar," he said. "Then I will put it through the neck of a bottle without breaking the shell. When the egg is inside the bottle it will resume its normal shape and the shell will become hard again. Then I will give the bottle with the egg in it to you. You can take it about with you wherever you go. People will want to know how you got the egg in the bottle. Don't tell them. Keep them guessing. That is the way to have fun with this trick."

Father grinned and winked at his visitor. Joe Kane decided that the man who confronted him was mildly insane but harmless. He drank the cup of coffee that had been given him and began to read his paper again. When the egg had been heated in vinegar. father carried it on a spoon to the counter and going into a back room got an empty bottle. He was angry because his visitor did not watch him as he began to do his trick, but nevertheless went cheerfully to work. For a long time he struggled, trying to get the egg to go through the neck of the bottle. He put the pan of vinegar back on the stove, intending to reheat the egg, then picked it up and burned his fingers. After a second bath in the hot vinegar, the shell of the egg had been softened a little, but not enough for his purpose. He worked and worked and a spirit of desperate determination took possession of him. When he thought that at last the trick was about to be consummated, the delayed train came in at the station and Joe Kane started to go nonchalantly out at the door. Father made a last desperate effort to conquer the egg and make it do the thing that would establish his reputation as one who knew how to entertain guests who came into his restaurant. He worried the egg. He attempted to be somewhat rough with it. He swore and the sweat stood out on his forehead. The egg broke under his hand. When the contents spurted over his clothes, Joe Kane, who had stopped at the door, turned and laughed.

A roar of anger rose from my father's throat. He danced and shouted a string of inarticulate words. Grabbing another egg from the basket on the counter, he threw it, just missing the head of the young man as he dodged through the door and escaped.

Father came upstairs to mother and me with an egg in his hand. I do not know what he intended to do. I imagine he had some idea of destroying it, of destroying all eggs, and that he intended to let mother and me see him begin. When, however, he got into the presence of mother, something happened to him. He laid the egg gently on the table and dropped on his knees by the bed as I have already explained. He later decided to close the restaurant for the night and to come upstairs and get into bed. When he did so, he blew out the light and after much muttered conversation both he and mother went to sleep. I suppose I went to sleep also, but my sleep was troubled. I awoke at dawn and for a long time looked at the egg that lay on the table. I wondered why eggs had to be and why from the egg came the hen who again laid the egg. The question got into my blood.[10] It has stayed there. I imagine, because I am the son of my father. At any rate, the problem remains unsolved in my mind. And that, I conclude, is but another evidence of the complete and final triumph of the egg—at least as far as my family is concerned.

Notes

[1] The description of an innocent, happy farmer who becomes ambitious for success is Anderson's metaphor for modern America, which has left the ideal of Jeffersonian, rural democracy and started down the road to industrialization and spiritual, cultural ruin.

[2] Garfield and Lincoln: American Presidents who began their lives from very humble origins.

[3] lying-in: the days of recovery after childbirth.

[4] People who have few possessions cling tightly to those they have: Anderson also means that people with few firm (but precious) ideas of truth remain stubbornly narrow-minded. This is his explanation of how people's characters become warped and deformed.

[5] They go quickly back to the hand of their maker: They soon die. Their maker is seen as a cruel, capricious God.

[6] the jolly innkeeper effect: there is a stereotype, from 18th and 19th century literature, of an inn or restaurant as a bright, welcoming place with a merry, warm-hearted manager. This was the impression which the father wanted to imitate.

[7] something prenatal: something in the Father's subconscious mind made him continue to express his ambition through the symbols of eggs. The unrecognized influence of the subconscious mind on human behavior is one of Sigmund Freud's principal theories.

[8] duplicity: deceitfulness.

[9] Christopher Columbus: the 16th century navigator who is supposed to have observed certain magnetic conditions under which an egg would stand on end. The father believed that Columbus cracked the egg in order to make it stand upright.

[10] The question got into my blood: The question began to worry my mind continuously.

Commentary

The Egg (1921) tells the story of a man who is turned miserable by ambitions of "getting up in the world". The narrator (the son) begins by explaining that his father was a happy young man whose life went awry after marrying and following his wife's advice to give up his job as a farmhand in order to start his own business as a chicken farmer. For ten years, the couple pour their resources into the fruitless enterprise of raising chickens, a "dreadfully stupid" and vulnerable animal beset with disease and death. Defeated by chicken farming, the couple open a restaurant outside the town. The father, now a bald, plump, middle-aged man, not unlike an egg in appearance, displays on a shelf his greatest treasure—jars of deformed chicks preserved in alcohol. Frustrated by poor business, he becomes convinced that he can draw customers by entertaining them with lively conversation. Trying to impress a customer one night, he attempts to squeeze a whole egg into a bottle. Unfortunately, he breaks one egg. He then throws another egg at the customer for laughing at him. He then storms upstairs to his wife and cries in her arms with his son looking on. In the end, the perplexed narrator ponders the defeating cycle of life represented by the chicken and the egg, ultimately finding some insight into his family's fate.

This is a humorous tale about a farmer from the countryside who becomes infected with the American passion for "success"—wealth and social position, the American ideals of the 1920's. Anderson's humor is ironic and grotesque, foreshadowing the "black humor" which entered American literature on a wide scale in the 1950's and 1960's. Yet, Anderson's intention was serious rather than simply humorous. He had watched with despair, and deplored the modern society's preoccupation with getting rich. He adopts the tone of a baffled spectator who stands in awe before all the mysteries of life. This literary role of a questioning observer later became typical of American Naturalist writers.

Questions and Exercises

1. How does the first-person point of view affect the style in this story?
2. Is the major conflict in the story internal or external?
3. What are the dominant tone and theme of the story?
4. Write a personal essay about something you tried but failed to do. The tone of the essay may be serious or humorous. Provide details to enable the reader to share your experience and your feelings.

William Faulkner

William Faulkner (1897—1962) was born to a once-wealthy Southern family in New Albany, Mississippi. Like Robert Frost, Faulkner was a regionalist, who spent most of his life in a small area in the Deep South of the United States, writing about the scenes and people he was most familiar with. He found his true voice and style with his important novels, *Sartoris* and *The Sound and the Fury* (both 1929). He successively advanced "stream of consciousness"—a writing technique in which the whole stories was told through the thoughts of one character. And later he used this same technique by putting the subconscious thoughts in the mind of a lunatic. Time sequences are often dislocated so that the reader feels himself to be a participant in the story rather than an observer.

Faulkner's frequent themes are about history and race. His stories try to explain the present time by examining the past, especially by telling the story of several generations of one family as history changed their lives. He generally presents a grim picture of human society where violence and cruelty are frequently included. In 1949, Faulkner was awarded the Nobel Prize for Literature. In *A Rose for Emily*, as in most of his works, he stresses such themes as the South's obsession with the past.

A Rose for Emily

I

When Miss Emily Grierson died, our whole town went to her funeral: the men through a sort of respectful affection for a fallen monument, the women mostly out of curiosity to see the inside of her house, which no one save an old man-servant—a combined gardener and cook—had seen in at least ten years.

It was a big, squarish frame house that had once been white, decorated with cupolas and spires and scrolled balconies in the heavily lightsome style of the seventies, set on what had once been our most select street.[1] But garages and cotton gins had encroached and obliterated even the august names of that neighborhood; only Miss Emily's house was left, lifting its stubborn and coquettish decay above the cotton wagons and the gasoline pumps—an eyesore among eyesores.[2] And now Miss Emily had gone to join the representatives of those august names where they lay in the cedar-bemused cemetery[3] among the ranked and anonymous graves of Union and Confederate soldiers who fell at the battle of Jefferson.

Alive, Miss Emily had been a tradition, a duty, and a care; a sort of hereditary obligation upon the town, dating from that day in 1894 when Colonel Sartoris,[4] the mayor—he who fathered the edict that no Negro woman should appear on the streets without an apron—remitted her taxes, the dispensation dating from the death of her father on into perpetuity. Not that Miss Emily would have accepted charity. Colonel Sartoris invented an involved tale to the effect that Miss Emily's father had loaned money to the town, which the town, as a matter of business, preferred this way of repaying. Only a man of Colonel Sartoris' generation and thought could have invented it, and only a woman could have believed it.

When the next generation, with its more modern ideas, became mayors and aldermen, this arrangement created some little dissatisfaction. On the first of the year they mailed her a tax notice. February came, and there was no reply. They wrote her a formal letter, asking her to call at the sheriff's office at her convenience. A week later the mayor wrote her himself, offering to call or to send his car for her, and received in reply a note on paper of an archaic shape, in a thin, flowing calligraphy in faded ink, to the effect that she no longer went out at all. The tax notice was also enclosed, without comment.

They called a special meeting of the Board of Aldermen.[5] A deputation waited upon her, knocked at the door through which no visitor had passed since she ceased giving china-painting lessons eight or ten years earlier. They were admitted by the old Negro into a dim hall from which a stairway mounted into still more shadow. It smelled of dust and disuse—a close, dank smell. The Negro led them into the parlor. It was furnished in heavy, leather-covered furniture. When the Negro opened the blinds of one window, they could see that the leather was cracked; and when they sat down, a faint dust rose sluggishly about their thighs, spinning with slow motes in the single sun-ray. On a tarnished gilt easel before the fireplace stood a crayon portrait of Miss Emily's father.

They rose when she entered—a small, fat woman in black, with a thin gold chain descending to her waist and vanishing into her belt, leaning on an ebony cane with a tarnished gold head. Her skeleton was small and spare; perhaps that was why what would have been merely plumpness in another was obesity in her. She looked bloated, like a body long submerged in motionless water, and of that pallid hue. Her eyes, lost in the fatty ridges of her face, looked like two small pieces of coal pressed into a lump of dough as they moved from one face to another while the visitors stated their errand.

She did not ask them to sit. She just stood in the door and listened quietly until the spokesman came to a stumbling halt. Then they could hear the invisible watch ticking at the end of the gold chain.

Her voice was dry and cold. "I have no taxes in Jefferson. Colonel Sartoris explained it to me. Perhaps one of you can gain access to the city records and satisfy yourselves."

"But we have. We are the city authorities, Miss Emily. Didn't you get a notice from the sheriff, signed by him?"

"I received a paper, yes," Miss Emily said. "Perhaps he considers himself the sheriff… I have no taxes in Jefferson."

"But there is nothing on the books to show that, you see. We must go by the—"

"See Colonel Sartoris. I have no taxes in Jefferson."

"But, Miss Emily—"

"See Colonel Sartoris." (Colonel Sartoris had been dead almost ten years.) "I have no taxes in Jefferson. Tobe!" The Negro appeared. "Show these gentlemen out."

II

So she vanquished them, horse and foot,[6] just as she had vanquished their fathers thirty years before about the smell.

That was two years after her father's death and a short time after her sweetheart—the one we believed would marry her—had deserted her. After her father's death she went out very little; after her sweetheart went away, people hardly saw her at all. A few of the ladies had the temerity to call, but were not received, and the only sign of life about the place was the Negro man—a young man then—going in and out with a market basket.

"Just as if a man—any man—could keep a kitchen properly," the ladies said; so they were not surprised when the smell developed. It was another link between the gross, teeming world and the high and mighty Griersons.

A neighbor, a woman, complained to the mayor, Judge Stevens, eighty years old.

"But what will you have me do about it, madam?" he said.

"Why, send her word to stop it," the woman said. "Isn't there a law?"

"I'm sure that won't be necessary," Judge Stevens said. "It's probably just a snake or a rat that nigger of hers[7] killed in the yard. I'll speak to him about it."

The next day he received two more complaints, one from a man who came in diffident deprecation.[8] "We really must do something about it, Judge. I'd be the last one in the world to bother Miss Emily, but we've got to do something." That night the Board of Aldermen met—three graybeards and one younger man, a member of the rising generation.

"It's simple enough," he said. "Send her word to have her place cleaned up. Give her a certain time to do it in, and if she don't..."

"Dammit, sir," Judge Stevens said, "will you accuse a lady to her face of smelling bad?"

So the next night, after midnight, four men crossed Miss Emily's lawn and slunk about the house like burglars, sniffing along the base of the brickwork and at the cellar openings while one of them performed a regular sowing motion with his hand out of a sack slung from his shoulder. They broke open the cellar door and sprinkled lime there, and in all the outbuildings. As they recrossed the lawn, a window that had been dark was lighted and Miss Emily sat in it, the light behind her, and her upright torso motionless as that of an idol. They crept quietly across the lawn and into the shadow of the locusts that lined the street. After a week or two the smell went away.

That was when people had begun to feel really sorry for her. People in our town, remembering how old lady Wyatt, her great-aunt, had gone completely crazy at last, believed that the Griersons held themselves a little too high for what they really were. None of the young men were quite good enough for Miss Emily and such.[9] We had long thought of them as a tableau, Miss Emily a slender figure in white in the background, her father a spraddled silhouette in the foreground, his back to her and clutching a horsewhip, the two of them framed by the back-flung front door.[10] So when she got to be thirty and was still single, we were not pleased exactly, but vindicated; even with insanity in the family she wouldn't have turned down all of her chances if they had really materialized.

When her father died, it got about that the house was all that was left to her; and in a way, people were glad. At last they could pity Miss Emily. Being left alone, and a pauper, she had become humanized. Now she too would know the old thrill and the old despair of a penny more or less.

The day after his death all the ladies prepared to call at the house and offer condolence and aid, as is our custom Miss Emily met them at the door, dressed as usual and with no trace of grief on her face. She told them that her father was not dead. She did that for three days, with the ministers calling on her, and the doctors, trying to persuade her to let them dispose of the body. Just as they were about to resort to law and force, she broke down, and they buried her father quickly.

We did not say she was crazy then. We believed she had to do that. We remembered all the young men her father had driven away, and we knew that with nothing left, she would have to cling to that which had robbed her, as people will.

III

She was sick for a long time. When we saw her again, her hair was cut short, making her look like a girl, with a vague resemblance to those angels in colored church windows—sort of tragic and serene.

The town had just let the contracts for paving the sidewalks, and in the summer after her father's death they began the work. The construction company came with riggers and mules and machinery, and a foreman named Homer Barron, a Yankee—a big, dark, ready man, with a big voice and eyes lighter than his face. The little boys would follow in groups to hear him cuss the riggers, and the riggers singing in time to the rise and fall of picks. Pretty soon he knew everybody in town. Whenever you heard a lot of laughing anywhere about the square, Homer Barron would be in the center of the group. Presently we began to see him and Miss Emily on Sunday afternoons driving in the yellow-wheeled buggy and the matched team of bays[11] from the livery stable.

At first we were glad that Miss Emily would have an interest, because the ladies all said, "Of course a Grierson would not think seriously of a Northerner, a day laborer." But there were still others, older people, who said that even grief could not cause a real lady to forget *noblesse oblige*[12]—without calling it *noblesse oblige*. They just said, "Poor Emily. Her kinsfolk should come to her." She had some kin in Alabama; but years ago her father had fallen out with them over the estate of old lady Wyatt,[13] the crazy woman, and there was no communication between the two families. They had not even been represented at the funeral.

And as soon as the old people said, "Poor Emily," the whispering began. "Do you suppose it's really so?" they said to one another. "Of course it is. What else could…" This behind their hands; rustling of craned silk and satin behind jalousies closed upon the sun of Sunday afternoon as the thin, swift clop-clop-clop of the matched team passed: "Poor Emily."

She carried her head high enough—even when we believed that she was fallen. It was as if she demanded more than ever the recognition of her dignity as the last Grierson; as if it had wanted that touch of earthiness to reaffirm her imperviousness. Like when she bought the rat poison, the arsenic. That was over a year after they had begun to say "Poor Emily," and while the two female cousins were visiting her.

"I want some poison," she said to the druggist. She was over thirty then, still a slight woman, though thinner than usual, with cold, haughty black eyes in a face the flesh of which was strained across the temples and about the eyesockets as you imagine a lighthouse-keeper's face ought to look. "I want some poison," she said.

"Yes, Miss Emily. What kind? For rats and such? I'd recon—"

"I want the best you have. I don't care what kind."

The druggist named several. "They'll kill anything up to an elephant. But what you want is—"

"Arsenic," Miss Emily said. "Is that a good one?"

"Is…arsenic? Yes, ma'am. But what you want—"

"I want arsenic."

The druggist looked down at her. She looked back at him, erect, her face like a strained flag. "Why, of course," the druggist said. "If that's what you want. But the law requires you to tell what you are going to use it for."

Miss Emily just stared at him, her head tilted back in order to look him eye for eye, until he looked away and went and got the arsenic and wrapped it up. The Negro delivery boy brought her the package; the druggist didn't come back. When she opened the package at home there was written on the box, under the skull and bones: "For rats."

IV

So the next day we all said, "She will kill herself"; and we said it would be the best thing. When she had first begun to be seen with Homer Barron, we had said, "She will marry him." Then we said, "She will persuade him yet," because Homer himself had remarked—he liked men, and it was known that he drank with the younger men in the Elks' Club—that he was not a marrying man. Later we said, "Poor Emily" behind the jalousies as they passed on Sunday afternoon in the glittering buggy, Miss Emily with her head high and Homer Barron with his hat cocked and a cigar in his teeth, reins and whip in a yellow glove.

Then some of the ladies began to say that it was a disgrace to the town and a bad example to the young people. The men did not want to interfere, but at last the ladies forced the Baptist minister—Miss Emily's people were Episcopal[14]—to call upon her. He would never divulge what happened during that interview, but he refused to go back again. The next Sunday they again drove about the streets, and the following day the minister's wife wrote to Miss Emily's relations in Alabama.

So she had blood-kin under her roof again and we sat back to watch developments. At first nothing happened. Then we were sure that they were to be married. We learned that Miss Emily had been to the jeweler's and ordered a man's toilet set in silver, with the letters H. B. on each piece. Two days later we learned that she had bought a complete outfit of men's clothing, including a nightshirt, and we said, "They are married." We were really glad. We were glad because the two female cousins were even more Grierson[15] than Miss Emily had ever been.

So we were not surprised when Homer Barron—the streets had been finished some time since—was gone. We were a little disappointed that there was not a public blowing-off,[16] but we believed that he had gone on to prepare for Miss Emily's coming, or to give her a chance to get rid of the cousins. (By that time it was a cabal,[17] and we were all Miss Emily's allies to help circumvent the cousins.) Sure enough, after another week they departed. And, as we had expected all along, within three days Homer Barron was back in town. A neighbor saw the Negro man admit him at the kitchen door at dusk one evening.

And that was the last we saw of Homer Barron. And of Miss Emily for some time. The Negro man went in and out with the market basket, but the front door remained closed. Now and then we would see her at a window for a moment, as the men did that night when they sprinkled the lime, but for almost six months she did not appear on the streets. Then we knew that this was to be expected too; as if that quality of her father which had thwarted her woman's life so many times had been too virulent and too furious to die.

When we next saw Miss Emily, she had grown fat and her hair was turning gray. During the next few years it grew grayer and grayer until it attained an even pepper-and-salt iron-gray, when it ceased turning. Up to the day of her death at seventy-four it was still that vigorous iron-gray, like the hair of an active man.

From that time on her front door remained closed, save for a period of six or seven years, when she was about forty, during which she gave lessons in china-painting. She fitted up a studio in one of the downstairs rooms, where the daughters and granddaughters of Colonel Sartoris' contemporaries were sent to her with the same regularity and in the same spirit that they were sent to church on Sundays with a twenty-five-cent piece for the collection plate. Meanwhile her taxes had been remitted.

Then the newer generation became the backbone and the spirit of the town, and the painting pupils grew up and fell away and did not send their children to her with boxes of color and tedious brushes and pictures cut from the ladies' magazines. The front door closed upon the last one and remained closed for good. When the town got free postal delivery, Miss Emily alone refused to let them fasten the metal numbers above her door and attach a mailbox to it. She would not listen to them.

Daily, monthly, yearly we watched the Negro grow grayer and more stooped, going in and out with the market basket. Each December we sent her a tax notice, which would be returned by the post office a week later, unclaimed. Now and then we would see her in one of the downstairs windows—she had evidently shut up the top floor of the house—like the carven torso of an idol in a niche, looking or not looking at us, we could never tell which. Thus she passed from generation to generation—dear, inescapable, impervious, tranquil, and perverse.

And so she died. Fell ill in the house filled with dust and shadows, with only a doddering Negro man to wait on her. We did not even know she was sick; we had long since given up trying to get any information from the Negro. He talked to no one, probably not even to her, for his voice had grown harsh and rusty, as if from disuse.

She died in one of the downstairs rooms, in a heavy walnut bed with a curtain, her gray head propped on a pillow yellow and moldy with age and lack of sunlight.

V

The Negro met the first of the ladies at the front door and let them in, with their hushed, sibilant voices and their quick, curious glances, and then he disappeared. He walked right through the house and out the back and was not seen again.

The two female cousins came at once. They held the funeral on the second day, with the town coming to look at Miss Emily beneath a mass of bought flowers, with the crayon face of her father musing profoundly above the bier and the ladies sibilant and macabre; and the very old men—some in their brushed Confederate uniforms—on the porch and the lawn, talking of Miss Emily as if she had been a contemporary of theirs, believing that they had danced with her and courted her perhaps, confusing time with its mathematical progression, as the old do, to whom all the past is not a diminishing road but, instead, a huge meadow which no winter ever quite touches, divided from them now by the narrow bottle-neck of the most recent decade of years.

Already we knew that there was one room in that region above stairs which no one had seen in forty years, and which would have to be forced. They waited until Miss Emily was decently in the ground before they opened it.

The violence of breaking down the door seemed to fill this room with pervading dust. A thin, acrid pall as of the tomb seemed to lie everywhere upon this room decked and furnished as for a bridal: upon the valance curtains of faded rose color, upon the rose-shaded lights, upon the dressing table, upon the delicate array of crystal and the man's toilet things backed with tarnished silver, silver so tarnished that the monogram was obscured. Among them lay a collar and tie, as if they had just been removed, which, lifted, left upon the surface a pale crescent in the dust. Upon a

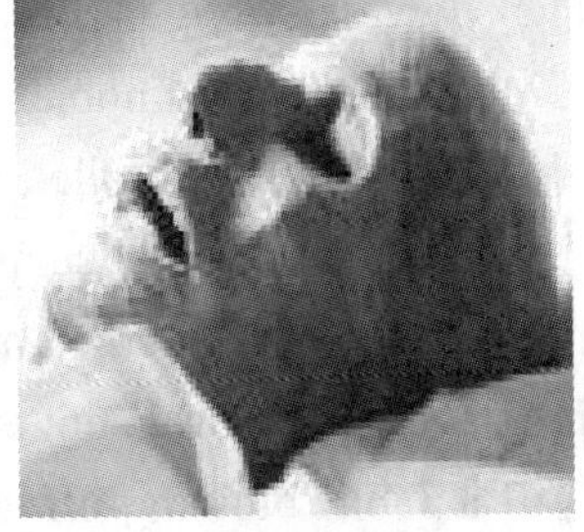

chair hung the suit, carefully folded; beneath it the two mute shoes and the discarded socks.

The man himself lay in the bed.

For a long while we just stood there, looking down at the profound and fleshless grin. The body had apparently once lain in the attitude of an embrace, but now the long sleep that outlasts love, that conquers even the grimace of love, had cuckolded him. What was left of him, rotted beneath what was left of the nightshirt, had become inextricable from the bed in which he lay; and upon him and upon the pillow beside him lay that even coating of the patient and biding dust.

Then we noticed that in the second pillow was the indentation of a head. One of us lifted something from it, and leaning forward, that faint and invisible dust dry and acrid in the nostrils, we saw a long strand of iron-gray hair.

Notes

[1] most select street: most decent street.

[2] an eyesore among eyesores: the ugly among the ugliest.

[3] the cedar-bemused cemetery: a cemetery surrounded with cedar trees that can cause a feeling of awe for people.

[4] Colonel Sartoris: an imaginary character in a novel by Faulkner.

[5] the Board of Aldermen: the city council.

[6] horse and foot: with all effort.

[7] nigger of hers: a Negro servant of Emily.

[8] in diffident deprecation: intending to express disapproval but with inadequate courage or power to do so.

[9] and such: and the like.

[10] Miss Emily a slender figure…the back-flung front door: The writer imagines this scene to be one on the stage—the father is sitting on the back of the horse with a whip in hand standing at the front part of the stage to protect his daughter from being courted by a repulsive trouble maker.

[11] the matched team of bays: a team of two well-matched reddish-brown horses.

[12] *noblesse oblige:* (French) literally meaning nobility obligates. The phrase suggests that persons of noble rank should behave nobly.

[13] Her father had fallen out…old lady Wyatt: The relationship between her father and old lady Wyatt became rather bad because of the latter's estate affair.

[14] Episcopal: governed by bishops.

[15] even more Grierson: even more arrogant than the Griersons.

[16] a public blowing-off: a disagreeable quarrel in public.

[17] cabal: plot; a small group of people working or plotting in secret.

Commentary

The Old South of America has long been idealized as a land of prosperous plantations, large white houses, cultured people, and a stable economy based on cotton. Yet, like any utopia, this picture is a distortion. It hides away many of the unpleasant, even appalling realities of plantation life. Still, long after the Civil War, with much of the south destroyed by economic hardship, the myth persisted among many white Southerners (like Emily and her neighbours) as a kind of nostalgia of a golden age.

A Rose for Emily is Faulkner's first published short story in April, 1930. The setting is in the southern town of Jefferson in Yoknapatawpha County, the same setting for a dozen of his novels. The protagonist Emily Grierson's personality has been twisted by forces beyond her control. Dominated by her aristocratic father, she has been prevented from getting married and after his death she is left alone and lives in poverty. She kills her lover Homer Barren in order that she can keep him with her. She does not accept change of the time and alienates herself from the community. She grows insane and her actions are abnormally grotesque, but she is a victim, a tragic woman who is sympathized by her townspeople. The main theme of this story is the relation of the individual and his actions to the past, present and future. Besides the exploration of psychological reality, the displaced chronological order in narration is also characteristic of Faulkner's style.

Questions and Exercises

1. How can you describe and account for Miss Emily Grierson's character?
2. What words convey the attitude the townspeople have toward Miss Emily? During the course of the story, does the attitude of the townspeople toward Miss Emily undergo a significant change?
3. Foreshadowing is an important way of telling a story. What in Miss Emily's character foreshadows the discovery of the body? Is there any event in the plot that prepares you for the horror of the ending?
4. Work in groups and discuss the meaning of the title of the story. Then write a paragraph stating and supporting your conclusions about the theme of *A Rose for Emily*.

Ernest Hemingway

Ernest Hemingway (1899—1961) was a novelist and short story writer who became one of the best known American writers in the 20th century. Hemingway is famous for his "telegraphic (or iceberg) style", which means that the language used is very explicit, and that the implied meanings are profound. What readers get is just the tip of an iceberg. The large part lies hidden for readers to search out. In 1952, he published his last successful novel, *The Old Man and the Sea*. In 1954, he was awarded the Nobel Prize for Literature.

Hemingway was a man of contradiction. He loved life, yet he continually pondered upon death. He wrote about men and women who were isolated from tradition, frightened, sometimes ridiculous, trying to find their own way of life, yet he gave no literary explanations, and no conventional happy endings to his stories. He wrote about the courage with which men face the tragedies of life that can never be remedied both physically and spiritually. His life was bold and courageous, yet his courage failed him in the end: he committed suicide by shooting himself with a hunting gun. It is worth being noted that, besides Ernest Hemingway himself, four more people in the family committed suicide: his father, brother, sister, and granddaughter Margaux.

A Clean Well-Lighted Place

It was very late and everyone had left the cafe except an old man who sat in the shadow the leaves of the tree made against the electric light. In the day time the street was dusty, but at night the dew settled the dust and the old man liked to sit late because he was deaf and now at night it was quiet and he felt the difference. The two waiters inside the cafe knew that the old man was a little drunk, and while he was a good client they knew that if he became too drunk he would leave without paying, so they kept watch on him.

"Last week he tried to commit suicide," one waiter said.

"Why?"

"He was in despair."

"What about?"

"Nothing."

"How do you know it was nothing?"

"He has plenty of money."

They sat together at a table that was close against the wall near the door of the cafe and looked at the terrace where the tables were all empty except where the old man sat in the shadow of the leaves of the tree that moved slightly in the wind. A girl and a soldier went by in the street. The street light shone on the brass number on his collar. The girl wore no head covering and hurried beside him.

"The guard will pick him up,"[1] one waiter said.

"What does it matter if he gets what he's after?"[2]

"He had better get off the street now. The guard will get him. They went by five minutes ago."

The old man sitting in the shadow rapped on his saucer with his glass. The younger waiter went over to him.

"What do you want?"

The old man looked at him. "Another brandy," he said.

"You'll be drunk," the waiter said. The old man looked at him. The waiter went away.

"He'll stay all night," he said to his colleague. "I'm sleepy now. I never get into bed before three o'clock. He should have killed himself last week."[3]

The waiter took the brandy bottle and another saucer from the counter inside the cafe and marched out to the old man's table. He put down the saucer and poured the glass full of brandy.

"You should have killed yourself last week," he said to the deaf man. The old man motioned with his finger. "A little more," he said. The waiter poured on into the glass so that the brandy slopped over and ran down the stem into the top saucer of the pile. "Thank you," the old man said. The waiter took the bottle back inside the cafe. He sat down at the table with his colleague again.

"He's drunk now," he said.

"He's drunk every night."

"What did he want to kill himself for?"

"How should I know."

"How did he do it?"

"He hung himself with a rope."

"Who cut him down?"[4]

"His niece."

"Why did they do it?"

"Fear for his soul."[5]

"How much money has he got?"

"He's got plenty."

"He must be eighty years old."

"Anyway I should say he was eighty."

"I wish he would go home. I never get to bed before three o'clock. What kind of hour is that to go to bed?"

"He stays up because he likes it."

"He's lonely. I'm not lonely. I have a wife waiting in bed for me."

"He had a wife once too."

"A wife would be no good to him now."

"You can't tell. He might be better with a wife."

"His niece looks after him. You said she cut him down."

"I know."

"I wouldn't want to be that old. An old man is a nasty thing."

"Not always. This old man is clean. He drinks without spilling. Even now, drunk. Look at him."

"I don't want to look at him. I wish he would go home. He has no regard for those who must work."

The old man looked from his glass across the square, then over at the waiters.

"Another brandy," he said, pointing to his glass. The waiter who was in a hurry came over.

"Finished," he said, speaking with that omission of syntax stupid people employ when talking to drunken people or foreigners. "No more tonight. Close now."

"Another," said the old man.

"No. Finished." The waiter wiped the edge of the table with a towel and shook his head.

The old man stood up, slowly counted the saucers,[6] took a leather coin purse from his pocket and paid for the drinks, leaving half a peseta[7] tip. The waiter watched him go down the street, a very old man walking unsteadily but with dignity.

"Why didn't you let him stay and drink?" the unhurried waiter asked. They were putting up the shutters.[8] "It is not half-past two."

"I want to go home to bed."

"What is an hour?"

"More to me than to him."

"An hour is the same."

"You talk like an old man yourself. He can buy a bottle and drink at home."

"It's not the same."

"No, it is not," agreed the waiter with a wife. He did not wish to be unjust. He was only in a hurry.

"And you? You have no fear of going home before your usual hour?"[9]

"Are you trying to insult me?"

"No, hombre,[10] only to make a joke."

"No," the waiter who was in a hurry said, rising from pulling down the metal shutters. "I have confidence. I am all confidence."

"You have youth, confidence, and a job," the older waiter said. "You have everything."

"And what do you lack?"

"Everything but work."

"You have everything I have."

"No. I have never had confidence and I am not young."

"Come on. Stop talking nonsense and lock up."

"I am of those who like to stay late at the cafe," the older waiter said. "With all those who do not want to go to bed. With all those who need a light for the night."

"I want to go home and into bed."

"We are of two different kinds," the older waiter said. He was now dressed to go home. "It is not only a question of youth and confidence although those things are very beautiful. Each night I am reluctant to close up because there may be some one who needs the cafe."

"Hombre, there are bodegas[11] open all night long."

"You do not understand. This is a clean and pleasant cafe. It is well lighted. The light is very good and also, now, there are shadows of the leaves."

"Good night," said the younger waiter.

"Good night," the other said. Turning off the electric light he continued the conversation with himself. It was the light of course but it is necessary that the place be clean and pleasant. You do not want music. Certainly you do not want music. Nor can you stand before a bar with dignity although that is all that is provided for these hours. What did he fear? It was not a fear or dread. It was a nothing that he knew too well. It was all a nothing and a man was a nothing too. It was only that and light was all it needed and a certain cleanness and order. Some lived in it and never felt it but he knew it all was nada y pues nada y nada y pues nada. Our nada who art in nada, nada be thy name thy kingdom nada thy will be nada in nada as it is in nada. Give us this nada our daily nada and nada us our nada as we nada our nadas and nada us not into nada but deliver us from nada; pues nada.[12] Hail nothing full of nothing, nothing is with thee. He smiled and stood before a bar with a shining steam pressure coffee machine.

"What's yours?" asked the barman.

"Nada."

"Otro loco mas,"[13] said the barman and turned away.

"A little cup," said the waiter.

The barman poured it for him.

"The light is very bright and pleasant but the bar is unpolished," the waiter said.

The barman looked at him but did not answer. It was too late at night for conversation.

"You want another copita?"[14] the barman asked.

"No, thank you," said the waiter and went out. He disliked bars and bodegas. A clean, well-lighted cafe was a very different thing. Now, without thinking further, he would go home to his room. He would lie in the bed and finally, with daylight, he would go to sleep. After all, he said to himself, it's probably only insomnia. Many must have it.

Notes

[1] pick him up: arrest him.

[2] What does it matter if he gets what he's after: This sentence implies that it is up to the policeman himself whether or not he will arrest the old man.

[3] He should have killed himself last week: When the young waiter says this, he doesn't mean to be cruel to the old man, because he knows the old man cannot hear him. He is only annoyed by the inconveniences the old man has caused him. He compensates for his words by filling the old man's glass so that the brandy slopped over.

[4] Who cut him down: Who saved him when he was committing suicide with the rope?

[5] Fear for his soul: For religious reasons, the old man's niece did not let him die. Roman Catholics believe that the soul of a person who commits suicide will not be admitted into heaven.

[6] The old man…counted the saucers: The customer pays for the drinks according to the number of saucers he uses for drinking.

[7] peseta: a unit of money in Spain.

[8] They were putting up the shutters: They were closing the business at the end of the day.

[9] You have no fear of going home before your usual hour: Aren't you afraid that you will catch your wife having an affair with some other man if you get home before your usual hour? Here the old waiter is joking on the young waiter.

[10] hombre: (Spanish) my good old man.

[11] bodegas: (Spanish) cafes; public houses.

[12] Some lived in it…but deliver us from nada; pues nada: This is a parody of a paragraph of a well known Christian prayer. "Our Father who art in Heaven, hallowed be thy name; Thy kingdom come, thy will be done, in Earth as it is in Heaven. Give us this day our daily bread, and forgive us our debts as we forgive our debtors; But deliver us from evil." nada: (Spanish) nothing; y: (Spanish) and; pues: (Spanish) then.

[13] Otro loco mas: Another lunatic.

[14] copita: a small cup.

Commentary

The plot of Hemingway's *A Clean Well-Lighted Place* is quite simple and unimportant. A quiet, dignified, deaf, old widower, who has recently attempted suicide, sits until late into the night drinking at a Spanish cafe while two waiters—one young, inconsiderate, eager to get home to his wife; the other older, more compassionate, pondering about the old man's plight and his own.

The younger waiter is impatient with the old man; he just wishes the customer would quit drinking and go home, so that the waiter could go home too. He cannot relate to whatever causes the old man to have so many drinks over so long a period, night after night, in the quiet cafe. He especially cannot fathom what could have led the old man to attempt suicide, because the old man "has plenty of money".

The older waiter, on the other hand, understands despair only too well. He is saddened when the young waiter insults the old man, and is even more grieved when the young waiter closes the cafe and sends the old man away. As he says to the young waiter, "You have youth, confidence, and a job. You have everything." The old man, on the other hand, has nothing—no one to go home to, nothing to look forward to, no pleasure left in life except the small comfort of being able to spend a little time in a clean, well-lighted cafe.

After the young waiter leaves to go home to his waiting bride, the older one continues the conversation with himself. He knows the value of his cafe; when you have nothing else to live for, a place like that can be a small fortress against the huge, all-encompassing darkness of existence. What lies beyond the warm glow of the cafe is nothingness: a great existential nothingness that turns the Christian faith in a loving God into something horrible.

What is so special about this very short story is the way Hemingway manages to evoke the universal disparities between the young waiter who, with his whole life ahead of him, is "all confidence" and the elderly who realizes there is literally nothing to live for.

Questions and Exercises

1. Jackson J. Benson states, "Blindness versus awareness is Hemingway's most pervasive theme, and it is borne on a rippling wave of irony into almost everything he writes." How do the contrasting perspectives of the two waiters in *A Clean Well-Lighted Place* express this theme? Who is blind? And who is aware?
2. Does the story present the human condition in optimistic or pessimistic terms? In what sense are the story's style and tone suited to this worldview?
3. The story's primary point of view is objective. At times, however, a limited point of view is adopted. Identify such instances, and try to explain the reason for each shift in point of view.

Isaac Bashevis Singer

Isaac Bashevis Singer (1904—1991) was a Polish-born American journalist, novelist, short-story writer, and essayist, who won the Nobel Prize for Literature in 1978. As an American writer, Singer is a most atypical American. He was born in Poland, but he still writes in Yiddish, and he did not become an American citizen until 1943. He is widely recognized as one of the greatest in a long tradition of Yiddish writers. His novels are moving depictions of Jewish life in Poland and America. His short stories are masterpieces of irony, wit, wisdom and folklore. He accepts whatever happens, not as coming from God, but as facts of life as it exists—things are what they are. His chief subject is the traditional Polish life in various periods of history, largely before the Holocaust of the Jews. He has especially examined the role of the Jewish faith in the lives of his characters, who are pestered with passions, magic, asceticisms and religious devotion.

Singer writes in Yiddish, then carefully translates his works into English. His works are far better known in English than in the original, but he has said: "I call myself a bilingual writer and say that English has become my "second original!" His popular short stories have been published in many collections, among them *Gimpel the Fool* (1957) and *A Crown of Feathers* (1973), which received a major award. Singer has written two books about his youth: *In My Father's Court* (1966) and *A Young Man in Search of Love* (1978). His style appears to be effortless and easy-going.

The Son from America

The village of Lentshin was tiny—a sandy market-place where the peasants of the area met once a week.

It was surrounded by little huts with thatched roofs or shingles green with moss. The chimneys looked like pots. Between the huts there were fields, where the owners planted vegetables or pastured their goats.

In the smallest of these huts lived old Berl, a man in his eighties, and his wife, who was called Berlcha (wife of Berl). Old Berl was one of the Jews who had been driven from their villages in Russia and had settled in Poland. In Lentshin, they mocked the mistakes he made while praying aloud. He spoke with a sharp "r". He was short, broad-shouldered, and had a small white beard, and summer and winter he wore a sheepskin hat, a padded cotton jacket, and stout boots. He walked slowly, shuffling his feet. He had a half acre of field, a cow, a goat, and chickens.

The couple had a son, Samuel, who had gone to America forty years ago. It was said in Lentshin that he became a millionaire there. Every month, the Lentshin letter carrier brought old Berl a money order and a letter that no one could read because many of the words were English. How much money Samuel sent his parents remained a secret. Three times a year, Berl and his wife went on foot to Zakrocaym and cashed the money orders there. But they never seemed to use the money. What for? The garden, the cow, and the goat provided most of their needs. Besides, Berlcha sold chickens and eggs, and from these there was enough to buy flour for bread.

No one cared to know where Berl kept the money that his son sent him. There were no thieves in Lentshin. The hut consisted of one room, which contained all their belongings: the table, the shelf for meat, the shelf for milk foods, the two beds, and the clay oven. Sometimes the chickens roosted in the woodshed and sometimes, when it was cold, in a coop near the oven. The goat, too, found shelter inside when the weather was bad. The more prosperous villagers had kerosene lamps, but Berl and his wife did not believe in newfangled gadgets.[1] What was wrong with a wick in a dish of oil? Only for the Sabbath[2] would Berlcha buy three tallow candles at the store. In summer, the couple got up at sunrise and retired with the chickens. In the long winter evenings, Berlcha spun flax at her spinning wheel and Berl sat beside her in the silence of those who enjoy their rest.

Once in a while when Berl came home from the synagogue[3] after evening prayers, he brought news to his wife. In Warsaw there were strikers who demanded that the czar abdicate. A heretic by the name of Dr. Herzl had come up with the idea that Jews should settle again in Palestine. Berlcha listened and shook her bonneted head. Her face was yellowish and wrinkled like a cabbage leaf. There were bluish sacks under her eyes. She was half deaf. Berl had to repeat each word he said to her. She would say, "The things that happen in the big cities."

Here in Lentshin nothing happened except usual events: a cow gave birth to a calf, a young couple had a circumcision party,[4] or a girl was born and there was no party. Occasionally, someone died. Lentshin had no cemetery, and the corpse had to be taken to Zakroczym. Actually, Lentshin had become a village with few young people. The young men left for Zakroczym, for Nowy Dwor, for Warsaw, and sometimes for the United States. Like Samuel's, their letters were illegible, the Yiddish[5] mixed with the languages of the countries where they were now living. They sent photographs in which the men wore top hats and the women fancy dresses like squiresses.

Berl and Berlcha also received such photographs. But their eyes were failing and neither he nor she had glasses. They could barely make out the pictures. Samuel had sons and daughters with Gentile names—and grandchildren who had married and had their own offspring. Their names were so strange that Berl and Berlcha could never remember them. But what difference do names make? America was far, far away on the other side of the ocean, at the edge of the world. A Talmud teacher[6] who came to Lentshin had said that Americans walked with their heads down and their feet up. Berl and Berlcha could not grasp this. How was it possible? But since the teacher said so it must be true. Berlcha pondered for some time and then she said, "One can get accustomed to everything."

And so it remained. From too much thinking—God forbid—one may lose one's wits.

One Friday morning, when Berlcha was kneading the dough for the Sabbath loaves, the door opened and a nobleman entered. He was so tall that he had to bend down to get through the door. He wore a beaver hat and a cloak bordered with fur. He was followed by Chazkel, the coachman from Zakroczym, who carried two leather valises with brass locks. In astonishment Berlcha raised her eyes.

The nobleman looked around and said to the coachman in Yiddish, "Here it is." He took out a silver ruble[7] and paid him. The coachman tried to hand him change but he said, "You can go now."

When the coachman closed the door, the nobleman said, "Mother, it's me, your son Samuel—Sam."

Berlcha heard the words, and her legs grew numb. Her hands, to which pieces of dough were sticking, lost their power. The nobleman hugged her, kissed her forehead, both her cheeks. Berlcha, began to cackle like a hen, "My son!" At that moment Berl came in from the woodshed, his arms piled with logs. The goat followed him. When he saw a nobleman kissing his wife, Berl dropped the wood and exclaimed, "What is this?"

The nobleman let go of Berlcha and embraced Berl.

"Father!"

For a long time Berl was unable to utter a sound. He wanted to recite holy words that he had read in the Yiddish Bible, but he could remember nothing. Then he asked, "Are you Samuel?"

"Yes, father, I am Samuel."

"Well, peace be with you." Berl grasped his son's hand. He was still not sure that he was not being fooled. Samuel wasn't as tall and heavy as this man, but then Berl reminded himself that Samuel was only fifteen years old when he had left home. He must have grown in that faraway country. Berl asked, "Why didn't you let us know that you were coming?"

"Didn't you receive my cable? Samuel asked.

Berl did not know what a cable was?

Berlcha had scraped the dough from her hands and enfolded her son. He kissed her again and asked, "Mother, didn't you receive a cable?"

"What? If I lived to see this, I am happy to die," Berlcha said, amazed by her own words. Berl, too, was amazed. These were just the words he would have said earlier if he had been able to remember. After a while Berl came to himself and said, "Berlcha, you will have to make a double Sabbath pudding in addition to the stew."

It was years since Berl had called Berlcha by her given name. When he wanted to address her, he would say, "Listen," or "Say". It is the young or those from the big cities who call a wife by her name. Only now did Berlcha begin to cry. Yellow tears ran from her eyes, and everything became dim. Then she called out, "It's Friday—I have to prepare for the Sabbath." Yes, she had to knead the dough and braid the loaves. With such a guest, she had to make a larger Sabbath stew. The winter day is short and she must hurry.

Her son understood what was worrying her, because he said, "Mother, I will help you."

Berlcha wanted to laugh, but a choked sob came out. "What are you saying? God forbid."

The nobleman took off his cloak and jacket and remained in his vest, on which hung a solid-gold watch chain. He rolled up his sleeves and came to the trough. "Mother, I was a baker for many years in New York," he said, and he began to knead the dough.

What! You are my darling son who will say Yiddish for me. She wept gaspingly. Her strength left her, and she slumped onto the bed.

Berl said, "Women will always be women." And he went to the shed to get more wood. The goat sat down near the ovens; she gazed with surprise at this strange man—his height and his bizarre clothes.

The neighbors had heard the good news that Berl's son had arrived from America and they came to greet him. The women began to help Berlcha prepare for the Sabbath. Some laughed, some cried. The room was full of people, as at a wedding. They asked Berl's son, "What is new in America?" And Berl's son answered, "America is all right."

"Do Jews make a living?"

"One eats white bread there on weekdays."

"Do they remain Jews?"

"I am not a Gentile."

After Berlcha blessed the candles, father and son went to the little synagogue across the street. A new snow had fallen. The son took large steps, but Berl warned him, "Slow down."

In the synagogue the Jews recited "Let Us Exult" and "Come, My Groom." All the time, the snow outside kept falling. After prayers, when Berl and Samuel left the Holy Place, the village was unrecognizable. Everything was covered in snow. One could see only the contours[8] of the roofs and the candles in the windows. Samuel said, "Nothing has changed here."

Berlcha had prepared fish, chicken soup with rice, meat, carrot stew. Berl recited the benediction[9] over a glass of ritual wine. The family ate and drank, and when it grew quiet for a while one could hear the chirping of the house cricket. The son talked a lot, but Berl and Berlcha understood little. His Yiddish was different and contained foreign words, After the final blessing Samuel asked, "Father, what did you do with all the money I sent you?"

Berl raised his white brows. "It's here."

"Didn't you put it in a bank?"

"There is no bank in Lentshin."

"Where do you keep it?"

Berl hesitated. "One is not allowed to touch money on the Sabbath, but I will show you." He crouched beside the bed and began to shove something heavy. A boot appeared. Its top was stuffed with straw. Berl removed the straw and the son saw that the boot was full of gold coins. He lifted it.

"Father, this is a treasure!" he called out.

"Well."

"Why didn't you spend it?"

"On what? Thank God, we have everything."

"Why didn't you travel somewhere?"

"Where to? This is our home."

The son asked one question after the other, but Berl's answer was always the same: they wanted for nothing. The garden, the cow, the goat, the chickens provided them with all they needed. The son said, "If thieves knew about this, your lives wouldn't be safe."

"There are no thieves here."

"What will happen to the money?"

"You take it."

Slowly, Berl and Berlcha grew accustomed to their son and his American Yiddish. Berlcha could hear him better now. She even recognized his voice. He was saying, "Perhaps we should build a larger synagogue."

"The synagogue is big enough," Berl replied.

"Perhaps a home for old people."

"No one sleeps in the street."

The next day after the Sabbath meal was eaten, a Gentile from Zakroczym brought a paper—it was the cable. Berl and Berlcha lay down for a nap. They soon began to snore. The goat, too, dozed off. The son put on his cloak and his hat and went for a walk. He strode with his long legs across the market place. He stretched out a hand and touched a roof. He wanted to smoke a cigar, but he remembered it was forbidden on the Sabbath. He had a desire to talk to someone, but it seemed that the whole of Lentshin was asleep. He entered the synagogue. An old man was sitting there, reciting psalms. Samuel asked, "Are you praying?"

"What else is there to do when one gets old?"

"Do you make a living?"

The old man did not understand the meaning of these words. He smiled, showing his empty gums,[10] and then he said, "If God gives health, one keeps on living."

Samuel returned home. Dusk had fallen. Berl went to the synagogue for the evening prayers and the son remained with his mother. The room was filled with shadows.

Berlcha began to recite in a solemn singsong, "God of Abraham, Isaac, and Jacob, defend the poor people of Israel and Thy name. The Holy Sabbath is departing; the welcome week is coming to us. Let it be one of health, wealth, and good deeds."

"Mother, you don't need to pray for wealth," Samuel said. "You are wealthy already."

Berlcha did not hear—or pretended not to. Her face had turned into a cluster of shadows.

In the twilight Samuel put his hand into his jacket pocket and touched his passport, his checkbook, his letters of credit. He had come here with big plans. He had a valise filled with presents for his parents. He wanted to bestow gifts on the village. He brought not only his own money but funds from the Lentshin Society in New York, which had organized a ball for the benefit of the village. But this village in the hinterland[11] needed nothing. From the synagogue one could hear hoarse chanting. The cricket, silent all day, started again its chirping. Berlcha began to sway and utter holy rhymes inherited from mothers and grandmothers:

Thy holy sheep
In mercy keep,
In Torah and good deeds;
Provide for all their needs,
Shoes, clothes, and bread
And the Messiah's tread.[12]

Notes

[1] newfangled gadgets: electrical appliances that are new but unnecessary or of no use.

[2] the Sabbath: the seventh day of the week; Saturday kept as a day of rest and worship by Jews and some Christians.

[3] the synagogue: Jewish temple; a place where Jews worship according to their religion.

[4] a circumcision party: a Jewish or Muslim religious ceremony at which to cut off the foreskin at the end of the sex organ of a man or a part of the clitoris of a woman.

[5] the Yiddish: the language spoken by Jews, esp. in eastern Europe.

[6] a Talmud teacher: a teacher who teaches the teachings of Talmud, the body of Jewish law concerned with religious or nonreligious life.

[7] a silver ruble: a measure of money (in the form of a silver coin) in former USSR.

[8] contours: the shape of the outer limits of a building or of an area.

[9] benediction: (the act of giving) a blessing.

[10] gums: areas of firm pink flesh in which the teeth are fixed at the bottom and the top of the mouth.

[11] hinterland: the inner part of a country.

[12] Thy holy sheep…the Messiah's tread: This holy poem can be paraphrased as follows: Your sacred followers of Jesus Christ, stay right in God's favor. If you act on the Jewish teachings and do good deeds, you will be provided with everything you need: including shoes, clothes, bread, and the chance to do Messiah and dance joyfully in the holy church.

Commentary

The story gives an accurate description of a small Jewish village in Poland before the Second World War. The village has been completely left out of the modern world and life there continues in its age-old tradition. The villagers remain very backward, and they feel it quite unnecessary to indulge themselves in the "luxurious style" of modern life. Young men, however, usually leave the village and go to work in towns, cities, and even the United States.

Samuel, the son of Berl and Berlcha, an old Jewish couple, now a rich American banker, comes home to see his parents after an absence of over forty years. He arrives home hoping to bring many changes and improvements to the village. Despite his good intentions, Samuel finds that the old Jews are rather satisfied with the possessions they have and contented with the way of life as it is. The true reason is that their peaceful life style make them see no need for any change—they prefer to remain backward. Though the story is an amusing contrast of different attitudes between two generations and between the old and new ways of Jewish life, it can also be significant and instructive in making readers of any nations ponder upon the actual qualities of the modern life.

Questions and Exercises

1. What kind of life do Samuel's parents live now? Why do they feel contented with their present backward way of life?
2. What kind of style does the author adopt? And how is it fit to the tone of the story?
3. Discuss what kind of life should be regarded as a happy one in your understanding, then write a paragraph to talk about the central theme of the story and your response toward this theme.

John Updike

John Updike (1932—), American novelist, short story writer and poet, internationally known for his novels *Rabbit, Run* (1960), *Rabbit Redux* (1971), *Rabbit Is Rich* (1981), *Rabbit at Rest* (1990), which follow the life story of Harry "Rabbit" Angstrom, a star athlete, from his youth through the social and sexual upheavals of the 1960s, to later periods of his life, and to final decline.

Updike's oeuvre has been large, consisting of novels, short stories, essays, poems, plays, and children's tales. His most recent novel is *Seek My Face* (2002). Updike has also published *Collected Poems* 7953—7993 (1993) and a collection of essays titled *The Afterlife and Other Stories* (1994). In 1998, Updike received the National Book Foundation Medal for Distinguished Contribution to American Letters.

A & P

In walks these three girls in nothing but bathing suits. I'm in the third check-out slot, with my back to the door, so I don't see them until they're over by the bread. The one that caught my eye first was the one in the plaid green two-piece. She was a chunky kid, with a good tan and a sweet broad soft-looking can[1] with those two crescents of white just under it, where the sun never seems to hit, at the top of the backs of her legs. I stood there with my hand on a box of HiHo crackers[2] trying to remember if I rang it up or not. I ring it up again and the customer starts giving me hell. She's one of these cash-register-watchers, a witch about fifty with rouge on her cheekbones and no eyebrows, and I know it made her day to trip me up.[3] She'd been watching cash registers forty years and probably never seen a mistake before.

By the time I got her feathers smoothed[4] and her goodies into a bag—she gives me a little snort in passing, if she'd been born at the right time they would have burned her over in Salem[5]—by the time I get her on her way the girls had circled around the bread and were coming back, without a pushcart, back my way along the counters, in the aisle between the check-outs and the Special bins. They didn't even have shoes on. There was this chunky one, with the two-piece—it was bright green and the seams on the bra were still sharp and her belly was still pretty pale so I guessed she just got it (the suit)—there was this one, with one of those chubby berry-faces, the lips all bunched together under her nose, this one, and a tall one, with black hair that hadn't quite frizzed right, and one of

these sunburns right across under the eyes, and a chin that was too long—you know, the kind of girl other girls think is very "striking" and "attractive" but never quite makes it,[6] as they very well know, which is why they like her so much—and then the third one, that wasn't quite so tall. She was the queen. She kind of led them, the other two peeking around and making their shoulders round. She didn't look around, not this queen, she just walked straight on slowly, on these long white prima donna[7] legs. She came down a little hard on her heels, as if she didn't walk in her bare feet that much, putting down her heels and then letting the weight move along to her toes as if she was testing the floor with every step, putting a little deliberate extra action into it. You never know for sure how girls' minds work (do you really think it's a mind in there or just a little buzz like a bee in a glass jar?) but you got the idea she had talked the other two into coming in here with her, and now she was showing them how to do it, walk slow and hold yourself straight.

She had on a kind of dirty-pink—beige maybe, I don't know—bathing suit with a little nubble all over it and, what got me, the straps were down. They were off her shoulders looped loose around the cool tops of her arms, and I guess as a result the suit had slipped a little on her, so all around the top of the cloth there was this shining rim. If it hadn't been there you wouldn't have known there could have been anything whiter than those shoulders. With the straps pushed off, there was nothing between the top of the suit and the top of her head except just her, this clean bare plane of the top of her chest down from the shoulder bones like a dented sheet of metal tilted in the light. I mean, it was more than pretty.

She had sort of oaky hair that the sun and salt had bleached, done up in a bun that was unravelling, and a kind of prim face. Walking into the A & P with your straps down, I suppose it's the only kind of face you *can* have. She held her head so high her neck, coming up out of those white shoulders, looked kind of stretched, but I didn't mind. The longer her neck was, the more of her there was.

She must have felt in the corner of her eye me and over my shoulder Stokesie in the second slot watching, but she didn't tip. Not this queen. She kept her eyes moving across the racks, and stopped, and turned so slow it made my stomach rub the inside of my apron, and buzzed to the other two, who kind of huddled against her for relief, and they all three of them went up the cat-and-dog-food-breakfast-cereal-macaroni-rie-raisins-seasonings-preads- spaghetti-soft-drinks-rackers-and-cookies aisle. From the third slot I look straight up this aisle to the meat counter, and I watched them all the way. The fat one with the tan sort of fumbled with the cookies, but on second thought she put the packages back. The sheep[8] pushing their carts down the aisle—the girls were walking against the usual traffic (not that we have one-way signs or anything)—were pretty hilarious. You could see them, when Queenie's white shoulders dawned on them, kind of jerk, or hop, or hiccup, but their eyes snapped back to their own baskets and on they pushed. I bet you could set off dynamite in an A & P and the people would by and large keep reaching and checking oatmeal off their lists and muttering "Let me see, there was a third thing, began with A, asparagus, no, ah, yes, applesauce!" or whatever it is they do mutter. But there was no doubt, this jiggled them. A few house-slaves in pin curlers even looked around after pushing their carts past to make sure what they had seen was correct.

You know, it's one thing to have a girl in a bathing suit down on the beach, where what with the glare nobody can look at each other much anyway, and another thing in the cool of the A & P, under the fluorescent lights, against all those stacked packages, with her feet paddling along naked over our checkerboard green-and-cream rubber-tile floor.

"Oh Daddy," Stokesie said beside me. "I feel so faint."

"Darling," I said. "Hold me tight." Stokesie's married, with two babies chalked up on his fuselage[9] already, but as far as I can tell that's the only difference. He's twenty-two, and I was nineteen this April.

"Is it done?" he asks, the responsible married man finding his voice. I forgot to say he thinks he's going to be manager some sunny day, maybe in 1990 when it's called the Great Alexandrov and Petrooshki Tea Company or something.

What he meant was, our town is five miles from a beach, with a big summer colony out on the Point, but we're right in the middle of town, and the women generally put on a shirt or shorts or something before they get out of the car into the street. And anyway these are usually women with six children and varicose veins mapping their legs and nobody, including them, could care less. As I say, we're right in the middle of town, and if you stand at our front doors you can see two banks and the Congregational church and the newspaper store and three real-estate offices and about twenty-seven old free-loaders tearing up Central Street because the sewer broke again. It's not as if we're on the Cape; we're north of Boston and there's people in this town haven't seen the ocean for twenty years.

The girls had reached the meat counter and were asking McMahon something. He pointed, they pointed, and they shuffled out of sight behind a pyramid of Diet Delight peaches. All that was left for us to see was old McMahon patting his mouth and looking after them sizing up their joints.[10] Poor kids, I began to feel sorry for them, they couldn't help it.

Now here comes the sad part of the story, at least my family says it's sad but I don't think it's sad myself. The store's pretty empty, it being Thursday afternoon, so there was nothing much to do except lean on the register and wait for the girls to show up again. The whole store was like a pinball machine and I didn't know which tunnel they'd come out of. After a while they come around out of the far aisle, around the light bulbs, records at discount of the Caribbean Six or Tony Martin Sings[11] or some such gunk[12] you wonder they waste the wax on, six packs of candy bars, and plastic toys done`up in cellophane that fall apart when a kid looks at them anyway. Around they come, Queenie still leading the way, and holding a little gray jar in her hand. Slots Three through Seven are unmanned and I could see her wondering between Stokes and me, but Stokesie with his usual luck draws an old party in baggy gray pants who stumbles up with four giant cans of pineapple juice (what do these bums *do* with all that pineapple juice? I've often asked myself) so the girls come to me. Queenie puts down the jar and I take it into my fingers icy cold. Kingfish Fancy Herring Snacks in Pure Sour Cream: 49¢. Now her hands are empty, not a ring or a bracelet, bare as God made them, and I wonder where the money's coming from. Still with that prim look she lifts a folded dollar bill out of the hollow at the center of her nubbled pink top. The jar went heavy in my hand. Really, I thought that was so cute.

Then everybody's luck begins to run out. Lengel comes in from haggling with a truck full of cabbages on the lot and is about to scuttle into that door marked MANAGER behind which he hides all day when the girls touch his eye. Lengel's pretty dreary, teaches Sunday school and the rest, but he doesn't miss that much. He comes over and says, "Girls, this isn't the beach."

Queenie blushes, though maybe it's just a brush of sunburn I was noticing for the first time, now that she was so close. "My mother asked me to pick up a jar of herring snacks." Her voice kind of startled me, the way voices do when you see the people first, coming out so flat and dumb yet kind of tony, too, the way it ticked over "pick up" and "snacks." All of a sudden I slid right down her voice into her living room. Her father and the other men were standing around in ice-cream coats and bow ties and the women were in sandals picking up herring snacks on toothpicks off a big plate and they were all holding drinks the color of water with olives and sprigs of mint in them. When my parents have somebody over they get lemonade and if it's a real racy affair Schlitz[13] in tall glasses with "They'll Do It Every Time" cartoons stencilled on.

"That's all right," Lengel said. "But this isn't the beach." His repeating this struck me as funny, as if it had just occurred to him, and he had been thinking all these years the A & P was a great big dune and he was the head lifeguard. He didn't like my smiling—as I say he doesn't miss much—but he concentrates on giving the girls that sad Sunday-school-superintendent stare.[14]

Queenie's blush is no sunburn now, and the plump one in plaid, that I liked better from the back—a really sweet can—pipes up, "We weren't doing any shopping. We just came in for the one thing."

"That makes no difference," Lengel tells her, and I could see from the way his eyes went that he hadn't noticed she was wearing a two-piece before. "We want you decently dressed when you come in here."

"We are decent," Queenie says suddenly, her lower lip pushing, getting sore now that she remembers her place, a place from which the crowd that runs the A & P must look pretty crummy.[15] Fancy Herring Snacks flashed in her very blue eyes.

"Girls, I don't want to argue with you. After this come in here with your shoulders covered. It's our policy." He turns his back. That's policy for you. Policy is what the kingpins want. What the others want is juvenile delinquency.

All this while, the customers had been showing up with their carts but, you know, sheep, seeing a scene, they had all bunched up on Stokesie, who shook open a paper bag as gently as peeling a peach, not wanting to miss a word. I could feel in the silence everybody getting nervous, most of all Lengel, who asks me, "Sammy, have you rung up this purchase?"

I thought and said "No" but it wasn't about that I was thinking. I go through the punches, 4, 9, GROC, TOT—it's more complicated than you think, and after you do it often enough, it begins to make a little song, that you hear words to, in my case "Hello *(bing)* there, you *(gung)* hap-py pee-pul *(splat"*—the splat being the drawer flying out. I uncrease the bill, tenderly as you may imagine, it just having come from between the two smoothest scoops of vanilla I had ever known were there, and pass a half and a penny into her narrow pink palm, and nestle the herrings in a bag and twist its neck and hand it over, all the time thinking.

The girls, and who'd blame them, are in a hurry to get out, so I say "I quit" to Lengel quick enough for them to hear, hoping they'll stop and watch me, their unsuspected hero. They keep right on going, into the electric eye; the door flies open and they flicker across the lot to their car, Queenie and Plaid and Big Tall Goony-Goony (not that as raw material she was so bad), leaving me with Lengel and a kink in his eyebrow.

"Did you say something, Sammy?"

"I said I quit."

"I thought you did."

"You didn't have to embarrass them."

"It was they who were embarrassing us."

I started to say something that came out "Fiddle-de-doo." It's a saying of my grand-mother's, and I know she would have been pleased.

"I don't think you know what you're saying," Lengel said.

"I know you don't," I said. "But I do." I pull the bow at the back of my apron and start shrugging it off my shoulders. A couple customers that had been heading for my slot begin to knock against each other, like scared pigs in a chute.

Lengel sighs and begins to look very patient and old and gray. He's been a friend of my parents for years. "Sammy, you don't want to do this to your Mom and Dad," he tells me. It's true, I don't. But it seems to me that once you begin a gesture it's fatal not to go through with it. I fold the apron, "Sammy" stitched in red on the pocket, and put it on the counter, and drop the bow tie on top of it. The bow tie is theirs, if you've ever wondered. "You'll feel this for the rest of your life," Lengel says, and I know that's true, too, but remembering how he made that pretty girl blush makes me so scrunchy inside I punch the No Sale tab and the machine whirs "pee-pul" and the drawer splats out. One advantage to this scene taking place in summer, I can follow this up with a clean exit, there's no fumbling around getting your coat and galoshes, I just saunter into the electric eye in my white shirt that my mother ironed the night before, and the door heaves itself open, and outside the sunshine is skating around on the asphalt.

I look around for my girls, but they're gone, of course. There wasn't anybody but some young married screaming with her children about some candy they didn't get by the door of a powder-blue Falcon station wagon. Looking back in the big windows, over the bags of peat moss and aluminum lawn furniture stacked on the pavement, I could see Lengel in my place in the slot, checking the sheep through. His face was dark gray and his back stiff, as if he'd just had an injection of iron, and my stomach kind of fell as I felt how hard the world was going to be to me hereafter.

Notes

[1] can: buttocks.

[2] HiHo crackers: the brand name of a kind of biscuits.

[3] trip sb. up: catch or trap sb. in a mistake.

[4] get sb.'s feathers smoothed: make sb. calm down.

[5] Salem: a town in Massachusetts. It is most widely known as the site of the Salem witchcraft trials of 1692, in which 19 witches were executed.

[6] but never quite makes it: never becomes attractive and beautiful enough.

[7] prima-donna (adj.): like the leading woman singer in an opera.

[8] sheep: Here the word refers to customers in the supermarket.

[9] with two babies…on his fuselage: (humorously used) already got two children. chalk up: credit, charge; fuselage: the main body of an aircraft or big gun; chalk up on one's fuselage: keep a record of the number of foes killed in the battle.

[10] joints: a large piece of beef from the cow's leg. Here the word humorously refers to the girls' fat bare legs.

[11] the Caribbean Six, Tony Martin Sings: the names of music band.

[12] gunk: dirty thing.

[13] Schlitz: the brand name of an alcoholic drink.

[14] Sunday-school-superintendent stare: an unpleasant look of a Sunday school official who is in charge of the children's conducts.

[15] getting sore now that…must look pretty crummy: (She) became painful and angry now that she has realized her lower social status compared with that of the people who run A & P.

Commentary

Throughout the 1950s, many Americans profited from the post World War II economic boom, enjoying a period of long-awaited material prosperity. Business, especially the corporate world, offered the promise of the good life (usually in the suburbs), with its real and symbolic marks of success—house, car, television, and the latest in home appliances. Attached to this ideal were assumptions concerning the "typical" American lifestyle, the "proper" family (in terms of its size and its rigidly defined gender roles), and codes of "appropriate" behavior, all of which contributed to the nation's conformist mentality.

The story *A & P* is a tale of a young man who lets his desires and his anger get a little too far ahead of him and in the end winds up quitting his job. The main character of the story is Sammy, an eighteen year old boy from a small suburb outside Boston who works at an A & P Supermarket. It's his effort to make an impression on a beautiful young lady with bathing suits in the shop that ends up leaving Sammy unemployed.

In this story, Updike draws on memories of his childhood and teenage years for the sort of "small" scenes and stories for which he quickly became famous. "There is a great deal to be said about almost anything," Updike comments in an interview in *Contemporary Authors*. "All people can be equally interesting. ... Now either nobody is a hero or everybody is. I vote for everybody. My subject is the American Protestant small-town middle class. I like middles. It is in middles that extremes clash..." What John Updike does is to remind us of the human costliness of an everyday situation. In *A & P*, there is cost, and a small triumph—and a young man's growing awareness of the "hard" world ahead.

Questions and Exercises

1. List some of the most obvious physical characteristics of the A & P's customers. How do these characteristics make them foils for Queenie and her friends?
2. What rules and conventions are customers expected to follow in a supermarket? How does the behavior of Queenie and her friends violate these conventions?
3. Given what you learn about Sammy in the story, what do you see as his primary motivation for quitting his job?
4. What do you understand from the conclusion of the story? What does Sammy mean when he realizes "how hard the world was going to be to me hereafter"?

John Cheever

John Cheever (1912—1982) was born in Quincy, Massachusetts. His father owned a shoe factory and was relatively wealthy until he lost his business in the 1929 stock market crash and deserted his family. The young Cheever was deeply upset by the breakdown of his parents' relationship. His formal education ended when he was seventeen.

John Cheever was a rather famous American fiction writer. He is often called the "Chekhov of the suburbs". His main subject was the spiritual and emotional emptiness of life. He especially described the manners and morals of middle-class, suburban America, with an ironic humor which softened his basically dark vision. Although he often used his family as material, his daughter Susan Cheever has reminded that "of course none of us *expected* accuracy from my father. He made his living by making up stories."

A number of Cheever's early works were published in *The New Republic*, *Collier's Story,* and *The Atlantic.* In 1935 he began a lifelong association with the *New Yorker*. His best work is his novel *The Wapshot Chronicle* (1957), which was given a National Book Award, and his sequel *The Wapshot Scandal* (1964). *The Stories of John Cheever* (1978) won the Pulitzer Prize for fiction, the National Books Critics Circle Award, and an American Book Award.

The Enormous Radio

Jim and Irene Wescott were the kind of people who seem to strike that satisfactory average of income, endeavor, and respectability that is reached by the statistical reports in college alumni bulletins. They were the parents of two young children, they had been married nine years, they lived on the twelfth floor of an apartment house near Sutton

Place, they went to the theater on an average of 10.3 times a year, and they hoped someday to live in Westchester.[1] Irene Wescott was pleasant, rather plain girl with soft brown hair, and a wide, fine forehead upon which nothing at all had been written, and in the cold weather she wore a coat of fitch skins dyed to resemble mink. You could not say that Jim Westcott looked younger than he was, but you could at least say of him that he seemed to feel younger. He wore his graying hair cut very short, he dressed in the kind of clothes his class had worn at Andover, and his manner was earnest, vehement, and intentionally naïve. The Westcotts differed from their friends, their classmates, and their neighbors, only in an interest they shared in serious music. They went to a great many concerts—although they seldom mentioned this to anyone—and they spent a good deal of time listening to music on the radio.

Their radio was an old instrument, sensitive, unpredictable, and beyond repair. Neither of them understood the mechanics of radio—or when the instrument faltered, Jim would strike the side of the cabinet with his hand. This sometimes helped. One Sunday afternoon, in the middle of the a Schubert[2] quartet, the music faded away altogether. Jim struck the cabinet repeatedly, but there was no response; the Schubert was lost to them forever. He promised to buy Irene a new radio, and on Monday when he came home from work he told her that he had got one. He refused to describe it, and said it would be a surprise for her when it came.

The radio was delivered at the kitchen door the following afternoon, and with the assistance of her maid and the handyman Irene uncrated it and brought it into the living room. She was struck at once with the physical ugliness of the large gumwood cabinet. Irene was proud of her living room, she had chosen its furnishings and colors as carefully as she chose her clothes, and now it seemed to her that her new radio stood among her intimate possessions like an aggressive intruder. She was confounded by the number of dials and switches on the instrument panel, and she studied them thoroughly before she put the plug into a wall socket and turned the radio on. The dials flooded with a malevolent green light, and in the distance she heard the music of a piano quartet. The quintet was in the distance for only an instant; it bore down upon her with a speed greater than light and filled the apartment with the noise of music amplified so mightily that it knocked a china ornament from a table to the floor. She rushed to the instrument and reduced the volume. The violent forces that were snared in the ugly gumwood cabinet made her uneasy. Her children came home from school then, and she took them to the Park. It was not until later in the afternoon that she was able to return to the radio.

The maid had given the children their suppers and was supervising their baths when Irene turned on the radio, reduced the volume, and sat down to listen to a Mozart quintet that she knew and enjoyed. The music came through clearly. The new instrument had a much purer tone, she thought, than the old one. She decided that tone was most important and that she could conceal the cabinet behind the sofa. But as soon as she had made her peace with the radio, the interference began. A crackling sound like the noise of a burning powder fuse began to accompany the singing of the strings. Beyond the music, there was a rustling that reminded Irene unpleasantly of the sea, and as the quintet progressed, these noises were joined by the many others. She tried all the dials and switches but nothing dimmed the interference, and she sat down, disappointed and bewildered, and tried to trace the flight of the melody. The elevator shaft in her building ran beside the living-room wall, and it was the noise of the elevator that gave her a clue to the character of the static. The rattling of the elevator cables and the opening and closing of the elevator doors were reproduced in her loudspeaker, and, realizing that the radio was sensitive to electrical currents of all sorts, she began to discern through the Mozart[3] the ringing of telephone bells, the dialing of phones, and the lamentation of a vacuum cleaner. By listening more carefully, she was able to distinguish doorbells, elevator bells, electric razors, and Waring mixers, whose sounds had been picked up from the apartments that surrounded hers and transmitted through her loudspeaker. The powerful and ugly instrument, with its mistaken sensibility to discord, was more than she could hope to master, so she turned the thing off and went into the nursery to see her children.

When Jim Wescott came home that night, he went to the radio confidently and worked the controls. He had the same sort of experience Irene had had. A man was speaking on the station Jim had chosen, and his voice swung instantly from the distance into a force so powerful that it shook the apartment. Jim turned the volume control and reduced the voice. Then, a minute or two later, the interference began. The ringing of telephones and doorbells set in, joined by the rasp of the elevator doors and the whir of cooking appliances. The character of the noise had changed since Irene had tried the radio earlier; the last of the electric razors was being unplugged, the vacuum cleaners had all been returned to their closets, and the static reflected that change in pace that overtakes the city after the sun goes down. He fiddled with the knobs but couldn't get rid of the noises, so he turned the radio off and told Irene that in the morning he'd call the people who had sold it to him and give them hell.

The following afternoon, when Irene returned to the apartment from a luncheon date, the maid told her that a man had come and fixed the radio. Irene went into the living room before she took off her hat or her furs and tried the instrument. From the loudspeaker came a recording of the "Missouri Waltz." It reminded her of the thin, scratchy music from an old-fashioned phonograph that she sometimes head across the lake where she spent her summers. She waited until the waltz had finished, expecting an explanation of the recording, but there was none. The music was followed by silence, and then the plaintive and scratchy record was repeated. She turned the dial and got a satisfactory burst of Caucasian music—thump of bare feet in the dust and the rattle of coin jewelry—but in the background she could hear the ringing of bells and a confusion of voices. Her children came home from school then, and she turned off the radio and went to the nursery.

When Jim came home that night, he was tired, and he took a bath and changed his clothes. Then he joined Irene in the living room. He had just turned on the radio when the maid announced dinner, so he left it on, and Irene went to the table.

Jim was too tired to make even pretense of sociability, and there was nothing about the dinner to hold Irene's interest, so her attention wandered from the food to the deposits of silver polish on the candlesticks and from there to the music in the other room. She listened for a few minutes to a Chopin[4] prelude and then was surprised to hear a man's voice break in. "For Christ's sake, Kathy," he said, "do you always have to play the piano when I get home?" The music stopped abruptly. "It's the only chance I have," the woman said. "I'm at the office all day." "So am I," the man said. He added something obscene about an upright piano, and slammed a door. The passionate and melancholy music began again.

"Did you hear that?" Irene asked.

"What?" Jim was eating his dessert.

"The radio. A man said something while the music was still going on—something dirty."

"It's probably a play."

"I don't think it *is* a play," Irene said.

They left the table and took their coffee into the living room. Irene asked Jim to try another station. He turned the knob. "Have you seen my garters?" A man asked. "Button me up," a woman said. "Have you seen my garters?" the man said again. "Just button me up and I'll find your garters," the woman said. Jim shifted to another station. "I wish you wouldn't leave apple cores in the ashtrays," a man said. "I hate the smell."

"This is strange," Jim said.

"Isn't it?" Irene said.

Jim turned the knob again. "On the coast of Coromandel where the early pumpkins blow," a woman with a pronounced English accent said, "in the middle of the woods lived the Yonghy-Bonghy-Bò. Two old chairs, and half a candle, one old jug without a handle…"

"My God!" Irene cried. "That's the Sweeneys' nurse."

"These were all his worldly goods," the British voice continued.

"Turn that thing off," Irene said." Maybe they can hear *us*." Jim switched the radio off. "That was Miss Armstrong, the Sweeneys' nurse," Irene said. "She must be reading to the little girl. They live in 17-B. I've talked with Miss Armstrong in the Park. I know her voice very well. We must be getting other people's apartments."

"That's impossible," Jim said.

"Well, that was the Sweeneys' nurse," Irene said hotly. "I know her voice. I know it very well. I'm wondering if they can hear us."

Jim turned the switch. First from a distance and then nearer, nearer, as if borne on the wind, came the pure accents of the Sweeneys' nurse again: *"Lady Jingly! Lady Jingly!"* she said, *"sitting where the pumpkins blow, will you come and be my wife?* said the Yonghy-Bonghy-Bò…*"*

Jim went over to the radio and said, "Hello" loudly into the speaker.

"I am tired of living singly," the nurse went on, "on this coast so wild and shingly, I'm a-weary of my life; if you'll come and be my wife, quite serene would be my life..."

"I guess she can't hear us," Irene said. "Try something else."

Jim turned to another station, and the living room was filled with the uproar of a cocktail party that had overshot its mark. Someone was playing the piano and singing the "Whiffenpoof Song,"[5] and the voices that surrounded the piano were vehement and happy. "Eat some more sandwiches," a woman shrieked. There were screams of laughter and a dish of some sort crashed to the floor.

"Those must be the Fullers, in 11-E," Irene said. "I knew they were giving a party this afternoon. I saw her in the liquor store. Isn't this too divine? Try something else. See if you can get those people in 18-C."

The Westcotts overheard that evening a monologue on salmon fishing in Canada, a bridge game, running comments on home movies of what had apparently been a fortnight at Sea Island, and a bitter family quarrel about an overdraft at the bank. They turned off their radio at midnight and went to bed, weak with laughter. Sometime in the night, their son began to call for a glass of water and Irene got one and took it to his room. It was very early. All the lights in the neighborhood were extinguished, and from the boy's window she could see the empty street. She went into the living room and tried the radio. There was some faint coughing, a moan, and then a man spoke. "Are you all right, darling?" he asked. "Yes," a woman said wearily. "Yes, I'm all right, I guess," and then she added with great feeling, "But, you know, Charlie, I don't feel like myself any more. Sometimes there are about fifteen or twenty minutes in the week when I feel like myself. I don't like to go to another doctor, because the doctor's bills are so awful already, but I just don't feel like myself, Charlie. I just never feel like myself." They were not young, Irene thought. She guessed from the timbre of their voices that they were middle-aged. The restrained melancholy of the dialogue and the draft from the bedroom window made her shiver, and she went back to bed.

The following morning, Irene cooked breakfast for the family—the maid didn't come up from her room in the basement until ten—braided her daughter's hair, and waited at the door until her children and her husband had been carried away in the elevator. Then she went into the living room and tried the radio. "I don't want to go to school," a child screamed. "I hate school. I won't go to school. I hate school." "You will go to school," an enraged woman said. "We paid eight hundred dollars to get you into that school and you'll go if it kills you." The next number on the dial produced the worn record of the "Missouri Waltz". Irene shifted the control and invaded the privacy of several breakfast tables. She overheard demonstrations of indigestion, carnal love, abysmal vanity, faith, and despair. Irene's life was nearly as simple and sheltered as it appeared to be, and the forthright and sometimes brutal language that came from the loudspeaker that morning astonished and troubles her. She continued to listen until her maid came in. Then she turned off the radio quickly, since this insight, she realized, was a furtive one.

Irene had a luncheon date with a friend that day, and she left her apartment a little after twelve. There were a number of women in the elevator when it stopped at her floor. She stared at their handsome and impassive faces, their furs, and the cloth flowers in their hats. Which one of them had been at Sea Island? She wondered. Which one had overdrawn her bank account? The elevator stopped at the tenth floor and a woman with a pair of Skye terriers joined them, her hair was rigged high on her head and she wore a mink cape. She was humming the "Missouri Waltz."

Irene had two Martinis at lunch, and she looked searchingly at her friend and wondered what her secrets were. They had intended to go shopping after lunch, but Irene excused herself and went home. She told the maid that she was not to be disturbed; then she went into the living room, closed the doors, and switched on the radio. She heard, in the course of the afternoon, the halting conversation of a woman entertaining her aunt, the hysterical conclusion of a luncheon party, and hostess briefing her maid about some cocktail guests. "Don't give the best Scotch to anyone who hasn't white hair," the hostess said. "See if you can get rid of the liver paste before you pass those hot things, and could you lend me five dollars? I want to tip the elevator man."

As the afternoon waned, the conversations increased in intensity. From where Irene sat, she could see the open sky above the East River. There were hundreds of clouds in the sky, as though the south wind had broken the winter into pieces and were blowing it north, and on her radio she could hear the arrival of cocktail guests and the return of children and businessmen from their schools and offices. "I found a good-sized diamond on the bathroom floor this morning," a woman said. "It must have fallen out of the bracelet Mrs. Dunston was wearing last night." "We'll sell it," a man said. "Take it down to the jeweler on Madison Avenue[6] and sell it. Mrs. Dunston won't know the difference, and we could use a couple of hundred bucks…" "Oranges and lemons, say the bells of St. Clement's," the Sweeneys' nurse sang. "Halfpence and farthings," say the bells of St. Martin's. "When will you pay me?" say the bells at old Bailey[7]… "It's not a hat," a woman cried, and at her back roared a cocktail party. "It's not a hat, it's a love affair. That's what Walter Florell said. He said it's not a hat, it's a love affair," and then, in a lower voice, the same woman added, "Talk to somebody, for Christ's sake, honey, talk to somebody. If she catches you standing here not talking to anybody, she'll take us off her invitation list, and I love these parties."

The Wescotts were going out for dinner that night, and when Jim came home, Irene was dressing. She seemed sad and vague, and he brought her a drink. They were dining with their friends in the neighborhood, and they walked to where they were going. The sky was broad and filled with light. It was of those splendid spring evenings that excite memory and desire, and the air that touched their hands and faces felt very soft. A Salvation Army[8] band was on the corner playing "Jesus Is Sweeter". Irene drew her husband's arm and held him there for a minute, to hear the music." They are really such nice people, aren't they?" she said. They have such nice faces. Actually, they are so much nicer than a lot of the people we know." She took a bill from her purse and walked over and dropped it into the tambourine. There was in her face, when she returned to her husband, a look of radiant melancholy that he was not familiar with. And her conduct at the dinner party that night seemed strange to him, too. She interrupted her hostess rudely and stared at the people across the table from her with an intensity for which she would have punished her children.

It was still mild when they walked home from the party, and Irene looked up at the spring stars. "How far the little candle throws its beams," she exclaimed. "So fine a good deed in a naughty world." She waited that night until Jim had fallen asleep, and then went out into the living room and turned on the radio.

Jim came home at about six the next night. Emma, the maid, let him in, and he had taken off his hat and was taking off his coat when Irene ran into the hall. Her face was shining with tears and her hair was disordered. "Go up to 16-C, Jim!" she screamed. "Don't take off your coat. Go up to 16-C. Mr. Osborn's beating his wife. They've been quarreling since four o'clock, and now he is hitting her. Go up there and stop him."

From the radio in the living room, Jim heard screams, obscenities, and thuds. "You know you don't have to listen to this sort of thing," he said. He strode into the living room and turned the switch. "It's indecent," he said. "It's like looking into windows. You know you don't have to listen to this sort of thing. You can turn it off."

"Oh, it's so terrible, it's so dreadful," Irene was sobbing. "I've been listening all day, and it's so depressing."

"Well, if it's so depressing, why do you listen to it? I bought this dammed radio to give you some pleasure," he said. "I paid a great deal of money for it. I thought it might make you happy. I wanted to make you happy."

"Don't, don't, don't, don't quarrel with me," she moaned, and laid her head on his shoulder. "All the others have been quarreling all day. Everybody's been quarreling. They're all worried about money. Mrs. Hutchinson's mother is dying of cancer in Florida and they don't have enough money to send her to the Mayo Clinic. At least, Mr. Hutchinson says they don't have enough money. And some woman in this building is having an affair with the handyman—with that hideous handyman. It's too disgusting. And Mrs. Melville has heart trouble, and Mr. Hendricks is going to lose his job in April and Mrs. Hendricks is horrid about the whole thing and that girl that plays the "Missouri Waltz" is a whore, a common whore, and the elevator man has tuberculosis and Mr.

Osborn has been beating his wife." She wailed, she trembled with grief and checked the stream of tears down her face with the heel of her palm.

"Well why do you have to listen?" Jim asked again. "Why do you have to listen to this stuff if it makes you miserable?"

"Oh, don't, don't, don't," she cried. "Life is too terrible, too sordid and awful. But we've never been like that, have we, darling? Have we? I mean, we've always been good and decent and loving to one another, haven't we? And we have two children, two beautiful children. Our lives aren't sordid, are they, darling? Are they?" She flung her arms around his neck and drew his face down to hers. "We're happy, aren't we, darling? We are happy, aren't we?"

"Of course we're happy," he said tiredly. He began to surrender his resentment. "Of course we are happy. "I'll have that dammed radio fixed or taken away tomorrow." He stroked her soft hair. "My poor girl," he said.

"You love me, don't you?" she asked. "And we're not hypercritical or worried about money or dishonesty, are we?"

A man came in the morning and fixed the radio. Irene turned it on cautiously and was happy to hear a California-wine commercial and a recording of Beethoven's Ninth Symphony, including Schiller's "Ode to Joy".[9] She kept the radio on all day and nothing untoward came toward the speaker.

A Spanish suite was being played when Jim came home. "Is everything all right?" he asked. His face was pale, she thought. They had some cocktails and went to dinner to the "Anvil Chorus" from *Il Trovatore*.[10] This was followed by Debussy's "La Mer".[11] "I paid the bill for the radio today," Jim said. "It cost four hundred dollars. I hope you'll get some enjoyment out of it"

"Oh, I'm sure I will," Irene said.

"Four hundred dollars is a good deal more than I can afford," he went on. "I wanted to get something that you'd enjoy. It's the last extravagance we'll indulge in this year. I see that you haven't paid your clothing bills yet. I saw them on your dressing table." He looked directly at her. "Why did you tell me you paid them? Why did you lie to me?"

"I just didn't want you to worry, Jim," she said. She drank some water. "I'll be able to pay my bills out of this month's allowance. There were the slipcovers last month, and that party."

"You've got to learn to handle the money I give you a little more intelligently, Irene," he said. "You've got to understand that we don't have as much money this year as we had last. I had a very sobering talk with Mitchell today. No one is buying anything. We're spending all of our time promoting new issues, and you know how long that takes. I'm not getting any younger you know. I'm thirty-seven. My hair will be gray next year. I haven't done as well as I hoped to do. And I don't suppose things will get any better."

"Yes dear," she said.

"We've got to start cutting down," Jim said. "We've got to think of the children. To be perfectly frank with you, I worry about money a great deal. I'm not at all sure of the future. No one is. If anything should happen to me, there's the insurance, but that won't go very far today. I've worked awfully hard to give you and the children a comfortable life," he said bitterly. "I don't like to see all my energies, all my youth, wasted in fur coast and radios and slipcovers and—"

"Please Jim," she said. "Please. They'll hear us."

"Who'll hear us? Emma can't hear us."

"The radio."

"Oh, I'm sick!" He shouted. "I'm sick to death of your apprehensiveness. The radio can't hear us. Nobody can hear us. And what if they can hear us? Who cares?"

Irene got up from the table and went into the living room. Jim went to the door and shouted from there. "Why are you so Christly all of a sudden? What's turned you overnight into a convent girl? You stole your mother's jewelry before they probated her will. You never gave your sister a cent of that money that was intended for her—not even when she needed it. You made Grace Howland's life miserable, and where was all your piety and all your virtue when you went to that abortionist? I'll never forget how cool you were. You packed your bag and went off to have that child murdered as if you were going to Nassau. If you'd had any reasons, if you had any good reasons—"

Irene stood for a minute before the hideous cabinet, disgraced and sickened, but she held her hand on the switch before she extinguished the music and the voices, hoping the instrument might speak to her kindly, that she might hear the Sweeney's nurse. Jim continued to shout at her from the door. The voice on the radio was suave and noncommital. "An early-morning railroad disaster in Tokyo," the loudspeaker said, "killed twenty-nine people. A fire in a Catholic hospital near Buffalo for the care of blind children was extinguished early this morning by nuns. The temperature is forty-seven. The humidity is eighty-nine."

Notes

[1] Sutton Place: a square in Manhattan, New York City where the wealthy live; Westchester: a wealthy suburban county just outside New York City.

[2] Schubert (1797—1828): Austrian composer.

[3] Mozart (1756—1791): Austrian composer.

[4] Chopin (1810—1849): Polish composer and pianist.

[5] Whiffenpoof Song: Yale University drinking song.

[6] Madison Avenue: a street in Manhattan, New York City, center of the advertising business.

[7] Oranges…at Old Bailey: Traditional English song.
[8] Salvation Army: International Christian religious and charitable movement organized and operated on military lines. Its purpose is to preach the Gospel (New Testament of the Bible) and achieve spiritual, moral, and physical reclamation.
[9] Beethoven's Ninth Symphony: The last movement includes a choir and soloists, singing "Ode to Joy", a poem by the famous German poet, Schiller.
[10] *Il Trovatore*—Anvil Chorus: music composition from Verdi, a great master of Italian opera.
[11] Debussy's "La Mer": music composition from Debussy, a great French composer.

Commentary

The Enormous Radio is usually seen as John Cheever's lyrical short story. It is about a middle class woman who mysteriously picks up her neighbors' intimate conversations over her radio, which acts as a wake-up call for Jim and Irene Westcott. The young couple at first seem to lead a good life and be exempt from any problems in their daily life, not at all inferior to any of their former schoolmates. However, the radio proves them wrong even though they have believed their life to be better than their neighbors'.

From the story we know that the Westcotts' life is simply like a freshly painted used car: nice and shiny on the outside but falling apart on the inside. What is ironic is that the Westcotts are far from being a "perfect family", and the community they try to conform to is just as flawed and imperfect as the Westcotts themselves. Jim and Irene (Jim in particular) begin to question the "perfection" of their own marriage. Finally, they end up having a violent confrontation about dishonesty and hypocrisy. As is widely accepted, dishonesty, hypocrisy, and physical abuse are not characteristic qualities of a "perfect" marriage.

What the enormous radio has done for the Westcotts is to make them see that they should get themselves out of hypocrisy and face reality objectively. And what John Cheever wants to tell the middle class people is to fix their own problems first rather than hypocritically worry about the outside images. The implied fact is clear: life nowadays is not easy, and in this modern world the lives of our neighbors are just as troubled as our own.

Questions and Exercises

1. Is there anything in the story besides the radio itself that could be labeled as an element of fantasy?
2. Is most of the information brought by the radio about the neighbors shocking or sordid? What do all the exposures of private lives add up to?
3. Does possession of the radio give the Wescotts any advantages or disadvantages over their neighbors? Imagine that you yourself had such a radio, what might it reveal to you about people's present life today?

Part 5

A Guide to Appreciating English Essays

1 Introduction

The primary aim of essays is to discuss a matter, to express a point of view, to persuade people to accept a thesis on any subject, to reveal certain emotional aspects of life, or simply to amuse or entertain the reader. An essay differs from a "treatise" or "dissertation" in that the former is addressed to a general rather than a specialized audience; as a result, the essay discusses its subject in non-technical fashion, and often with a liberal use of such devices as anecdote, striking illustration, and humor to enhance its appeal.

Essay as a literary genre has a long history. The Greeks and the Romans wrote essays long before the genre was given what became its standard name by Montaigne's French *Essais* in 1580. Francis Bacon, later in the 16th century, started the English use of the term in his own *Essays,* most of which are short discussions such as "Of Studies", "Of Truth," "Of Marriage and the Single Life." Alexander Pope adopted the term for his expository compositions in verse, *The Essay on Criticism* (1711) and *The Essay on Man* (1733). In the early 18th century Joseph Addison and Sir Richard Steele's *Tattler* and *Spectator,* with their many successors, gave to the essay written in prose its standard modern form.

In the early 19th century the founding of new types of magazines gave great impetus to the writing of essays and made them a major genre of literature. This was the age when William Hazlitt, Charles Lamb, and later in the century, Robert Louis Stevenson brought the English essay—especially the personal essay—to a level that has not been surpassed. Major American essayists in the 19th century include Washington Irving, Ralph Waldo Emerson, Henry David Thoreau, James Russell Lowell, and Mark Twain. In our own era the many periodicals pour out scores of essays every week, most of which are formal in type. Virginia Woolf, George Orwell, E. M. Forster, James Thurber, E. B. White, Joan Didion, Susan Sontag, and Toni Morrison, are notable 20th-century practitioners of the English essays.

In terms of stylistic division, an essay fits the category of non-fictional prose, and it has the distinction between formal and informal.

The formal essay, or article, is relatively impersonal. The author writes as an authority, or at least as a highly knowledgeable person, and expounds the subject in an orderly way. Examples can be found in various scholarly journals, as well as among the serious articles on current topics and issues in any of the magazines addressed to a thoughtful audience, such as *Harper's Commentary, Scientific American,* and so on.

In the informal essay (or "familiar" or "personal essay"), the author assumes a tone of intimacy with his audience, tends to deal with everyday things rather than with public affairs or specialized topics, and writes in a relaxed, self-revelatory, and sometimes whimsical fashion. Popular examples of modern essays are to be found in any issue of *The New Yorker* and *Readers' Digest.*

2 Main Types of English Essays

According to subjects and forms, essays may fall into five main types: they are the classic essay, the periodical essay, the philosophical essay, the autobiographical essay, and the critical essay, though such divisions may sometimes be too arbitrary. For instance, Bacon's essays are classical because they have revealed the spirit of classicism, but it is hard to deny that they are highly philosophical. Therefore, our classifications are just to meet the convenience of teachers and students in the course of class teaching and learning.

2.1 The classic essay

The term "classic" may imply three meanings: 1) the work of the highest rank in any nation that is seen as the greatest masterpiece; 2) any work that follows the Greek and Roman tradition of writing; and 3) the work that conforms to strict rules or elegant forms, produced from intellect rather than imagination, and avoiding obscurity or self-indulgence.

The classic essay possesses in much the same way the following characteristics of classic literature:

(1) The classic essay is of clarity, splendour, sublimity, and philosophicality.

(2) The classic essay adopts much of a lasting trait from classic literature in subjects, styles, and even language itself. So it is of typical classic beauty and strength.

(3) The classic essay places great importance upon strict rules, elegant forms, refined diction, confined syntax, and balanced structure.

(4) In subject matter, the classic essay deals with a variety of themes, such as philosophy, literary criticism, arts, politics, history, social problems, travels, and other important aspects of life.

2.2 The periodical essay

The periodical essay usually refers to the type of essay that appeared in the journals, as in *The Rambler*, *The Tatler* and *The Spectator*.

In the late 17th and early 18th centuries there appeared the London coffeehouse, of which the most famous were Button's and Will's, and coffeehouses had become popular places for the exchange of news and opinions. It was in London coffeehouses that the most famous of the early "periodicals" were born. These writers include Sir Richard Steele, Joseph Addison, and so on.

By the 19th century, most eminent men of letters attempted to broaden their audiences by means of essays in the press, and in the 20th century, the influence of journalism pervaded the most important works of some authors. Such famous writers include G. B. Shaw, H. G. Wells, Virginia Woolf, Aldous Huxley, etc.

2.3 The philosophical essay

The philosophical essay is a classification not of form, but of subject matter. It covers a variety of subjects ranging from philosophy to politics, religion, morals and aesthetics, etc. Early writers of this genre include Aristotle on rhetoric and metaphysics, Cicero on the pleasantness of old age, and Saint Augustine on theology. The Frenchman Montaigne made the form of essay achieve better than possibly any other form of writing by pursuing an ethical purpose without pompousness.

With the advent of a keener political awareness in the 18th-century Enlightenment, the essay became all-important as a vehicle for criticism of society and religion. Because of its flexibility, brevity, and potentiality both for ambiguity and for allusions to current conditions and events, it was an ideal tool for philosophical reformers.

The role of the essay in the American literature of ideas is significant, as can be seen in several of Emerson's philosophical essays. John Dewey continued the efforts of such predecessors as Thomas Jefferson and Benjamin Franklin to advocate his philosophical ideas.

2.4 The biographical essay

The biographical essay is a form of nonfictional writing of biography or autobiography. As a branch of imaginative literature, it seeks to convey a sense of the individuality and significance of the subject through creative insight.

The origins of the biographical essay are remote. Examples in Western languages are found in the Old Testament stories, in the Greek and Scandinavian epics. The sayings and teachings of wise and holy men, such as Plato who provided many passages of the biographical essay. The Renaissance England produced biographical essays of considerable interest, achievements including Sir Thomas More's *Life of John Picas, Earl of Mirandola*

(1510), Francis Bacon established himself as the representative of the Elizabethan writers of biographical essays, with *The History of Henry VII* (1622).

The 17th century was the most important period for the development of the English biographical essay, and prepared much for the appearance of the 18th century masterpieces of the genre: *The Lives of the English Poets* (1779—1781) by Samuel Johnson, and *The Life of Johnson* (1791) by James Boswell. Johnson is one of the most influential and accomplished biographical essayists, presenting rounded and detailed portraits of people. And Boswell's *Life of Johnson* is considered by many as the supreme example of this genre. Notable British and American essayists include: Coleridge, Southey, Carlyle, Aldous Huxley, Bertrand Russell, and Benjamin Franklin.

2.5 Literary criticism

Literary criticism is a term applied to the comparison, analysis, interpretation and evaluation of works of literature. There are many ways in which criticism may be classified. Generally speaking, it consists of theoretical criticism and practical criticism (sometimes called applied criticism). Theoretical criticism undertakes to establish, on the basis of general principles, a set of terms, distinctions, and categories to be applied to the identification and analysis of literature, as well as the criteria by which these works and their writers are to be evaluated.

Practical criticism concerns itself with the discussion of particular works and writers. The earliest great work of theoretical criticism was Aristotle's *Poetics* (the 4th century B.C.). Another well-known author is John Dryden who wrote *Lives of the English Poets* (1779—1781).

Modern time is the greatest critical age. Literary criticism, as the art of judging literature, has greatly prospered. Owing to a vast expansion of human knowledge in all fields, old notions of criticism have been reviewed and reinterpreted, and new approaches to criticism have often cross-fertilized one another. In a sense literary criticism seemed to be of greater importance and significance than ever before.

3 Main Techniques in Essay Writing

Broadly speaking, essayists use the following six techniques in developing their essays: argumentation, exposition, characterization, narration, description, and cause-and- effect.

3.1 Argumentation

Argumentation is a form of discourse in which reason is used to influence or change people's ideas or actions. Writers adopt argumentation most frequently when writing formal essays or speeches.

Persuasion is the main type of argumentation. It is intended to make its readers adopt a certain opinion or perform an action or do both. Modern examples of persuasion include political speeches, television commercials, and newspaper editorials.

To be persuasive, writers must back up their opinions with objective evidence—acts, incidents, and examples. Helen Keller in her essay *Three Days to See* backs up an opinion with evidence when she writes that many husbands do not know the color of their wife's eyes. Persuasive writers also offer logical arguments, or reasons, in support of their opinions. Helen Keller, again, gives a logical argument for appreciating the sense of sight when she recounts that she has only been able to touch the objects at the Museum of Natural History.

3.2 Exposition

Exposition is the kind of writing that is intended primarily to present information. Although it is used in fiction as well as nonfiction, the most familiar form it takes is in essays.

Unlike narration or description, exposition aims at the clear presentation or explanation of ideas. In general, it answers the questions how and why. The writer of an exposition is always a man thinking, interpreting, informing and persuading by the use of evidence and reasoning. Exposition, therefore, discusses its subject not in time or space, but by logic.

Expository paragraphs contain two different classes of statements. The first—a general, rather abstract statement—is called *the topic sentence.* In the topic sentence, the writer asserts his belief, opinion, evaluation or conclusion about the subject of a paragraph. The second type of statements in a paragraph consists of particular facts, examples, illustrations, and supporting details to prove writer's point.

The principles of effective exposition are the same as those for narrative or descriptive writing, but the patterns of organization are different simply because the goals of writing are different. An exposition writer may employ common methods of logic and thinking and develop his material by offering examples as evidence, by comparing and contrasting, by showing cause and effect, by defining, by arguing, and so on, and each of these methods describes a particular form of development or arrangement of ideas. In many cases, there will be one method that dominates in an exposition, but it is not uncommon that these methods are often employed in combinations suited to the subject matter.

3.3 Characterization

Characterization means the creation of imaginary persons so that they seem lifelike. Although this method is mostly used in fiction writing, it can also be effective in writing an essay when some incidences of characters are involved. There are three fundamental methods of characterization: (a) the explicit presentation by the author of the character through direct exposition; (b) the presentation of the character in action, with little or no explicit comment by the author; and (c) the presentation from within a character about the character's inner self.

3.4 Narration

Narration is the major technique used in expository writing of essays. It can be fiction or nonfiction, depending on whether the characters and events in the story are imagined or real. A biography or an autobiography belongs to nonfiction narration.

A central figure in every narrative is the narrator, or the person who tells the story. Successful narration gives an exact picture of things as they occur, so it must grow out of good observation and clear arrangement of details in logical sequence. What's more, the narrator's attitudes may add a distinct or personal flavor to the story.

At the core of most effective narration is a conflict or problem. Successive events in the story lead to a climax, or emotional high point. After that comes the resolution, the final outcome of the story. In the resolution, seemingly unrelated details may be tied together, questions answered, or conflicts resolved.

3.5 Description

Description can be found in almost all kinds of essay writings. It is a part of storytelling, whether the story is fictional or real. Good descriptive writing is made up of many details: specific pictures, colors, shapes, sounds, smells, tastes, textures, and even emotions. With description, the writer tries to make the reader see, feel, and hear by showing rather than by merely telling. It is through the use of specific details and concrete language that abstract thoughts are made vividly real. By showing sensory impressions and the thought these impressions evoke, the essayist can make a profound comment about an experience or condition in life.

3.6 Cause-and-effect

A cause-and-effect essay refers to a piece of writing in which the events in the story are often interrelated by cause and effect. That is, one event—*the cause*—is the reason that another event—*the effect*—takes place. There are three fundamental ways of organizing a cause-and-effect essay: (a) the single-cause and many-effects, (b) the many-causes and single-effect, and (c) a combination of (a) and (b).

The effectiveness and convincingness of this kind of essay are mainly achieved by citing specific facts and precise statistical figures. Apart from these, the writer may also resort to the device of contrast and comparison to further enhance the reader's awareness of the severity or urgency of a situation or problem.

But please note that the above listed writing techniques are not at all exclusive from one another. More often than not, great essayists usually mingle them together skillfully in writing according to actual cases.

Selected Readings of English Essays

Francis Bacon

Francis Bacon (1561—1626) was the great British writer of renaissance and one of the pioneers of modern scientific thought. His essays chiefly fall into three categories: philosophical, purely literary, and professional.

Bacon was accused of bribery and corruption. Found guilty, he was imprisoned in the Tower, fined and debarred from holding public office. The disgrace hurt him deeply, but it enabled him to settle down to his real life-work as a writer and a philosopher.

In 1605, Bacon had already published *The Advancement of Learning,* a study of scientific progress. In the 1620s, he devoted himself to his immensely ambitious scheme for reconstructing the foundations of all human knowledge. He planned to base all knowledge upon scientific observation—an undertaking which was quite beyond the powers of any single man. It was his never stopping pursuit of truth that eventually caused his death. One winter day in 1626, he left his coach to gather snow for some scientific experiment—a study of the effects of cold as a preservative. During this experiment he caught pneumonia, and died in April the same year.

Bacon's literary fame chiefly rests on his Essays. There are "metaphysical" qualities in his prose which links it to early 17th century verse. He has been entitled "the first modern mind" and "father of inductive reasoning".

Bacon's works were extremely successful and much liked by the public for at least three reasons. Firstly, his literary form was fresh to the English public. The French philosopher Montaigne first called his prose writing *essays,* and Bacon borrowed the title from him. But different from Montaigne's personal and informal style, Bacon's style is more formal and more tightly organized. Then, his essays cover a variety of subjects, ranging from abstract subjects such as "the composition of beauty" to practical matters such as "friendship". Bacon's essays greatly helped people to form a new attitude towards life and death, stimulate a stronger desire to explore the unknown fields of knowledge, and develop a better understanding of one's inner self in relation to the outside world. Finally, these essays, though short, are elegantly phrased, extremely terse and clear in expression, and full of wisdom. They cannot only offer people useful and practical advice in personal affairs, but also encourage people to play more active roles in their social lives.

Of Studies

Studies serve for delight, for ornament, and for ability. Their chief use for delight, is in privateness and retiring;[1] for ornament, is in discourse; and for ability, is in the judgment and disposition of business. For expert men[2] can execute, and perhaps judge of particulars, one by one; but the general counsels, and the plots and marshalling of affairs,[3] come best, from those that are learned. To spend too much time in studies is sloth; to use them too much for ornament, is affectation; to make judgment wholly by their rules, is the humor of a scholar. They perfect nature, and are perfected by experience; for natural abilities are like natural plants, that need pruning[4] by study; and studies themselves do give forth directions too much at large, except they be bounded in by experience. Crafty men[5] contemn studies, simple men admire them, and wise men use them, for they teach not their own use; but that is a wisdom without them, and above them, won by observation. Read not to contradict and confute, nor to believe and take for granted, nor to find talk and discourse, but to weigh and consider. Some books are to be tasted, others to be swallowed, and some few to be chewed and digested; that is, some books are to be read only in parts; others to be read, but not curiously;[6] and some few to be read wholly, and with diligence and attention. Some books also may be read by deputy, and extracts made of them by others, but that would be only in the less important arguments and the meaner sort of books; else distilled books are like common distilled waters, flashy things[7]. Reading maketh a full man; conference a ready man; and writing an exact man. And therefore, if a man write little, he had need have a great memory; if he confer little, he had need have a present wit;[8] and if he read little, he had need have much cunning, to seem to know, that he doth not. Histories make men wise; poets, witty; the mathematics, subtle; natural philosophy, deep; moral, grave; logic and rhetoric, able to contend. Abeunt studia in mores.[9] Nay, there is no stond[10] or impediment in the wit, but may be wrought out by fit studies; like as diseases of the body, may have appropriate exercises. Bowling is good for the stone and reins;[11] shooting for the lungs and breast; gentle walking for the stomach; riding for the head; and the like. So if a man's wit be wandering, let him study the mathematics; for in demonstrations, if his wit be called away never so little, he must begin again. If his wit be not apt to distinguish or find differences, let him study the schoolmen;[12] for they are *cumini sectores*.[13] If he be not apt to beat over matters,[14] and to call up one thing to prove and illustrate another, let him study the lawyers' cases. So every defect of the mind, may have a special receipt.[15]

Notes

[1] in privateness and retiring: when alone and away from work.

[2] expert men: men who learn much from experience and little from study.

[3] the plots and marshalling of affairs: the planning and handling of practical matters.
[4] pruning: cultivating.
[5] crafty men: shrewd and cunning men.
[6] not curiously: not attentively; without much care.
[7] distilled waters: infusions of herbs, used as home remedies; flashy things: tasteless and insipid matters.
[8] a present wit: a ready mind.
[9] Abeunt studia in mores: (Quoted from Ovid, Heroides, XV, 83) Studies pass into the characters; studies go to make a man's character.
[10] stond: obstacle.
[11] the stone and reins: the bladder and kidneys.
[12] the schoolmen: scholastic philosophers.
[13] *cumini sectores*: dividers of cumin seeds; hair splitters.
[14] beat over matters: examine things with great care.
[15] receipt: cure, prescription.

Commentary

Bacon's *Of Studies* has long been a classic in English prose throughout history. Though it is made up of only one short paragraph, its message is conveyed with sweeping effect and overwhelming power. The text forcibly focuses on the controlling idea "studies serve for delight, for ornament, and for ability." The author employs many devices in his writing, among which ellipsis, parallel construction and antithesis are perhaps the most striking.

Of Studies effectively expresses the wit and wisdom that are characteristic of Bacon as both a scholar and a philosopher. "To spend too much time in studies is sloth;" he wrote, "to use them too much for ornament is affectation; to make judgement wholly by their rules is the humor of a scholar." Obviously, Bacon did not value book knowledge without putting it into real practice. This essay, compact in style, terse in expression, and profound in thoughts, certainly belong to the high rank of prose in world literature.

Questions and Exercises

1. Bacon's maxims have always been famous. Locate in the selected essay some lines that have now become common sayings.
2. Bacon has often been entitled "the first modern mind" and "father of inductive reasoning". Do you agree? Find examples from the above essay to support your statement.
3. Compare your study habits, and try to draw something valuable from this selected essay.

Samuel Johnson

Samuel Johnson (1709—1784) is perhaps the most quoted of English writers next only to William Shakespeare. The latter part of the 18th century is often (in English-speaking countries, of course) called, simply, the Age of Johnson.

Before 1748, Johnson published practically nothing under his own name. Then he began to work on *A Dictionary of the English Language*. In June 1746 he signed an agreement with a group of publishers who would pay him 1,575 pounds. With six copyists to help him, he read through numerous books by "standard authors" and marked their use of various words. Johnson then wrote definitions for over 40,000 words, with different shades of meaning, illustrating the meanings with about 114,000 quotations that he had gathered. His work has served as the basis for all English dictionaries since. The Dictionary was published in 1755. Oxford University rewarded him with a Master of Arts degree, which came in time for him to include it on the title page of the Dictionary.

Apart from his immense contribution as a lexicographer, Johnson is also remembered as an essayist, a biographer, a critic, a poet, a playwright, and a literary leader. His reputation also rests upon his large personality, mostly revealed by his biography *Life of Johnson* written by James Boswell.

On Idleness

Many moralists have remarked, that Pride[1] has of all human vices the widest dominion, appears in the greatest multiplicity of forms, and lies hid under the greatest variety of disguises; of disguises, which, like the moon's veil of brightness, are both its luster and its shade, and betray it to others, though they hide it from ourselves.

It is not my intention to degrade Pride from this preeminence of mischief, yet I know not whether Idleness may not maintain a very doubtful and obstinate competition.[2]

There are some that profess Idleness in its full dignity, who call themselves the Idle, as Busiris[3] in the play "calls himself the Proud"; who boast that they do nothing, and thank their stars that they have nothing to do; who sleep every night till they can sleep no longer, and rise only that exercise may enable them to sleep again; who prolong the reign of darkness by double curtains, and never see the sun but to "tell him how they hate his beams";[4] whose whole labor is to vary the postures of indulgence, and whose day differs from their night but as a couch or chair differs from a bed.

These are the true and open votaries of Idleness,[5] for whom she weaves the garlands of poppies, and into whose cup she pours the waters of oblivion; who exist in a state of unruffled stupidity, forgetting and forgotten; who have long ceased to live, and at whose death the survivors can only say, that they have ceased to breathe.

But Idleness predominates in many lives where it is not suspected; for being a vice which terminates in itself, it may be enjoyed without injury to others; and is therefore not watched[6] like Fraud, which endangers property, or like Pride, which naturally seeks its gratifications in another's inferiority. Idleness is a silent and peaceful quality, that neither raises envy by ostentation, nor hatred by opposition; and therefore nobody is busy to censure or detect it.

As Pride sometimes is hid under humility, Idleness is often covered by turbulence and hurry.[7] He that neglects his known duty and real employment, naturally endeavors to crowd his mind with something that may bar out[8] the remembrance of his own folly, and does any thing but what he ought to do with eager diligence, that he may keep himself in his own favor.

Some are always in a state of preparation, occupied in previous measures, forming plans, accumulating materials, and providing for the main affair. These are certainly under the secret power of Idleness. Nothing is to be expected from the workman whose tools are forever to be sought. I was once told by a great master, that no man ever excelled in painting, who was eminently curious about pencils and colors.[9]

There are others to whom Idleness dictates another expedient,[10] by which life may be passed unprofitably away without the tediousness of many vacant hours. The art is, to fill the day with petty business, to have always something in hand which may raise curiosity, but not solicitude, and keep the mind in a state of action, but not of labor.

This art has for many years been practiced by my old friend Sober, with wonderful success. Sober is a man of strong desires and quick imagination, so exactly balanced by the love of ease,[11] that they can seldom stimulate him to any difficult undertaking; they have, however, so much power, that they will not suffer him to lie quite at rest, and though they do not make him sufficiently useful to others, they make him at least weary of himself.

Mr. Sober's chief pleasure is conversation; there is no end of his talk or his attention; to speak or to hear is equally pleasing; for he still fancies that he is teaching or learning something, and is free for the time from his own reproaches.[12]

But there is one time at night when he must go home, that his friends may sleep; and another time in the morning, when all the world agrees to shut out interruption. These are the moments of which poor Sober trembles at the thought. But the misery of these tiresome intervals, he has many means of alleviating.[13] He has persuaded himself that the manual arts are undeservedly overlooked; he has observed in many trades the effects of close thought, and just ratiocination.[14] From speculation he proceeded to practice, and supplied himself with the tools of a carpenter, with which he mended his coalbox very successfully, and which he still continues to employ, as he finds occasion.

He has attempted at other times the crafts of the shoemaker, tinman, plumber, and potter; in all these arts he has failed, and resolves to qualify himself for them by better information. But his daily amusement is chemistry. He has a small furnace, which he employs in distillation, and which has long been the solace[15] of his life. He draws oils and waters, and essences and spirits, which he knows to be of no use; sits and counts the drops as they come from his retort,[16] and forgets that, whilst a drop is falling, a moment flies away.

Poor Sober! I have often teased him with reproof, and he has often promised reformation; for no man is so much open to conviction as the Idler, but there is none on whom it operates so little. What will be the effect of this paper I know not; perhaps he will read it and laugh, and light the fire in his furnace; but my hope is that he will quit his trifles, and betake himself to rational and useful diligence.

Notes

[1] Pride: The person whose name is called Pride. The author uses the name in an allegorical sense. Other examples such as "Idleness", "Fraud", "Sober" also appear in this essay.

[2] It is not my intention…a very doubtful and obstinate competition: I do not intend to lessen the serious harm caused by Pride, but I am afraid that Idleness might win over Pride by incurring more serious harm to man.

[3] Busiris: In Greek mythology, Busiris was a king of Egypt who sacrificed all visitors to the Gods, hoping to avert a famine.

[4] who prolong the reign of darkness…to "tell him how they hate his beams": This sentence implies Mr. Idleness indulges in the habit of oversleeping so much that he even develops hatred for the lovely sunshine. but: except.

[5] votaries of Idleness: worshippers of the Goddess of Idleness.

[6] watched: guarded against.

[7] turbulence and hurry: being restless and busy.

[8] bar out: prevent; get rid of.

[9] Some are always in a state of preparation…who was eminently curious about pencils and colors: This paragraph simply suggests that those who are always busy with trivial preparations for some big schemes can hardly achieve any essential success in the end.

[10] expedient: some action that is thought of useful, helpful or advisable for a particular purpose, though not necessarily fair or moral.

[11] balanced by the love of ease: feeling relaxed or striking a balance of mind by the

love of an easeful way of life.

[12] and is free for the time from his own reproaches: and is exempt from self-blame for his own waste of time.

[13] many means of alleviating: many ways to lessen his worry or pain.

[14] ratiocination: speculation; process of logical and methodical reasoning.

[15] solace: comfort or relief from pain, trouble or distress.

[16] retort: glass vessel with a long narrow neck turned downwards, used for distilling liquids.

Commentary

In the fall of 1748, while working on the Dictionary, Samuel Johnson wrote a 368-line poem, *The Vanity of Human Wishes*. It is the first work that he published under his own name. However, this became the starting point of his writing career. Rather than poetry, he continued writing prose essays as a moralist. From March of 1750 to March of 1752, for two years, every Tuesday and Saturday he published a periodical he called *The Rambler*, each issue consisting of an essay written by himself, 208 essays in all. *On Idleness* is just one of them.

In *On Idleness*, the author combines several commonly-used writing techniques to develop the essay. First, since he intends to write as a moralist, he adopts the technique of allegory by personifying the characters as "Idleness", "Fraud", "Pride", and "Sober". Second, Johnson uses effective illustration to characterize the funny and thought-provoking features of "Mr. Sober". Third, Johnson's talent of using hyperbole also leaves the reader a permanent impression. How can we forget the Idlers' profound love for oversleeping, so much so that they will "prolong the reign of darkness by double curtains, and never see the sun but to 'tell him how they hate his beams'"! Fourth, oxymoron is another important method Johnson uses in writing. "As Pride sometimes is hid under humility, Idleness is often covered by turbulence and hurry." The irony here is clear: Mr. Idleness is truly a busy Idler! More interestingly, Mr. Sober, simply an incarnation of Mr. Idler, is an even more paradoxical pitiable figure: Mr. Sober, a clear-headed Idler, enjoys doing anything but his own trade. At the end of the essay, Johnson puts forward a humorous yet serious warning for the numerous Sober-minded Idlers in the world to quit trifles, and betake themselves to rational and useful diligence.

Questions and Exercises

1. What kind of writing techniques does Johnson adopt to develop this essay? Are they effective or not? Give your reasons.
2. What moral lessons can we learn from the essay *On Idleness*? Compose an essay of your own to expound on your idea of idleness.

Henry David Thoreau

Henry David Thoreau (1817—1862) was a great American writer, philosopher, poet, and

a most practical man who taught nothing that he was not prepared to practice in himself. He was born in Concord, a village near Boston. After graduating from Harvard, and teaching school for some years, he went to live with Emerson, his Concord neighbor and transcendentalist, both to study with him and to work as a handyman. In 1845, when he was 26, he built a cabin on the shores of Walden Pound and lived there for two years while writing the two books: *A Week on the Concord* and *Merrimack Rivers and Walden.* It was while he was at Walden that he was arrested for refusing to pay his poll taxes as a protest against Negro slavery and spent a night in jail. This event found some expression in his best known essay *Civil Disobedience*, which became highly influential in the 20th century.

Civil Disobedience

(*Excerpts*)

I heartily accept the motto—"That government is best which governs least"; and I should like to see it acted up to more rapidly and systematically. Carried out, it finally amounts to this, which also I believe—"That government is best which governs not at all"; and when men are prepared for it, that will be the kind of government which they will have. Government is at best but an expedient;[1] but most governments are usually, and all governments are sometimes, inexpedient. The objections which have been brought against a standing army, and they are many and weighty, and deserve to prevail, may also at last be brought against a standing government. The standing army is only an arm of the standing government. The government itself, which is only the mode which the people have chosen to execute their will, is equally liable to be abused and perverted before the people can act through it. Witness the present Mexican War, the work of comparatively a few individuals using the standing government as their tool; for, in the outset, the people would not have consented to this measure.[2]

This American government—what is it but a tradition, though a recent one, endeavoring to transmit itself unimpaired to posterity,[3] but each instant losing some of its integrity? It has not the vitality and force of a single living man; for a single man can bend it to his will. It is a sort of wooden gun to the people themselves. But it is not the less necessary for this; for the people must have some complicated machinery or other, and hear its din,[4] to satisfy that idea of government which they have. Governments show thus how successfully men can be imposed on, even impose on themselves, for their own advantage. It is excellent, we must all allow. Yet this government never of itself furthered any enterprise, but by the alacrity[5] with which it got out of its way. *It* does not keep the country free. *It* does not settle the West. *It* does not educate. The character inherent in the American people has done all that has been accomplished; and it would have done somewhat more, if the government had not sometimes got in its way. For government is an expedient by which men would fain[6] succeed in letting one another alone; and, as has been said, when it is most expedient, the governed are most let alone by it. Trade and commerce, if they were not made of India rubber, would never manage to bounce over the obstacles which legislators are continually putting in their way;[7] and, if one were to judge these men wholly by the effects of their actions, and not partly by their intentions, they would deserve to be classed and punished with those mischievous persons who put obstructions on the railroads.

But, to speak practically and as a citizen, unlike those who call themselves no-government men, I ask for, not at once no government, but *at once* a better government. Let every man make known what kind of government would command his respect, and that will be one step toward obtaining it.

After all, the practical reason why, when the power is once in the hands of the people, a majority are permitted, and for a long period continue, to rule, is not because they are most likely to be in the right, nor because this seems fairest to the minority, but because they are physically the strongest. But a government in which the majority rule in all cases cannot be based on justice, even as far as men understand it. Can there not be a government in which majorities do not virtually decide right and wrong, but conscience?—in which majorities decide only those questions to which the rule of expediency is applicable? Must the citizen ever for a moment, or in the least degree, resign his conscience to the legislator? Why has every man a conscience, then? I think that we should be men first, and subjects afterward. It is not desirable to cultivate a respect for the law, so much as for the right. The only obligation which I have a right to assume is to do at any time what I think right. It is truly enough said that a corporation has no conscience; but a corporation of conscientious men is a corporation *with* a conscience. Law never made men a whit more just; and, by means of their respect for it, even the well-disposed are daily made the agents of injustice. A common and natural result of an undue respect for law is, that you may see a file of soldiers, colonel, captain, corporal, privates, powder-monkeys,[8] and all, marching in admirable order over hill and dale to the wars, against their wills, ay, against their common sense and consciences, which makes it very steep marching indeed, and produces a palpitation of the heart. They have no doubt that it is a damnable business in which they are concerned; they are all peaceably inclined.

Now, what are they? Men at all? or small movable forts and magazines, at the service of some unscrupulous man in power? Visit the Navy Yard,[9] and behold a marine, such a man as an American government can make, or such as it can make a man with its black arts—a mere shadow and reminiscence of humanity, a man laid out alive and standing, and already, as one may say, buried under arms with funeral accompaniments, though it may be,

"Not a drum was heard, not a funeral note,
As his corse to the rampart we hurried;
Not a soldier discharged his farewell shot
O'er the grave where our hero we buried."[10]

The mass of men serve the state thus, not as men mainly, but as machines, with their bodies. They are the standing army, and the militia, jailers, constables, *posse comitatus*,[11] etc. In most cases there is no free exercise whatever of the judgment or of the moral sense; but they put themselves on a level with wood and earth and stones; and wooden men can perhaps be manufactured that will serve the purpose as well. Such command no more respect than men of straw or a lump of dirt. They have the same sort of worth only as horses and dogs. Yet such as these even are commonly esteemed good citizens. Others, as most legislators, politicians, lawyers, ministers, and office-holders, serve the state chiefly with their heads; and, as they rarely make any moral distinctions, they are as likely to serve the devil, without *intending* it, as God. A very few, as heroes, patriots, martyrs, reformers in the great sense, and *men*, serve the state with their consciences also, and so necessarily resist it for the most part; and they are commonly treated as enemies by it. A wise man will only be useful as a man, and will not submit to be "clay", and "stop a hole to keep the wind away",[12] but leave that office to his dust at least: —

"I am too high-born to be propertied,
To be a secondary at control,
Or useful serving-man and instrument
To any sovereign state throughout the world."[13]

He who gives himself entirely to his fellow-men appears to them useless and selfish; but he who gives himself partially to them is pronounced a benefactor and philanthropist.

How does it become a man to behave toward this American government today? I answer, that he cannot without disgrace be associated with it. I cannot for an instant recognize that political organization as *my* government which is the *slave's* government also.

All men recognize the right of revolution; that is, the right to refuse allegiance to, and to resist, the government, when its tyranny or its inefficiency are great and unendurable. But almost all say that such is not the case now. But such was the case, they think, in the Revolution of '75.[14] If one were to tell me that this was a bad government because it taxed certain foreign commodities brought to its ports, it is most probable that I should not make an ado about it, for I can do without them. All machines have their friction; and possibly this does enough good to counterbalance the evil. At any rate, it is a great evil to make a stir about it. But when the friction comes to have its machine, and oppression and robbery are organized, I say, let us not have such a machine any longer. In other words, when a sixth of the population of a nation which has undertaken to be the refuge of liberty are slaves, and a whole country is unjustly overrun and conquered by a foreign army, and subjected to military law, I think that it is not too soon for honest men to rebel and revolutionize. What makes this duty the more urgent is the fact that the country so overrun is not our own, but ours is the invading army.[15]

Notes

[1] expedient: useful, helpful or advisable for a particular purpose, though not necessarily fair or moral.

[2] Witness the present Mexican War...the people would not have consented to this measure: Thoreau wrote *Civil Disobedience* at the time of the Mexican War (1846—1848), which many New Englanders saw as a stratagem to aid the spread of southern slavery. The essay was first presented as a lecture at the Concord Lyceum on January 26, 1848, under the title "The Rights and Duties of the Individual in Relation to Government." standing: permanent and established.

[3] to transmit itself unimpaired to posterity: pass itself integral to descendants.

[4] din: continuing loud confused noise.

[5] alacrity: prompt and eager readiness.

[6] fain: with pleasure.

[7] India rubber: Made from the latex of tropical plants, "India" because it came from the West Indies, and "rubber" from its early use as an eraser. Here it means: Trade and commerce are rather flexible in dealing with bureaucratization so as to rid themselves of the obstacles set by the government.

[8] powder-monkeys: boys who carried powder to cannon.

[9] the Navy Yard: presumably a reference to the United States Navy in Boston, Massachusetts.

[10] From *The Burial of Sir John Morre at Corunna* by Charles Wolfe (1791—1823).

[11] *posse comitatus*: Group empowered to uphold the law, a sheriff's posse. Here it refers to citizens authorized to help keep the peace.

[12] From *Hamlet* written by English dramatist William Shakespeare (1564—1616).

[13] From *King John* by William Shakespeare.

[14] the Revolution of '75: The American Revolution began in Concord & Lexington from 1775 to 1783.

[15] the invading army: a reference to slavery in the U.S, and to the invasion of Mexico by the U.S.

Commentary

While *Walden* can be applied to almost anyone's life, Thoreau's *Civil Disobedience* was like a highly-honored and quite influential architectural landmark. Thoreau advocated quite similar ideas with those of Mohandas Gandhi and Martin Luther King, who supported the idea of non-violent resistance to injustices. In the 1940s, *Civil Disobedience* was read by the Danish resistance; in the 1950s it was cherished by people who opposed McCarthyism; in the 1960s it produced strong influence in the struggle against racial segregation in South Africa; and in the 1970s it was discovered by a new generation of anti-war activists.

Civil Disobedience is an eloquent and philosophical protest against the inefficient government and unjust law. Thoreau asserted the motto "the government is best which governs least". In the essay he made two notable contributions to American ideas: one was people should live instead of working for living; the other was if people thought a law was unjust they could resist it by civil disobedience. In addition, as a transcendentalist, he highly valued the integrity of an individual, believing that men should let one another alone instead of serving the State as "machine", and that "we should be men first, and subjects afterward." Owing to his amazing incisive logic, it is not without reason that his works are written for all time.

In addition, Thoreau is a master of style in prose: learned and homely, eloquent and salty, rhetorical and concise, straightforward and concrete.

Questions and Exercises

1. According to Thoreau, how does the government become expedient? And what should people do accordingly as a response to an inefficient government and the unendurable laws?
2. What do you think of the Utopian State "which can afford to be just to all men, and to treat the individual with respect as a neighbor"?

Aldous Huxley

Aldous Huxley (1894—1963) was born to a family in the south of England. Unable to take part in the First World War because of his weak eyes, he attended Oxford University, where he cultivated his life-long curiosity about a great number of subjects. He became a very learned and erudite man, but at Oxford he grew cynical and disgusted with the world of that time, and became increasingly pessimistic during the 1930s.

Huxley wrote four novels, three collections of poems and a book of short stories and essays all in a tone of cynicism. He firmly believed that science divorced from social values would eventually destroy the civilized human society and undermine the political progress. He wondered what life would be like if every activity from birth to death was preoccupied and controlled by scientific technology.

By temperament, Huxley was an observer of life and a collector of human curiosities. With this attitude in mind, he acted as an outraged idealist and sought ways to preserve traditional humanistic values against the onslaughts of modern technology. People were very interested in reading his ideas about modern life because he wrote with a polished, elegant style and his profound knowledge provided his books with philosophical and prophetic insights.

The Beauty Industry

The only American industry unaffected by the general depression of trade is the beauty industry. American women continue to spend on their faces and bodies as much as they spent before the coming of the slump—about three million pounds a week. These facts and figures are "official", and can be accepted as being substantially true. Reading them, I was only surprised by the comparative smallness of the sums expended. From the prodigious number of advertisements of aids to beauty[1] contained in the American magazines, I had imagined that the personal appearance business must stand high up among the champions of American industry—the equal, or only just less than the equal, of bootlegging and racketeering, movies and automobiles. Still, one hundred and fifty-six million pounds a year is a tidy sum. Rather more than twice the revenue of India, if I remember rightly.

I do not know what the European figures are. Much smaller undoubtedly. Europe is poor, and a face can cost as much in upkeep as a Rolls-Royce. The most that the majority of European women can do is just to wash and hope for the best. Perhaps the soap will produce its loudly advertised effects; perhaps it will transform them into the likeness of those ravishing creature as who smile so rosily and creamily, so peachily and pearlily, from every hoarding. Perhaps, on the other hand, it may not. In any case, the more costly experiments in beautification are still as much beyond most European means as are high-powered motor-cars and electric refrigerators. Even in Europe, however, much more now is spent on beauty than was ever spent in the past. Not quite so much more as in America, that is all. But, everywhere, the increase has been undoubtedly enormous.

The fact is significant. To what is it due? In part, I suppose, to a general increase in prosperity. The rich has always cultivated their personal appearance. The diffusion of wealth—such as it is—now permits those of the poor who are less badly off than their fathers to do the same.

But this is, clearly, not the whole story. The modern cult of beauty is not exclusively a function (in the mathematical sense) of wealth. If it were, then the personal appearance industries would have been as hardly hit by the trade depression as any other business.

But, as we have seen, they have not suffered. Women are retrenching on other things than their faces. The cult of beauty must therefore be symptomatic of changes that have taken place outside the economic sphere. Of what changes? Of the changes, I suggest, in the status of women; of the changes of our attitude towards "the merely physical".

Women, it is obvious, are freer than in the past. Freer not only to perform the generally unenviable social functions hitherto reserved to the male, but also to exercise the more pleasing, famine privilege of being attractive. They have the right, if not to be less virtuous than their grandmothers, at any rate to look less virtuous. The British Matron, not long since a creature of austere and even terrifying aspect, now does her best to achieve and perennially preserve the appearance of what her predecessor would have described as a Lost Woman.[2] She often succeeds. But we are not shocked—at any rate, not morally shocked. Aesthetically shocked—yes; we may sometimes be that. But morally, no. We concede that the Matron is morally justified in being preoccupied with her personal appearance. This concession depends on another of a more general nature—a concession to the Body, with a large B, to the Manichaean principle of evil.[3] For we have now come to admit that the body has its rights. And not only rights—duties, actually duties. It has, for example, a duty to do the best it can for itself in the way of strength and beauty. Christian-ascetic ideas[4] no longer trouble us. We demand justice for the body as well as for the soul. Hence, among other things, the fortunes made by face-cream manufacturers and beauty-specialists, by the vendors of rubber reducing belts and massage machines, by the patentees of hair-lotions and the authors of books on the culture of the abdomen.

What are the practical results of this modern cult of beauty? The exercises and the massage, the health motors and the skin foods—to what have they led? Are women more beautiful than they were? Do they get something for the enormous expenditure of energy, time, and money demanded of them by the beauty-cult? These are questions which it is difficult to answer. For the facts seem to contradict themselves. The campaign for more physical beauty seems to be both a tremendous success and a lamentable failure. It depends on how you look at the results.

It is a success in so far as more women retain their youthful appearance to a greater age than in the past. "Old ladies" are already becoming rare. In a few years, we may well believe, they will be extinct. White hair and wrinkles, a bent back and hollow cheeks will come to be regarded as medievally old-fashioned. The crone of the future will be golden, curly and cherry-lipped, neatankled and slender. The Portrait of the Artist's Mother will come to be almost indistinguishable, at future picture shows, from the Portrait of the Artist's Daughter. This desirable consummation will be due in part to skin foods and injections of paraffin-wax, facial surgery, mud-baths, and paint, in part to improved health, due in its turn to a more rational mode of life. Ugliness is one of the symptoms of disease, beauty of health. In so far as the campaign for more beauty is also a campaign for more health, it is admirable and, up to a point, genuinely successful. Beauty that is merely the artificial shadow of these symptoms of health is intrinsically of poorer quality than the genuine article. Still, it is a sufficiently good imitation to be sometimes mistakable for the real thing. The apparatus for mimicking the symptoms of health is now within the reach of every moderately prosperous person; the knowledge of the way in which real health can be achieved is growing, and will in time, no doubt, be universally acted upon. When that happy moment comes, will every woman be beautiful—as beautiful, at any rate, as the natural shape of her features, with or without surgical and chemical aid, permits?

The answer is emphatically: No. For real beauty is as much as an affair of inner as of the outer self. The beauty of a porcelain jar is a matter of shape, of color, of surface texture. The jar may be empty or tenanted by spiders, full of honey or stinking slime—it makes no difference to its beauty or ugliness. But a woman is alive, and her beauty therefore is not skin deep. The surface of the human vessel is affected by the nature of its spiritual contents. I have seen women who, by the standards of a connoisseur of porcelain, were ravishingly lovely. Their shape, their color, their surface texture were perfect. And yet they were not beautiful. For the lovely vase was either empty or filled with some corruption. Spiritual emptiness or ugliness shows through. And conversely, there is an interior light that can transfigure forms that the pure aesthetician would regard as imperfect or downright ugly.

There are numerous forms of psychological ugliness. There is an ugliness of stupidity, for example, of unawareness (distressingly common among pretty women). An ugliness also of greed, of lasciviousness, of avarice. All the deadly sins,[5] indeed, have their own peculiar negation of beauty. On the pretty faces of those especially who are trying to have a continuous "good time", one sees very often a kind of bored sullenness that ruins all their charm. I remember in particular two young American girls I once met in North Africa. From the porcelain specialist's point of view, they were beautiful. But the sullen boredom of which I have spoken was so deeply stamped into their fresh faces, their gait and gestures expressed so weary a listlessness, that is unbearable to look at them. These exquisite creatures were positively repulsive.

Still commoner and no less repellent is the hardness which spoils so many pretty faces. Often, it is true, this air of hardness is due not to psychological causes, but to the contemporary habit of over-painting. In Paris, where this over-painting is most pronounced, many women have ceased to look human at all. Whitewashed and ruddled, they seem to be wearing masks. One must look closely to discover the soft and living face beneath. But often the face is not soft, often it turns out to be imperfectly alive. The hardness and deadness are from within. They are the outward and the visible signs of some emotional or indistinctive disharmony, accepted as a chronic condition of being. We do not need a Freudian to tell us that this disharmony is often of a sexual nature.

So long as such disharmonies continue to exist, so long as there is good reason for sullen boredom, so long as human beings allow themselves to be possessed and hagridden by monomaniacal vices, the cult of beauty is destined to be ineffectual. Successful in prolonging the appearance of youth, or realizing or simulating the symptoms of health, the campaign inspired by this cult remains fundamentally a failure. Its operations do not touch the deepest source of beauty—the experiencing soul. It is not by improving skin foods and point rollers, by cheapening health motors and electrical hair-removers, that the human race will be made beautiful; it is not even by improving health. All men and women will be beautiful only when the social arrangements give to every one of them an opportunity to live completely and harmoniously, when there is no environmental incentive and no hereditary tendency towards monomaniacal vice. In other words, all men and women will never be beautiful. But there might easily be fewer ugly human beings in the world than there are at present. We must be content with moderate hopes.

Notes

[1] aids to beauty: various beautifying products.

[2] a Lost Woman: an woman with immoral behavior.

[3] the Manichaean principle of evil: the evil in the Manichaean religion in Iran during 216—276, which believes that the human spirit is virtuous and his body is evil. So material is the source of evil.

[4] Christian-ascetic ideas: the Christian belief that true Christians should exercise strict control over their physical desires and needs.

[5] All the deadly sins: According to Christianity, there are chiefly seven deadly sins: pride, covetousness, lust, anger, gluttony, envy, and sloth.

Commentary

In discussion of the development of beauty industry in the 1930s, Aldous Huxley got rather dismayed to find that American women spent on their faces and bodies as much as about three million pounds a week, more than twice the revenue of India. However, what worried him most was that, while pursuing outer beauty, people in developed countries have neglected their inner beauty and harmony of their soul.

The whole essay can be divided into four parts. The first part (paras. 1 & 2) describes the fact that the European and American women have paid over scrupulous attention to their facial beauty. The second part (paras. 3 to 5) expounds the real causes for the over-enthusiastic cult for outer beauty. The third part (paras. 6 & 7) assumes that the pursuit of outer beauty may obtain some purpose to a certain extent in terms of facial beauty. The fourth part (paras. 8 to 10) is a discussion of the critical essence of true beauty. Huxley especially emphasizes the crucial importance of possessing beauty in the true sense of the word—a harmonious combination between body and soul. And in the last concluding paragraph, the author proposes that the practical solution to the beautification problem actually rests in the amelioration of the overall social structure rather than in the rapid growth of beauty products.

Questions and Exercises

1. What is the distorted modern conception of human beauty according to Huxley?
2. Write a short essay entitled "How to Achieve Genuine Beauty".

Mark Twain

Mark Twain (1835—1910) was born Samuel Langhorne Clemens in Florida, Missouri, but lived as a child in Hannibal, Missouri, on the Mississippi River. He took the name Mark Twain from the call of the pilots on the river steamers, which indicated that the water was twelve feet deep, a safe depth for a steamer. During his early years, he worked as a riverboat pilot, newspaper reporter, printer, and gold prospector. But then he turned to writing, and became one of the greatest of American writers. Although his popular image is as the author of such humorous works, *The Adventures of Tom Sawyer* and *The Adventures of Huckleberry Finn,* Twain had the other side that may be resulted from the bitter experiences of his life—financial failure and the deaths of his wife and daughters. His last writings are savage, satiric, and pessimistic in content and tone. The following essay is taken from *Letters from the Earth,* one of Mark Twain's later works.

On the Damned Human Race

I have been studying the traits and dispositions of the lower animals (so-called), and contrasting them with the traits and dispositions of man. I find the result humiliating to me. For it obliges me to renounce my allegiance to the Darwinian theory of the *Ascent of Man from the Lower Animals*; since it now seems plain to me that the theory ought to be vacated in favor of a new and truer one, this new and truer one to be named the *Descent of Man from the Higher Animals*.

In proceeding toward this unpleasant conclusion I have not guessed or speculated or conjectured, but have used what is commonly called the scientific method. That is to say, I have subjected every postulate that presented itself to the crucial test of actual experiment, and have adopted it or rejected it according to the result. Thus I verified and established each step of my course in its turn before advancing to the next. These experiments were made in the London Zoological Gardens, and covered many months of painstaking and fatiguing work.

Before particularizing any of the experiments, I wish to state one or two things which seem to more properly belong in this place than further along. This, in the interest of clearness. The massed experiments established to my satisfaction certain generalizations, to wit:

(1) That the human race is of one distinct species. It exhibits slight variations (in color, stature, mental caliber, and so on) due to climate, environment, and so forth; but it is a species by itself, and not to be confounded with any other.

(2) That the quadrupeds are a distinct family, also. This family exhibits variations (in color, size, food preferences, and so on; but it is a family by itself).

(3) That the other families (the birds, the fishes, the insects, the reptiles, etc.) are more or less distinct, also. They are in the procession. They are links in the chain which stretches down from the higher animals to man at the bottom.

Some of my experiments were quite curious. In the course of my reading I had come across a case where, many years ago, some hunters on our Great Plains organized a buffalo hunt for the entertainment of an English earl. They had charming sport. They killed seventy-two of those great animals; and ate part of one of them and left the seventy-one to rot. In order to determine the difference between an anaconda and an earl (if any) I caused seven young calves to be turned into the anaconda's cage. The grateful reptile immediately crushed one of them and swallowed it, then lay back satisfied. It showed no further interest in the calves, and no disposition to harm them. I tried this experiment with other anacondas; always with the same result. The fact stood proven that the difference between an earl and an anaconda is that the earl is cruel and the anaconda isn't; and that the earl wantonly destroys what he has no use for, but the anaconda doesn't. This seemed to suggest that the anaconda was not descended from the earl. It also seemed to suggest that the earl was descended from the anaconda, and had lost a good deal in the transition.

I was aware that many men who have accumulated more millions of money than they can ever use have shown a rabid hunger for more, and have not scrupled to cheat the ignorant and the helpless out of their poor savings in order to partially appease that appetite. I furnished a hundred different kinds of wild and tame animals the opportunity to accumulate vast stores of food, but none of them would do it. The squirrels and bees and certain birds made accumulations, but stopped when they had gathered a winter's supply, and could not be persuaded to add to it either honestly or by chicane. In order to bolster up a tottering reputation the ant pretended to store up supplies, but I was not deceived. I know the ant. These experiments convinced me that there is this difference between man and the higher animals: he is avaricious and miserly; they are not.

In the course of my experiments I convinced myself that among the animals man is the only one that harbors insults and injuries, broods over them, waits till a chance offers, then takes revenge. The passion of revenge is unknown to the higher animals.

Roosters keep harems, but it is by consent of their concubines; therefore no wrong is done. Men keep harems but it is by brute force, privileged by atrocious laws which the other sex were allowed no hand in making. In this matter man occupies a far lower place than the rooster.

Cats are loose in their morals, but not consciously so. Man, in his descent from the cat, has brought the cats looseness with him but has left the unconsciousness behind (the saving grace which excuses the cat). The cat is innocent, man is not.

Indecency, vulgarity, obscenity (these are strictly confined to man); he invented them. Among the higher animals there is no trace of them. They hide nothing; they are not ashamed. Man, with his soiled mind, covers himself. He will not even enter a drawing room with his breast and back naked, so alive are he and his mates to indecent suggestion. Man is "The Animal that Laughs." But so does the monkey, as Mr. Darwin pointed out; and so does the Australian bird that is called the laughing jackass. No! Man is the Animal that Blushes. He is the only one that does it or has occasion to.

At the head of this article we see how three monks were burnt to death a few days ago, and a prior put to death with atrocious cruelty. Do we inquire into the details? No; or we should find out that the prior was subjected to unprintable mutilations. Man (when he is a North American Indian) gouges out his prisoners eyes; when he is King John,[1] with a nephew to render untroublesome, he uses a red-hot iron; when he is a religious zealot dealing with heretics in the Middle Ages, he skins his captive alive and scatters salt on his back; in the first Richard's[2] time he shuts up a multitude of Jew families in a tower and sets fire to it; in Columbus's time he captures a family of Spanish Jews and—(but that is not printable; in our day in England a man is fined ten shillings for beating his mother nearly to death with a chair, and another man is fined forty shillings for having four pheasant eggs in his possession without being able to satisfactorily explain how he got them). Of all the animals, man is the only one that is cruel. He is the only one that inflicts pain for the pleasure of doing it. It is a trait that is not known to the higher animals. The cat plays with the frightened mouse; but she has this excuse, that she does not know that the mouse is suffering. The cat is moderate—unhumanly moderate: she only scares the mouse, she does not hurt it; she doesn't dig out its eyes, or tear off its skin, or drive splinters under its nails—man-fashion; when she is done playing with it she makes a sudden meal of it and puts it out of its trouble. Man is the Cruel Animal. He is alone in that distinction.

The higher animals engage in individual fights, but never in organized masses. Man is the only animal that deals in that atrocity of atrocities, War. He is the only one that gathers his brethren about him and goes forth in cold blood and with calm pulse to exterminate his kind. He is the only animal that for sordid wages will march out, as the Hessians[3] did in our Revolution, and as the boyish Prince Napoleon did in the Zulu war, and help to slaughter strangers of his own species who have done him no harm and with whom he has no quarrel.

Man is the only animal that robs his helpless fellow of his country, takes possession of it and drives him out of it or destroys him. Man has done this in all the ages. There is not an acre of ground on the globe that is in possession of its rightful owner, or that has not been taken away from owner after owner, cycle after cycle, by force and bloodshed.

Man is the only Slave. And he is the only animal who enslaves. He has always been a slave in one form or another, and has always held other slaves in bondage under him in one way or another. In our day he is always some man's slave for wages and does that man's work; and this slave has other slaves under him for minor wages, and they do his work. The higher animals are the only ones who exclusively do their own work and provide their own living.

Man is the only Patriot. He sets himself apart in his own country, under his own flag, and sneers at the other nations, and keeps multitudinous uniformed assassins on hand at heavy expense to grab slices of other people's countries, and keep them from grabbing slices of his. And in the intervals between campaigns, he washes the blood off his hands and works for the universal brotherhood of man, with his mouth.

Man is the Religious Animal. He is the only Religious Animal. He is the only animal that has the True Religion, several of them. He is the only animal that loves his neighbor as himself, and cuts his throat if his theology isn't straight. He has made a graveyard of the globe in trying his honest best to smooth his brother's path to happiness and heaven. He was at it in the time of the Caesars,[4] he was at it in Mahomet's time, he was at it in the time of the Inquisition, he was at it in France a couple of centuries, he was at it in England in Mary's day, he has been at it ever since he first saw the light, he is at it today in Crete (as per the telegrams quoted above) he will be at it somewhere else tomorrow. The higher animals have no religion. And we are told that they are going to be left out, in the Hereafter. I wonder why? It seems questionable taste.

Man is the Reasoning Animal. Such is the claim. I think it is open to dispute. Indeed, my experiments have proven to me that he is the Unreasoning Animal. Note his history, as sketched above. It seems plain to me that whatever he is he is not a reasoning animal. His record is the fantastic record of a maniac. I consider that the strongest count against his intelligence is the fact that with that record back of him he blandly sets himself up as the head animal of the lot: whereas by his own standards he is the bottom one.

In truth, man is incurably foolish. Simple things which the other animals easily learn, he is incapable of learning. Among my experiments was this. In an hour I taught a cat and a dog to be friends. I put them in a cage. In another hour I taught them to be friends with a rabbit. In the course of two days I was able to add a fox, a goose, a squirrel and some doves. Finally, a monkey. They lived together in peace; even affectionately.

Next, in another cage I confined an Irish Catholic from Tipperary, and as soon as he seemed tame I added a Scotch Presbyterian from Aberdeen. Next a Turk from Constantinople; a Greek Christian from Crete; an Armenian; a Methodist from the wilds of Arkansas; a Buddhist from China; a Brahman from Benares. Finally, a Salvation Army Colonel from Wapping. Then I stayed away two whole days. When I came back to note results, the cage of Higher Animals was all right, but in the other there was but a chaos of gory odds and ends of turbans and fezzes and plaids and bones and flesh, not a specimen left alive. These Reasoning Animals had disagreed on a theological detail and carried the matter to a Higher Court.

One is obliged to concede that in true loftiness of character, Man cannot claim to approach even the meanest of the Higher Animals. It is plain that he is constitutionally incapable of approaching that altitude; that he is constitutionally afflicted with a Defect which must make such approach forever impossible, for it is manifest that this defect is permanent in him, indestructible, ineradicable.

I find this Defect to be the Moral Sense. He is the only animal that has it. It is the secret of his degradation. It is the quality which enables him to do wrong. It has no other office[5]. It is incapable of performing any other function. It could never have been intended to perform any other. Without it, man could do no wrong. He would rise at once to the level of the Higher Animals.

Since the Moral Sense has but the one office, the one capacity (to enable man to do wrong) it is plainly without value to him. It is as valueless to him as is disease. In fact, it manifestly is a disease. Rabies is bad, but it is not so bad as this disease. Rabies enables a man to do a thing, which he could not do when in a healthy state: kill his neighbor with a poisonous bite; one is the better man for having rabies: The Moral Sense enables a man to do wrong. It enables him to do wrong in a thousand ways. Rabies is an innocent disease, compared to the Moral Sense. No one, then, can be the better man for having the Moral Sense. What now, do we find the Primal Curse to have been? Plainly what it was in the beginning: the infliction upon man of the Moral Sense; the ability to distinguish good from evil; and with it, necessarily, the ability to do evil; for there can be no evil act without the presence of consciousness of it in the doer of it.

And so I find that we have descended and degenerated, from some far ancestor—some microscopic atom wandering at its pleasure between the mighty horizons of a drop of water perchance—insect by insect, animal by animal, reptile by reptile, down the long highway of smirch less innocence, till we have reached the bottom stage of development—namable as the Human Being. Below us, nothing.

Notes

[1] King John: King John of England (1199—1216), the youngest son of Henry II. During his brother Richard I's absence on the third Crusade, John had himself declared king and later held his brother in captivity. He was believed to have murdered his nephew Arthur I of Brittany. This and many other cruel things he did made him extremely unpopular. Finally a civil war broke out and he died during the war, presumably poisoned.

[2] Richard: Richard I, King of England (1157—1199), the second son of Henry II, also known as the Lion-Hearted. As a symbol of bravery, he spent only six months of his 10-year reign in the kingdom; the rest of the years, he spent in crusade or as a hostage in Austria.

[3] the Hessians: German mercenaries serving with the British during the American Revolution. The Germans constituted about one third of the king's troops in America. For these mercenaries, Britain paid the German rulers a total of 1.77 million pounds.

[4] Caesar: This was a name of a powerful Roman family which became a title borne by the successor to the imperial throne. Julius Caesar (100—44 B.C.) was the Roman general who ruled the country.

[5] office: function.

Commentary

In this satirical essay *On the Damned Human Race*, Mark Twain, by making fun of Charles Darwin's theory of "The Ascent of Man", unmistakably directs his target toward the dark qualities of the whole human race. The most sarcastic of all is that Twain claims that moral sense of human beings dictates good versus evil, with evil being the outcome. Since animals have no moral sense, all of what they do is just innocent instinct, and none of it would ever be judged as evil. Only humans have the ability to commit immoral acts by going against the moral codes established by themselves. Due to inferior physical and moral attributes, when compared to the "higher animals", there is no way we could logically consider humans as above the other "lower animals" of the Earth.

Twain also ridicules the various religious groups of the human race. He humorously describes an imaginary cage where he has succeeded in making various animals become friends. He then goes on to describe another cage, where he put in a number of men from different areas and religions, who, instead of living peacefully together, have torn each other to pieces trying to force their beliefs on others.

Although we may feel Twain is going a bit too overboard, as with any satire, we generally have to agree with what he said. We find very little of what Twain says to be offensive, since it is not at all uncommon that man has abused his very powers and gifts to destroy his natural habitat and his own species in his endless search for more convenience. Any self respecting higher animals would be ashamed if their immoral actions are being similar to those of man's.

Questions and Exercises

1. What is the main idea of this essay? Is Mark Twain serious when he says that he has done many months of painstaking and fatiguing work in the London Zoological Gardens? What kind of effect do you think he hopes to achieve with this mock seriousness?
2. What specific human traits and dispositions does Twain condemn? Isn't there some saving grace for the human race? Mark Twain wrote this essay about a century ago. Would you say that people have changed for the better or just the opposite?
3. Do you agree with the statement that human beings are the greatest menace to this world and they are the least fit for survival? State your reasons.

Helen Keller

At the age of 19 months, Helen Keller was a happy, healthy child. She was already saying a few words. Then she had a high fever which caused her to become deaf and blind. No longer could she see nor hear. Helen was a very bright child. She learned to do many things by feeling of people's hands to try to find out what they were doing. She could also recognize people by feeling of their faces or their clothes.

The story of Helen Keller and her triumph, with the help of her teacher and companion Anne Sullivan Macy over the twin handicaps of blindness and deafness has been told many times. Miss Sullivan herself had been blind, but had an operation and regained her sight. So she understood what Helen was feeling and knew quite well how to teach her the signs for the letters of the alphabet. Then she would spell the words in Helen's hand to communicate with her.

Anne taught her for years. Helen learned to read Braille language, a system of raised dots representing letters. In 1904, she graduated from Radcliff College of Harvard

University with high honours, and proceeded to support herself by lecturing and writing. When she went to college, Anne went with her and tapped out the words of the instructors into her hand. Anne stayed with her for 50 years and was the most important person in Helen's life.

Helen had an amazing memory, and she also had skills that very few people have ever been able to develop. She could put her fingers to a person's lips and understand the words which were being spoken. While she was in college she wrote her book called *The Story of My Life*. She later became famous and traveled around the world making many speeches to various groups of people. Although Helen published several books, she is now chiefly celebrated as a symbol of the strength and high courage of the human spirit.

Three Days to See

All of us have read thrilling stories in which the hero had only a limited and specified time to live. Sometimes it was as long as a year; sometimes as short as twenty-four hours. But always we were interested in discovering just how the doomed man chose to spend his last days or his last hours. I speak, of course, of free men who have a choice, not condemned criminals whose sphere of activities is strictly delimited.

Such stories set us thinking, wondering what we should do under similar circumstances. What events, what experiences, what associations should we crowd into those last hours as mortal beings? What happiness should we find in reviewing the past, what regrets?

Sometimes I have thought it would be an excellent rule to live each day as if we should die tomorrow. Such an attitude would emphasize sharply the values of life. We should live each day with a gentleness, a vigor, and a keenness of appreciation which are often lost when time stretches before us in the constant panorama of more days and months and years to come. There are those, of course, who would adopt the Epicurean motto[1] of "Eat, drink, and be merry," but most people would be chastened by the certainty of impending death.

In stories the doomed hero is usually saved at the last minute by some stroke of fortune, but almost always his sense of values is changed: he becomes more appreciative of the meaning of life and its permanent spiritual values. It has often been noted that those who live, or have lived, in the shadow of death bring a mellow sweetness to everything they do.

Most of us, however, take life for granted. We know that one day we must die, but usually we picture that day as far in the future. When we are in buoyant health, death is all but unimaginable. We seldom think of it. The days stretch out in an endless vista. So we go about our petty tasks, hardly aware of our listless attitude toward life.

The same lethargy, I am afraid, characterizes the use of all our faculties and senses. Only the deaf appreciate hearing, only the blind realize the manifold blessings that lie in sight. Particularly does this observation apply to those who have lost sight and hearing in adult life. But those who have never suffered impairment of sight or hearing seldom make the fullest use of these blessed faculties. Their eyes and ears take in all sights and sounds hazily, without concentration and with little appreciation. It is the same old story of not being grateful for what we have until we lose it, of not being conscious of health until we are ill.

I have often thought it would be a blessing if each human being were stricken blind and deaf for a few days at some time during his early adult life. Darkness would make him more appreciative of sight; silence would teach him the joys of sound.

Now and then I have tested my seeing friends to discover what they see. Recently I was visited by a very good friend who had just returned from a long walk in the woods, and I asked her what she had observed. "Nothing in particular," she replied. I might have been incredulous had I not been accustomed to such responses, for long ago I became convinced that the seeing see little.

How was it possible, I asked myself, to walk for an hour through the woods and see nothing worthy of note? I who cannot see find hundreds of things to interest me through mere touch. I feel the delicate symmetry of a leaf. I pass my hands lovingly about the smooth skin of a silver birch, or the rough, shaggy bark of a pine. In the spring I touch the branches of trees hopefully in search of a bud the first sign of awakening Nature after her winter's sleep. I feel the delightful, velvety texture of a flower, and discover its remarkable convolutions; and something of the miracle of Nature is revealed to me. Occasionally, if I am very fortunate, I place my hand gently on a small tree and feel the happy quiver of a bird in full song. I am delighted to have the cool waters of a brook rush through my open finger. To me a lush carpet of pine needles or spongy grass is more welcome than the most luxurious Persian rug. To me the page ant of seasons is a thrilling and unending drama, the action of which streams through my finger tips.

At times my heart cries out with longing to see all these things. If I can get so much pleasure from mere touch, how much more beauty must be revealed by sight. Yet, those who have eyes apparently see little. The panorama of color and action which fills the world is taken for granted. It is human, perhaps, to appreciate little that which we have and to long for that which we have not, but it is a great pity that in the world of light the gift of sight is used only as a mere convenience rather than as a means of adding fullness to life.

If I were the president of a university I should establish a compulsory course in "How to Use Your Eyes". The professor would try to show his pupils how they could add joy to their lives by really seeing what passes unnoticed before them. He would try to awake their dormant and sluggish faculties.

Perhaps I can best illustrate by imagining what I should most like to see if I were given the use of my eyes, say, for just three days. And while I am imagining, suppose you, too, set your mind to work on the problem of how you would use your own eyes if you had only three more days to see. If with the on-coming darkness of the third night you knew that the sun would never rise for you again, how would you spend those three precious intervening days? What would you most want to let your gaze rest upon?

I, naturally, should want most to see the things which have become dear to me through my years of darkness. You, too, would want to let your eyes rest on the things that have become dear to you so that you could take the memory of them with you into the night that loomed before you.

If, by some miracle, I were granted three seeing days, to be followed by a relapse into darkness, I should divide the period into three parts.

The First Day

On the first day, I should want to see the people whose kindness and gentleness and companionship have made my life worth living. First I should like to gaze long upon the face of my dear teacher, Mrs. Anne Sullivan Macy, who came to me when I was a child and opened the outer world to me. I should want not merely to see the outline of her face, so that I could cherish it in my memory, but to study that face and find in it the living evidence of the sympathetic tenderness and patience with which she accomplished the difficult task of my education. I should like to see in her eyes that strength of character which has enabled her to stand firm in the face of difficulties, and that compassion for all humanity which she has revealed to me so often.

I do not know what it is to see into the heart of a friend through that "Window of the soul", the eye. I can only "see" through my finger tips the outline of a face. I can detect laughter, sorrow, and many other obvious emotions. I know my friends from the feel of their faces. But I cannot really picture their personalities by touch. I know their personalities, of course, through other means, through the thoughts they express to me, through whatever of their actions are revealed to me. But I am denied that deeper understanding of them which I am sure would come through sight of them, through watching their reactions to various expressed thoughts and circumstances, through noting the immediate and fleeting reactions of their eyes and countenance.

Friends who are near to me I know well, because through the months and years they reveal themselves to me in all their phases; but of casual friends I have only an incomplete impression, an impression gained from a handclasp, from spoken words which I take from their lips with my finger tips, or which they tap into the palm of my hand.

How much easier, how much more satisfying it is for you who can see to grasp quickly the essential qualities of another person by watching the subtleties of expression, the quiver of a muscle, the flutter of a hand. But does it ever occur to you to use your sight to see into the inner nature of a friend or acquaintance? Do not most of you seeing people grasp casually the outward features of a face and let it go at that?

For instance can you describe accurately the faces of five good friends? Some of you can, but many cannot. As an experiment, I have questioned husbands of long standing about the color of their wives' eyes, and often they express embarrassed confusion and admit that they do not know. And, incidentally, it is a chronic complaint of wives that their husbands do not notice new dresses, new hats, and changes in household arrangements.

The eyes of seeing persons soon become accustomed to the routine of their surroundings, and they actually see only the startling and spectacular. But even in viewing the most spectacular sights the eyes are lazy. Court records reveal every day how inaccurately "eyewitnesses" see. A given event will be "seen" in several different ways by as many witnesses. Some see more than others, but few see everything that is within the range of their vision.

Oh, the things that I should see if I had the power of sight for just three days!

The first day would be a busy one. I should call to me all my dear friends and look long into their faces, imprinting upon my mind the outward evidences of the beauty that is within them. I should let my eyes rest, too, on the face of a baby, so that I could catch a vision of the eager, innocent beauty which precedes the individual's consciousness of the conflicts which life develops.

And I should like to look into the loyal, trusting eyes of my dogs—the grave, canny little Scottie, Darkie, and the stalwart, understanding Great Dane, Helga, whose warm, tender, and playful friendships are so comforting to me.

On that busy first day I should also view the small simple things of my home. I want to see the warm colors in the rugs under my feet, the pictures on the walls, the intimate trifles that transform a house into home. My eyes would rest respectfully on the books in raised type which I have read, but they would be more eagerly interested in the printed books which seeing people can read, for during the long night of my life the books I have read and those which have been read to me have built themselves into a great shining lighthouse, revealing to me the deepest channels of human life and the human spirit.

In the afternoon of that first seeing day, I should take a long walk in the woods and intoxicate my eyes on the beauties of the world of Nature trying desperately to absorb in a few hours the vast splendor which is constantly unfolding itself to those who can see. On the way home from my woodland jaunt my path would lie near a farm so that I might see the patient horses ploughing in the field, (perhaps I should see only a tractor!) and the serene content of men living close to the soil. And I should pray for the glory of a colorful sunset.

When dusk had fallen, I should experience the double delight of being able to see by artificial light which the genius of man has created to extend the power of his sight when Nature decrees darkness.

In the night of that first day of sight, I should not be able to sleep, so full would be my mind of the memories of the day.

The Second Day

The next day—the second day of sight—I should arise with the dawn and see the thrilling miracle by which night is transformed into day. I should behold with awe the magnificent panorama of light with which the sun awakens the sleeping earth.

This day I should devote to a hasty glimpse of the world, past and present. I should want to see the pageant of man's progress, the kaleidoscope of the ages. How can so much be compressed into one day? Through the museums, of course. Often I have visited the New York Museum of Natural History to touch with my hands many of the objects there exhibited, but I have longed to see with my eyes the condensed history of the earth and its inhabitants displayed there—animals and the races of men pictured in their native environment; gigantic carcasses of dinosaurs and mastodons which roamed the earth long before man appeared, with his tiny stature and powerful brain, to conquer the animal kingdom; realistic presentations of the processes of development in animals, in man, and in the implements which man has used to fashion for himself a secure home on this planet; and a thousand and one other aspects of natural history.

I wonder how many readers of this article have viewed this panorama of the face of living things as pictured in that inspiring museum. Many, of course, have not had the opportunity, but I am sure that many who have had the opportunity have not made use of it. there, indeed, is a place to use your eyes. You who see can spend many fruitful days there, but I with my imaginary three days of sight, could only take a hasty glimpse, and pass on.

My next stop would be the Metropolitan Museum of Art, for just as the Museum of Natural History reveals the material aspects of the world, so does the Metropolitan show the myriad facets[2] of the human spirit. Throughout the history of humanity the urge to artistic expression has been almost as powerful as the urge for food, shelter, and procreation. And here, in the vast chambers of the Metropolitan Museum, is unfolded before me the spirit of Egypt, Greece, and Rome, as expressed in their art. I know well through my hands the sculptured gods and goddesses of the ancient Nile-land. I have felt copies of Parthenon friezes,[3] and I have sensed the rhythmic beauty of charging Athenian warriors. Apollos and Venuses and the Winged Victory of Samothrace[4] are friends of my finger tips. The gnarled, bearded features of Homer[5] are dear to me, for he, too, knew blindness.

My hands have lingered upon the living marble of Roman sculpture as well as that of later generations. I have passed my hands over a plaster cast of Michelangelo's[6] inspiring and heroic Moses; I have sensed the power of Rodin;[7] I have been awed by the devoted spirit of Gothic wood carving. These arts which can be touched have meaning for me, but even they were meant to be seen rather than felt, and I can only guess at the beauty which remains hidden from me. I can admire the simple lines of a Greek vase, but its figured decorations are lost to me.

So on this, my second day of sight, I should try to probe into the soul of man through this art. The things I knew through touch I should now see. More splendid still, the whole magnificent world of painting would be opened to me, from the Italian Primitives, with their serene religious devotion, to the Moderns, with their feverish visions. I should look deep into the canvases of Raphael, Leonardo da Vinci, Titian, Rembrandt.[8] I should want to feast my eyes upon the warm colors of Veronese, study the mysteries of El Greco,[9] catch a new vision of Nature from Corot.[10] Oh, there is so much rich meaning and beauty in the art of the ages for you who have eyes to see!

Upon my short visit to this temple of art I should not be able to review a fraction of that great world of art which is open to you. I should be able to get only a superficial impression. Artists tell me that for deep and true appreciation of art one must educated the eye. One must learn through experience to weigh the merits of line, of composition, of form and color. If I had eyes, how happily would I embark upon so fascinating a study! Yet I am told that, to many of you who have eyes to see, the world of art is a dark night, unexplored and unilluminated.

It would be with extreme reluctance that I should leave the Metropolitan Museum, which contains the key to beauty—a beauty so neglected. Seeing persons, however, do not need a metropolitan to find this key to beauty. The same key lies waiting in smaller museums, and in books on the shelves of even small libraries. But naturally, in my limited time of imaginary sight, I should choose the place where the key unlocks the greatest treasures in the shortest time.

The evening of my second day of sight I should spend at a theatre or at the movies. Even now I often attend theatrical performances of all sorts, but the action of the play must be spelled into my hand by a companion. But how I should like to see with my own eyes the fascinating figure of Hamlet, or the gusty Falstaff amid colorful Elizabethan trappings! How I should like to follow each movement of the graceful Hamlet, each strut of the hearty Falstaff! And since I could see only one play, I should be confronted by a many-horned dilemma, for there are scores of plays I should want to see. You who have eyes can see any you like. How many of you, I wonder, when you gaze at a play, a movie, or any spectacle, realize and give thanks for the miracle of sight which enables you to enjoy its color, grace, and movement?

I cannot enjoy the beauty of rhythmic movement except in a sphere restricted to the touch of my hands. I can vision only dimly the grace of a Pavlowa,[11] although I know something of the delight of rhythm, for often I can sense the beat of music as it vibrates through the floor. I can well imagine that cadenced motion must be one of the most pleasing sights in the world. I have been able to gather something of this by tracing with my fingers the lines in sculptured marble; if this static grace can be so lovely, how much more acute must be the thrill of seeing grace in motion.

One of my dearest memories is of the time when Joseph Jefferson allowed me to touch his face and hands as he went through some of the gestures and speeches of his beloved Rip Van Winkle. [12] I was able to catch thus a meager glimpse of the world of drama, and I shall never forget the delight of that moment. But, oh, how much I must miss, and how much pleasure you seeing ones can derive from watching and hearing the interplay of speech and movement in the unfolding of a dramatic performance! If I could see only one play, I should know how to picture in my mind the action of a hundred plays which I have read or had transferred to me through the medium of the manual alphabet.

So, through the evening of my second imaginary day of sight, the great fingers of dramatic literature would crowd sleep from my eyes.

The Third Day

The following morning, I should again greet the dawn, anxious to discover new delights, for I am sure that, for those who have eyes which really see, the dawn of each day must be a perpetually new revelation of beauty.

This, according to the terms of my imagined miracle, is to be my third and last day of sight. I shall have no time to waste in regrets or longings; there is too much to see. The first day I devoted to my friends, animate and inanimate. The second revealed to me the history of man and Nature. Today I shall spend in the workaday world of the present, amid the haunts of men going about the business of life. And where can one find so many activities and conditions of men as in New York? So the city becomes my destination.

I start from my home in the quiet little suburb of Forest Hills, Long Island. Here, surrounded by green lawns, trees, and flowers, are neat little houses, happy with the voices and movements of wives and children, havens of peaceful rest for men who toil in the city. I drive across the lacy structure of steel which spans the East River, and I get a new and startling vision of the power and ingenuity of the mind of man. Busy boasts chug and scurry about the river—racy speed boat, stolid, snorting tugs. If I had long days of sight ahead, I should spend many of them watching the delightful activity upon the river.

I look ahead, and before me rise the fantastic towers of New York, a city that seems to have stepped from the pages of a fairy story. What an awe-inspiring sight, these glittering spires, these vast banks of stone and steel-structures such as the gods might build for themselves! This animated picture is a part of the lives of millions of people every day. How many, I wonder, give it so much as a second's glance? Very few, I fear, Their eyes are blind to this magnificent sight because it is so familiar to them.

I hurry to the top of one of those gigantic structures, the Empire State Building, for there, a short time ago, I "saw" the city below through the eyes of my secretary. I am anxious to compare my fancy with reality. I am sure I should not be disappointed in the panorama spread out before me, for to me it would be a vision of another world.

Now I begin my rounds of the city. First, I stand at a busy corner, merely looking at people, trying by sight of them to understand something of their lives. I see smiles, and I am happy. I see serious determination, and I am proud, I see suffering, and I am compassionate.

I stroll down Fifth Avenue. I throw my eyes out of focus, so that I see no particular object but only a seething kaleidoscope of colors. I am certain that the colors of women's dresses moving in a throng must be a gorgeous spectacle of which I should never tire. But perhaps if I had sight I should be like most other women—too interested in styles and the cut of individual dresses to give much attention to the splendor of color in the mass. And I am convinced, too, that I should become an inveterate window shopper, for it must be a delight to the eye to view the myriad articles of beauty on display.

From Fifth Avenue I make a tour of the city—to Park Avenue, to the slums, to factories, to parks where children play. I take a stay-at-home trip abroad by visiting the foreign quarters. Always my eyes are open wide to all the sights of both happiness and misery so that I may probe deep and add to my understanding of how people work and live. My heart is full of the images of people and things. My eye passes lightly over no single trifle; it strives to touch and hold closely each thing its gaze rests upon. Some sights are pleasant, filling the heart with happiness; but some are miserably pathetic. To these latter I do not shut my eyes, for they, too, are part of life. To close the eye on them is to close the heart and mind.

My third day of sight is drawing to an end. Perhaps there are many serious pursuits to which I should devote the few remaining hours, but I am afraid that on the evening of that last day I should again run away to the theater, to a hilariously funny play, so that I might appreciate the overtones of comedy in the human spirit.

At midnight my temporary respite from blindness would cease, and permanent night would close in on me again. Naturally in those three short days I should not have seen all I wanted to see. Only when darkness had again descended upon me should I realize how much I had left unseen. But my mind would be so crowded with glorious memories that I should have little time for regrets. Thereafter the touch of every object would bring a glowing memory of how that object looked.

Perhaps this short outline of how I should spend three days of sight does not agree with the program you would set for yourself if you knew that you were about to be stricken blind. I am, however, sure that if you actually faced that fate your eyes would open to things you had never seen before, storing up memories for the long night ahead. You would use your eyes as never before. Everything you saw would become dear to you. Your eyes would touch and embrace every object that came within your range of vision. Then, at last, you would really see, and a new world of beauty would open itself before you.

I who am blind can give one hint to those who see—one admonition to those who would make full use of the gift of sight: Use your eyes as if tomorrow you would be stricken blind. And the same method can be applied to the other senses. Hear the music of voices, the song of a bird, the mighty strains of an orchestra, as if you would be stricken deaf tomorrow. Touch each object you want to touch as if tomorrow your tactile sense would fail. Smell the perfume of flowers, taste with relish each morsel, as if tomorrow you could never smell and taste again. Make the most of every sense: glory in all the facets of pleasure and beauty which the world reveals to you through the several means of contact which Nature provides. But of all the senses, I am sure that sight must be the most delightful.

Notes

[1] the Epicurean motto: a short sentence used as a guide of rule which believes that people should devote to pleasure, esp. refined sensuous enjoyment.

[2] the myriad facets: the countless dimensions.

[3] Parthenon friezes: ornamental band or strip along the walls of Parthenon Temple in Athens, Greece.

[4] Apollos and Venuses and the Winged Victory of Samothrace: Apollo: Sun God; Venus: Goddess of Love/Beauty; the Winged Victory of Samothrace: the goddess of victory of Samothrace, a Rhodian sculptor, between 220 and 190 B.C.

[5] Homer: a legendary early Greek poet traditionally credited with the composition of *Iliad* and *Odyssey*, commonly assumed to have lived in the 8th century B.C.

[6] Michelangelo: the most representative artist of the 16th-century Italy, a very influential sculptor, painter, architect, and poet.

[7] Rodin: Auguste Rodin (1840－1917), French art sculptor whose masterpiece sculpture is *The Thinker*.

[8] Raphael: Raphael Sanzio (1483－1520), Italian painter during the period of High Renaissance; Leonardo da Vinci: Florentine painter, sculptor, architect, engineer, and scholar, and one of the greatest minds of the Renaissance, Italy; Titian: Tiziano Vecelli or Vecellio, better known in English as Titian, one of the most versatile of

Italian painters, was recognized as the leader of the 16th-century Venetian school of the Italian Renaissance; Rembrandt: Holland's greatest 17th-century painter.

[9] El Greco: the most unusual painter in 16th-century Europe, who combined the strict Byzantine style of his homeland, Greece, with influences received during his studies in Venice and the medieval tradition of the Spanish country where he worked.

[10] Corot: Jean-Baptiste-Camille Corot (1796—1875), French painter.

[11] Pavlowa: Anna Pavlowa, the glorious Russian ballet star, became famous for her premiere of *The Dying Swan* on May 19, 1909 in Paris.

[12] Rip Van Winkle: a famous short novel written by Washington Irving (1783—1859).

Commentary

Persuasion is a kind of writing in which an author tries to make the reader accept an opinion or take an action. To be persuasive, writers must back up their opinions with objective evidence—facts, incidents, and examples. *Three Days to See* written by Helen Keller offers a fine example of persuasion and argument in essay writing. Keller backs up her opinion with convincing evidence when she writes that many husbands do not know the color of their wife's eyes.

Furthermore, persuasive writers also offer logical arguments, or sensible reasons to support their opinions. Keller here successfully gives a logical argument for appreciating the sense of sight when she recounts that she has only been able to touch the objects at the Museum of Natural History.

Questions and Exercises

1. Why should Helen Keller select young adulthood rather than some other period of life as the time when a person ought to experience temporary deafness and blindness?
2. Helen Keller has planned her three days of sight with great care. Try to state briefly the central theme around which she has organized each day's viewing.
3. Choose a hot issue that is currently talked about at present, and write an essay expressing your opinion on it. Remember to use facts, incidents, and logical arguments to support yourself, so that other people will be persuaded.

Part 6

Short Glossary of Literature Terms

accent: the word which describes a stressed syllable.

acting: the last of the four steps in characterization in a performed play.

action: an imagined event or series of events in fiction.

Alexandrine: a verse of six iambic feet.

allegory: a kind of literature in which concrete things—characters, events, and objects—represent ideas. In an allegory the comparison is extended to include an entire work or large portion of a work.

alliteration: the repetition of initial consonant sounds, especially at the beginning of words or of stressed syllables. For example, "Pale beyond porch or portal". (Swinburne)

allusion: a brief reference to a person, place or event, either in history or in previous literature, which the reader is assumed to know.

ambiguity: the use of a word or expression to mean more than one thing.

amphibrach: an unstressed syllable, followed by a stressed and an unstressed; the foot used in limericks as a variant of the anapestic foot.

analogy: an extended comparison based on certain resemblances between things that are otherwise unlike.

anapest: a metrical form in which each foot consists of two unstressed syllables followed by a stressed one.

antagonist: a neutral term for a character who opposes the leading character.

anticlimax: a continuation of the plot after the story's climax. Its intent is to relieve from the tension of the climax, or to present further complications of the plot.

apostrophe: the addressing of a discourse to a real or imagined person who is not present; a speech to an animal, object or a personified abstraction.

archaism: the use of words and phrases no longer current.

archetype: a basic pattern of human values, such as the stock plot archetypes of romantic love, and the good triumphing over the evil.

argument: the development of an idea, including the introduction of a hypothesis, supporting details, and logical conclusions.

argumentation: one of the four basic types of discourse, the attempt of which is to convince the reader of the truth of the author's position by presenting objective evidence or by using logic.

assonance: the repetition of vowel sounds, especially in stressed syllables.

atmosphere: the mood prevailing in a literary work. It often relates to the writer's tone, and also to whatever sets up certain expectations in the reader.

audience: the people attending a theatrical production; the intended group of readers for whom a writer writes.

autobiography: an account of a person's life written by himself or herself.

ballad: a narrative poem that is meant to be sung. Characterized by repetition and often by a repeated refrain, ballads were originally a folk creation, transmitted orally from person to person and age to age.

ballad stanza (also called *ballad measure*): a common stanza form, consisting of a quatrain in which lines of iambic tetrameter alternates with iambic trimester, rhyming *xaxa*.

biography: an account of a person's life written by another person.

blank verse: the verse form that consists of unrhymed lines in iambic pentameter. Many of Shakespeare's plays are in blank verse.

block quotation: a longer quotation, set off from the text by additional indentation.

brainstorming: When generating ideas for developing an essay, we use brainstorming by making random associations and jotting down ideas informally.

Burns Stanza (also called habbie stanza or Scottish stanza): a six-line stanza rhyming *aaabab*, with a metrical count of 4-4-4-2-4-2 feet (or accents) for the six lines. It was a favorite metrical form adopted by the Scottish poet Robert Burns, and thus the name.

cadence: (of free verse) a coherent word group spoken as a single rhythmical unit, such as a noun phrase or prepositional phrase.

caesura, caesurae: a natural break falling inside a line of poetry.

***carpe diem* poetry:** poetry concerned with the shortness of life and the need to act now and enjoy the present. *carpe diem* means "seize the day".

character: (1) a fictional personage who acts or appears in a work; (2) a combination of a person's qualities, especially moral qualities.

characterization: the fictional or artistic presentation of a fictional personage.

chorus: the stanza of a song that is repeated, usually after the verse which is different each time; In classical Greek plays, members of the chorus were often masked and relied alternatively on song, dance, and recitation of a chorus to make their commentary.

Chronological order: plot arrangement in the order of calendar or of occurrence.

City poem: a poem about life in a city or about the city itself; a modern counterpart to poems about rural life known as *idylls* or *pastorals*. A city poem might be ironically called an "urban pastoral". The rise of such poems coincides with the Industrial Revolution just before the turn of the 19th century. Blake's *London*, and Wordsworth's *Composed upon Westminster Bridge* are such examples.

classicism: a form of literature that emphasizes the classic qualities of form, reason, restraint, and is based on distinguished artistic models of the past.

climax: the point at which the conflict reaches the highest top and the action stops rising and begins falling or reversing. It is the third part of plot structure and is also called *the turning point of the plot*.

comedy: a broad category of dramatic works that are intended primarily to entertain and amuse the audience through exaggeration and incongruity.

complication: a stage of narrative and dramatic structure in which the major conflicts are brought out; *the rising action* of a drama.

conceit: a figure of speech which establishes a striking witty parallel between two basically dissimilar things or situations. The metaphysical poets tend to yoke violently together dissimilar ideas, yet the emotions can be clearly and often passionately felt by the reader.

conclusion: the fifth part of plot structure, the point at which the situation that was destabilized at the beginning of the story becomes stable once more.

concrete poetry: also called *shaped verse*; poetry shaped to look like an object.

conflict: a struggle between opposing forces, such as between two people, between a person and something in nature or society, or even between two parts of the self.

connotation: what is suggested by a word, apart from what it explicitly describes.

controlling metaphor: a metaphor which is carried throughout all or a part of a work. Also called extended or conceptual metaphor.

criticism: the evaluative or interpretive work written by professional interpreters of literary texts.

cosmic irony: irony which implies that a god or fate controls and toys with human actions, feelings, lives, and outcomes.

couplet (distich): lines of poetry rhyming in pairs. The most normal type in English poetry is the heroic couplet.

crisis: the point of uncertainty and tension or the turning point of a story.

dactyl (dactylic): the metrical pattern in which each foot consists of a stressed syllable followed by two unstressed syllables.

denotation: a dictionary definition or the direct and specific meaning of a word as opposed to *connotation* or implied meanings.

denouement: The point at which the aftermath of the climax is presented to the author. Literally, "the untying of a knot" in French.

dialogue: the speeches of two or more characters in a story, play or poem.

diction: word choice, types of words, and the level of language that an author chooses to use.

didactic: referring to a work designed to demonstrate, or to present persuasively, a moral, religious, or political doctrine; didactic poetry aims to teach something, in other words, the primary purpose of didactic poetry is to instruct.

dilemma: two choices facing a protagonist, usually in a tragic situation, with either choice being unacceptable or damaging.

dimeter: a line of poetry of two metrical patterns.

distich (couplet): a Greek term meaning two line verse; sometimes used synonymously with *couplet*.

disyllable: any word of two syllables.

double foot: two metrical feet in combination. In English, the common double foot is double iamb (∪ ∪— —), a pyrrhic foot and a spondee. The rhythm is endemic to the English language, occurring in many phrases: "the absurd act", "with a blank look", "an obscure face".

drama: an individual play or plays considered as a group; one of the three major genres of literature with others being poetry and fiction..

dramatic irony: a kind of *situational irony* in which a character perceives his or her plight in a limited way while the audience and one or more of the other characters understand it entirely.

dramatic monologue: poem spoken by a character or through a persona (Greek for "mask), rather than by the poet or an unidentified speaker; a type of poem, derived from theater, in which a speaker addresses an imaginary audience or the reader at length. The form is related to the *soliloquy*.

dramatic poetry: poetry written for performance as a play. It is one of the three genres of poetry, others being lyric poetry and narrative poetry.

dramatis personae: the list of characters that appears either in the play's program or at the top of the first page of the written play.

dynamic characters: characters who change during the course of drama and narrative fiction.

elegy: poem for someone who is dead or any poem on any subject written in elegiac meter. Thomas Gray's *Elegy—Written in a Country Churchyard* is a good case in point.

elegiac couplet: a line of dactylic hexameter followed by a line of dactylic pentameter.

emblematic poem (concrete poem, shaped poem, visual poem): a poem in which the words or letters form a typographical picture, either imitating how something looks or suggesting what the subject does. George Herbert depicts an altar and a pair of wings to show the religious themes of his poem.

end rhyme: rhymed words that appear at the ends of lines of poetry.

end-stopped line: a line of poetry that has a definite pause or strong halt at the end.

English sonnet: also called *Shakespearean sonnet*; a sonnet form that divides the poem into three units of four lines each and a final unit of two lines. Its classic rhyme scheme is *abab cdcd efef gg*.

enjambment: verse in which the sense runs on without a pause from one line to the next, and thus an enjambed line is also called a *run-on line*. It is the opposite of an *end-stop line*.

epic: a long narrative poem that centers on a heroic figure, upon whose actions the fate of a nation or a race often depends. It has elevated language and a grand, high style.

epigram: a short pithy comic or satirical poem; but in modern usage a very short, usually witty verse with a quick turn at the end.

epitaph (elegy): verse that commemorates a person or a group of people who have died. Epitaph are often inscribed upon tombs or gravestones.

essay: a prose composition of undefined length that usually treats a single theme or subject.

exposition: that part of the plot structure that sets the scene, introduces characters, and establishes the situation at the beginning of a story or play. Additional exposition is often scattered throughout the work.

extended metaphor: see *controlling metaphor*.

external conflicts: conflicts that take place outside characters—between characters or between characters and physical realities, such as storms, earthquakes, hostile terrain, etc.

eye rhyme: words that seem to rhyme because parts of them are spelled identically but pronounced differently, such as *bear, fear; fury, bury; moved, loved; wonder, yonder.*

fable: a story, in verse or prose, whose characters are animals and which points out a moral. Aesop's fables from ancient Greek tell such stories in the form of a fable.

fairy tales: a story immersed in a magic dream world in which frightening or marvelous things happen. *The Nightingale and the Rose* written by Oscar Wilde is an example of a fairy tale.

falling action: the events that occur after the climax. See *denouement*.

fantasy: a work or part of a work that is fantastic or nonrealistic. Not taking place in the real world.

farce: a play characterized by broad humor, wild antics, and often slapstick, pratfalls, or other physical humor.

feminine rhyme: lines of verse which rhyme with one stressed syllable followed by one unstressed syllable.

feminist criticism: an interpretive approach in literature designed to raise the consciousness about the importance and unique nature of women.

figurative language: a way of saying one thing and suggesting another so that the words have significance beyond the literal meaning.

figures of speech: literary devices such as metaphor and simile, personification, apostrophe, in which what is stated not literally but literarily.

first-person point of view: a character "I", who tells the story and necessarily has a limited point of view.

fixed form: poetry written according to traditional closed patterns such as sonnet or villanelle, as apposed to open form poetry widely used in free verse.

flashback: a plot-structuring device whereby a scene from the fictional past is inserted into the fictional present or dramatized out of order.

flat character: a fictional character, often but not always a minor character, who is relatively simple, thus does not change much in the course of a story, as opposed to a *round character*.

foil: one character, usually minor, designed to highlight the major character.

foot: the basic unit of measure in a metrical line.

foreshadowing: hinting at events yet to come later in the plot.

form (shape): an established pattern to which a poem conforms. For example, a typical sonnet consists 14 iambic pentameter lines written to a fixed rhyme scheme.

formal diction: language that is lofty, dignified, and impersonal, as opposed to colloquial diction and informal diction.

fourteener: a line consisting of seven iambic feet; iambic heptameter.

free verse: also called "open form". Poetry characterized by varying line lengths, lack of traditional meter, and with non-rhyming lines.

genre: the largest category for classifying literature—fiction, poetry, drama, essay, biography. The great traditional *genres* of literature were: tragedy, comedy, satire, epic, elegy, pastoral, lyric.

Harlem Renaissance: an African American literary movement centered in Harlem in the 1920s. Influenced by jazz and blues, these poets celebrated black culture and attacked the forces that oppressed the American blacks.

heptameter: a seven-foot line of verse, also called the *fourteener* when the metrical pattern is iambic.

hero/heroine: the leading male/female character, usually larger than life, sometimes almost godlike.

heroic couplet: rhymed pairs of lines in iambic pentameter.

hexameter: a line of poetry consisting of six metrical feet.

historical criticism: literary criticism that studies how historical events, intellectual beliefs, and cultural patterns relate to works of literature.

hymn: a sacred lyric or a hymnal poem.

hyperbole: overstatement characterized by exaggerated language.

iamb: a metrical form in which each foot consists of an unstressed syllable followed by a stressed one.

idyll (idyl): short poem depicting rural life or country scenes. The adjective *idyllic* refers to something that is natural, simple, harmonious, and picturesque.

image (imagery): broadly defined, any sensory detail in a work; more narrowly, the use of figurative language to evoke a feeling, or to call to mind an idea.

imagism: a poetic movement invented by Ezra Pound around 1909 as an antidote to the rhetorical excesses of the Victorian poetry and the pastoral complacency of Georgian verse.

imperfect foot: a metrical foot consisting of a single syllable, either heavily or lightly stressed.

informal diction: language that is not as lofty as formal diction; language similar to everyday speech.

internal conflict: conflict that takes place within the minds of characters.

internal rhyme: rhymed words that occur within a line of poetry or that appear close together in prose.

in-text citation: a source citation appearing within the essay rather than in the list of works cited at the end.

inversion: the reversal of an unexpected metrical foot, as when a trochee is substitute for one or more of the feet in an iambic line (called a trochaic inversion), as in "Gather ye rosebuds while ye may." (— ∪ |∪ —|∪ —|∪ —|); a wrenching or disruption of the usual word order in a sentence.

irony: a situation or statement characterized by a significant difference between what is expected and what actually happens. Language that states the opposite of what is intended is *verbal irony*. The placement of characters in a state of ignorance is *dramatic irony*. The emphasis on powerlessness is *cosmic* or *situational irony* that is connected with a pessimistic or fatalistic view of life.

Italian sonnet: a sonnet form that divides the poem into one section of eight lines (octave) and a second section of six lines (sestet), usually following the rhyme scheme of *abba abba cdecde*.

limerick: a light or humorous verse form of mainly anapestic verses of which the first, second, and fifth lines are of three feet; the third and fourth lines are of two feet; and the rhyme scheme is *aabba*.

limited point of view: a perspective pinned to a single character, whether a first-person- or a third-person-centered consciousness, so that we cannot know for sure what is going on in the minds of other characters.

line: one or more words arranged in a line, which is the most immediately visible structural unit of poetry.

list poem: a poem that names or enumerates a series of things; a catalogue as in many of Walt Whitman's poems.

literary criticism: the analysis and interpretation of works of literature.

literary critics: professional interpreters or evaluators, of literary texts.

literature: written or oral compositions that tell stories, dramatize situations, express emotions, and analyze and advocate ideas. Literature is designed to engage readers emotionally as well as intellectually, with major genres of *fiction, poetry, drama,* and *nonfiction prose*, and with many separate sub-forms.

low (physical) comedy: humor that employs burlesque, horseplay, or the representation of unrefined life, as opposed to high (verbal) comedy.

lyric: originally a song set to the music of the lyre; then any poem intended to be sung; more recently, any short poem presenting a single speaker who expresses a state of mind involving thought and feeling.

major (main) characters: those characters whom we see and learn about the most.

masculine rhyme: a rhyme pattern in which the final syllable of one line rhymes with the final syllable of another, also called *single rhyme* or *true rhyme*.

melodrama: a sentimental dramatic form with an artificially happy ending.

metaphor: (1) one thing pictured as if it were something else, suggesting a likeness or analogy between them; (2) an implicit comparison of one thing with another unlike itself without the use of a verbal signal.

meter: the more or less regular pattern of stressed and unstressed syllables in a line of poetry; the recurrence in a poetic line of a regular rhythmic unit.

minor characters: those figures who fill out the story but who do not figure prominently in it.

monologue: a long speech made by a single character to himself or herself, to the audience, or to an off-stage character.

monometer: a line of poetry consisting of one metrical foot.

mood: the prevailing tone or atmosphere of a literary work.

moral: the ethical lesson of a literary work.

motif: a recurrent situation that deliberately connects a work with common patterns of existing thought.

motivation: plausible grounds for a character's actions.

musical comedy: a modern prose play integrated with lyrics set to specially composed music.

narration: the recounting of an event or a series of events or actions.

narrative poetry: poetry that tells a story. It is one of the three genres of poetry, others being dramatic and lyric poetry.

narrative structure: a textual organization based on sequences of connected events usually presented in a straightforward chronological framework.

narrator: the character who "tells" the story.

nature: a term suggesting something inborn, inherent, and thus predictable in a person's character.

near rhyme: also called "imperfect, eye, slant rhyme" as in "love" and "move". Rhyming words have approximate rather than identical sounds.

neoclassicism: a late 17th and 18th centuries school of literature that attempts to revive the principles of classicism. Man is viewed as imperfect and dualistic, and restrained emotions dominate the writing. Dryden, Milton, Pope, and Johnson are representative of neoclassicism.

new criticism: literary criticism that deemphasizes the value of biography and history for interpreting literature and that instead focuses on the form and unity of literary works.

nonfiction prose: a genre of literature consisting of essays, articles, and books that are concerned with real as apposed to fictional writings.

novel: a form of complex fictitious prose that contains the three main elements of plot, characters, and setting.

novelette: a work of prose fiction that is longer than the short story but shorter than the novel.

occasional poem: poem written for a special event or occasion, public or private. The poet laureate, for example, is often called upon to write poems for royal anniversaries and other public events.

octameter: a line of poetry consisting of eight metrical feet.

octave (octet): a stanza of poetry consisting of eight lines; the first eight lines of a Petrarchan/Italian sonnet.

octava rima: a special kind of eight-line stanza which Lord Byron uses in *Don Juan*, rhyming *abababcc*.

ode: a long lyric poem, serious in subject, elevated in style, and elaborate in stanzaic structure. In English poetry there are three types of odes: the Pindaric ode, following the pattern originated by the ancient Greek poet Pindar; the Horatian ode, named after the ancient Roman poet Horace; and the irregular ode which has no set rhyme scheme and no set stanza pattern. The irregular ode has employed all manner of formal possibilities, while often retaining the tone and thematic elements of the classical ode.

omniscient point of view: an organization device in which the reader has access to the perceptions and thoughts of all the characters in the story; the point of view that can wander like a camera from one character to another but cannot get inside anyone's head, thus does not present from the inside any character's thoughts.

onomatopoeia: the use of a word that imitates the sound of what the word means, such as *dingdong, bang, sizzle, buzz,* and *puff.*

open form: opposite for "*closed or fixed form*" in poetry writing. See *free verse.*

opera: a dramatic form in which some of the dialogues are sung instead of spoken.

overstatement: exaggerated language; also called *hyperbole.*

oxymoron: a figure of speech that combines two apparently contradictory elements, as in *wise fool (sophomore).*

parable: a short fiction that illustrates an explicit moral lesson.

paradox: a statement that seems contradictory but may actually be true.

parallelism: a figure of speech in which the same grammatical structures are repeated.

parody: a work that imitates another work for comic effect by exaggerating the style and changing the content of the original.

pastoral: also called an *eclogue,* a poem that describes the simple life of country folk, usually shepherds who live a timeless, painless life in a world full of beauty, music, and love.

pentameter: a line of poetry consisting of five feet.

pentastich: a five-line stanza especially if the stanza is unrhymed.

persona: a character used by the author as the narrative voice.

personification: treating an abstraction as if it were a person by endowing it with humanlike qualities.

Petrarchan sonnet: See ***Italian sonnet***.

plagiarism: a theft of the intellectual property of others. the presentation of other people's ideas, work, and facts as one's own.

plot: the arrangement of the action in a fictional work.

poem, poet/poetess, poetry: a rhythmic, unified composition characterized by imagination and the use of figurative language. A poem is one poetic work. A poet/poetess is a person who writes poems. Poetry may refer to the poems of one poet, to all poems generally, or to the aesthetics of poetry considered as an art.

poetic license: the privilege to depart from normal logic, diction, or rhyme in order to achieve a particular desired effects in poetry writing.

point of view: the point from which people, events, and other details in a story are viewed.

Pre-Raphaelite movement: a literary movement characteristic of Italian art before Raphael. A group of artists and writers in the 19th century believed in a return to a simple, straightforward presentation in art and literature.

primary source: the original work of literature under discussion (as opposed to the "secondary source" that comments on the primary work.

prose: writing that does not have a regular rhythmic pattern.

prosody: the systematic study of versification, including meter, rhyme, stanza forms, etc.

protagonist: the major character in a narrative play or story.

pun: a play upon words that are identical or similar in sound but have sharply different meanings, such as "7 days without water makes one week (weak)".

pyrrhic foot: two unstressed syllables together. This foot occurs only occasionally in English as a variant on some other foot.

quatrain: a four-line stanza, employing various meters and rhyme schemes.

quintet (quintrain, cinquain): a five-line stanza.

Quintilla: a Spanish five-line stanza containing eight syllables per line and rhyming *ababa, abbab, abaab,* or *aabba.*

reader response critical approach: an interpretive approach based on the proposition that literary works are not fully created until readers make transactions with them in the light of their own knowledge and experience.

realism: a general term meaning accuracy of detail and true presentation of actuality.

refrain: the repetition of a phrase, a line or a series of lines at the same point in each stanza throughout a poem. The refrain is a feature of many metrically powerful poems, such as ballads and nursery rhymes, where it creates an effect close to ritual.

Renaissance: the rebirth of culture throughout Europe in the later Middle Ages. It is often said to have begun in Italy in the late 14th century and did not reach England until the 16th century, where it had a late flowering in the Elizabethan and Jacobean periods in England.

rhetoric: the principles and theory dealing with the logical, clear, convincing presentation of facts and ideas in speech or composition.

rhyme: the identity or strong similarity between terminal sounds of words. The use of rhyme at the ends of lines in poetry is normal, especially in the well-known stanza forms.

rhyme scheme: any pattern of end rhyme, which is a traditional method of organizing stanzas and poems.

rhythm: the modulation of stressed and unstressed elements in the flow of speech. In most conventional poetry, rhythm was often expressed in regular, metrical forms; in prose and in free verse, rhythm is present but in a much less predictable and regular manner called *cadence*.

rising action: the second of the five parts of plot structure, in which events complicate the situation that existed at the beginning of a work, intensify the conflict or introduce new conflict.

romanticism: the belief and assumption that reliance on emotion provides a valid and powerful means of knowing and also a reliable guide to ways of living. The period is roughly from 1789 (the date of the French Revolution) to 1837 or from Blake to early

Tennyson.

round characters: complex characters, often major characters, who can grow and change, or act in a way that you did not expect from what had gone before.

run-on lines: see *enjambment.*

sarcasm: a form of verbal irony in which apparent praise is actually harshly or bitterly critical.

satire: a literary work that holds up human failings to ridicule and censure.

scansion: the process of scanning a poem by analyzing the metrical structure in a line of poetry.

second-person narrator: a character, "you", who tells the story and necessarily has a limited point of view, and may be seen as an extension of the reader and thus an unreliable narrator.

secondary source: a work that is a commentary upon the primary source under discussion, including critical essays, articles of analysis, interviews, and other materials related to interpreting a primary work.

sestet: a line of poetry consisting of six lines; the final six lines of a Petrarchan sonnet.

sestina: a six-line stanza or poem. It is a sestet, except that the term does not apply to the sonnet.

set: the design, decoration, and scenery of the stage during a play.

setting: the time, place, or social background of the action in a story, poem, or play.

Shakespearean sonnet: See ***English sonnet***.

shaped verse: See ***concrete poetry***.

simile: a direct comparison between two essentially different things, introduced by the words *like* or *as*.

situational irony: a type of irony emphasizing that human beings are trapped in forces beyond their comprehension and control. Also called *cosmic irony* or *irony of fate*.

slant rhyme: rhyme in which the sounds are similar but not exactly the same. It is also called *near rhyme* or *approximate rhyme*.

soliloquy: a monologue in which the character in a play is alone and speaking only to himself or herself.

sonnet: a fixed verse form consisting of fourteen lines usually in iambic pentameter. See ***Italian sonnet*** and ***Shakespearean sonnet***.

speaker: the person, not necessarily the author, who is the voice of a poem. The reader should not assume that the speaker equals the author.

Spenserian stanza: the nine-line stanza of *The Faerie Queene*: the first eight lines are iambic pentameters, the last is an iambic hexameter (or Alexandrine). The rhyme scheme is *ababbcbcc*.

spondee: a metrical foot consisting of two stressed syllables together as in *singsong*. This foot occurs only occasionally in English poetry as a variant on some other foot.

sprung rhythm, accentual rhythm: a method of accenting, developed by Gerald Manley Hopkins, in which major stresses are "sprung" from the poetic line.

stage directions: a playwright's instructions concerning lighting, scenery, tone of voice, action, entrances, exits, and the like.

stanza: a verse paragraph or a division of a poem demarcated by extra line spacing.

stereotype: a character who is so ordinary and unoriginal that he/she seems to have been cast in a mold.

stock character: a character that appears in a number of stories or plays, such as the cruel stepmother, the braggart, and so forth.

stream-of-consciousness novel: the type of psychological novel developed by James Joyce and William Faulkner in which the characters' consciousness is explored.

stress: See ***accent***.

strophe: a stanzaic unit of poetry specifically associated with the Pindaric ode.

structure: the organization or arrangement of the various elements in a work.

style: a distinctive manner of expression; each author's style is expressed through his/her diction, rhythm, imagery, and so on.

subgenre: division within the category of a genre; *novel, novella,* and *short story* are subgenres of the genre *fiction.*

subject: (1) the concrete and literal description of what a story is about; (2) the general or specific area of concern of a poem—also called *topic*.

subplot: another name for an under-plot; a subordinate plot in fiction or drama.

surrealism: a modern literary and artistic movement that grew out of Dadaism and Futurism. It stressed the importance of dreams, the unconscious, non-rational thought, free association, and strange juxtaposition. In one word, it attempts to depict things beyond reality or in a surreal manner.

suspense: the expectation of and doubt about what is going to happen next.

symbol: a person, place, object, or event in a literary work that figuratively "stands for" something else.

symbolism: a modern literary movement in reaction to realism, replacing the objectivity and directness of the realists' methods with symbolic techniques that attempted to present a true reality beyond objective reality.

synecdoche: a figure of speech in which a part of something represents the whole, as in "wagging tongues" to represent " gossiping neighbours".

temporal setting: the time of a literary text.

tercet: a three-line stanza.

terza rima: an interlocking form of verse consisting of three-line stanzas in which the second line of each stanza rhymes with the first and third of the next: *aba bcb cdc*, etc.

tetrameter: a line of poetry consisting of four metrical feet.

theme: a generalized, abstract paraphrase of the inferred central or dominant idea of a work; a poem's attitude towards its subject.

third-person limited point of view: in narrative fiction, the telling of a story by an apparently all-knowing or omniscient narrator who enters the mind of only one character. The narrator may refer to all the characters in the third person, as "he" or "she".

third-person narrator: a character, "he" or "she", who tells the story.

third-person objective (dramatic) point of view: in narrative fiction, the telling of a story by an apparently all-knowing or omniscient narrator who enters the mind of no characters. We learn the characters from the outside just as we do when watching a play, thus the term *dramatic*. The narrator may refer to all the characters in the third person, as "he" or "she".

third-person omniscient point of view: in narrative fiction, the telling of a story by an apparently all-knowing or omniscient narrator who enters the minds of more than one characters, who may refer to all the characters in the third person, as "he" or "she".

three unities: According to Aristotle's descriptions of drama in his *Poetics*, the three unities are those of *action*, *place*, and *time*. This theory insists that the creation of drama should resemble reality as much as possible. Therefore, a play should dramatize a single major *action* that takes place in a single *place* during the approximate *time* it would take for completion, from beginning to end. During the Renaissance, some critics considered the three unities to be rules of regular drama. Later, critics still considered the unity of *action* important, but minimized the unities of *place* and *time*.

tone: the emotional attitude a literary work takes toward its subject and theme.

topic: See ***subject***.

traditional symbols: symbols that, through years of usage, have acquired an agreed-upon significance or an accepted meaning.

tragedy: a literary work in which a character, usually a good and noble person of high rank, is brought to a disastrous doom in his or her confrontation with a superior force such as fortune, gods, social forces, universal values or a direct result of a fatal flaw in his or her character. A tragedy should evoke fear and pity in the audience.

tragicomedy: a literary work containing a mixture of tragic and comic elements.

trochee (trochaic meter): a metrical form in which each foot consists of a stressed syllable followed by an unstressed one.

turning point: See ***climax***.

underplot: See ***subplot***.

understatement: language that avoids obvious emphasis; litotes is one form of it.

unstressed syllable: a syllable that is not emphasized, like *a* in *appear* or *er* in *utter*.

verbal irony: a statement in which the literal meaning differs from the implicit meaning.

villain: the one who opposes the hero and heroine.

villanelle: a verse form consisting of nineteen lines divided into six stanzas—five tercets and one quatrain. The first and third lines of the first tercet rhyme, and this rhyme is repeated through each of the next four tercets and in the last two lines of the concluding quatrain.

voice: the speaker of a poem; the "person" who tells the story.

wit: a brief and well-phrased expression contrived to give one a shock of amused surprise. The distinctive "metaphysical wit" is a well-known critical term.

References

[1] Abrams M A. *A Glossary of Literary Terms*. Beijing: Foreign Language Teaching and Research Press, 2004.

[2] Beaty J, Booth A, Hunter J, et al. *The Norton Introduction to Literature*. New York: W. W. Norton & Company, Inc., 2002.

[3] Booz E. *A Brief Introduction to Modern American Literature*. Shanghai: Shanghai Foreign Language Education Press, 1982.

[4] Cassidy J, DiYanni R. *Discovering Literature*. [s.l.]: Glencoe/McGraw-Hill, 1991.

[5] DiYanni R. *Drama: An Introduction*. [s.l.]: McGraw-Hill Higher Education, 2000.

[6] DiYanni R, Rompf K. *Book of Fiction*. [s.l.]: McGraw-Hill Inc., 1995.

[7] Drabble M. *The Oxford Companion to English Literature*. Beijing: Foreign Language Teaching and Research Press, 2005.

[8] Doyle P. *Best Poems*. [s.l.]: Jamestown Publishers, 1998.

[9] Kearns G, et al. *British and Western Literature*. [s.l.]: Macmillan/McGraw-Hill, 1987.

[10] Rozakis E L. *How to Interpret Poetry*. Shanghai: Shanghai Translation Press, 2005.

[11] Gaskell P. *Landmarks in English Literature*. Edinburgh: Edinburgh University Press, 2006.

[12] Gordon J B, Kuehner K. *Fiction—An Introduction to the Short Story*. Lincohnwood (Illinois): NTC / Contemporary Publishing Group, Inc., 1999.

[13] Griffith K. *Writing Essays About Literature*. Beijing: Beijing University Press, 2006.

[14] Kirszner G, Laurie M, Stephen R. *Literature Reading, Reacting, Writing*. Beijing: Beijing University Press, 2006.

[15] Wilson E, Goldfarb A. *Anthology of Living Theater*. [s.l.]: Macmillan/McGraw-Hill, 1998.

[16] 戴继国. 英国诗歌教程. 北京：对外经济贸易大学出版社，2005.

[17] 何功杰. 英诗选读. 合肥：安徽教育出版社，1998.

[18] 胡荫桐等. 美国文学新编. 北京：外语教学与研究出版社，2001.

[19] 李正栓，吴晓梅. 英美诗歌教程. 北京：清华大学出版社，2004.

[20] 刘炳善. 英国文学简史. 开封：河南人民出版社，1993.

[21] 刘溶波. 英美文学名著欣赏. 广州：华南理工大学出版社，2005.

[22] 刘海平，朱雪峰. 英美戏剧：作品与评论. 上海：上海外语教育出版社，2004.

[23] 林六辰. 英美小说要素解析. 上海：上海外语教育出版社，2004.

[24] 龙毛忠等. 英美文学精华导读. 上海：华东理工大学出版社，2004.

[25] 罗选民. 英美文学赏析教程. 北京：清华大学出版社，2002.

[26] 邵金娣，白劲鹏. 文学导论. 上海：上海外语教育出版社，2002.
[27] 陶洁. 美国文学选读. 北京：高等教育出版社，2000.
[28] 王宝童. 金域行——英诗教程. 开封：河南大学出版社，1993.
[29] 汪冷，田丽. 美国文学作品选读. 上海：上海交通大学出版社，2003.
[30] 王守仁. 英国文学选读. 北京：高等教育出版社，2001.
[31] 吴定柏. 美国文学大纲. 上海：上海外语教育出版社，1998.
[32] 吴定柏. 美国文学欣赏. 上海：上海外语教育出版社，2002.
[33] 袁宪军，钱坤强. 英语小说导读. 北京：北京大学出版社，2004.
[34] 张伯香，龙江. 英美经典小说赏析. 武汉：武汉大学出版社，2005.
[35] 张定铨，吴刚. 新编简明英国文学史. 上海：上海外语教育出版社，2002.
[36] 左金梅. 西方文学. 青岛：中国海洋大学出版社，2006.

图书在版编目 (CIP) 数据

英美文学鉴赏导读 = A Guide to Appreciating English Literature: 英文 / 魏健主编. —杭州：浙江大学出版社，2008.7 (2021.1 重印)

ISBN 978-7-308-06090-5

I. 英… II. 魏… III. ①英语－阅读教学－高等学校－教材②文学欣赏－英国③文学欣赏－美国 IV. H319. 4: I

中国版本图书馆 CIP 数据核字 (2008) 第 097180 号

英美文学鉴赏导读

主　编　魏　健

副主编　温中兰

审　校　〈美〉Michael C. Milam

责任编辑　诸葛勤

封面设计　刘依群　周　灵

出版发行　浙江大学出版社

(杭州天目山路 148 号　邮政编码 310007)

(网址: http://www.zjupress.com)

排　　版　浙江时代出版服务有限公司

印　　刷　杭州良诸印刷有限公司

开　　本　710mm×1000mm　1/16

印　　张　28.5

字　　数　832 千

版 印 次　2013 年 11 月第 2 版　2021 年 1 月第 11 次印刷

印　　数　13501—14500

书　　号　ISBN 978-7-308-06090-5

定　　价　68.00 元

浙江大学出版社市场运营中心联系方式　(0571) 88925591; http://zjdxcbs.tmall.com